Worldview, the Orichas, and Santería

UNIVERSITY PRESS OF FLORIDA

Florida A&M University, Tallahassee
Florida Atlantic University, Boca Raton
Florida Gulf Coast University, Ft. Myers
Florida International University, Miami
Florida State University, Tallahassee
New College of Florida, Sarasota
University of Central Florida, Orlando
University of Florida, Gainesville
University of North Florida, Jacksonville
University of South Florida, Tampa
University of West Florida, Pensacola

Worldview, the Orichas, and Santería

Africa to Cuba and Beyond

Mercedes Cros Sandoval

University Press of Florida
Gainesville/Tallahassee/Tampa/Boca Raton
Pensacola/Orlando/Miami/Jacksonville/Ft. Myers/Sarasota

First cloth printing, 2006
First paperback printing, 2009

Library of Congress Cataloging-in-Publication Data
Cros Sandoval, Mercedes.
Worldview, the orichas, and Santeria : Africa to Cuba and beyond /
Mercedes Cros Sandoval.
p. cm.
Includes bibliographical references and index.
ISBN: 978-0-8130-3020-3 (alk. paper)
ISBN: 978-0-8130-3452-2 (pbk.)
1. Santeria—Cuba. 2. Orishas—Cuba. 3. Cuba—Religion.
4. Cuba—Religious life and customs. I. Title.
BL2532.S3C77 2007
299.6'740972919–dc22   2006022834

The University Press of Florida is the scholarly publishing agency
for the State University System of Florida, comprising Florida A&M
University, Florida Atlantic University, Florida Gulf Coast University,
Florida International University, Florida State University, New College of Florida, University of Central Florida, University of Florida,
University of North Florida, University of South Florida, and University of West Florida.

University Press of Florida
15 Northwest 15th Street
Gainesville, FL 32611-2079
http://www.upf.com

To the memory of my parents, Dr. Juan Cros Capote and Elena Arrúe Demar, for having broadened my experiences and whetted my appetite for the love of music, art, poetry, nature, history, and all humanist pursuits.

Contents

Illustrations

Informants

Aguilar, Javier. *Babalao.*

Alfaro, Olimpia. A famous *akpuon,* or soloist, who died in 2002. The author knew Alfaro over the course of many years.

Armenteros, Virgilio, M.D. (Ifá Omí). *Babalao.*

Baró, Florencio. Talented percussionist, d. 1994. Baró collaborated with the author on several projects.

Barrios, Niurka (Olomidara). Daughter of Yemayá Olokun.

Céspedes, Leonel. *Babalao* "El Chino." A prestigious *Osainista.*

Díaz, Oswaldo. Senior *santero* initiated in the worship of Ochún over forty years ago in the city of Matanzas and member of the famous Ferminita lineage. Each year, on September 24, Díaz and his godchildren promote a procession in Miami, headed by a Catholic priest and two assistants who celebrate a mass beforehand. The image of the Virgin of Mercy that Díaz keeps in his home is then paraded through the streets. The procession features a small band and is attended by more than one hundred persons.

Eires, Silvia (Efún Okún Lorún). Senior *santera/iyalocha* Yemayá.

Erice, Manolo (Ojuani Araketu). Prestigious *babalao* frequently consulted by the author.

Fernández, Wilfredo, Jr. *Babalao* and key informant. His father was a prestigious *babalao* and *olúo* who had Olofin. Both men belonged to the respected lineage founded by Bernardo Rojas, who was initiated by the legendary Adechina, the founder of the Regla de Ifá in Cuba.

García Cortez, Julio. An *omoricha* and author of several books about Santería.

Guerra, John (Osoroso). *Babalao.* Close friend of the author.

Hernandez, Abelardo. *Omoricha,* 1972–2003. Son of Ochún and a prestigious *babaoricha* initiated in the 1940s in Cuba. The author received the fundamental sacred necklaces from Hernandez in 1973.

Pichardo, Ernesto. A well-known *oriaté* who has been instrumental in bringing Santería into the open. His famous lawsuit against the city of Hialeah resulted in a Supreme Court of the United States decision that legalized the sacrifice of animals in religious ceremonies. The author conducted interviews with Pichardo in Miami.

Ramos, Miguel "Willie." A talented *akpuon,* or soloist, as well as a highly respected *oriaté* and a successful curator of museum exhibits on Santería. The author and Ramos have collaborated on numerous projects since 1987.

Torrado, Norma (Egüin Cholá). Senior *iyalocha.*

Torres, Ezequiel (Ocha Alaché). An *oloaña* (consecrated to the *oricha* of the drums). Torres is a prestigious player of the sacred drums. His sister Nery is a well-known Afro-Cuban dancer. Torres belongs to the lineage *La Pimienta* that originated with Ferminita Gómez.

Zamora, Rigoberto. A well-known and outspoken *babalao.*

Foreword

This remarkable study of Santería, an Afro-Cuban religion first brought to the attention of scholars by Fernando Ortiz, makes a major contribution to the rich religious history of the New World, to the field of comparative religion, and to our understanding of processes of culture change. It also provides insight into various aspects of both the history and culture of Cuba and West African Yoruba.

Mercedes Cros Sandoval stretches our view to encompass broad historical processes. She also expands our awareness of the myriad humanistic details reflected in the mythology of this religion. It is matters such as these, combined with explorations of other aspects of life and circumstance in the Cuban setting that allow her to trace changing elements in the Yoruban religion after it was introduced to, accepted by, altered, and elaborated upon by various segments of the Afro-Cuban population.

I feel honored by the invitation to write this foreword, but since I have known Mercedes Sandoval for more than thirty years, I wish to express not only the high praise I have for her work but, also, the respect I have for her as a colleague and a remarkable human being.

From the time she became involved in the programs of the Department of Psychiatry at the University of Miami School of Medicine in the early 1970s, she has demonstrated keen intelligence, a commitment to hard work, a loyalty to colleagues and friends, and courage under difficult life circumstances. She has shown a willingness to take on research, training, and teaching roles that would have been daunting to many others with fewer personal responsibilities than she carried. She has always taken stands based upon the strength of convictions derived from all the evidence available to her, and that is what she offers now.

Mercedes Cros Sandoval has a persona that is large and impressive. It is reflected in the scope of this volume, which she has had to set aside on so many prior occasions throughout the years. Finally, she has offered her readers a way of understanding the origins, structure, functions, and transformations of the religious system called "Santería." She has done so with both a breadth and an intimacy that few others can match.

A major component of this book is about the orishas (divinities) in Africa and the *orichas* (gods/saints) in Cuba, their changes through time, and their functions in the lives of those who worship them. She has presented the material within the theoretical framework of worldview analysis. In so doing, her descriptions of the complex interplay of history and circumstance contribute immensely to our understanding of processes of religious borrowing, accommodation, and transformation that gave rise in Cuba to a new religious form.

Much has been written about this religion since Cros Sandoval, building upon the work of the earliest Cuban scholars and other early contributors to the field of inquiry, began a pioneering study. Her research in the mid-1960s attempted to identify specific changes in conceptualizations and perceived functions of those African divinities that survived in Cuba. That study was unique, and we are fortunate to have English translations of some of her earlier work included here.

More important, however, Mercedes Cros Sandoval has introduced into the discourse on Santería the value of a worldview approach as a means of understanding the dynamics of culture change within a religious framework. This will bring fresh insights and theoretical challenges to scholars in the field. It will also bring new conceptualizations and knowledge to readers who may not otherwise appreciate the full significance of what she has undertaken.

Cros Sandoval has provided the reader with an essential understanding of a broad sweep of history and offered important insight into its inner workings regarding religious tradition and change. She has done this both from the perspective of an insider and an outsider. She personally observed Santería's cultural position in Cuba during the 1940s and 1950s. She has personally experienced the trauma of upheaval and exile. She has mastered both the personal transformations involved in biculturalism and the professional requirements of cultural brokerage. Few anthropologists are trained, as she is, in both culture history and functionalism as analytical approaches to cultural phenomena. Such an orientation, coupled with her own "Cubanness," and the sensitivities that this implies, allows her to speak with an authority that few other scholars command.

Cros Sandoval's data are based upon an enduring, questioning interest in this religious system, upon historical materials, formal interviews, participant observation, intimate personal conversations, recorded oral histories and musical reminiscences, as well as the resources of the notebooks of Santería's priests and priestesses.

Over a period of forty years her patience and dedication have borne remarkable fruit. She is able to place the contributions of successive generations of Santería's practitioners and followers into both social and historical context, thereby bringing meaning and coherence to otherwise confusing and seemingly contradictory interpretations presented in the literature.

Her descriptions and interpretations allow us to see something of the "soul" of this Afro-Cuban religion and to understand why, as she suggests, it will continue to be sufficiently open to accommodate changed circumstances in new settings. It is hoped that an extension of her worldview approach will allow us to comprehend better the new forms and functions that may be expected.

Mercedes Cros Sandoval's work is seminal and enduring. Her informed, complex, multifaceted approach sets a challenging standard for students of religious studies from a variety of disciplines. It also provides a remarkable experience for those general readers who simply want to know something about, more about, or a lot about Santería. This is not a lightweight book, but it offers something of interest and value to many kinds of readers.

Hazel Hitson Weidman, Ph.D.
Professor of Social Anthropology and Director, Office of Transcultural
Education and Research Emerita, Department of Psychiatry
University of Miami School of Medicine

Preface

Theoretical Framework

In this work the author has chosen to use the concept of worldview as an organizing framework and a tool of analysis. While scholars of religion continue to use the concept of worldview, it has been largely in disuse in recent years within anthropological theory and research. The anthropologist Michael Kearney suggests, however, that worldview: ". . . is a potentially powerful tool for exploring the recesses of socially constructed human consciousness . . ." (1984:ix). He sees worldview as the cognitive framework supporting a group's lifestyle (42). As such, worldview provides a logical or cognitive matrix that may be used as a basis for comparison when people from different cultures are placed in situations of coexistence regardless of the manner in which such a situation comes about.

If we consider the concept of ethos as referring to the life-style of a group, its social organization, and socially sanctioned ways of behaving, then ethos is an indicator of specific principles of social structure and behavior that are ordered by worldview assumptions about the nature of reality. Worldview assumptions offer a means of analysis that may help us understand cultural continuities as well as processes of cultural borrowing, syncretism (the coming together), and merging (transculturation). These are processes of change embedded in the history of all religious forms, including those under consideration here.

Models for Worldview Analysis

Michael Kearney

In a recent thorough review of the history of the worldview concept, David K. Naugle (2002:244) concludes with the comment that Kearney's model, as it stands, "is one of the most complete worldview models available today in any discipline." It is for this reason that it has been heavily utilized in the work to follow.

In Kearney's view (1984:42), "Each society is a particular arrangement of ideas and behavior. The overall cognitive framework of these ideas and behavior is that society's world view." Furthermore, "The world view of a people is their way of looking at reality. It consists of basic assumptions and images that provide a more or less coherent, though not necessarily accurate, way of thinking about the world. A world view comprises images of Self and of all that is recognized as not-Self, plus ideas about relationships between them, as well as other ideas" (41).

Kearney identifies five worldview universals: 1) the Self and Other; 2) Relationship; 3) Classification; 4) Causality; and 5) Space and Time. (65-107). He argues that these are necessary aspects of any human worldview, but sees these categories as being affected by two basic factors, both of which are involved in logico-structural integration.

According to Kearney, logico-structural integration reflects "the ways in which the assumptions of worldview are interrelated and the way they, in turn, affect cultural behavior. . . . The organization of world-view assumptions is shaped in two ways. The first of these is due to internal equilibrium dynamics among them. This means that some assumptions and the resultant ideas, beliefs, and actions predicated on them are *logically* and *structurally* more compatible than others, and that the entire world view will 'strive' toward maximum logical and structural consistency. The second and main force giving coherence and shape to a world view is the necessity of having to relate to the external environment" (52).

Taking the subject further, Kearney proposes that "human social behavior, social structure, institutions, and customs are consistent with the assumptions about the nature of the world. Therefore, in given environments, some such assumptions are more functional than others, and are therefore more subject to positive selective pressures" (52).

Additionally, Kearney suggests that "'external inconsistencies' in a world view result when its images or assumptions are maladaptive or otherwise inappropriate for the reality that the world view presumably mirrors. Thus, at a given point in its history a world view may be a satisfactory cognition of the environment. That is, the culturally patterned perceptions of that environment and the organization of those percepts into concepts are not only internally consistent . . . but also serve to organize behavior such that it is meaningful and adaptive. The study of culture change in general . . . is fundamentally the analysis of this fit or lack of fit between world view and environment" (54).

I draw upon Kearney's theoretical model throughout this volume. I utilize it most heavily in chapter 1 (pp. 14–17) and in chapter 22. As we shall see in part 2 of this study, Kearney's concept of logico-structural integration may help to explain the loss or diminished role in Cuba of some of the Yoruban orishas (divinities).

Florence Kluckhohn

Another useful model for identifying worldview assumptions is that of Florence Kluckhohn (1953), who sees values as crucial dimensions of worldview.

According to Kluckhohn, these values manifest themselves in the ". . . limited number of basic human problems for which all peoples at all times and in all places must find some solution" (346). She hypothesizes that all societies must develop ways to deal with five universal problems she identifies that relate to 1) the character of human nature; 2) the significant time dimension; 3) the valued modality of human activity; 4) the valued relationship of man to other men; and 5) the valued relationship of man to nature (and supernature).[1]

The Kluckhohn-Strodtbeck Value Orientation Schedule (Kluckhohn and Strodtbeck 1961) was developed as an instrument to establish as objectively as possible the dominant (first-ranked) and variant (second- and third-ranked) patterns of value orientation held by diverse groups of people throughout the world. The scale provides choices in each of the five universal problem areas:

1) The character of human nature: a) good, b) both good and evil, c) evil.
2) The significant time dimension: a) past, b) present, c) future.
3) The valued modality of human activity: a) being, b) doing.
4) The valued relationship of man to other men: a) lineal, b) collateral, c) individual.
5) The valued relationship of man to nature (and supernature): a) mastery over nature (and supernature), b) subjugation to nature (and supernature), c) in harmony with nature (and supernature).

In chapter 2, I utilize the Kluckhohn and Strodtbeck model in a post hoc fashion. In the absence of formal instruments to measure the extent of similarities and differences between a coherent worldview of the Yoruba who entered Cuba and a coherent worldview of those populations in the receiving society, it is necessary to develop inferential constructs on the basis of available historical and descriptive materials. Aspects of ethos during both the colonial and republican periods in Cuba are well represented in the main discourse of this volume. It is on the basis of this information that an attempt is made to infer the value orientation profiles of both black and white lower-income groups in colonial and republican Cuba.

The value of a worldview approach to understanding continuity and change in religious forms that emerged as Santería will become more apparent as I proceed. For example, worldview analysis helps us see the extent of congruencies or lack thereof in the lifestyles of groups in contact. Congruencies facilitate transculturation while incompatibilities do not. Chapter 22 in Part 3 is particularly helpful in this regard. The discussion in that context covers important matters related to basic assumptions as well as issues pertaining to logico-structural integration—factors that throw light on cultural dynamics in the emergence of Santería.

Acknowledgments

My thanks to the soul of my dear friend Florencio Baró, who for several years visited my home each Friday, filling it with his music and his haunting memories of his native town, Carlos Rojas.

There are no words to thank my friend Celia Suarez for editing this work and turning unending sentences into meaningful paragraphs. I don't know how our friendship has endured the detailed and challenging task that she undertook!

Thanks to Hazel Weidman, who encouraged me to write this book. She insisted that I had something to contribute to the understanding of Santería from the broadest possible yet most intimate perspective.

I am deeply grateful to Terry Rey for his kind interest in my work, for having edited the manuscript one more time, for his precise and accurate comments and recommendations, and for his assistance in helping me find the proper publisher.

Doris Sandigo's patience and efficiency has played a most important part in getting the manuscript ready for printing, and I am grateful.

Special thanks go to Idania Carpio and Debi Singh from the Miami Dade College North Campus Library and to Marta Cosculluela, Lily Menes, and Gloria de la Mancha from the Inter-American Campus Library for their professional and warm assistance and support.

May the *orichas* (gods of the Yoruban pantheon) keep all of them in good health!

My gratitude goes to the souls of Lydia Cabrera and Titina de Rojas for their friendship. I learned a lot about Santería and Cuba from them, but above all else they were living examples of the real meaning of aristocracy: duty and commitment, not privilege.

My warm gratitude goes to Miguel "Willie" Ramos, with whom I have collaborated on several projects throughout the years. I greatly appreciate his valuable friendship and unlimited patience with my eternal prodding and discussion. I am quite indebted to Ezequiel Torres, the great *olubatá*. Only the best memories and feelings are evoked by the name of Blanca Nieves Tamayo. She could bring Cuba into my living room while drinking rum and playing on the piano the music she composed for Rolando. I will never forget the classy "Violin to Yemayá" that she offered in Washington, D.C. I agree with her that in her time she was "the most beautiful *negra* in Havana."

I am indebted to Jesus Fernández Cano, who was born in Spain and bonded to Cuba. Through cassette tapes, videotapes, and unmatched conversation, he has generously shared with me his rich experiences with Santería in Cuba in the 1990s. My gratitude goes to Wilfredo Fernández Jr. for his support, for his Cubanness, and for allowing me inside his rich life experiences. I give thanks also to the *babalaos* (priest of Orúla or Orúnmila) Manolo Erice, Virgilio Armenteros, John Guerra, and Jorge Torres, whose friendship and knowledge have greatly enlightened me. I will forever be grateful to Silvia Eire and Nancy Torrado, senior *iyalochas (santeras),* whose trustworthy friendship I treasure greatly.

My gratitude goes to the soul of Enrique Cougat, the unforgettable medium whose *libreta de santero* (notebook of Santería) had the most beautiful *patakís* (legends). I am also grateful to the souls of Juan Candela and his wife, Neida. I spent many evenings in their home, where I was transported by their magic back to the Cuba of the 1940s and 1950s. My heart is full of warmth and gratitude for the soul of Abelardo Hernández, my *padrino* (godfather), who gave me the *collares* (consecrated necklaces).

Life has brought me the friendship of Javier Echevarría, a young man recently arrived from the island, whose documentaries have been internationally recognized and honored. It has been encouraging to discover through him that the images and worldview that were elaborated by several generations of Cubans are still alive despite adversity. It has also been important to know I share with such a sensitive, inquisitive young man the same point of view concerning the role of "popular piety" (which he calls "popular imagery") in the path of Santería in Cuba.

Special thanks go to Ernesto and Fernando Pichardo and their mother, Carmen, whose points of view on Santería and other matters I have learned to appreciate.

My gratitude goes to the souls of living and departed *santeros* and *santeras* (Santería's priests and priestesses), *babalaos* (priests dedicated to the cult of the god of oracles), spiritualists (followers of Allan Kardec's spiritualist practices), and *muerteros* (mediums engaged in communicating with the dead), who graced me with their friendship and opened their hearts and homes, enabling me to be part of their mystical experience. Among them, I am especially indebted to Epifanía Jané, Anita Arpazón, Oswaldo Díaz, Olimpia Alfaro, Erconides Sanamé, Julio García Cortes, Lydia Casanova, Ezequiel Torres, Nenita and Tita.

My thanks go to my former student-assistants Alicia Agramonte, María de los Angeles Gas, Beatriz Montón, and Celia Pellón, who transcribed tapes and notes into some type of order. I am indebted to my friend Dr. Julio García Gómez, who enthusiastically assisted me every time I needed to learn a scientific term for a specific Cuban botanical or zoological specimen. I am also indebted to Carmen Vazquez, who cheered me on through this endeavor. Thanks to Marta Corbea, who read and commented on a few chapters of the manuscript.

My task would have been far more difficult without them.

Note to the Reader

In this work many Lucumí/Lukumí and Spanish words, which are part of the language of Santería, are used. Lucumí is the name used for the sacred language of the Afro-Cuban religion called "Santería." It derives from the Yoruba language and is mixed with Spanish and *bozal*,[1] the form of communication used by African-born slaves in Cuba. *Lucumí* and Spanish words appear in the text in italics. A glossary is included at the end of the text that identifies and defines such words. Spanish phonetics are used to transcribe *Lucumí* and Yoruba words prevalent in Cuba. For the Yoruba language, English phonetics are used but without the Yoruba accents.

Most of the informants consulted by the author were Spanish-speakers, and the author has translated the substance of these conversations. In the case of written statements such as that given by *Babalao* Virgilio Armenteros, M.D., and information quoted from texts written in Spanish, such as Lydia Cabrera's *El Monte* and Juan Sosa's *Sects, Cults and Syncretisms*, the translation has been *ad verbatim*.

The author has also translated into English large sections from her own book *La Religión Afrocubana*, particularly reflected in Part 2 but also in Part 1. These sections include a great number of *patakís*/myths from that book. A few new *patakís*/myths from *libretas de santeros/santeras* have been translated into English and included when appropriate.

The author's publications will be found under Cros Sandoval, Mercedes even if they were originally written under other names such as Mercedes Cros Arrúe, or Mercedes C. Sandoval, and Mercedes S. Sandoval.

Yoruba deities are known by many different names both in Nigeria and in Cuba. Moreover, these names have been spelled in different manners by authors, believers, and by the priests and priestesses who, in Cuba, wrote or dictated the *libretas de santeros*. For instance, the *oricha* Agayú in some *ilé ochas* is known as Aganyú and in others as Agallú Sola. In Nigeria the name is normally spelled using the *j*, but in Spanish phonetics, the *j* sound is pronounced by the *y* and the *ll* letters. On the other hand, Elegguá is also known as Elegbara, Legba; Yemayá is also known as Yemanyá.

In the narrative, I have chosen to use one of the names to facilitate the reader's comprehension but to respect the spelling of the *libretas de santeros* when I am transcribing. The same situation is faced when I am dealing with terms such as *odu*, *oro* and others. Some informants pronounce it and spell is as *odún*, *oddún*, or *oru*.

Prologue

Ochún, the goddess of the river, love, and all sweet things, found out that some of her children had been shipped to Cuba as slaves. There, they were lonely and sad. So, she decided to go to Cuba to keep them company, to give them comfort, and to join in their dances, to share their sorrows and their joys.

Ochún, worried and apprehensive about the long voyage, decided to visit her sister Yemayá, the owner of the sea. Ochún said, "Yemayá, I have to cross the sea to go to Cuba. I want to be with my children, but I am afraid of the long trip."

Yemayá replied, "Don't be afraid, Ochún, I'll take care of you. I will take you to the bottom of the ocean, and we will cross it without hazards." Appeased, Ochún said, "You have reassured me, but tell me Yemayá, you, who reach all the way to Cuba and visit its shores and beaches, how is Cuba and how are the Cubans?"

Yemayá replied to Ochún, "Cuba is very much like Africa; it is never cold there and the tropical nights are long and warm. Its rivers and streams flow quietly, shaded by coconut and palm tree fronds. However, Ochún, not all Cubans are black, as the people here; some are white and others are mulattos."

Ochún, apprehensively, told Yemayá, "I am worried, since I am not used to people different from us." Then, she quickly added, "I would like you to grant me two wishes: As we voyage toward Cuba, straighten my hair just a little bit with the waves of the ocean; and, with the foam of the waves, lighten my skin just a little bit. Thus, when I arrive in Cuba, I will be neither black nor white. These changes will make me acceptable to all the Cubans, those who are black, white, and mulatto. I will resemble them, and they will be my children."

In her queenly and maternal demeanor, Yemayá granted Ochún the two wishes; and that is the reason Cubans were graced with a patron saint, a mother whose physical features match those of the Cuban people. That is why she is our Lady of Charity . . . Ochún.[1]

Moforibale Erekusu, Iyá Mi!
(I Revere Thee, Cuba, My Mother!)

Introduction

During the 1940s, when I was a teenager in Cuba, I became interested in the religious beliefs and practices of the Cuban people. In Baracoa (the first town founded by the Spaniards in 1512), where I spent my childhood, I was fascinated by frequent references in adult conversations to the interaction of people with the spirits of the dead. Comments about supernatural phenomena were also prevalent.

On some evenings one could see La Luz de Yara, a vision resembling the moon navigating along the horizon on the surface of the ocean. According to popular beliefs it was the soul of an Indian woman called Yara. According to my father (a physician) that light was produced by the mineralized remains of microorganisms that live in the ocean.

There were also stories about *jigues*, [1] fearsome beings, or dark dwarfs which resembled manatees, that emerged in the evenings from the rivers. The belief in *jigues* reputedly had roots in the aboriginal Indian population.

Many people told stories about *aparecidos* (ghosts), especially in the countryside. Some of these *aparecidos* conversed with their living relatives, scolding them when they misbehaved and giving them advice. *Luces* (lights) and *aparecidos* also showed people the places where money had been buried.

It was common for individuals, especially women, to fall into a trance while being possessed by a large variety of spirits. The daughter of our cook[2] often had *ataques* (possession by spirits) generally during arguments with her drunken husband. The *ataques* elicited the neighbors' attentions, which served to interrupt the altercations. The cook's oldest daughter, who was black, was a seer. She went into imperceptible trances and foretold the future.

These behaviors and beliefs were prevalent among whites and blacks of the lower-income groups and among some members of the middle class.

It should be noted, also, that the belief in miracles was all pervasive. When I was eight or nine years old, I told my father that I wished to become a physician. He tried to dissuade me, explaining with a smile: "Merceditas, in Cuba being a physician is not easy. When a patient dies the physician is blamed; but, if the patient gets well, the miracles of the Virgin or a saint are credited with the recovery."

In 1945 my parents moved our family to Guantánamo in the province of Oriente. Next to our home there was a tenement with three one-bedroom apartments. In the common yard of that building on most Sunday afternoons, *bembés*[3] were held in which Santería and *muertería* practices mixed. It is noteworthy that the family involved was originally from Havana, one of the cradles of Santería.

In Guantánamo I was a guest at a sophisticated "violin for Ochún" that took place in the home of a well-to-do mulatto accountant. In this middle-class setting, a musician was hired to play the violin to honor the Virgin of Charity/Ochún, whose altar was placed in the living room.

At that time in Cuba, even though some popular songs such as "Babalú Ayé" and "Me boté a Guanabacoa" (I went to Guanabacoa) were already popularizing Santería's practices and the names of its gods, many people did not know much about it or had not even heard of it.

In Guantánamo I also witnessed a Tumba Francesa,[4] a Haitian-derived celebration, which regularly took place in a large house on the street of Máximo Gómez North. Women, dressed in beautiful colonial garments with rich embroidery, danced with their partners, who also were attired in elegant colonial suits. My impression was that they danced a courtly dance reminiscent of a minuet. All the participants were black, while most of the *bembés* I had attended or watched had a mixed gathering.

As a young adult attending the University of Havana, I worked as an interviewer for the 1952 Cuban National Population Census and for Mestre y Conill, Ltd., a well-known publicity firm in Havana. These field surveys were methodologically sound. They required random interviews of people in a particular area, block by block, to obtain data reflective of the population of Cuba. Even though in the cities the mystical ambiance prevalent in the countryside and in the small towns lost ground, the heterogeneity of religious practices prevailed. I still cherish these fluid human interactions that transcended all racial and class prejudices—experiences that were not at all atypical in the Cuba of the 1940s.

Especially interesting to me were Jesús María, Regla, Marianao, and other lower-income neighborhoods, because they were mixed in character and included substantial concentrations of practitioners and followers of Santería. The close interaction between people of different races and socioeconomic levels was also part of the daily routine in neighborhoods such as El Cerro, La Víbora, and El Vedado, where middle-class and even upper-class homes were situated next to tenements.

One of the projects in which I was involved was a survey concerning Clavelitos, a white country-music singer, who had a daily radio program. He did not have much of a following until he began telling the audience that he had the power to magnetize water. He added that if, during the program, people placed glasses full of water on top of the radio, the energized water would acquire healing and otherwise benevolent powers. His ratings soared, to the chagrin of the more educated classes.

There was racial prejudice and discrimination in Cuba, but not to the extent that it was practiced in other countries. Alejandro de la Fuente (2001: 10–19) points out the uniqueness of the "Cuban case" relative to racial relations. In Cuba following the inauguration of the republic, all public services were integrated—schools, churches, trains, buses, stores, bathrooms, hospitals, and offices. Most neighborhoods were integrated with the exception of the most exclusive and expensive neighborhoods in the larger cities. These circumstances encouraged the development of friendships and close relationships across racial, social class, and economic boundaries.

Normally, *bembés*, secular drumming parties, and all types of religious gatherings (spiritualist séances, *muertería*, spirit possession) went on in an ambiance of tolerance. Those people, mostly white, who believed that these practices were the superstitions of uneducated people, avoided, ignored, or endured them.

The following story from the 1940s, referred to me by Wilfredo Fernández Jr., reflects Cuba's and Santería's former mystical ambiance, devoid of ethnic or cultural barriers. The informant was around eight years old at that time, and he was living in his family's old plantation house. At three o'clock in the morning, someone started to bang on the front door. His mother, alarmed, opened the door to an employee, who urged her: "Señora, please open the door of the chapel; Yemayá wants to wash Saint Francis of Assisi." The lady of the house complied and opened the chapel for a black woman possessed by Yemayá. The woman proceeded to go to the statue of Saint Francis on an altar and wash it with great care and devotion.

This magical ambiance and ethos of the Cuba in which I grew up creatively nourished the inspiration of writers, painters, sculptors, and musicians, but it could also be manipulated by opportunists seeking to increase and maintain their power. For example, following Cuba's opportunistic traditions and playing into the religiosity and miracle seeking of many Cubans, it was popularly believed that Batista, the Cuban dictator from 1952 through 1958, was backed and protected by the soul of an Indian. He gave his close associates, as presents, rings with the colored enameled face of a feathered Plains Indian chief, which they proudly wore.

Within this background and amid the growing discontent with Batista, I graduated from the University of Havana with a Ph.D. in social sciences and public law. Afterward, at Florida State University I obtained an M.A. in anthropology. Then, as the wife of an Air Force officer, I lived in Puerto Rico for three years (1957–60), followed by two years in New York City. By then, Castro had set a date for the beginning of the Cuban Diaspora so significant to the future of Santería. It was in 1962 that the growing Sandoval family moved to Spain for a four-year stay.

These life experiences in different Hispanic countries and in the United States strengthened my sensitivity to similarities and differences among the various Latin American, Cuban, Caribbean, Spanish, and American cultures. In Spain I applied this appreciation and knowledge to earn a Ph.D. in culture and history of the Americas from the University of Madrid.

More than forty years have elapsed since I began working on my doctoral dissertation, which examined Yoruban elements in Afro-Cuban Santería. When I began this lifelong dedication to the study of Santería, I hoped to continue that tradition begun by Fernando Ortiz, nourished by Rómulo Lachatañeré, Lydia Cabrera, and others who studied the African impact upon Cuban culture. This interest had some causal connections with Cuba's history and the work of Cuban scholars. In a sense Cuba was unique, because the slave trade lasted until the abolition of slavery during the last quarter of the nineteenth century. Africa, therefore, was closer to Afro-Cubans than to the descendants of Africans brought to other colonies in the New World. Cuba was also unique in that Cuban scholars and writers like Fernando Ortiz became interested in researching Afro-Cuban themes following the early inception of the republic in 1902.

My dissertation of 1966 was based upon extensive academic research and personal experiences in the field in Cuba. It had a historical focus that sought answers to questions about the origins of the Yoruban religion in Africa and the changes that the African religion underwent while being adapted to the Cuban environmental, social, economic, religious, and cultural milieu. The study provided a systematic comparison of Yoruban deities on both sides of the Atlantic, something that had not been done before. Such juxtaposition allowed the identification of changes that occurred or did not occur in the character, essence, and attributes of the Yoruban gods when worshipped in the Cuban setting. It emphasized those strategic adaptations that enabled the religion to survive and, ultimately, become a vehicle for the retention of elements of Yoruban language, music, and dance. The dissertation also suggested the extent to which this African religion significantly affected the Cuban population at large. Its title was *"Lo Yoruba en la Santería Afrocubana"* (Yoruba elements in Afro-Cuban Santería).

When I moved to Miami in 1967, I continued to explore and study Santería. It was Lydia Cabrera who encouraged me to publish my doctoral dissertation in order to make it available for broader use. Her prologue graced an updated and expanded version, which was published in Spanish in 1975 by Editorial Playor of Madrid. The new title was *La Religión Afrocubana* (The Afro-Cuban Religion).

The friendship that developed between Lydia and me was extremely rewarding. I enjoyed her acute sense of humor, her vast humanist education, her love of life and country, and the ease with which she communicated with people of all classes and races. I will never forget our discussions about Santería, about the many changes that were occurring—which she decried. She regretted the presence of some new *santeros* who were not really knowledgeable about their religion. She feared that Santería was losing its secret mysteries, its magical heart, and its mystical-spiritual ambiance that she loved so dearly.

At the time of our discussions during the late 1960s and early 1970s, there were not many scholars or authors interested in the subject, but Lydia knew those who were. Although Lydia had close relationships with Paul Verger and Roger Bastide, both well-known scholars in the field, I did not have the opportunity to meet them in person. However, when William Bascom and his wife, Carmelita, came to Miami in the mid-1970s Lydia and I spent an entire day with them, discussing changes in Santería, the *botánicas*,[5] the obvious merging with Palo Mayombe[6] and spiritualist beliefs, as well as the impact the overwhelming presence of whites was having on this religion.

When we discussed the matter of syncretic processes involved in culture change, Bascom's view was different from ours. Bascom looked at Santería from the perspective of the Yoruban religion. Lydia and I looked at it from the Cuban point of view. We saw Santería as a manifestation of the syncretic processes that were generating Cuban culture and were nourished by a mystical worldview prevalent in both Cuba and Africa. Worldview is a key concept and a matter that will be discussed more fully in chapters 1 and 2 and throughout the book.

During the 1970s and 1980s I did extensive field research in Miami while working as a Cuban "culture broker," mediator, and interpreter (Weidman 1973, 1975) for the Department of Psychiatry in the School of Medicine at the University of Miami. At this time my interest focused primarily on the synchronic aspects of Santería, that is, its function as a support system for people experiencing culture shock, problems of survival, the stress of acculturation, and multiple health problems.

I visited and interviewed a great number of *santeros, santeras,* spiritualists, and other healers, especially those who were consulted by the clients of the hospital and clinics where I worked. I sought their support and cooperation with the clinical treatment plan of our common clients. I was intrigued by Santería's resilience in confronting the new conditions of the postindustrial society. It was more vibrant and open than I would have expected, and most of the practitioners were white.

It was during this period that Abelardo Hernández, a *santero* who was the *padrino* (godfather) of one of our clients, advised me of the need to receive the *collares de fundamento*. I accepted the necklaces with gratitude and great respect for the practitioner who honored me, even though I had told him I was not a believer. I chose not to continue the process of initiation out of respect for the religion and because, in my own estimation, it would have been unethical to do so.

Over the last twenty years I have continued gathering information, participating in Santería's rituals when invited to do so, and observing both enduring traditions and changes, always seeking answers to new questions about such changes or the lack thereof. Overall, the extensive period of inquiry, which encompasses close to half a century, often has been difficult. Many prestigious *santeros* and *babalaos* did not wish to share their knowledge with the uninitiated. Nevertheless, through dedication, honesty in relationships, professional credibility, shared interests, and more than superficial knowledge of Santería, I was personally and professionally rewarded by the development of strong friendships with many key informants. At the same time, it took long hours and great patience with other key persons to be able to move beyond their hermetic stance.

The world has changed dramatically during the past fifty years, and Santería has also changed. It has changed from a religion practiced on the dirt floors of the poor temple-houses of the practitioners in Cuba to rituals performed in elegant banquet halls in the United States. It has changed from having a primarily lower-income Cuban black following to attracting people of different nationalities, races, and income groups. It has moved from secrecy to having practitioners participate in international scholarly meetings, press conferences, and radio and television programs.

Internal forces, such as pragmatism and tendencies to incorporate elements from other religious realms, have contributed to its transformation. These constitute a genuine part of its central adaptive dynamism.

External circumstances have been significant catalysts for change as well. In Cuba, Castro's totalitarian regime, its religious policies combined with its attempts to sponsor a folkloric and tourist version of Santería, have brought fundamental changes.

Santería's adaptation to exile conditions and a significant increase in the presence of white practitioners have also brought great changes. Other pressures have been wrought by the black American "Yoruban reversionism," which, in spite of its origins in Cuban Santería, has distanced itself from it by renouncing and denouncing Catholic and Cuban elements in the religion. Yoruban reversionism assumes an exclusive Afro-centric posture. It may be that, in a sense, these circumstances threaten the former essence of Afro-Cuban Santería.

There is also a significant Nigerian influence resulting from an interest in the expressions of the Yoruban religion in the New World. Thus, there is an abundance of available new literature on Yoruban religion and Santería.

This has generated new knowledge, understandings, and consequent internal change.

It is difficult to judge how much information gathered nowadays was preserved by Cuban practitioners or was obtained from African documentaries, books, conferences, and other sources. Understandably, through the years, my appraisal of Santería has changed. I have pondered the different conclusions to which I have been drawn while observing Santería over long periods of time. Of one thing I am certain: those conclusions were based upon all the available information I had in the course of my studies.

In the 1950s this religion was known and practiced by a minority of the Cuban population. It was perceived by many middle- and upper-class Cubans as a religion of blacks and the underclass. Many members of the poorer classes viewed it as witchcraft and sorcery. Even though, at that time, it was unknown to many Cubans, including many of African descent, Santería counted a number of followers from the middle and even the higher strata of society. Some participated openly, but more frequently they were secretly involved in it. Today, due to the Cuban Diaspora, the present conditions in Cuba, and other worldwide factors, Santería is widely known in the New World, in parts of Europe, and other regions of the world.

Santería and its Yoruban parent religion have always demonstrated the flexibility to adjust to different settings and to attract participants of diverse racial and socioeconomic backgrounds. They have been open and inclusive rather than closed and exclusive despite elements of secrecy within the religious structure itself. The functions that the Yoruban religion traditionally fulfilled were emphasized or de-emphasized according to the conditions and demands of the new milieux. Yet, I could never have predicted, while writing my doctoral dissertation so many years ago—and much less when, as a teenager in the 1940s I first became interested in Santería—that, at the threshold of the twenty-first century, it would become such a widespread emergent phenomenon.

Santería has been the subject of study by Cuban and non-Cuban scholars. The present work attempts to give a broad, comprehensive overview of this religious system. It aims to follow the trajectory of the Yoruban religion, the path of the orishas from Nigeria to Cuba on into a second exile. It attempts to recreate the ambiance of the ecological niches in which this religion flourished. It also strives to identify the changes that it has undergone in the process of being incorporated by individuals into these new sociocultural settings. According to Ninian Smart (1995: 20), the study of religion requires a poly-methodic approach, which uses methods drawn from a variety of disciplines. I have used multiple perspectives, to the extent possible, in an attempt to understand Santería and the directions in which it is evolving.

The concept of worldview frames much of the material introduced here.

From personal experiences and memories anchored in the sociocultural context in which I was reared and reached adulthood, I have attempted to convey some of the religious practices of that ethos in Cuba during the 1940s and 1950s. I have also tried to convey to the reader something of the religious ambiance in the Cuban countryside at approximately the same period of time. The latter picture portrayed rests upon the personal experiences and memories of an individual anchored in a sociocultural context very different from but still very similar to my own.

My understanding of Santería derives from a broad cultural knowledge of archaeology, historical events, Cuban literature, art, music, political ideologies, and trends. I was also part of a generation in search of solutions to Cuban social, political, and economic problems. Many of my generation wanted to fully incorporate blacks in a protagonistic fashion into the national scene and to free Cuba from outside interference. In essence this orientation reflected a search for a Cuban national identity in line with Martí's all encompassing ideology: "More than White, more than Black: Cuban," or as de la Fuente (2001: 12) said, paraphrasing Martí, "with all and for all" suggests "a nation for all."

Studying Santería was, to me, a way of reaching out and understanding significant segments of the Cuban population; as was the study of black literature, black music, and the impact they had on Cuban life and Cuban ethos. Much of the material presented here is from historical records and secondary sources; other information comes from intimate personal conversations, formal interviews, and participant observation, as well as notebooks from *santeros* and *babalaos*.

Whatever the levels of heterogeneity in the emergence of both Yoruban "ethnicity" and Santería (Lucumí) it is the congruence of value orientations within sociocultural systems in contact that allows "syncretic" processes to make a difference or not. I argue that transculturative processes occur more easily and rapidly when there are many congruencies in worldview assumptions than when there are few such congruencies; that is, when syncretism can occur easily.

Earlier work along these lines (my own included) has emphasized syncretic processes primarily and has looked less intensely at the worldview assumptions underlying those syncretisms. As I look at them here, it is my opinion that worldview approaches better explain transculturative processes that support cultural continuities in the face of change. In my view they better explain those areas of meaning that allow people to continue on an identifiable sociostructural path that also allows variations while preserving a fundamental meaning-system. Kearney's discussion of logico-structural integration helps make these points clear: "In constructing a model of a world view we expect to replicate these logico-structural relations in the derived basic propositions that represent assumptions in the various world-view universals. Therefore, we can say that certain propositions about some of the various universals of a world view tend to imply compatible and preclude incompatible propositions in both the same and other dimensions. Thus at any given time in its history a world view is to some degree a more-or-less logically consistent and structurally integrated set of assumptions" (Kearney 1984: 123–24). As I will point out in chapter 2, compatibilities that were present in the worldview brought by the Yoruban slaves to Cuba and that of many whites, especially those of the lower strata of society, facilitated the transculturative process and the merging of religious beliefs and practices.

Part 1 of this book deals with the origins of Santería. It describes aspects of the worldview of what has been labeled the Yoruban religion and aspects of the worldview of large segments of the Cuban population that were shared. It also describes the inception and emergence of this religion in Cuba, its structure, paraphernalia, and practices. Included is a biographical account that sheds light and information on Santería's functions and accommodations in a rural setting. One chapter discusses the loss of some of the Yoruban beliefs about reincarnation and the consequences of this loss within the religion. Another chapter discusses the great importance that Santería's function as a health-delivery system has had in attracting a new following, especially Cuban whites and people of non-Cuban extraction.

Part 2 provides a systematic comparison of the orishas in Africa and their counterparts that are known in Cuba. This section is a translation into English, updated and expanded, of my book *La Religión Afrocubana*, which was published in 1975. It includes a great deal of Nigerian and Afro-Cuban mythology in an effort to engage the reader in the humanistic elements and the magical ambiance of Santería in order to provide a substantial basis for interpreting types and degrees of change.

Part 3 discusses the moral dimensions of Santería. It also elaborates upon the significance of worldview analysis as related to basic assumptions and matters of logico-structural integration—both involved in contributing toward a better understanding of continuity and change in cultural and religious systems. Part 3 then focuses on the changes that have occurred in Santería on the island and in exile since the Cuban Revolution. It concludes with a discussion of issues and trends and suggests that worldview analysis of Santería in new historical, sociocultural, religious, political, and ecological contexts will be important, perhaps essential, for our understanding of cultural continuities and change in this specific religion's form in the future.

Santería is both a part of and a manifestation of a somewhat ambiguous (mystical and yet pragmatic) worldview. The accompanying ambivalent stance of individuals involved in Santería is linked to accommodations made to diverse and sometimes conflicting traditions that created Cuban culture. Examples are the embracing of mysticism and practicality, emotionalism and rationalism; the valuing of both traditional and trendy behaviors; adherence to both ethical and opportunistic inclinations; being both gullible and shrewd; accepting of both scientific endeavor and miracle seeking; believing and participating in both humanism and utilitarianism, and so forth. These conflicting themes were and continue to be representative of the core, or ethos, of being Cuban. They are "built into" Cuban personality. Ernest Hemingway sensitively identified these characteristics of the Cuban ethos and chose to offer his Nobel Prize medal to the Virgin of Charity as a way to honor the people of Cuba. The Yoruban religion was one that found fertile ground within the framework of such an ethos. The "match" was sufficiently strong to support the emergence of an Afro-Cuban religion called "Santería."

As a social scientist, I find nothing more challenging than the study and understanding of the dynamic processes of cultural association, borrowing, and adaptation prompted by the abrupt contact of groups of people from different cultural traditions. The process that gives rise to something new, yet old, by means of what Dr. Fernando Ortiz labeled "transculturación" (Ortiz 1963:129–35) has been the focus of my attention over many years. In essence, transculturation is what this book is about.

It is also about the application of a worldview approach to understanding the transculturative process itself. My overarching concern has been to illustrate congruencies between worldviews that may not only account for cultural continuity in the face of change but also those aspects of worldview that may, in turn, be more susceptible to change in diverse sociocultural settings during different historical periods.

My hope is that a worldview approach to understanding processes of transculturation reflected in the emergence of Afro-Cuban Santería will offer a stimulus to more detailed inquiry along such lines in the future.

Part 1

Santería's Development and Structure

The Yoruban Background of Santería/Regla Lucumí

Cuba's historical and social development supported the merging of traditions of different cultural origins. This chapter will offer a general overview of the history of the Yoruban people. Chapter 2 will deal with Cuba's colonial and early republican period: the institutions, circumstances, and milieu that enabled the survival of African religious beliefs in this new land.

Historical Overview: West Africa and Nigeria

The opening of the New World to colonization coincided with the successful Portuguese explorations of the West African Coast and the establishment of regular trade with the local kings. Until that time, geographic and other factors had kept the people living in sub-Saharan Africa isolated from the more technologically advanced people living in the northern Mediterranean coastal area. The desertification of the Sahara during the last thousands of years is probably the most important factor. A coastline largely devoid of safe harbors also contributed to this relative isolation.

The great river systems offered ample means for internal transport and communication. However, according to Robert W. July (1970: 8), before emptying into the sea, these rivers spilled over the continental edge in waterfalls and rapids that were impediments to communication between the interior and the coast. James L. Gibbs (1966: 549–50) in specific reference to Nigeria claimed that "most of Yoruba country lies on a denuded peneplain of ancient crystalline rocks. . . . In the crystalline country the rivers are choked with boulders and are quite unnavigable."

The prevalence of dreaded diseases such as malaria and yellow fever also acted as deterrents to explorers and traders. For all of these reasons Europeans did not venture into this region of Africa until well into the fifteenth century, though they were already exploring faraway regions in Asia and the New World. In the words of Robert W. July (1970:8): "It was not until the nineteenth century that Europe came to know anything substantial about the African interior, while only the occasional traveler from the Middle East was able to make his way into Africa beyond the Sahara."

Several empires had flourished during medieval times in the western Sudan. These empires, located at the bend of the Niger River, dominated the region from the fourth to the sixteenth century C.E. According to Robert W. July

(1970:61), "The savannah kingdoms infrequently possessed cultural and ethnic homogeneity; they were built on military conquest; imperial expansion often outran imperial administration; the problem of internal policing was never satisfactorily solved nor was the matter of orderly transfer of power through recognized succession." However, it seemed unreasonable to him to impute weakness to the states that lasted as long as they did (1970: 60).

The Ghana Empire, bounded on the north by the desert and extending westward from the bend of the Niger to the Atlantic, was founded around 300 B.C.E. and flourished for over six centuries, from approximately the beginning of the eighth century to the thirteenth century. It was based upon a strong monarchy, an efficient tax-collecting system, a hierarchy of officials, and extensive trade among numerous cities. Its gold-based economy lured Arabs, who crossed the desert on camels from the northern Mediterranean and established exclusive trade with these sub-Saharan people over the course of eight centuries. Arabic became the language of trade, and the religious penetration of Islam began. In 1076 the Almoravids conquered the Ghana Empire. After its fall, Ghana lingered for another two centuries, having been greatly weakened by that blow.

Following the decline of the Ghana Empire, the Mali Empire (thirteenth to sixteenth centuries) flourished. One of its famous cities, Timbuktu, boasted famous scholars, holy men, and a university. Later the Songhai Empire (1350s–1650s) replaced the Mali. Our knowledge about these empires is limited and is based primarily on archaeological findings and the accounts of Islamic visitors and traders.

The dramatic changes that occurred during the fifteenth century in the western Mediterranean greatly affected the history of West Africa and the New World. In 1415 the Portuguese conquered the Arab stronghold of Ceuta in Northwest Africa. Subsequently, Portuguese traders and explorers manned annual expeditions down the West African coast to establish trading posts and missions. In 1486 Alfonso d'Aveiro came to Benin with a small trading mission. According to Sanche De Gramont (1977:58): "The Portuguese were the first white men the Niger delta people had ever seen. The Benin king, or oba, who had slaves for his own use, began to sell them to his white visitors in exchange for copper bracelets. This was the start of the greatest forced migration in history, which scattered West Africans all over the globe."

The availability of this new slave labor force fostered the establishment of the plantation system in parts of the New World. This system had its origins in the Mediterranean during the Crusades and was tied to labor-intensive sugar agriculture and industry for the European market. According to Curtin, et al. (1978:215): "The whole system of plantation agriculture is sometimes called the South Atlantic system. Its productive centers were in the Americas, supplied by slave labor from Africa, managerial staff from Europe, and producing tropical staples, for the European market."

In 1492, Queen Isabel of Castile expelled the Arabs from their last stronghold in Granada and sponsored Columbus in the successful expedition that opened the New World to the Europeans. Eventually, the colonists from these areas clamored for slaves. When the colonists demanded slave labor, the Europeans accommodated them; they had direct access to an inexhaustible source: sub-Saharan Africa, especially the West Coast.

In search of cheap labor, the Spanish crown authorized the importation of African slaves to its new colonies in the Caribbean early in the sixteenth century. This action was taken at the urging of the colonists, including some pious members of religious orders who meant to protect the Indian population, which was perceived as fragile. Thus, the transatlantic slave trade began on a regular basis.

Portuguese ships, which had been exploring the coast of West Africa, were the first to engage in this inhumane business. Later, European sea powers such as the Dutch, the Royal Company of French Guinea, and others competed for the spoils of the profitable trade. Following the Treaty of Utrecht in 1713, Great Britain practically monopolized this trade until it was declared illegal by treaties signed by Spain and Great Britain in 1817 and 1820. Even after those treaties were signed, the trade continued to flourish in the form of profitable contraband until the last decades of the nineteenth century.

Even before the arrival of Europeans in West Africa, local political authority was not very stable. Empires and political hegemony did not last very long, being rapidly replaced by the hegemony of others. Sometimes empires would be dissolved into small kingdoms or chieftainships which comprised a few villages. The towns and the patrilineal lineages were the enduring sociopolitical units where all members knew their specific places. To understand the strength and survival of this culture, it is necessary to delve into the history of the Yoruba-speaking people of Southwest Nigeria.

It is always hazardous to make generalized statements about a culture, drawing from literature that covers a period stretching over many years and in some cases, several centuries. Cultures are dynamic, in a constant process of flux and change, but cultures also have core features that are identifiable and enduring. Such features manifest stability and coherence in the face of change as well as integrity of meaning through time. In an attempt to shed light on the roots and worldview of Santería I have no choice but to assume the risk of error by utilizing data about Nigerian and Cuban culture gathered by observers and researchers over the course of several centuries but especially during the last two centuries. The intent is to identify congruencies of form and meaning between Yoruban religion and Cuban popular religiosity. Also, the intent is to identify the transformations and accommodations that gave birth to Santería in the process of adapting to the Cuban milieu.

The Yoruba-speaking people have been one of the most artistically, politically, and religiously advanced in West Africa. They live in the southwest of the present nation-state of Nigeria. Until fifty years ago, it was believed that the Yoruba migrated to West Africa from the east, from somewhere near what ancient Egyptians called the Upper Nile, during the early centuries of the Christian era. The prevalent opinion today is that they are people of great antiquity in the area they occupy. According to linguists, their language has been spoken as a separate branch of the Kwa group for thousands of years.

The Yoruba-speaking people were never under a single ruler at any time in their history. Their language never included a name that might indicate they were conscious of a shared homogeneous identity. They identified themselves according to the kingdom or chieftainship into which they were born.

In the nineteenth century, Europeans used the term Yoruba to refer to the language of the people who inhabited the old Oyo kingdom in the northern regions of Yorubaland; they also used it to refer to the language of those people who spoke dialects related to Old Oyo. According to Peel (2000:28): "Despite their shared linguistic and cultural traits and regard for Ile-Ife as the origin of their most sacred traditions, the speakers of 'Yoruba' dialects did not as yet share a common and distinctive name: they knew themselves as Egba, Ijesha, or Awori, or else just by the ilu, or 'town.'" Ade Ajayi and Smith (1964:2) report that the neighbors of the Yoruba-speaking people used the word Anago to refer to Yoruba language. Among Afro-Cubans the word Anagó is also used to refer to Lucumí and/or the Yoruban language (Cabrera 1957). Anago is also the name of a town in western Yorubaland.

Ile Ife, the sacred city of the Yoruba, established in an evergreen forest, played a very prominent role in the historical and cultural experience of the Yoruba-speaking people. Ile Ife's oral traditions claim that Oduduwa, the mythical ancestor of the Yoruban people, arrived from the east. "Ile Ife was the place where he (Oduduwa) settled and it was from there that his children and grandchildren went forth to found the various ruling dynasties among the Yoruba and neighboring peoples. All the important traditional rulers who have the right to wear beaded crowns trace their origin there, and many of them used to send to Ile-Ife for sacred symbols to use at their coronations in order to legitimize themselves. The rulers of imperial Oyo and of Shabe, Old Ketou, Abeokuta, and other regions were among them" (Ade Ajayi and Smith 1964:1).

Robert F. Thompson (1976:CH1/1) provides additional information about Ile Ife, Oduduwa, and the governance structure: "Yorubaland divides into traditional states, the oldest by tradition founded by the mythic founder of the kingship and father of all Yoruba, the great deity Oduduwa. The capital of each state is at the same time, in most instances, a center of art. These states, viewed from their sacred center, the holy city of Oduduwa, Ile-Ife, include: Oyo and Igbomina in the north; Ijesha, Efon, and the petty kingships of the Ekiti in the east; Ode, Ondo, and Owo in the southeast; Ijebu in the south; Shabe, Ketou, Ohori Anago, Aworri, Ibarapa, Egba, and Egbado in the southwest. Farther to the west there are enclaves of Yoruba in north central Dahomey and Togo."

According to Pemberton and Afolayan (1996:26): "Today almost every Yoruba kingdom or mini-state claims descent from Ile Ife and that the crown of their Oba was bestowed by Oduduwa. There is little doubt about the antiquity and cultural importance of Ile Ife in Yoruba history. Archeological, art historical, and linguistic evidence trace the history of Ife to the ninth century and confirm its status as a well-developed city-state by the twelfth century."

Ile Ife's dominance lasted over five hundred years, from the tenth to the fifteenth centuries. Its influence and worldview profoundly affected Yoruban culture, especially in the arts, politics, and religion. Ile Ife terra-cotta heads and bronzes have received worldwide recognition as great artistic achievements. In addition, Ile Ife's elaboration of the belief in divine kingship had a great impact on Yoruban political and religious culture. This influence is apparent when one takes into account that the most important dynastic families of regional kingdoms claimed to be descendants of the legendary founders of Ile Ife.

Among the Yoruba-speaking people there was a trend toward urbanism unparalleled among their neighbors.

> More than two thirds of the population of the traditional city, according to Peter Lloyd, was composed of cultivators who maintained houses in the town and also farming huts, the latter sometimes located at some distance from the town. Other sectors of the urban groupings included traders and craftsmen, the latter specializing in various patterns (ona), the Yoruba word for art. Wealth from the farms assured leisure and patronage to lineages of sculptors, brass-casters, blacksmiths, bead embroiderers, and so forth. These men were enabled to address themselves to the professional creation of beauty. In the ancient centers, such as Ijebu-Ode and Ketu, the concentration of chiefly and sacred authority assured the artists of patronage and prestige. Their works and their designs helped bring the gods to the town and maintain the glory of the kingships. (Thompson 1976:CH1/1)

In addition to the arts, adds Thompson (P/1), Yoruban society valued personal qualities such as composure and character. "The nine million Yoruba of southwestern Nigeria and Dahomey value power and command (ashe), composure (itutu); and character (iwa)... Command resided in the king, the deputy of the gods. The arts of kingship suggested divine energy in juxtaposition with a composed human mask of equilibrium and control.... Doctor-diviners were specialists in composure and coolness (itutu), assuaging fevers and dislocations of the body politic.... It is good to be cool, but it is also necessary to be manly and dynamic. Here the role of the warriors is introduced. These brave men guarded the security of the cities."

Yoruban leaders demonstrated having successfully balanced the three cultural values of command, composure, and character to master the necessary foundations for urban living. According to Thompson (1976:P/1): "Urbanism demands many achievements, among them political organization, standards of health, and military security. The arts of the Yoruba assure us these issues were on the minds of the leaders of the past and that the problems were dealt with intelligently, involving among other decisions, differential weightings of the values of command, composure, and character."

In matters of religious beliefs, Ile Ife's influence was paramount. In Ile Ife the cult to orishas (deities), such as Orunmila, the god of wisdom and the oracles, Olodumare, the sky god, and Elegbara Eshu, the god of the unpredictable, became very elaborate, and from Ile Ife these cults spread far and wide among the Yoruba. Consequently, Ile Ife's orishas became more generic, displacing or outshining other regional orishas who had similar attributes or characteristics.

Even though most of the local regional rulers claimed descent from Ile Ife's sacred kingship, their particular gods, in some instances, showed characteristics that set them apart from those of Ile Ife. Nevertheless, for the Yoruba the concept of an ancestral city was of paramount importance from a political, social, and religious perspective. This view meant that people's sense of identity did not transcend the city and region from which their ancestors came. As such, people owed allegiance to the area's rulers and rendered cult to the area's orishas.

As time passed, other orishas besides those originally worshipped in Ile Ife attained significance, and their cults spread throughout Yorubaland. Among the most significant were the creator god, Obatala; the goddess of the river, Oshun; the mother of fish and of many orishas, Yemonja; the god of thunderstorms, Shango; and his consort, Oya, the goddess of the Niger River. The cult to Ogun, the god of metals and war, and the cult to the sacred twins, or Ibeji, also spread throughout most of Yorubaland.

The worldview of the Yoruba-speaking people, as described by Pemberton and Afolayan (1996:136), is very mystical: "Among the Yoruba the universe of gods, ancestors, and the living is a shared realm of continuous ritual activity."

This cosmological construct is the product of intuitive sympathy with nature. Western man loses this empathy in his quest to control nature by pragmatic means instead of spiritual ones. In the religion of the Yoruba-speaking people, the source of all the life force, sacred energy, or ashe, of the world is a remote creator. Ashe is manifested in natural phenomena, especially those related to the earth.

In West Africa, perceptions about nature, man, life, and death were different from those of the educated elite of western Europe. For example, in West Africa a person has his own character and personality, but, in a sense, individual identity is superseded by group identity. The western value of individuality is alien to most people in a society where social status, residence, ownership, worship, and other social attributes are determined by the place the individual holds in the patrilineal lineage.

Also, in traditional West African society the realms of the sacred and the profane were not separate but engaged in an interactive flow, not unlike European perceptions during medieval times. The realms of the secular and the sacred were contiguous, as were the realms of the living and the dead. Religion was such a part of the fabric of life that people needed constantly to consult oracles, give offerings, and negotiate an endless number of taboos to engage positively the supernatural powers that presided over every aspect of their lives. William Fagg (1982: 33, 34), who did fieldwork among the Yoruba 1949 to 1981, claims that most pre-industrial societies share the following: ". . . their ontology is based on some form of dynamism, the belief in immanent energy, in the primacy of energy over matter in all things. . . . Thus, it is energy and not matter, dynamic and not static being, which is the true nature of things. This conception is more readily intelligible to those versed in modern physics than to others, and indeed it would appear, at least when stated in this summary form, to be closer to the objective scientific truth than is the static conception of matter by which we live." As we shall see later, this concept of "immanent energy" is the Yoruban concept of "ashe" (and the Afro-Cuban *"aché"*). Adds Fagg (1982:53): "Ashe is . . . a Yoruba concept by which (one) may understand the diversity in Yoruba art as creative acts of interpretation and realize that this activity is an essential characteristic of Yoruba culture."

Also, central in traditional West African religions was the belief that sympathetic as well as dangerous and hostile spirits were around the living, and that they could and did intervene in their daily lives. Consequently, the individual spent a great amount of time attempting to deal with the spiritual world in order to attract benevolent spirits and disentangle himself from the others. His life was an endless liturgy whereby practical behavior was intertwined with mystical beliefs and ritual practices that, ultimately, were indistinguishable.

Such a view is illustrated in the words of Sanche De Gramont, the Pulitzer Prize-winner who traveled extensively through West Africa in 1972 gathering data for his book on the story of the Niger River and its explorers:

> The African's thought process is alien to the European. It is based on different notions of nature, society, and death, and it survives to a surprising degree in modern African states, coexisting with Western-inspired technology and learning. In traditional, rural West African societies, man is in such close communion with nature, and is so dependent on natural phenomena such as rainfall, that he tends to see cause and effect as the coincidence between two completely unrelated phenomena. Just as he sees rain falling and millet growing, so, if a man crosses his path as his head begins to ache, he will think: that man is the cause of my headache. More than that, he will attach some symbolic significance to the event, as he does to natural phenomena. He will think: that man who crossed my path and gave me a headache must be a member of a tribe antagonistic to mine. (De Gramont 1977:39–40)

In a world conceived of as if it were governed by supernatural forces, access to control is perceived as still being possible through magical practices. Such practices are based on the assumptions that like produces like, that opposite produces opposite, and that by manipulating an object that has been in contact with someone or something, one can effectively achieve a desired result.

De Gramont (1977:39) reported on magical practices in Nigeria. There, for example, an egg, which is perceived as not having a mouth, is buried to insure that a secret will be kept. In the Niger Delta, a tribe stops rain by sprinkling coal dust in the fields, because fire is assumed to be the opposite of water.

De Gramont's observations are based upon his experiences in West Africa nearly a century after the contraband of slaves to Cuba had ceased. There are great similarities in the worldview assumptions of Santería's followers and those described by De Gramont. It seems very likely that such assumptions and practices that have survived in modern West Africa were brought to the New World by slaves, where they also survived, coexisted with, and complemented Western technology in Afro-Cuban Santería and Afro-Brazilian Candomblé.

In contrast to De Gramont, Peter McKenzie (1997:38), who has done extensive research on Yoruban religiosity in the nineteenth century during the period when great numbers of Yoruba were brought to Cuba, sees in the religion a different focus: "Yoruba religion in the nineteenth century would seem to be a religion of the earth rather than of the sky." Earthly natural phenomena such as mountains, volcanoes, hills, rocks, piles of stones, water, rivers, streams, lagoons, the sea, and the ocean are perceived as manifestations of ashe. Ashe is also manifested in some trees, commonly in groves, in some plants and herbs, and in some animals, particularly snakes, snails, lizards, and birds, especially vultures. The power of ashe is channeled or manifested in different ways: orishas, consecrated stones, oracles, trees, symbolic objects fashioned by man, such as amulets, and so forth. The objective of rituals is to procure the force necessary for subsistence, the propagation of the people, and the ability to cope with life.

Atmospheric phenomena, such as lightning, thunder, rain, tornadoes, and the wind, which greatly affect the lives of earthly dwellers, are also considered important sources of supernatural power. The rainbow is admired and revered, but not as much as the more dynamic and destructive atmospheric phenomena. Moreover, the sun, the moon, and the stars are admired for their magnificence and are viewed as manifestations of the greatness of the creations of the Supreme Being, but they are not the objects of much religious interest.

Insightfully, J. D. Y. Peel (2000:92), focusing on the ethos of Yoruban religious practices, which are also observable in Santería, comments:

> "Making country fashion"[1] was above all a quest for power. This might take the form of personal endowments, such as health, wealth, and fertility; or (because these good things were felt to depend in large part on how you stood with other people) of relational powers, power over other people, or protection from the power of others. In societies like this, an adequate history of religion has to be a political history too, while political history, if it is not to be unpardonably thin, has to take a strong streak of religion in it. More specifically, the political narratives of the last two chapters form an essential backdrop to the mainly "religious" focus of what is to come, for two principal reasons: first because relations with *orisa* and other unseen powers are modeled on those with chiefs and powerful people, who are often regarded as different from them in degree rather than in kind; and second, because the point of "making country fashion" was largely to affect power relations in the community.

The Yoruba occasionally practiced human sacrifice. According to P. A. Talbot (1926 3:859): "The greatest numbers of human sacrifices among the Yoruba were probably those offered at the sacred city of Ife. Here the British Government had great difficulty in securing their abolition; the Awni insisted that the sacrifices were made for the well-being of the whole human race, and further that if those performed in his own behalf were discontinued, his superior knowledge and arts derived there from would leave him." Talbot (1926:32, 46, 88) also reports on victims offered to Shango on special occasions, to Olokun, to Ogun, and to other orishas. There is no hard evidence that in Cuban Santería human sacrifices have ever been offered.[2]

After the decline of Ile Ife during the second half of the fifteenth century, new successor kingdoms and city-states arose. According to J. A. Atanda (1980:19), "The key political unit on which government was based in all the Yoruba kingdoms was the town, *ilú*. Each kingdom consisted of many towns, but this did not mean that there were many independent governments in each kingdom. What happened was that the government of the capital served as the central government of the kingdoms, while those of the subordinate towns served as local government units." Among these kingdoms, the most important was Oyo, which was located in the northwestern part of Yoruba country, in the savanna area, close to the Niger River. Tradition claims that Oranyan, Oduduwa's son or grandson, founded Oyo. This was among the latest kingdoms founded by the Yoruba, and it became the most powerful. Oyo, having contact with all of the markets around the area, became the most important trading center south of the Niger.

Oyo's hegemony was in part due to the imposing cavalry that the priest-ruler, or Alafin, commanded. In addition, Oyo had excellent weavers and blacksmiths whose products were in great demand. Oyo also obtained large profits from importing horses, which gave it great military and political advantage. Cavalry revolutionized warfare, especially in the savanna areas where horses became military assets. Moreover, in the savannas, the tzetze fly, which proved deadly for horses, was not as prevalent as in the heavily forested zones.

As the Oyo Empire flourished, old myths were elaborated in efforts to legitimize Oyo's authority and preeminence; in some subjugated regions this authority was challenged in the ritual field. Apter (1992:33) thinks that this conflict is reflected and manifested in Oyo-centric versus Ife-centric fields of ritual: "According to the ritual-field theory, Ife-centric traditions were preserved by rituals which emphasized The autonomy of Ife's successor states vis-à-vis Oyo's imperial interests. It was not traditionalistic piety for Ife's past grandeur which kept its founding myths and dynastic traditions vigorously alive, but the political opposition of its successor states to Oyo's growing hegemonic claims." As we shall later see this conflict is a source of contradictions in mythology and rituals in Yoruba religion and in Santería.

Oyo flourished for over two centuries and began to decline at the end of the eighteenth century. Its final demise caused the terrible civil wars that ravaged Yoruba country during the nineteenth century. These wars facilitated the expansion of the slave trade, which further disrupted the Yoruba homeland, society, and culture. When at the end of the eighteenth century the old Oyo Empire started to decline, a new Oyo Empire emerged to the south, but it also went into decline in the early nineteenth century.

According to C. W. Newbury (1961:36), the evidence shows that the slave trade in Yoruban country was not considerable before 1820. Slaving had not caused much disruption because of the political arrangements between the alafin of Oyo and the obas of Ife, Ekiti, Ijebu, Ondo, and Ilesha, who claimed a common origin. As a consequence of the collapse of the Oyo Empire, the slave trade flourished, in spite of being outlawed by Great Britain in the 1820s.

Another unsettling consequence of the demise of the Oyo Empire was intercity civil wars, which were prevalent in the 1850s and, in many instances, were fueled by the eagerness to capture prisoners to be sold as slaves. Simultaneously, social disruption prevented the development of legitimate trade, further eroding the social and political basis of Yoruban society. Ravaging civil wars, population displacements, and unparalleled slave raiding generated highly disruptive processes within the social and political fabric of Yoruban society. As summed up by Robert W. July (1970:11): "In the final analysis, as they were to demonstrate during their nineteenth-century civil wars, the Yoruba had little internal cohesion and were incapable of living and working together in peace."

During this period the encroaching pressures of two world religions, Christianity and Islam, began to be felt in Nigeria. Anglicans and Methodists established Christian missions. Also, former slaves, who had been given freedom by the abolitionist crusade heralded by the Christians, returned to their homeland. Many of the returnees were imbued with the new ideas to which they had been exposed (Peel 2000:8) and were grateful for the advocacy of Christian missionaries. At the same time, in the north and northwest, Islam was making extraordinary gains. Nevertheless, orisha worshippers could still count on the backing of the authorities for the practice of their religion during these changing times.

The Yoruba-speaking people remained independent of foreign hegemony until the end of the nineteenth century. After devastating civil wars and the fall of the new Oyo Empire, most of the area they occupied became part of the British Protectorate that was established in 1900. In a short period of time great percentages of the population embraced different denominations of Christianity, while others converted to Islam.

At present, the Yoruba-speaking people reside in and constitute the most populous ethnic group of the nation-state of Nigeria, which was created in 1960. Nigeria borders on the south with the sea, to the north and east with the River Niger, and to the west with the Republic of Benin, formerly called Dahomey or French Nigeria. Large numbers of Yoruba live in the Republic of Benin in the towns of Pobe, Ketou, and Shabe, close to the border with Nigeria. Smaller groups live in the Republic of Togo and on the Gold Coast, in the Republic of Ghana.

Traditional Yoruban Ethos and Worldview

Aspects of Yoruban ethos and worldview have been touched upon above. In this section, however, I wish to elaborate more specifically upon the two concepts. As I mentioned in the preface, ethos is considered to be the life-style of a group; while worldview is, as Kearney (1984:42) suggests, the cognitive framework supporting a group's life-style. In addition, ethos reflects specific principles of social structure and behavior that are ordered by worldview assumptions.

Although she did not use the term, Alma Lowery-Palmer (1980), a graduate student under the supervision of Michael Kearney (1984), provides a description of Yoruban ethos based upon research in Osegere, a farming community located in southwestern Nigeria sixteen miles north of Ibadan, the capital of the state of Oyo. The study was done in 1976 and 1977, but it is of particular importance to the present discussion. It descriptively encapsulates a way of life that is compatible with earlier ethnographic material on the Yoruba. Furthermore, utilizing Kearney's model for the analysis of worldview, this study also reveals the logico-structural integration of values and assumptions that support the way of life of this agricultural community.

The integrity of interrelationships along behavioral parameters in all aspects of life is impressive. The clear-cut principles that structure behavior in family and community spheres of activity constitute a basis for order and harmony that is striking. And even though Yoruban ethos in the mid-1970s may not reflect perfectly the ethos of the Yoruban groups from which slaves were exported to Cuba during the colonial period, Lowery-Palmer's dissertation research cannot be dismissed lightly. It serves as a guide to understanding much of present day Yoruban behavior as well as a guide for questioning inquiry into aspects of Yoruban behavior described from the past. Lowery-Palmer argues (and there is ample evidence to support her assertion) that even though Yoruban subgroups may differ in details of certain ceremonies and behaviors, ". . . yet in Yorubaland the different Yoruban groups do share a consciousness of the world" (Lowery-Palmer 1980:40).

Space limitations prohibit an extensive review of the Osegere Yoruban ethos described by Lowery-Palmer (1980:9–39), but following her descriptions along various parameters of social organization and behavior, she captures the image of what might be considered the good life in Osegere by quoting Osborne as follows: "The presence of adult children and grandfatherhood are evidence of a man's wisdom and ability to live harmoniously with the family, neighbors, gods, and ancestors" (Osborne 1972:83; Lowery-Palmer 1980:15).

As Lowery-Palmer moves from a description of ethos into an analysis of worldview assumptions based upon Kearney's prepublication teaching model, she concludes that the "three basic principles reflecting their world view assumptions, by which the Yoruba structure their social patterns, are: 1) patrilineal social organization reflecting Yoruba images of Self-Other; 2) rules of seniority reflecting images of time; and 3) spatial images of rural-urban relationship" (Lowery-Palmer 1980: 38).

Lowery-Palmer then enters into an extensive examination of Osegere residents' perceptions and behaviors along Kearney's universal dimensions for the analysis of worldview outlined above in the preface. Her insightful and detailed findings cannot be reviewed here, but three important quotations from her work are included below. According to Lowery-Palmer (1980:63), citing Awolalu (1972:112), "Man is not created to be alone. He is created to be a being-in-relation. The whole existence from birth to death is organically embodied in a series of associations, and life appears to have its full value only in those close ties. Those close ties will include extended family members, the clan and village, the various societies and organizations in the community together with the close ties to the ancestors and gods who are interested in the day-to-day life of men." This echoes the words of Mbiti (1970:141), whom Lowery-Palmer (1980:63) quotes: "I am because we are; and since we are, therefore I am."

Kearney (1984:74) refers to this student's work in his published theoretical model for worldview analysis. He comments that "The way in which people see their relationship to the Other affects the way they act toward it. If a people see themselves as intimately interconnected with the Other in general, then they see their well-being as dependent on its well-being. In such a case it might be appropriate to speak of an 'ecological consciousness.'"

Continuing, Kearney indicates that the image of Self as an aspect of and as dependent on the group is congruent with Yoruban assumptions about causality.

> . . . [A]ll visible and invisible phenomena are assumed to result from the presence of varying concentrations and forms of ubiquitous energy. . . . All persons and things are part of a web of relationships that depend on this energy. It is contrary to this image to think of people or things in isolation; they exist only as aspects of relationships, linked together by this pervasive power. . . . One of the forms of this power is human thought, which is assumed to be effective in the sense that wishes and emotions can have an effect at a distance. What another may think of you can potentially affect your personal condition. The individuals of the local community are intimately connected in this way. And it follows that you are concerned about how others regard you, for your state of well-being is dependent not only on how they act toward you but also on what they think about you. (Kearney 1984: 75)

Kearney also notes that attitudes toward nonhuman aspects of the world are consistent with Yoruban assumptions about interpersonal relationships, and that the image of pervasive power is central in this regard. He quotes Lowery-Palmer as follows:

> The unity of "wholeness" of the universe is dependent on man who is at the center, relating himself to natural phenomena, including other men, in a manner which facilitates balance or harmony. The underlying principle on which balance is achieved and maintained is that of proper respect for the unifying principle of power or energy exchange between all created forms. In order to understand and make use of power, the Yoruba individual seeks knowledge by continuously improving his skills and abilities in deciphering the meaning of the invisible as manifested by the visible. To the Yoruba natural phenomena, including the physical body, are a source of knowledge and wisdom. The dynamic relationship of Self and nature is characterized by knowledge seeking activities in a cooperative harmonious manner. (Lowery-Palmer: 75–76, in Kearney: 1984:75)

According to Kearney (1984:75), "This view of perceptible forms as but manifestations of a more fundamental 'spiritual' principle is logico-structurally consistent with Yoruba world-view classification."

Once again Kearney (1984:75) quotes Lowery-Palmer, who had relied upon earlier statements by Kearney (N.D.):

> To the Yoruba, while particular persons (or entities) appear outwardly different, behind surface appearances they are only manifestations of an underlying power which unifies all creation. As in the Yoruba image of Self-Other, in which the Self is completely identified, in an undifferentiated way, with the group, so is person/not-person not qualitatively different from all life; it is a visible aspect of the underlying process of interactions and interdependence of all living systems. Living beings—man, plants, animals, spirits—are viewed as a continuum of beings differing only in amounts of power. The Yoruba image of life is that of an energy system that can maintain itself as a self-centered, self-regulating, balanced unity irrespective of the form in which it inheres. . . . (Lowery-Palmer 1980:84)

A great deal more could be said on the matter of Yoruban ethos and worldview, but for present purposes the intent is to suggest two things: The first is the degree to which Yoruban ethos structures a life of order in daily activities, of morality in dealing with others, of respect for those above and below in social hierarchies, of consideration among cohorts in cross-cutting social categories, along with balance and harmony among human beings, the natural environment, the ancestors, and the gods. Reflected in the structure of such an ethos are ideals of self-composure, integrity of character, of power in the form of knowledge and wisdom, and measured behavior in relation to others, to the natural environment, and to the supernatural realm.[3]

The second suggestion to be made here is the degree to which both social order and the logico-structural integration of values and assumptions supporting that order were shattered with the experience of civil wars in Africa and of slavery during the Cuban colonial period. In Cuba particularly, the Yoruban ethos and worldview were no longer in accord with dramatically altered socioenvironmental conditions in the new setting. Lowery-Palmer's study helps us infer an ethos and worldview baseline from which to better understand Yoruban beliefs and their contribution to the emergence of Santería.

The Cuban Colonial and Republican Background of Santería/Regla Lucumí

If, to comprehend Santería, it is vital to have some understanding of the Yoruba-speaking people's experience, it is also important to consider the Cuban colonial and republican experience. These were societies in which slaves were settled and where their descendants were born; societies in which strategies and institutions were developed that allowed the preservation of some of the African cultural traditions.

In a sense those societies nourished but also transformed the African religions that were brought by slaves. Some aspects of the religions survived; others were changed, and still others were merged with a variety of religious beliefs and practices. The final outcome fulfilled the needs of many members of the new society, including people of European descent.

Colonial Cuba

Columbus arrived in Cuba during his first voyage to the New World on October 27, 1492, when Amerindian groups sparsely populated the island. Bartolomé de Las Casas, one of the earliest chroniclers, distinguished two distinct groups: the Siboneyes or Ciboneyes and the Taínos (1951 1:246). This terminology is still being used today (Dacal Moure and Rivero de la Calle (1996:10). The Siboneyes were food collectors who roamed the coastal areas and the river mouths in search of food. The horticulturist Taínos lived in villages. They were linguistically related to the Arawak, who were originally from the Amazon basin. The Arawak had sailed a northwesterly migratory course in their dugout canoes, first settling the Lesser Antilles and then the most easterly islands of the Greater Antilles (Puerto Rico, Hispaniola) until they finally reached Cuba.

The contribution of these Amerindian ethnic groups to post-conquest Cuban culture was meager. Their population was decimated shortly after the establishment of the Spanish colonial settlements in 1512. The ravaging effect of epidemics upon their immune systems, which had no resistance to common European childhood and other diseases, like syphilis, killed many. The harsh servitude to which many of them were subjected also proved too much for them. Those who survived intermingled with the Spanish colonists, their descendants, and the African slaves who were brought with them. Their legacy remains in the names of geographic locations, rivers, trees, and fruits; also, in their transmitted knowledge of the cultivation of tobacco, which later became the most important export product of the colony of Cuba for over three hundred years.

The Iberian Peninsula had witnessed great demographic and cultural upheavals before and during this period. It was originally inhabited by the Iberians, Mediterranean Caucasians who had a Neolithic culture. Later, parts of the peninsula were occupied by Celtic tribes. Phoenicians and Greeks settled the Mediterranean and Atlantic coastal areas and established colonies that culturally influenced the local population. Later, Rome conquered, colonized, and occupied the peninsula, imprinting its culture, languages, and dialects with as much force as it had in Italy. In the fifth century C.E. Germanic tribes, especially the Visigoths, occupied the peninsula. During the eighth century, Muslim warriors, in some instances led by heirs of Persian dynastic families, occupied most of the peninsula. Later on, in the eleventh century, other waves of Muslims, originally from Morocco, entered in great numbers. Consequently, over time cultural and religious heterogeneity has dominated the life of the inhabitants of the Iberian Peninsula. The merging of these contrasting cultural traditions resulted in a rich, unique, and diversified cultural legacy evidenced in the music, painting, literature, cuisine, and other social characteristics in what is now Spain. Overall, the cultural heritage of Spain greatly influenced Cuban culture.

Muslim Arabs brought Africans from the sub-Sahara regions as slaves to Spain. Even though the Moorish power vanished coincidentally during the same year the New World was discovered, limited numbers of African slaves and freeborn blacks remained in Catholic Spain. A few of them were brought to the New World and to Cuba from the beginning of its colonization.

The Spanish colonial system was characterized by an inefficient centralization of political power, and by economic and religious monopolies. These factors did very little to stimulate democratic institutions, bureaucratic efficiency, private economic enterprise, and/or free ideological discourse.

The urban orientation of the Spanish civilization can be discerned clearly in the patterns of colonization it followed. The Spanish founded *villas* or towns with a central area or park around which the Catholic Church, the local government headquarters, other official buildings, and the homes of important officers and individuals [of that town] were built. Each town was named and placed under the protection of a saint, a path of the Virgin, or other religious figure.

The Catholic Church that came to the Americas was, to all intents and purposes, a Spanish national church based on an agreement made by Queen Isabel of Castile with the papacy. The church became an arm of the government of the metropolis, aligned with the interests of the privileged classes.

Catholicism was brought to the Americas at the end of the Middle Ages just after a wave of *Marianismo* (cult of the Virgin Mary) had swept over Western Christianity, especially Mediterranean Catholicism. In the New World the church encouraged devotion to the Virgin in her different manifestations. The Virgin was perceived as presenting herself in visions to different people in the Americas. In many instances she showed in her semblance the racial features of the population of each area. This phenomenon began when, early in the colonial period, the Virgin Mary resembling a Mexican was seen by a Mexican Indian. This appearance of Mary is called Guadalupe and is the patron of all Mexicans.

During the colonial period (1512–1898) the Catholic Church was the official religion of the colony. The Catholic Church in Cuba lacked the evangelical zeal and inspiration that were the engines of its proselytizing efforts during the sixteenth century in Mexico and later in California and other places. The church managed the few parochial schools that offered meager instruction to a limited number of townspeople. The vast majority of the island's inhabitants, freemen and slaves alike, were illiterate. Private tutors instructed children of the Creole[1] elite.

Some children of the middle class attended the few private schools that were opened in the nineteenth century. Many children of the middle and upper classes were cared for by black nannies who, in many instances, exposed them to the values and beliefs of the magical and mystical African worldview.

The island of Cuba languished during the first three centuries of the colonial period. Spanish colonists were lured away by the opportunities in new colonies established in Bolivia, Peru, and Mexico. Nevertheless, some population growth resulted from intermarriage among the surviving descendants of the decimated Indian population with the few Spanish colonists and African slaves who had settled on the island.

Only Cuba's capital city, Havana, engaged significantly in foreign trade. For nearly three centuries, because of Havana's advantageous geographic location, the Spanish fleet, full of the treasures extracted from other exploited colonies, gathered in the harbor before departing for Spain. Outside of Havana the inhabitants of the interior of the island managed to obtain scarce goods by engaging in illegal trade, sometimes even with merchants sailing under enemy flags.

Cuba, at first, was a colony of exploitation rather than settlement. The conditions of slaves during this period were not as harsh as they would become after 1790, when large sugar cane and coffee plantations began to flourish on the island. Herbert S. Klein (1967) shows that even after 1790 Cuban slaves lived under more humane conditions than slaves in the former British colony of Virginia and later a State of the Union.

According to Hanke (1949) and Klein (1967), the Catholic Church took a more humane position regarding the treatment of slaves and Amerindians than was the case with other Christian churches in North American colonies. Moreover, the policy of the Catholic Church, whose doors were open to all people regardless of race and status, was that slavery is against natural law. It could only be justified when imposed as a temporary state on people who were being Christianized.

In general, the Catholic Church also took a more lenient position in the Americas regarding the religious practices of newly Christianized Amerindians and Africans than it had in Europe with newly Christianized Jews or Muslims or the general population. A good example of this is the posture of the bishop of Cuba, Morell de Santa Cruz, described by Castellanos and Castellanos (1988 1:98, 99).

This bishop arrived in Cuba in the second half of the eighteenth century during a time of great economic and social change, which turned the island into a successful plantation economy. These plantations required a great number of slaves. Bishop Morell of Santa Cruz was aware of the importance of *cabildos*,[2] influential mutual-aid religious brotherhoods or associations of Africans of the same "nation" and their descendants, some of which were affiliated with the parochial system while others were not. In these *cabildos* slaves and freemen alike participated in traditional behaviors and celebrated African-style dances and ceremonies.

The bishop did not persecute these organizations. Instead, he incorporated those that were not already part of the parochial system by assigning a priest to each. He advised the priests not to interfere with their celebrations (which he considered abominations) but to learn the language of the Africans and to wait for them to realize the "truth," open their eyes, and recognize their aberrations. He also strongly recommended that the priests foster the worship of the Virgin Mary so that the slaves would seek her protection. This calculated but ambiguous policy may have been the result of impotence in the face of enduring cultural practices. It may also have reflected paternalism, which, although not fostering tolerance, undoubtedly fostered patience and hope of the possibility of a gradual Christianization.

Until the last quarter of the eighteenth century there were adequate numbers of priests in Cuba. For example, the census of 1778 reports a priest for every 1,687 persons. However, things changed drastically in the nineteenth century when the great surge of slaves and other immigrants arrived. There was an acute shortage of priests and nuns. Moreover, the church had little success in recruiting Cuban-born individuals into the sacred orders. This situation limited its ability to demonstrate more interest in the welfare of the lower classes.

Dramatic events occurred during the last quarter of the eighteenth century that changed the lives of the impoverished inhabitants of Cuba as well as of those people living on the other shore of the Atlantic Ocean. In January 1762 the British crown declared war against Spain, prompted by the "Family Pact" treaty signed by the Spanish and French Bourbon monarchs. During that war (1762–63) Great Britain conquered the city of Havana, the harbor, and the area surrounding it. British occupation lasted only a year, but its influence was significant, because Havana harbor was opened to free trade. This development caused a commercial flowering in the capital city.

After reoccupying Havana in 1763, the Spanish colonial system could not avoid a liberalization of its restrictive trade policies. During this time Cuba was also blessed with better colonial administrators chosen by Carlos III, the "enlightened despot" who ruled Spain at the time. The incoming administrators supported the creation of new townships and fostered education, immigration, agriculture, and trade.

Additionally, the French Revolution in 1789 struck the Old and the New Worlds like a thunderbolt. Within a generation, Napoleon occupied Spain, from 1808 to 1812, taking the king and his heir as hostages. During the period of Napoleon's occupation of Spain, Juntas de Gobierno (colonial governing boards) were formed in the New World. These unofficial governmental entities administered the colonies in the name of the imprisoned king, rejecting Napoleon's emissaries.

After the defeat of Napoleon in 1812, and under the rule of Ferdinand VII, many colonists felt restless with the return of absolutist ways of governance, because they had savored some degree of self-government with the juntas. This situation precipitated the wars of emancipation, which, in less than twenty years, resulted in the emergence of twenty or more new republics in South and Central America. Only the islands of Cuba and Puerto Rico remained in the hands of the Spanish crown. By 1830, after Spain had lost all of its colonies except Cuba and Puerto Rico, the policies of the colonial government hardened. The military head of the government of the island, a captain general, had the power of the ruler of a city under siege.

The independence of South and Central America from Spain greatly affected Cuba beyond the political arena. During the nineteenth century many Spanish emigrants preferred to settle in Cuba and Puerto Rico instead of in the newly created republics. This demographic factor had a significant influence on the political, economic, and sociocultural development of Cuba.

During the French Revolution, Saint-Domingue, a French plantation colony in the Antilles that would become the Republic of Haiti, witnessed successful slave revolts in the 1790s. Under the leadership of inspired religious and military leaders, Haiti overthrew white rule in world history's only successful national slave revolt and became an independent nation.

Many French colonists escaped and settled on the neighboring island of Cuba. Some of these former plantation owners brought their slaves. They also brought knowledge of coffee and sugar cultivation. When Haiti's plantation economy collapsed, it left a vacuum in the market of sugar production that the Spanish colony of Cuba and the Portuguese colony of Brazil were eager to fill. In a short period of time, both were replenishing the sugar bowls of Europe.

In Cuba, sugar plantations and production required slave laborers for profitability. Later, coffee plantations also needed slaves as a labor force. Accordingly, in 1789, by decree, all restrictions to the introduction of slaves from Africa were removed.

During the next fifteen years the population of the island grew. One of the reasons was the importation of slaves; another was the immigration of white settlers. Thus, in 1774, under the administration of the Marquis de la Torre (1771–77), the first population census of Cuba was completed. According to that record there were 171,620 inhabitants: 96,440 whites, 30,847 free blacks, and 44,333 slaves. The subsequent census of 1791, barely three years after the free slave trade had been decreed, recorded 272,300 inhabitants. Blacks were more than 50 percent of the population, and the majority of these black residents were slaves (Santovenia and Shelton 1966:223).

Even though African slaves were brought to Cuba from the time it was first colonized, at the end of the eighteenth century the importation of slaves accelerated and the slaves' conditions worsened. Africans were brought to Cuba primarily from the regions of the western coast of Africa but some east Africans were also captured and brought as slaves.[3] Moreno Fraginals (1977) gathered information on the slave trade and the conditions in which slaves were kept in Cuba. Data from 1789 to 1820, the period when the trade was legal, include port of entry, name of the ship, port of departure from Africa, and other information. After 1820, when the slave trade was declared illegal, the information is somewhat more elusive because slaves were brought as contraband. Slaves were brought until the last decades of the nineteenth century, though "officially" the last year of record was 1873.

According to Moreno Fraginals' calculations, 1,012,386 Africans were brought to Cuba during the entire colonial period (1977:212–28). This figure shows that 86.36 percent of them arrived in Cuba after 1790. At first, the infamous trade was oriented toward bringing in field laborers. Thus, from 1746 to 1790, 90.38 percent of the slaves imported were males and 9.62 percent were females. The very low percentage of females, and possibly the high infant mortality rate, created conditions that forced plantation owners constantly to import slaves to replace those who died or were too old to work. According to Curtin, et al. (1978:221–22): "West Indian planters of the early eighteenth century believed that the price of slaves was so low in Africa that it actually cost less to buy a newly imported field hand than it did to pay the cost of subsistence for a child from birth to working age at about fourteen."

A factor that contributed to the retention of aspects of African culture and the consequent merging with aspects of the dominant culture was the presence of large numbers of free blacks and mulattos in colonial society. As indicated by Castellanos and Castellanos (1988 1:77–84) it was easier for urban slaves in Cuba to obtain their freedom than it was in the British colonies. The Siete Partidas (laws) gave servants and slaves in Spain, and later in the colonies, the means of obtaining their freedom. According to the law, slaves had the right to own property. Some of them obtained tools and mastered a trade. This enabled them to contract with their owners who, for a fixed amount, allowed them to seek outside work. Any income earned could be used to gradually purchase their freedom. At the same time, it was common for white men to grant freedom to their children born to slave women and to help or emancipate their slave lovers. This important free urban population of color became a bridge between the two worlds of slaves and masters. Its members served as role models not only for their urban counterparts who were not free but, ultimately, for all slaves.

Great changes began to occur at the end of the eighteenth century. The Seminario San Carlos (San Carlos Seminary) opened. In its classrooms the sensualist school of philosophy, with its emphasis on empiricism and experimentation, made its way onto the island. In addition, courses in constitutional law, imbued with the liberal ideas of the Enlightenment, were taught at the seminary. These courses challenged the archaic views of the University of Havana, which had previously followed a scholastic tradition in accordance with a worldview and theology at the service of the truths of the Catholic Church's dogma.

At the dawn of the nineteenth century, there was not much of a cultural core of what later came to be perceived as "Cuban." In other words, Cuba's cultural features were still preciously nascent at the beginning of the nineteenth century. It was at this time that awareness of an identity different from that of their parents or from others born in Spain began to be felt by some members of the elite of the white Creole population.

Subsequently, among some members of the new, enlightened, white, liberal, and Creole minority, ideas of change began to flourish. Some started to promote ideas of independence from Spain. (After all, only Cuba and Puerto Rico remained as part of the Spanish Empire.) Others promoted social and economic reforms, and some pressed for the emancipation of slaves. They had serious concerns about the development and growth of a black uneducated underclass, which would be difficult to assimilate into the fibers of the emerging nation. Still others were afraid that the emancipation of slaves would erode their economic base. They wanted to preserve slavery and were afraid of both abolitionist ideas and slave revolts.

At the same time, the period from 1790 to 1822 was the time of Cuba's great sugar and coffee boom, during which a new land-owning aristocracy made great fortunes. According to Moreno Fraginals (1977: 218), approximately 240,000 Africans were brought to work the plantations in the period from 1790 to 1822. Once the plantation economy was established, the social conditions of the slaves on those plantations were brutal. There were few, if any, slave families, and the slaves belonged to *dotaciones,* or gangs, where the plantation owners intentionally mixed slaves of different African tribes, with their different languages and cultures. The purpose of such measures was to prevent the development among the slaves of feelings of solidarity that might result in rebellious behavior.

The prosperity that a few on the island enjoyed was a source of needed income for the decadent government of the metropolis. That prosperity was based on harsh treatment of slave labor at the expense of Africans brought at first legally and then illegally by contraband. There was fear among members of the colonial government, the elite plantation owners, the privileged Spanish merchant class, and the white population in general of a repetition of events in Haiti, where successful rebellious slaves had destroyed the colonial government. The French colonists who managed to survive had to flee the island.

When Spain and Great Britain signed treaties banning slavery north (1817) and south (1820) of the equator, the price of slaves (now bought by contraband) increased. From then on emphasis was placed on a more balanced ratio between female and male imported slaves. Moreno Fraginals (1977: 218) reports that until the 1790s only 10.73 percent of the slaves were women. From 1823 to 1844 the ratio of women rose to 34.15 percent, and from 1845 to 1868 it increased to 44.54 percent.

These changes in the policy concerning the introduction of African women slaves fostered a large black Creole population. According to Moreno Fraginals (1977: 218), the Afro-Creoles, or Cuban-born Blacks, constituted 11.58 percent of the slave population by 1790. The percentage diminished after restrictions to the slave trade were lifted. Thus, in the period from 1791 to 1822 the percentage of Creole, or Cuban-born, slaves was reduced to 3.85 percent.

Moreno Fraginals adds that a policy of "good treatment" (better food and care) was implemented during the later period. These measures signaled a dramatic increase of Cuban-born black Creoles. Coincidentally, these children of slaves felt the same attachment to the new land that the white Creoles felt.

The white population was also experiencing a significant increase in numbers. Besides the French immigrants who had come from Haiti, other French and Spanish settlers came to Cuba when the United States acquired Louisiana and Florida. During the same period, immigrants from all over Spain, especially from the northern provinces (Catalonia, Galicia, Basque country, and Asturias) settled on the island.[4]

The influx of immigrants from the Canary Islands, which had always been slow but steady, also increased at this time. The authorities openly encouraged them to settle in the countryside to "whiten" the island, as concerns over the ultimate effects of slavery were dealt with. The Spanish authorities and the white population, though reliant on slavery for the production of wealth, were afraid Cuba would become another Haiti. Regardless of origin, during the nineteenth century, immigrants constituted large segments of the island's population. Some had come voluntarily, others as a result of political upheaval and change, many as slaves and, some as indentured servants.[5] According to Fernando Ortiz,

> Among all peoples historical evolution has always meant a vital change from one culture to another at tempos varying from gradual to sudden. But in Cuba the cultures that have influenced the formation of its folk have been so many and so diverse in their spatial position and in their structural composition that this vast blend of races and cultures overshadows in importance every other historical phenomenon. Even economic phenomena, the most basic factors of social existence, in Cuba are almost always conditioned by the different cultures. In Cuba the terms Ciboney, Taino, Spaniard, Jew, English, French, Anglo-American, Negro, Yucatec, Chinese, and Creole do not mean merely the different elements that go into the make-up of the Cuban nation, as expressed by their different indications of origin. (F. Ortiz 1970:98, 99)

Most white and black Creoles became attached to Cuba, to its insular and tropical charms and sensuality—a sensuality manifested in the beaches, the moonlight, the sway of the palm trees, the aroma of the wilderness, of cigars, and of coffee, and the sweetness of sugar cane, pineapples, and mangos. There was also sensual intimacy from the breezes and in the melody of the rivers. Cuba was perceived in human terms. Cuba, this sensual female, invited Cubans to live and enjoy life. This personalistic view was shared by Creoles across racial lines and became a source of inspiration for artists of all races. It was expressed in the richness and quality of Cuban music, literature, painting, dancing, and humor.

During the nineteenth century several political trends emerged in the now expanding and more populous colony. The reformist, the *anexionista*, and the separatist movements addressed economic, social, and political issues in different fashion. The reformist movement hoped to introduce reforms in the colonial system within the framework of the Spanish monarchy. Its vision was of Cuba as a province of Spain and not a colony of the metropolis. This view was defended by prominent leaders such as Felix Varela and Jose Antonio Saco well into the century. In the last two decades, autonomists such as Rafael Montoro, Eliseo Giberga, and others argued for autonomy from Spain. The *anexionistas* hoped to make Cuba a pro-slavery state of the United States. They had the support of many members of the rich land-owning Creole class, such as Miguel Aldama, Gaspar Betancourt Cisneros, and others, as well as some members of the U.S. Congress. By 1865 their cause was lost following the defeat of the South in the Civil War.

In the final decades of the nineteenth century a wave of spiritualist ideas made their appearance in Cuba. The ideas and beliefs of Allan Kardec (1803–69) became very popular. Allan Kardec was the pen name of a French writer, Hipolyte Leon Denizard Rivail.[6] He authored *The Spirit's Book: Spiritualist Philosophy* (1857), *The Book of the Mediums* (1861), *The Gospel According to Spiritualism* (1864), and some selected prayers. Kardec's teachings became very popular among many members of the white Creole upper-class, white peasants, and the small urban middle class.

In the political arena several attempts by reformists to extract reforms from the Spanish government met with failure. In 1861 the famous Information Board went to Spain to advise the government about necessary changes in the administration of the island. By 1865 it was apparent that the retrograde Spanish monarchy was both unwilling and incapable of granting reforms.

Separatist ideas and movements had the upper hand, and the First War of Independence was launched in 1868. This war lasted ten years, and from its beginning black men (freemen and slaves alike) figured conspicuously in the ranks and also as officers in the insurgent's army. It is remarkable that so many Cuban former slaves joined the revolutionary forces during the Second War of Independence (1895–98), especially since slavery already had been abolished.

The Second War of Independence, inspired by José Martí's all-inclusive ideology "More than White, more than Black,—A Nation for All Cubans," began in 1895. Martí, who had lived in the United States as an exile, could foresee that the U.S. government's ambitions to take over the island left few other alternatives.

During the Wars of Independence, the church hierarchy and the Spanish clergy openly sided with the metropolis. However, as indicated by Francisco Gonzales del Valle in Manuel P. Maza Miguel (1993: 73–74), the Cuban-born clergy did side with the best interests of the Cuban people for emancipation, independence, and freedom.

In 1898 the United States, which had failed in its attempts to buy the island and which had been following with great interest the events occurring on the island, declared war against Spain. This declaration of war was prompted by the destruction of the warship *Maine*, which blew up in the harbor of Havana. The Americans argued that it was sabotaged by the Spaniards (a point disproved by evidence of internal explosion within the engine room).

The U.S. intervention abruptly ended the long struggle. Cuba was granted independence in 1902, after four years of U.S. military occupation. Independence was compromised, however, because the conditions for independence required acceptance of the Platt Amendment as an addition to the Constitution. This greatly limited Cuba's sovereignty, since it gave the U.S. government the prerogative to intervene on the island any time the lives or properties of U.S. citizens were in jeopardy.[7]

The U.S. interventionists used their power to try to persuade the members of the Cuban Constitutional Assembly to refuse blacks the right to vote, to segregate the public schools of the nascent nation, and to take other measures that could greatly harm the Afro-Cubans. According to de la Fuente (2001: 50), "Repression of African-based cultural practices was not new, but the U.S. occupation government had given the process renewed impetus and legitimacy. Shortly after the occupation, processions and public demonstrations by Afro-Cuban religious societies were prohibited. North Americans viewed Afro-Cuban religions as a 'mass of foolishness' in which Catholicism and 'African demon-worship' had become 'grotesquely mixed.'" However, the almost-white assembly refused to implement such measures against Afro-Cubans, who had been a sizable component of the Cuban revolutionary forces against Spain. Thus, all males over the age of twenty-one were granted the right to vote, and all public schools and facilities were integrated.

Despite integration and universal suffrage for all adult men, the nascent republic did not give blacks proper recognition or equal opportunities. In addition, many white Cubans who had sacrificed family members and their fortunes in the struggle for independence but who were against the Platt Amendment were also pushed aside.

Many blacks, discontented with treatment during the early years of the republic, attempted to create a political party for blacks. When this strategy was denied, unrest erupted into a rebellion of blacks who then wanted to create an independent republic in Oriente. The repression was brutal and the attempt at an independent black republic also met with failure.

In spite of the difficulties and setbacks many blacks took advantage of the public school system and, using the power of the vote, they were able to make significant advances. Gradually, an influential black middle class emerged.

As previously indicated, Cuban colonial society had been plagued by social upheaval, rank injustice, epidemics, political arbitrariness, bureaucratic inefficiency, and authoritarianism. Moreover, during the colonial period, the island suffered from serious health issues. Debilitating diseases such as malaria and yellow fever were endemic and epidemic. Typhus took a large toll, as did tuberculosis. Other infectious diseases and intestinal parasites had deleterious effects on the total population, freemen and slaves alike. Occasionally, a plague such as cholera ravaged parts of the island. There was a lack of medical facilities. Furthermore, at that time modern, preventive, and social medicine had not yet developed. This left the population in the cities, and especially in the countryside, utilizing home remedies with heavy reliance on an extensive Spanish pharmacopoeia further enriched by that of the Amerindians and major contributions from African slaves and their descendants. Medical problems normally triggered a number of religious procedures ranging from masses and rosaries, to promises to saints and the Virgin, to the use of amulets, and, also, to visits to a variety of healers, including African and Afro-Cuban healers.

A policy initiated by the U.S. military occupation government to eradicate stagnant water, to teach the population to boil drinking water, and to adopt other hygienic measures was rigorously implemented. In 1909 Cuba became the first country in the world to create a ministry of health, which focused on social and preventive medicine. The focus on preventive medicine was effective—Cuba's last plagues (bubonic and small pox) occurred in 1914. Thanks to the discovery by the Cuban doctor Tomás Finlay that the mosquito was a transmitter of yellow fever, this disease, also, was practically eradicated.

Republican Cuba

With the advent of the republic, the Catholic Church ceased to be the official religion of the state. It lost some of its authority, but it continued to have a measure of official influence. Other Christian churches were given more recognition and began to flourish, opening very good schools, which were important sources of recruitment. Nevertheless, the Cuban ambiance remained imbued with Cuban-style Catholicism. The Catholic Church, with its widely dispersed schools and churches, preserved a presence in all of the towns and cities of the island. In a very real sense, it enjoyed a semi-official status. Moreover, in colonial times the streets of towns and cities were normally given the names of saints. Even though during the republic, street names were changed to those of Cuban patriots, most people knew the streets by their former names. The Catholic Church was always a guest or the protagonist at significant national events such as the cutting of a ribbon for the inauguration of a new road or a new aqueduct.

The Catholic Church, however, endured a dual reputation. Many members of the middle class were aware of its extremely one-sided posture in favor of Spanish absolutism during the Wars of Independence. In the popular (lower-income) groups the Catholic Church had a reputation for siding with the rich. Many did not agree with its position concerning divorce, birth control, and other issues. This posture was expressed in the popular phrase "Yo soy Católico a mi manera" (I am Catholic my own way). For many this meant, "I am baptized; I go to church every so often; I will marry in the church; if I have to I will get a divorce but will continue to be Catholic; and when I'm dying I want to be given the last rites."

At the same time, as mentioned previously, not many Cubans were attracted to the priesthood. Thus, churches and convents were manned primarily by Spanish priests and nuns. Carlos Velasco (1915:94) indicates that 1,462 religious personnel had immigrated to Cuba from Spain between 1902 and 1914, while Louis Perez (1986:61) remarks that "the [Cuban] Catholic Church continued to be substantially a Spanish church."

Many of the upper and middle classes favored a Catholic education for their children on the grounds that they would be given the moral fiber that was necessary in life. However, some of the Spanish-born clergy, in their role as teachers, pronounced themselves opposed to Cuban nationalism and identity. In this respect Carlos Velasco (1915:96–111) writes that the textbooks used in Catholic schools by Spanish priests did not teach students pride in either their country or their heroes. In 1937 legislation was passed prohibiting individuals who had not been born in Cuba to teach either Cuban history or geography. Nevertheless, the central parks of Cuban towns and cities continued to be presided over by the Catholic Church.

The short-lived democratic republic (1902–59), in spite of corruption, political instability, and limited sovereignty, was able to address some of the grave social and economic problems of Cubans with some degree of success. By 1950 there was a local hospital in every municipality and a regional hospital with specialists in each province. These facilities were integrated and free of charge. By 1950 Cuba was ranked by the United Nations as a country that did not require tourists to have special vaccinations for travel there, as was the case with many other countries. Clinics that, for a moderate price, offered inpatient and outpatient care to residents of most towns and cities were decisive in making health services available to large proportions of the population. A large body of physicians was created, because any high-school graduate could enter the School of Medicine by paying a registration fee that was under $50 per year. Fee waivers were available to those who could not afford this amount.

In the field of education there were also impressive results. Cuba's percentage of the budget dedicated to education (22 percent) was the largest in the world. By 1953, 76.40 percent of the population was literate, compared with

56.55 percent in 1907 (Alvarez Díaz, et al. 1964: 70). By 1959 there was a university in each province and the rate of illiteracy was down to 20 percent according to census calculations (Alvarez Díaz, et al. 1964: 71).

According to census figures, unemployment in 1899 was 37.49 percent and in 1959 it was 20.08 percent. The Cuban National Economic Council estimated that in 1959 unemployment was 10.94 percent (Alvarez Díaz, et al. 1964: 73), a figure that may not reflect sugarcane workers' seasonal unemployment. Thus, between 1902 and 1959 the republic provided important social, educational, and health benefits for many of its citizens.

Popular Piety in Republican and Colonial Cuba

In this section the intent is to elaborate to the extent possible the unique ambiance and worldview of both Yoruban slave society and Cuban colonial and republican society. These portrayals of ethos and worldview suggest the ease with which cultural borrowing and transformations may have occurred. Whatever the full extent of the process, one overriding result was the merging of aspects of Spanish Catholicism, African religious traditions, and Spiritualism, which became Santería.

During the colonial period the cultural and social conditions of the island of Cuba included a heterogeneous population of uprooted people. Despite catechism classes offered by the Catholic Church, most of the population was not fully evangelized, in part due to a shortage of priests. Consequently, what flourished among the masses in Cuba was some sort of folk Catholicism or what is now known as popular piety.

POPULAR PIETY

Known by many as the "people's religion," "popular religiosity," or "popular Catholicism," this religious phenomenon was called by Pope Paul VI "popular piety." According to Father Juan Sosa (1999: 127): "Together with celebrations of the Virgin Mary, the universal and local celebrations of the saints constitute the core of the devotions in which the theme of popular piety develops." Furthermore, "The popular piety of the people, consequently, constitutes the totality of these devotions, and, at the same time it establishes itself as one of the best pastoral instruments for getting the people close to God in a 'pedagogy of Evangelization'" (Sosa 1999:128).

The Catholic Church's emphasis on evangelizing by teaching about the exemplary lives of the saints and stressing the importance of the Virgin as an intermediary to Christ fostered popular piety in a sense. The church's goal was to eventually lead the people to a full understanding of the message and meaning of Christ at a time when reading the Bible was not encouraged by the church. The church hoped that this pedagogy of evangelization would, in time, strengthen faith. In Sosa's words (1999:76, 77): "Faith is a gift that grows with time."

In Cuba, popular piety was expressed in the form of devotion to saints and specific paths of the Virgin. Other expressions of piety related to spiritualist beliefs and practices, beliefs in the evil eye, witchcraft, sorcery, and other types of religious phenomena outside of orthodox Catholicism.

THE SAINTS

The Catholic Church has always placed emphasis on the cult of the saints and different paths of the Virgin. Within every church there are several small chapels with altars where people offer prayers and light candles to these saints and the many manifestations of the Virgin. The fostering of such worship was expressed in other ways as well. In the 1940s in Santiago de Cuba, for example, small portable chapels (around a yard in height and half-a-yard in width and depth) were sent by the local church to the homes of parishioners, where they stayed for four or five days to gather alms and encourage worship. In addition, religious stores sold statues and chromolithographs that people placed on altars in their homes where prayers, candles, and flowers were offered to them.

Patrons

It is noteworthy that Cuban towns and cities were founded under the protection of a saint or Virgin. Each town had a saint or Virgin as patron, and the annual celebrations of the town took place on the day of that saint or Virgin in the Catholic calendar. For instance, in Guantánamo these festivities took place on the day of Santa Catalina de Ricci, the patron saint of that city. The famous carnivals of Santiago are still celebrated around July 26, which is the day of Santiago Apostle, the patron of Spain and of that city.

It was customary for people to be named after the saint in the Catholic calendar who presided over the day of their birth. Even if one was given another name, in pre-Castro's Cuba, people celebrated their saint's day more often than their birthday. When one was named after a saint or a Virgin, there was an understanding that that saint assumed responsibility as a protector of the individual.

Children were taught to pray to their *angel de la guardia,* or guardian angel. Generally, chromolithographs, statues, and medals of the guardian angel were placed near the crib or bed of children.

Miracles and Promises

Belief in miracles was all pervasive. When in need, people made promises to saints and to different manifestations of the Virgin Mary, seeking miraculous assistance primarily when sickness, unemployment, or any other crisis affected them or someone dear.

It was common to see a woman dress in a *promesa* (promise) garment for a period of one or two years to fulfill a promise made to a saint or Virgin after having been granted a special request or favor that was perceived as a miracle. Garments made of burlap were used to repay Saint Lazarus, who was considered exceptionally miraculous and had a following throughout the island. Similarly, a yellow robe with a yellow belt twisted as a rope was worn for the Virgin of Charity.

It was also very common for people to wear *escapularios* or *detentes* (images of Catholic saints and Virgins embroidered in cloth) around their necks for protection. Almost everyone who could afford it wore a necklace with a medal of Jesus, a Virgin, or a saint attached.

Moreover, it was popular to participate in *cadenas* (chains) addressed to a particular saint to request some miracle. *Cadenas* were anonymous letters received through the mail that explained that the recipient had been chosen to be part of this chain. If the recipient agreed, he or she had to recruit by the same method one hundred people who might be interested in joining and furthering this linkage.

Also part of popular religiosity was the belief that power resides in certain types of religious relics, such as dirt from the Holy Land, chips of wood from a miraculous cross, the hair or bone of a saint, and so forth.

Catholic Calendar

In towns and cities the important celebrations were tied primarily to the Catholic calendar. In many ways the calendar established the rhythm of the town: the celebrations of Holy Week, Christmas, festivals to honor a town's patron saint, and important saints' days.

Holy Week

The celebration of Holy Week was a period of great spirituality. During that time, churches were crowded with people (mostly women) praying the rosary. All the church images were covered with purple material as signs of mourning. During these celebrations, the church, situated in the park at the center of the town, was the focus of everyone's attention.

In the town of Baracoa, in the northeastern region of the province of Oriente, where I spent my childhood, the religious festivities described below took place. Similar celebrations occurred all over the island.[8]

In Baracoa on Palm Sunday, the priest distributed *guano bendito* (blessed palm leaves), which everyone placed at the head of the bed for protection. A small procession then followed.

On Holy Thursday, the residents celebrated the Monumento (exhibit of Christ in the sarcophagus). The church was full of people praying rosaries, and many people at every station of the Via Crucis (Path of the Cross) said their prayers. The fragrance of burning incense and candles contributed to a mysterious ambiance and to the congregation's sense of mourning.

On Holy Friday the church bells rang a mournful steady tone all day and all night, tolling solemnly, while radio stations played only requiems and sacred music. All ordinary daily activities ceased. One was not supposed to sweep, cook, play the piano, sing, engage in games, and so forth. Holy Friday was a national holiday, and nobody worked.

At midday the street procession called El Encuentro (the Encounter) took place. The images of Mary and Jesus of Nazareth (dressed in purple, carrying the cross) were paraded along the two main streets in different processions. When they met, Christ's statue was lowered three times as a sign of greeting, and the statue of his mother also "bowed" three times.

In the afternoon the image of Christ in a glass sarcophagus was paraded in procession. His image was accompanied by the statue of the Virgin dressed in black, a dagger in her heart, and tears streaming down her cheeks, symbolizing her profound pain.

The following morning at ten o'clock the bells of the church rang joyfully, announcing Saturday of Glory. The next day the jubilant procession of Resurrection Sunday took place.

Christmas

The celebration of Christmas also generated a special ambiance of merriment, generosity, family reunions, and charity throughout the island. The churches and convents displayed *nacimientos* (nativity scenes), and children sang *villancicos* (Spanish Christmas carols). *Nacimientos* were also displayed in some homes. On Christmas Eve people celebrated the birth of Jesus in their homes, and many attended the Misa del Gallo (midnight mass). During the three-week-long Christmas season, poor people and children in the towns would come to serenade people's homes, singing *villancicos* and seeking *aguinaldo* (presents of food or money). The *aguinaldo* (a bonus consisting of an extra month's salary paid to government employees) was meant to help families celebrate Christmas.

On the eve of the day of Epiphany (January 6), the Three Magi were expected to come and bring presents to the children. A parade took place in Santiago de Cuba and other cities, in which the three kings, mounted on camels, greeted the children. The Magi were a display of ecumenism: one of them was black, another one white, and the third was Hindu.[9]

Other important celebrations took place throughout the year to honor locally and nationally worshiped Virgins and saints.

Virgin of Charity

Throughout the nation, around September 8, celebrations were held in honor of the Virgin of Charity,[10] with processions in most towns and cities of the island. Also, great numbers of people went as pilgrims to the shrine of this Virgin in the city of El Cobre.

In Baracoa three processions were held to honor the Virgin of Charity. The main one came from the Catholic Church. Normally the mayor, the judge, and the chief of police accompanied the priest presiding over it. Women followed, and next came men from the lower-income groups. Generally, three girls dressed in yellow, green, and pink garments (symbolizing the three cardinal virtues: Faith, Hope, and Charity) preceded the image of the Virgin that was carried by six or eight men. The local band played the "Skater's Waltz."

The following Sunday in September, the procession of José Frómeta from the neighborhood of La Laguna (the Lagoon) paraded the streets, accompanied by a small orchestra. José Frómeta was a respected mulatto political activist, the head of a large family, and a watch repairman. The skin color of the image of the Virgin of Charity in this procession was a little darker than the one from the Catholic Church.

The following week the procession from the neighborhood of La Playa (The Beach) paraded the streets. This procession was sponsored by Herminio Frómeta, a mulatto nicknamed "Maquey" (Hermit Crab). Maquey was a former altar boy and devout Catholic who had in his home a room-sized chapel with benches for family and friends to sit on while worshiping. The procession was accompanied by a band called Los Troncosos (the Trunks), and the Virgin in this procession also gave the appearance of a mulatto.

Santa Bárbara

Celebrations to welcome Saint Barbara, the patron of artillery, occurred throughout the island on the eve of December 4. People honored the saint in churches and private homes. In Baracoa at the home of "El Manco" (One Hand) Estevez *chilindrón* (mutton stew) was prepared for the guests. Manco Estevez was not a practitioner of Santería. In fact, many people in Cuba who were not involved in the practice of Santería were devoted to Saint Barbara and wore necklaces and medals with her image and amulets in the shape of a sword with a ruby or a red piece of crystal (symbols of Saint Barbara).

San Lázaro

On December 17 there were celebrations across the island but especially in the eastern province of Oriente and in El Rincón, a small town near the city of Havana where there was a leprosarium under the auspices of Saint Lazarus, the leper. Currently, El Rincón is still the destination of great numbers of pilgrims who go there in throngs, sometimes moving on their knees to make good on a promise to the miraculous healer. As in the case of Saint Barbara, most of the devotees were not followers of Santería.

Throughout the island, there were many private celebrations to honor this saint. I remember a female member of the Guzman family in Baracoa, who, under trance, would sing "Padre mío, San Lázaro . . ." (My father, Saint Lazarus . . .).

Virgin of el Carmen

Another important celebration took place in Baracoa on July 16 to honor the Virgin of el Carmen, the Catholic patron of sailors. People would gather at La Punta (the peninsula at the entrance of the bay), and young men competed for a prize by attempting to climb a greased pole.

THE DEAD

Beliefs concerning *el más allá* (the other side) were also part of popular religiosity that was prevalent throughout the island, especially in the countryside. Even though they did not engage in any specific practice, great numbers of people in Cuba believed that the dead were always watching over the living and interfering in their lives, sometimes positively and sometimes negatively. Many believed that the dead had to be appropriately taken care of by means of Catholic masses and rosaries, spiritualist masses, and flowers at the gravesite and in homes in front of a displayed picture of the deceased. According to Lydia Cabrera (1980: 343), "This eschatological vision of life after death exists among people who are free of all black influence and even among some Catholics."

Clothing constitutes an example of the important status the dead had in the lives of the living. After the deaths of their fathers or their husbands women were expected to wear *luto* (black garments) for a period of mourning (one or more years). Afterward, for two or three years more, they would wear *medio luto* (garments made of black and white material), symbolizing a gradual return to normalcy and the end of mourning.

There were substantial numbers of people on the island who practiced Spiritualism. Spiritualist beliefs were prevalent among the white middle class. Some followed Allan Kardec's teachings; others engaged in *espiritismo de cordón* (an unstructured gathering of believers who normally sat with hands locked in a circle of energy and became possessed by spirits). There was a large enough following to support a Kardec spiritualist center in the upstairs of the corner-house in the block where our home was situated in Baracoa.

Among many members of the poorer classes it was common for people to be mounted by a dead spirit.[11] These undifferentiated practices were generally called *muertería*. During possession the dead communicated with the living and requested favors. In this regard, I personally witnessed what were to me somewhat frightening experiences with a live-in maid. On those many evenings when my parents were out, the maid would go into a trance, during which she "passed" (was possessed by) many types of spirits. She would always request rum, cigars, and cigarettes. I learned very soon that to avoid being possessed by the spirits I had to cross my fingers and my legs while singing songs requesting that the spirits get "light" and lose their concern with our material world.

THE EVIL EYE

Beliefs in the nefarious effects of the "evil eye" were also very prevalent. Many children and babies wore amulets, or charms (some made of onyx, others made of metal portraying a pair of eyes) attached to their necklaces to ward off the evil eye. Many used coral charms for good luck and protection.

WITCHCRAFT AND SORCERY

Beliefs in witchcraft and sorcery were prevalent. A Cuban saying, "Yo no creo en brujería pero la respeto" (I don't believe in witchcraft but I respect it), is a common acknowledgment of the prevalence of these two practices in Cuba.

Congruencies in Ethos and Worldview

Kearney has stated that the main force "giving coherence and shape to a worldview is the necessity of having to relate to the external environment" (1984: 52). There is no question but that the external environment for both blacks and whites during the colonial and republican periods in Cuba dramatically affected African slaves as well as white immigrants to the island. In this section an attempt is made to suggest congruencies in ethos and worldview from the perspective of both Yoruban and Spanish Catholic backgrounds, but with the emphasis upon traditions within black and white Creole populations.

Marginality was a common life experience—socially, economically, politically, and medically—for both black and white Creoles. So was religiosity, within the framework of orthodox Catholic dogmatic beliefs. Marginality was partly caused by the heterogeneous origins (even among members of the same race) and recent uprooting experienced by both blacks and whites. This set of circumstances had a leveling effect in terms of ethos and worldview. Many white Creoles shared with many black Creoles basic assumptions about their world and their perceptions of reality. It is my opinion that the identification

of many elements of shared worldview images helps to explain both the retention of aspects of the Yoruban religion in Cuba and many of the factors that
supported its accommodations and transformations on Cuban soil.

There are many similarities, superficial and otherwise, between the behavior and images of reality of slaves from Nigeria and their Creole descendants
and those prevalent among various segments of lower-income white groups
and their Creole descendants in colonial Cuba. Many of the original white immigrants came from Andalusia, where the Moorish influence, culturally and
genetically, was very strong and the Jewish presence was also important.

Spain, for centuries, had been a meeting ground of different cultures. In
some instances ethnic groups conserved their own way of life and culture, but
in most instances merging occurred through processes of borrowing and adaptation. This is especially true of the people of southern Spain, who had been
exposed to Muslim and Jewish cultures, particularly through the sharing of life
in crowded medieval towns and quarters. They were also in contact with black
African slaves brought by the Muslims. Many Spaniards who came to Cuba
were familiar with mixed populations, cultural borrowing, and exchange.[12]

Yoruban culture and Spanish culture are both urban oriented. Of all the
African groups south of the Sahara the Yoruba have been considered the most
experienced in urban life. They prefer to live in towns and settlements surrounded by their agricultural lands.

Both the Yoruba and the Spanish are socially oriented, valuing fluid interpersonal relationships with others. Life for the Yoruba is shared with others.
And life for the Spaniards, especially those from the southern part of Spain,
is lived outdoors in parks, cafés, and on sidewalks, interacting with others,
engaging in conversation.

In both cultures each town or city has a patron saint or orisha that protects
it. Each year celebrations which include processions, ceremonies, music, and
dancing take place the day assigned by the religious calendars to these orishas
and saints. People in the towns feel allegiance to their patrons and seek their
protection.

Both groups are oriented toward the extended family. Seniority and lineage
are organizing principles in both traditions. Family life is conceived of as being
lived with other family members. Privacy has little meaning.

In both cultures names are given great importance; especially family names
that reveal lineage affiliation. Furthermore, given names have religious connotations. In the case of Spanish culture the link is to the saint whose name
one carries. In the case of the Yoruba two important elements reflect ties to the
name of an ancestor and the Supreme Being.

Social orientation in both groups is manifested through membership in
clubs and other types of cross-cutting associations. Closeness in interac-

tion with others is highly valued. Friendliness and familiarity with neighbors, friends of your friends, and of your family members is expected. Reciprocity and mutual aid are important in both cultures that are so socially and family oriented.

In both cultures there is a shared view that the dead continue to remain around the living and interfere in their lives. Also shared is the understanding in each that it is important to know how to propitiate them in order to rid oneself of the effects of those whose influences are more negative than positive.

Both groups consider music, singing, and dancing as important parts of a full life, notwithstanding their ritual aspects. In both cultures there is a recognized hierarchical ordering of power in heaven and on earth as reflected in the family, the Catholic Church, the Yoruba pantheon, and other institutions. In the secular sphere both marginal populations of newcomers and their descendants resented authority. They reacted to arbitrariness and anything perceived as expressions of illegitimate authority with passive resistance verbalized in the idiom "Obedezco pero no cumplo" ("I obey but I don't accomplish").

In the field of religion, for white Creoles, this attitude underlay the vitality of popular piety despite the Catholic Church's guidelines, which, preferably, would have suppressed it. This attitude toward religious inclusiveness was also shared by devotees of the Yoruban religion, as historical records have demonstrated.

In both religions there is a Supreme Being who is the source of all power in the universe. In both, there are intermediaries between the Supreme Being and human beings. The cult of saints and different paths of the Virgin are intermediaries in the Catholic Church. The orishas of the polytheistic pantheon of the Yoruba are also intermediaries, but they have the power (legitimized by the Supreme Being) to act independently as representatives of the highest power.

The inclusive posture of both the Yoruban religion and Catholicism encouraged the adoption of popular Catholic saints into the Yoruban framework, as did the acceptance of Yoruban orishas into the framework of meaning regarding Catholic saints. Both of these inclusive postures fostered the emergence and growth of Santería. Following its emergence, this inclusive posture permitted some Catholics to be initiated into Santería without having to renounce their primary religion.

In both cultures it is common to have chapels or altars in the homes for private worship. In addition, the people of both cultures make offerings and promises to the deities, especially to the intermediaries in efforts to recruit their assistance.[13]

In both Catholicism and Yoruban culture great importance is given to symbolism, elaborate rituals, and public processions. Colors have special meanings as do attributes of the saints and the orishas. For both white and black Creoles, these traditions continued, and emphasis was placed on the correct way to carry out well-defined ritual procedures in Santería.

In both cultures individuals are susceptible to being possessed by supernatural entities. In both cultures there is a pervasive belief in witchcraft and sorcery as well as in the evil eye. In both Creole cultures emotional display (anger, joy, contentment, and sadness) is considered human and not necessarily a manifestation of loss of control. Consequently lack of control and mastery were prevalent and in both cultures magical techniques were sought to cope with daily situations of bare survival.

In both cultures certain inanimate objects are assumed to be receptacles of supernatural power. In the practice of popular piety, medals and amulets are used as protections against all evil, especially the evil eye. Just as consecrated stones, necklaces, and attributes of the Yoruba orishas are considered containers of supernatural power, so also are relics considered to be by practitioners of popular piety.

Both cultures had extensive knowledge of pharmacopoeias, which facilitated exchange of information. In the case of blacks, the cultural antecedent for knowledge and use of medicinal substances was incorporated into religious beliefs and practices. As whites began to expand their own understandings and use of medicinal plants and herbs, the link to Yoruba-influenced practices in the religious sphere became stronger.

Finally, it might be noted that both cultures (and genes) contributed to the appearance in Cuba of images of the Virgin reflective of the physical appearance of large segments of the population. For example, in the realm of popular piety, the Virgin of Charity who accompanied the Cuban pro-independence soldiers in the war against Spain resembled the mulatto physical synthesis of the Creole mixture.[14]

It is my opinion that the identification of elements of shared worldview images and assumptions helps to explain the retention of many aspects of the Yoruban religion. It is assumed that such factors supported its accommodations and transformations on Cuban soil in a way that would not have been possible had there been fewer congruencies (such as might have been the case in a Protestant country or in a situation in which too few members of an immigrant population could retain substantial features of the ethos and worldview of their homeland).

Even when there was a lack of congruence in some areas of life, living, and religion, the descendants of both cultural groups shared an openness that favored religious inclusiveness, religious syncretism, and merging, or transculturation. The accommodations and adaptations that occurred were prevalent among whites and blacks of the lower-income groups and among some members of the middle class.

In the case of Santería the concept of worldview transcends both Euro-centric and Afro-centric orientations and allows us to identify the many similarities between the imported African religion and the total socioenvironmental configuration of the new setting. These congruencies help us to better understand the trajectory of African religious beliefs in Cuba specifically, then on into the United States. They also help us to understand the capacity of a religion of the so-called oppressed to attract a new following that included members of the so-called oppressors.

Factors That Contributed to the Survival of African Religions in Cuba

There were many factors that contributed to the survival of African religions in Cuba. The worldview and policies of the Catholic Church, the familiarity servants enjoyed in households, the prevalence of spiritualist beliefs and the presence of a significant middle class of colored people were all part of the process. The large number of slaves brought to the island at the end of the eighteenth century and during the nineteenth century also supported the development of Santería and other Afro-Cuban religions.

The Catholic Church played a very important role. Its mysticism and enduring emphasis on the worship of saints and the different paths of the Virgin contributed to the development of popular piety in large segments of the population. Its paternalistic stance concerning slaves' religious beliefs and practices was also influential. Even when the church judged them to be "primitive" and "disgusting" it tolerated them in most instances.

The close familiarity of ties and forms of communication that occurred between domestic slaves and servants with the master and his or her family, common among many Spanish Caribbean societies, was another contributing influence. Individuals of the middle and upper classes were often exposed to experiences, beliefs, and values of the people of lower socio-economic background. An example might be my own childhood experience with the household servant who went into trances, thus exposing me to aspects of religious behavior I might not have encountered otherwise.

An extremely important factor was the successful transplantation and transformation of the Spanish medieval institutions called *cabildos* to the special conditions of the Cuban slave society. Likewise, the blossoming of other neo-African clubs and social organizations contributed to the survival of African religions in Cuba.

The *cabildos,* as will be discussed in the next chapter, became centers of religious acculturation. At the same time they played an important role in cushioning the parameters of culture shock—creating islands of safety that supported traditional styles of interaction—thereby facilitating the survival of the slaves' religious beliefs as these beliefs began to merge with Catholicism.

Moreover, the arrival in a short period of time of a great number of white immigrants in addition to slaves and indentured servants resulted in a situation where people of different cultural traditions intermingled. The low-income white population often lived in neighborhoods where free blacks also resided, or lived very close by.

The popularity of spiritualist beliefs, a matter that will be considered in greater detail in the next chapter, contributed to the religious heterogeneity and to the merging of these different traditions.

Another important factor in Santería's development was the fact that slavery was abolished in Cuba shortly after the last contingent of Africans arrived. Many former slaves, who were born in Africa and still had vivid memories of their ancestry and cultural ethos, became free early enough to savor circumstances that helped sustain their African ways.

The impressive presence of large numbers of free blacks and mulattos in colonial society made a large difference insofar as the retention of African culture was concerned. They constituted an important part of the urban lower-middle and lower classes through economic means. In a very real sense they monopolized occupational roles such as those of tailor, seamstress, shoemaker, blacksmith, and other semiprofessional occupations such as those of midwifery and musicianship. They were instrumental in preserving African cultural forms and were also protagonists in the vital process of creolization. They became vehicles for the blending of the African and the mixed Spanish-other worldviews into the Cuban worldview. They greatly contributed to the emergence of a Creole culture, and to an artistic definition of Cubanness above and beyond racial distinctions.[15] Popular piety was another major factor that facilitated the survival of aspects of African religions in Cuba.

In summary, all of these factors greatly contributed to the survival of African religions in Cuba. But most important, perhaps, was the need for relationships with others in line with the Nigerian Yoruban ethos and worldview. Also important was the search for meanings compatible with prior understandings that provided a sense of well-being in the form of harmony and balance in overall lifestyle and basic assumptions about the nature of reality that supported it.

Ethos and Worldview Analysis of Lower-Income Groups in Colonial and Republican Cuba

As described in the preface, Kluckhohn and Strodtbeck (1961) developed a schedule to determine value orientation profiles as components of worldview.

The choices provided by the scale were designed to derive answers to five universal problems that are repeated here:

1) The character of human nature: a) good, b) both good and evil, c) evil.
2) The significant time dimension: a) past, b) present, c) future.
3) The valued modality of human activity: a) being, b) doing.
4) The valued relationship of man to other men: a) lineal, b) collateral, c) individual.
5) The valued relationship of man to nature (and supernature): a) mastery over nature (and supernature), b) subjugation to nature (and supernature), c) in harmony with nature (and supernature).

On the basis of descriptive materials provided about the ethos of lower-income groups in colonial and republican Cuba, inferences can be made about the probable positions that might have been taken by both black and white respondents to such an instrument.

THE CHARACTER OF HUMAN NATURE

In the face of repression, abuse, and arbitrary actions by those in positions of power and authority, lower-income groups in Cuba may well have perceived human nature as bordering on evil. However, given the profound Yoruban assumptions about neutral power in the universe that can be used for both good and evil, it is more likely that they perceived the disorder in their lives as being heavily influenced by evil, but that human nature itself was basically both good and evil. For white Creoles, fundamental principles of reciprocity and patronage may have softened a perception of human nature as evil into an assumption that the character of human nature was both good and evil. Congruent with such assumptions are those related to the ways in which human beings can call upon higher powers to bring more good into their lives to counterbalance negative circumstances of existence.

THE SIGNIFICANT TIME DIMENSION

For both black and white groups and their Creole descendants, basic assumptions about the most important time orientation would very likely have been the present. In situations of unpredictability and precarious means of survival, daily attention to problem solving must have taken precedence over a past orientation that was also important to both groups. The importance of lineage affiliations, the role of the dead, and deference to seniority in many aspects of life very likely placed the past as a secondary but also important dimension of time.

THE VALUED MODALITY OF HUMAN ACTIVITY

Given a present time orientation, it is very likely that a being activity orientation would be preferred to a doing activity orientation. If one is involved in daily solutions to a variety of life's problems, it is important to be "present" in whatever action is required. "Being" is an expression of "presence," and the more joyful aspects of life (music, singing, dancing, sharing food, and so forth) would be congruent with such an orientation. Nevertheless, assumptions about sources of supernatural assistance and ways of eliciting help from the spiritual realm would lead to a secondary orientation of doing in line with personal practice and guidance from those in the religious hierarchy.

THE VALUED RELATIONSHIP OF MAN TO OTHER MEN

Given the well-established order of Yoruban life in Nigeria, one would expect a continuation of the first-ranked lineal, second-ranked collateral, and a weak third-ranked individual orientation. But adaptation to the ethos of colonial and republican Cuba might well have fostered a more mixed orientation in the secular sphere while the emergence of Santería may have supported this traditional orientation in the religious sphere.

Even though a lineal orientation in the white immigrant and white Creole populations was expressed in the importance of family lineages, governmental structure, and church hierarchy, there was a secondary orientation to collateral relationships. But many Cubans learned to strategize in seeking personal goals so that an individualistic orientation was too highly valued to be placed in a weak third-ranked position.

It may be that the "jostling" for logico-structural integration (Kearney 1984) of assumptions to better fit the ethos and socioenvironmental circumstances of the period led to a more mixed result on the relational value dimension for this population. If this was the case for white immigrants and their Creole descendants in Cuba, how much more of a strain toward logico-structural integration there must have been for Yoruban immigrants and their Creole descendants in Cuba. For slaves deprived of their homelands, their extended families, their patrilineal ancestors, and their cross-cutting social clubs and associations, there must have been a necessary shift toward greater individuality than could ever have been the case in their homeland. It is very likely that there would be a more mixed value orientation profile for them in Cuba, with a much stronger emphasis on individualism in the secular sphere. However, within the ethos and safe space of the *cabildos*, the logico-structural integration of the traditional value profile may have been able to be retained in the foundations of Santería.

THE VALUED RELATIONSHIP OF MAN TO NATURE (AND SUPERNATURE)

Among the Nigerian Yoruba, the ideal relationship of man to nature and supernature would surely have been an "in-Harmony-with-Nature-and-Supernature" orientation (Lowery-Palmer 1980). However, given the ambiance of incertitude for black and white immigrants and their Creole descendants, one might surmise that for the lower-income inhabitants of the island feelings of subjugation toward nature (and supernature) were more congruent with reality and, therefore, prevalent. Relative lack of order and control in their lives would most likely contribute to feelings of helplessness and being "acted upon" rather than to assumptions of being in harmony with nature (and supernature).

A "Subjugation-to-Nature-(and-Supernature)" orientation, combined with lineality along a relational dimension, evokes images of causality and implicit power in the universe (Kearney 1984) along with the means of restoring balance and order in human lives. It is very likely that a first-ranked assumption of "subjugation to nature and supernature" would predispose both white immigrants and their Creole descendants and black immigrants and their Creole descendants to utilize whatever resources were available to them in the realms of religion, magic, healing, and other areas of societal functioning to achieve something closer to an "in Harmony-with-Nature-and-Supernature" orientation. Cuban value orientation has changed over time, as reflected in the findings of the *Health Ecology Report* (1978) and *Mariel and Cuban National Identity* (1986).

Summary of Inferential Constructs

For both black immigrants and their Creole descendants in lower-income groups and white immigrants and their Creole descendants in lower-income groups, the descriptive materials suggest the following:

1) The character of human nature is both good and evil, with a tendency toward evil in second-ranked position.
2) The significant time dimension is the present, with a tendency toward the past in second-ranked position.
3) The valued modality of human activity is being, with a tendency toward doing, particularly in the religious sphere.
4) The valued relationship of man to other men is lineal, with a strong collateral orientation in second-ranked position, and an individual orientation in third-ranked position, particularly in relation to the religious sphere. But there appears to be tension in this value profile that may be producing a more mixed orientation than is portrayed here.

5) The valued relationship of man to nature (and supernature) is subjugation to nature (and supernature), followed by an in-harmony-with-na-
ture (and supernature) in second-ranked position.

What does such a value orientation profile mean for the beliefs and actions
of ordinary people in their daily lives? We might utilize Kearney's (1984) analytic approach to reason as follows: If good and evil reside in all human beings
(and all things created), then the Self's relationship with other human beings
(and all "other than self") is fundamentally ambiguous or potentially harmful.
Also, if the Self is subjugated to nature (and supernature), then power lies in
the realm of the Other, and this relationship, also, is fraught with danger and
is potentially harmful.

The existence of these two value orientations alone has consequences for
human perceptions or images of "reality." For example, human beings are constantly exposed to impinging forces that may be helpful (good) but may also
bring evil in the form of poverty, sickness, disordered social relationships, and
disruption of other types.

The addition of a third value orientation regarding the valued relationship
of man to other men as first lineal, then collateral, then individual reinforces
both the vertical and horizontal dimensions of social reality. Negative influences may come along a vertical dimension from others above one in whatever
hierarchy of power exists. This might include elders, persons of authority in
social organizations, spirits of the family dead, and of the angry dead, the *orichas,* or even the Supreme Being. Harm may also come from others below the
self in the hierarchy of power as a consequence of envy. Negative influences
may also come to the self along a horizontal dimension from others: family
members, spouses, lovers, friends, neighbors, and strangers, as well as from
nature and malign magic.

A dominant value orientation of this configuration could well influence a
preferred time dimension focused on the present. With so many potentialities
for harm to enter one's life, survival in a comfortable state may depend upon
activity directed toward ensuring that good prevails and negative influences
are thwarted.

A dominant orientation of present time, itself, may influence the preferred
mode of activity. On the one hand, a being orientation may be linked to maintaining an equilibrium of goodness and harmony in one's life; while disorder
and disruption may require a doing orientation in the religious sphere to restore order to the self in the context of all others.

There is coherence in the relation of these value dimensions to each other.
They make "logical" sense, and it is in this way that Kearney's concept of logico-

structural integration becomes clear and meaningful in relation to cultural continuities and change.

We turn now to other social and historical factors that undoubtedly contributed to the emergence of Santería. It is my opinion that the similarities outlined above contributed to continuities of the Yoruban religion in Cuba. The ethos of marginalized persons in colonial and republican Cuba was supported by congruent worldviews that provided fertile soil for the emergence of a new religious form called "Santería." Some of the factors outlined above were clearly supportive of cultural continuity in the face of great change.

The Origins of Santería/Regla Lucumí

Slaves in Cuba took refuge in their religion. It was through their religion that some of their music, dances, mythology, and languages were preserved. Religion was the vehicle for the transmission of the beliefs, moral ideas, and aspects of the worldview of Africa, as well as a means of preserving as much of their way of life as was possible. While doing so, African religions in Cuba spontaneously opened to new influences and interpretations. Their intrinsic dynamism and flexibility made them acceptable and popular and facilitated evolution and growth into new religious forms that were uniquely Afro-Cuban.

There were some differences in the way African religions evolved and were integrated into Cuba's cultural history. Afro-Cubans in Havana and the large cities were exposed to a wide range of cultural influences from other ethnic backgrounds. Nevertheless, they had the *cabildos,* which, in many ways, functioned to preserve ethnic identities. In the countryside, however, within a small perimeter there were different African traditions, Catholicism, and European Spiritualism, all interacting, in an ambiance of tolerance and cross-fertilization.

The lasting influence of the Yoruban religion on Cuban culture was due to the demonstrated ability of priests—some brought as slaves; others ordained in Cuba—to preserve much of the complex organization of the Yoruban religion, the diverse and elaborate rituals, the mythology, the intricate divination systems, and the rich music. These accomplishments were made possible by the ability of the founding priests to train and guide new priests along with their willingness to change rituals and adapt them to meet the demands of new situations.

Santería/Regla Lucumí

Santería and Regla Lucumí are the names commonly given to the most popular and influential Afro-Cuban religion. It is also known as Regla de *Ocha* and Regla de Santo and is recognized as the religion of the *babaorichas, iyáorichas,* and *omorichas.*[1] Regla Lucumí is probably the most appropriate name for this religion, since Santería's believers use the word Lucumí to refer to themselves and to their sacred language.

According to some sources the word Lucumí is derived from the name of a kingdom northwest of Benin that was called Ulkami or Ulkama. In this regard, Percy Amaury Talbot (1926 1:282–83) includes the following quote from Olfert Dapper's 1668 book on geography: "The kingdom of Ulkami or Ulkama, a mighty country, lies to the East of Arder between the kingdoms of Arder and Benin, in the Northeast, but does not reach the sea. From this Kingdom many slaves, who had either been captured in war or been reduced to slavery for misdeeds, are brought to Little Arder (Porto Novo) and there sold to the Dutch and Portuguese, who brought them to the West Indies." Talbot thinks that Ulkami, or Ulkama, was the name by which the Kingdom of Oyo, which flourished during the sixteenth and seventeenth centuries, was first known to Europeans. There is no mention of Ulkami in eighteenth-century accounts. Thus, it could be inferred that with the passing of time such a kingdom disappeared or became known by another name.

Another source, Ade Ajayi and Smith (1964:2), says that the neighbors of the Yoruba called them Olukumi and that Europeans used the name Lucumi to designate Oyo and the people of the region around Oyo. However, according to some sources, among them Timothy A. Awoniyi (1881:104): "These terms *Ulkami/Ulkumi/Alkami* were probably a contraction of the nominal *Oluku mi* which literally in the language meant, My Confidant . . . a term which is still used when the actual name of the addressee is avoided or unknown. It may be that this term '*Oluku mi*'(My fellow tribesman) was frequently used by some of the Yoruba peoples when addressing one another. . . . The early Explorers, perhaps using some Yoruba people as informants, and frequently hearing the term '*Oluku mi*,' supposedly misconstrued the words to mean the name of the Yoruba people as well as their language."

Castellanos and Castellanos (1988–94:1:30) report that, according to Escalante, Lucumí is the name given to the Yoruba in Colombia and in Mexico. Since Lucumí was the name given to slaves brought from Yorubaland to New World colonies, it may be inferred that Yoruba-speaking people were brought to the New World from at least the middle of the seventeenth century, when the term Lucumi was used to designate the Oyo Empire and the Yoruba-speaking people.

In his comparative study of Yoruba and Lucumí, the linguist David L. Olmstead (1953:157–64) suggests that Yoruba-speaking people were brought to Cuba in large numbers from the last decades of the seventeenth century until the end of the contraband of slaves in the 1870s. During the 1840s, after the fall of the new Oyo Empire, thousands of refugees who had fled their homeland were captured by slave traders and were sent to Cuba and Brazil (S. Johnson 1921:192). They were called Lucumíes, following the criteria already established. They were probably scattered over the island, but the great majority settled in areas where sugar cane and coffee plantations were booming (the provinces of Havana and Matanzas).

The Inception of Santería

Even though the Yoruban people didn't comprise the largest ethnic group that was brought to Cuba, still they were brought in considerable numbers, especially after the slave trade became illegal. A significant contributor to their influence was the social background of at least some of the slaves. Because large parts of Yorubaland, including the new and the old Oyo Empires and the sacred city of Ile Ife, were ravaged by civil wars, many of its residents from all levels and spheres of society were sold into slavery. Among those slaves were a substantial number of well-trained priests and individuals versed in the complexity of Yoruban music. Some priests came to Cuba with knowledge of the use of sophisticated divination systems; others had mastery of the complex sacred music associated with the worship of the orishas; others were prepared to undertake the rigorous training of new priests; and still others demonstrated the ability to make necessary changes and adopt strategies that helped salvage their religion in Cuba.

Many reliable sources make reference to the presence of priests in the slave cargo. Abelardo Hernandez (June 1999), a late senior *santero* who had been initiated in the cult of Ochún over sixty years ago, claimed that "the first *santera* was an African who had Ochosi, and her son had Yewá." In his autobiographical accounts to be introduced later, Florencio Baró frequently makes references to three African priestesses who were founders of large religious lineages in Matanzas. Moreover, Wilfredo Fernández Jr.(June 2002), a *babalao* who was initiated in the prestigious house-temple of Bernardo Rojas, confided to me that in that house there was a photograph of Adechina (Adde' Shiná), the founder of the Regla de Ifá.[2] The photograph clearly shows the tribal scars on Adechina's face. This information suggests that Adechina was indeed born in Africa. It further supports the argument that priests, chiefs, and kings were part of the slave cargo.

The imposing presence in Cuba of the cult to Changó (the historical fourth Alafin, or king, of Oyo), gives credence to the notion that a number of priests and priestesses who specialized in Changó's worship came from territories where the Oyo Empire had great influence, if not from Oyo proper. Moreover, the preservation of the intricacies of Ifa divination suggests that many babalawos dedicated to the cult of Orunmila, who were experts in the Ifa divination system, were also brought as slaves to Cuba. In the same manner the cult of other *orichas,* such as Ochún, which flourished in Cuba, also suggests the presence of well-trained priests from Oshogbo and Ilesha, the cradle of Oshun's cult.

Miguel Ramos (2000; 2003:38–69) takes the position that the influence of the Yoruban people from the Oyo area was overwhelming in the inception and development of Santería. Ramos asserts that a Havana-based Oyo-centric orientation affected the growth and development of Santería's inner core and practices. As Ramos points out, the initiation procedures and rituals that prevail in Santería closely follow the Oyo model. He also stresses the importance in Cuban Santería of those orishas that were important in Oyo, or were closely associated with Shango, the tutelary patron of Oyo.

Another contributing factor in Santería's development was that, as pointed out before, slavery was abolished in Cuba shortly after the last contingent of Africans arrived. Many of these most recent arrivals, born in Africa and retaining clear memories of their ancestry and cultural traditions, became free early enough to thrive under conditions that helped sustain some of their African beliefs and behaviors.

With the end of the slave trade, legitimate trade with Africa began, which enabled believers on the island to purchase religious paraphernalia such as the palm nuts, or *ikínes,* used in divination. Some freed slaves returned to their homeland. Others went to Africa and later decided to come back to Cuba. All of these factors were significant in the emergence of a cultural and religious heritage that, to some extent, was preserved and continues to be preserved and transmitted through Santería and Cuban culture at large.

Yoruban traditional religion, which became intertwined in its homeland with Christianity and Islam, was being reformulated in a significant way in Cuba and Brazil. Even though great functional changes took place across the ocean from Africa, fundamentals of the Yoruban religion managed to survive and expand while developing qualities that attracted people of diverse ethnic backgrounds.

The Afro-Creole population in Cuba experienced a dramatic increase in numbers during the second half of the nineteenth century. Also, the Yoruban presence in the last waves of forced immigration, when women formed a significant percentage of the slave cargo, is amply documented. Moreno Fraginals' research (1977:212–28) shows the presence of heavy concentrations of Yoruban slaves in the provinces of Havana and Matanzas by the second half of the nineteenth century. These provinces became the cradles of Santería.

Though slaves were sold all over the island, great concentrations of Yoruban slaves were settled in and around the city of Havana and in the adjacent provinces of Matanzas and Las Villas. Some slaves were placed in the cities to serve as domestic servants or artisans, but the largest numbers were forced to labor in the sugar and coffee plantations. The life-styles of slaves in the cities and the countryside were thus very different. Therefore, it is necessary to at least gaze into the divergent experiences of slaves in the city and the countryside in order to have an understanding of the embryonic processes in the birth of Santería.

Cabildos emerged as institutions that were the spawning grounds of Santería in and around the large cities, especially the city of Havana, its neighborhoods, and nearby towns. A biographical account of life experiences in the small town of Carlos Rojas, in the province of Matanzas, illustrates a different, but also legitimate, nursery bed of Santería—the countryside.

THE CITY: *CABILDOS*

The *cabildos de nación* were religious brotherhoods of black slaves, primarily of the same ethnic background or region, and their descendants (slaves and freemen alike). Generally, they were organized under the tutelary protection of a saint or Virgin. In colonial Cuba they functioned as religious centers, as social clubs, and as mutual aid societies. They also provided entertainment. Members would meet every Sunday to dance secular dances and, also, to worship their gods in an atmosphere of freedom from government authorities. Generally they served to perpetuate or help create an ethnic identity—an identity reflecting a more coherent ethos and worldview than was possible in any other sphere of activity on the island.

Cabildos, although not called that at the time, originated in Spain during the reign of King Alfonso el Sabio of Castile, who, in the year 1200, ordered the inhabitants of Seville to organize into guilds and to establish religious brotherhoods, or *cofradías.* These institutions grouped the white inhabitants of Seville. Black slaves from the same ethnic background or region were also organized into *cofradías.*

Fernando Ortiz (1921b:4) cites de Zúñiga as reporting that, in Seville, around 1390, during the reign of Enrique III, there were slave organizations presided over by a foreman. The foreman, also a slave, acted as chief and judge of the slaves under his jurisdiction. He was responsible to the master for their behavior. He also presided over the festivities organized by his group. His role (reflecting traditional images of authority) was a direct antecedent of the captain, or king, of an Afro-Cuban *cabildo.* By the sixteenth century, the word *cabildo* was used in Spain to refer to the meetings of religious brotherhoods or *cofradías.*

Justino Matute y Gaviria (1866:78) refers to the existence, in the mid-1500s of a mulatto brotherhood in Seville. There was also a brotherhood of blacks in Seville in 1601, which, due to conflict with Cardinal de Guevara, was denied permission to march in a street procession.

The model of the slave *cabildos* of Seville was brought to the Americas during the colonial period. There were *cabildos* in Cuba, and, also, in other areas of Hispanic America where there were concentrations of black people. Ricardo Palma (1949: 152) reports on their presence in colonial Peru in the sixteenth century.

The first information about black *cabildos* in Cuba dates to 1598 when a brotherhood was incorporated as part of the Church of Santo Domingo in Havana. Slaves, reputedly of the same "nation," also formed social clubs and mutual aid societies called *cabildos*, which were not affiliated with any church. Through time, as *cabildos* became more numerous, many began to gain independence from the parochial system to which they had been incorporated; others had been independent of the church from the beginning. In 1755, as previously mentioned, Morell de Santa Cruz, the bishop of Havana, incorporated all of them into the church system.

In 1792 the authorities mandated that *cabildos* establish their locales outside the walled perimeter of the city. Their growing presence in the inner city represented a threat to the authorities and to white residents.

As mentioned earlier, *cabildos* became social and political organizations that were considered to represent blacks of specific ethnic background. Members elected their own officials, among them a king, one or two queens, a master of ceremonies, and others who were placed in charge of elaborate celebrations full of pomp and ingenuity. The king and queen would often dress luxuriously in European-style garments, while the priests would don African costumes. The king was always the most prestigious member of the "nation," and, invariably, a respected elder. The officers were responsible for the administration of the *cabildo* and for the settling of disputes among members.

Members paid a monthly fee for the maintenance of the organization. Frequent collections were made to aid the needy, to help pay for the funeral of a member, or for the freedom of members too old or too weak to work.

Cabildos organized *comparsas* and *congas*,[3] festive street processions, in which slaves paraded with the images of their gods. When the authorities forbade them from doing so, they began parading with images of Catholic saints, who, for various reasons, had been associated with African deities.

This evolution marks one of the first steps toward religious merging. At first, the Catholic images may have served as a cover for the African *orichas*. Later, in a presumed quest for meaning and access to every available form of power and redress, a closer association between the statue of some of the Catholic saints and the African *orichas* occurred. At that point, the image of the saint was taken to the *cabildo* to preside over the *toque de tambor* (celebrations) and other African rituals. According to Fernando Ortiz (1921b:19), when the colonial authorities realized that the images of the saints did not guarantee a pious Christian meeting, but that, instead, the saints were presiding over African rituals, they forbade the use of Catholic images in the *cabildos*.

Roger Bastide (1971:9) and others reported that associations of Africans of the same nation were encouraged by the Portuguese and Spanish colonial governments as a means of social control. In Brazil, *batuques* that were similar to the *cabildos* were formed. According to Raimundo Nina Rodríguez (1934:253), at the beginning of the nineteenth century, the count of Arcos confirmed that the Portuguese government provided support to the *batuques* as a political measure.

These institutions reinforced ethnocentrism and bred a sense of rivalry among slaves from different African ethnic origins or regions. Disunity among the slaves made it unlikely that they would unite against the common white master. When revolts occurred, instead of joining in, slaves of other ethnic groups remained indifferent. Strong ethnic identity could engender hostility not only towards whites, but also toward blacks of other ethnic backgrounds.

Aside from such political considerations, from the time of their inception in Seville, *cabildos* functioned primarily as social, religious, and mutual aid societies. Possibly *cabildos* also served to awaken and later strengthen a paramount ethnic identity among their members. For example, as mentioned previously, in the case of the Yoruba-speaking people, individuals from Oyo, Egbado, Ijesha, Oshogbo, and other areas who spoke the same language were officially labeled by the authorities as Lucumíes.

Cabildos de nación were organized by people who shared a common language and culture, but who in most cases identified themselves only with the region of Nigeria from which they came. Such organizations might have triggered in them an awareness of commonalities in language, religion, family structure, and other cultural features that they shared and were not necessarily conscious of before. The term Lucumí may then have superseded Oyo, Egbado, Ijesha, Oshogbo, and other points of origin as the paramount identity of the *cabildo* members. Such a new identity is compatible with the fact that the Yoruban language spoken in Cuba is called Lucumí, as is the religion derived from that area. This reflects one aspect of a process that Palmié (1993) describes as "ethnogenesis." The original label, Lucumí, however, most likely originated with outsiders.

Given the probable range of variation in the membership of some *cabildos*, such processes may well have contributed to the genesis of other "new," ethnic labels or identities. Whether consensually derived or truly reflective of a numerically dominant group, cultural practices were retained, reinforced, refined, or created with sufficient meaning and coherence to be transmitted to marginal members or newcomers to the group. Nowhere is this more evident than in the religious functions of the *cabildos*. A striking example of such processes in action is provided by Brandon (1997: 73): "El Cabildo Africano

Lucumi expelled members for any taint of vice; it prohibited non-lucumi drum rhythms at its dances. . . ."[4]

It should be noted that social clubs of Spaniards originally from the same province (Catalonia, Galicia, Canary Islands, Asturias, and others) also flourished in colonial and republican Cuba. The aims were similar to those of the *cabildos*: recreation, mutual aid, education, and, in the more recent past, outpatient and in-patient medical services.[5]

In the final decades of the nineteenth century, the importance of *cabildos* began to wane. The authorities forbade street parades, or *comparsas,* and attempted to place *cabildos* under the parochial system to ensure their supervision by the Catholic Church. In other words, the Spanish authorities attempted to reconstruct the original system of *cabildos,* curbing their independence, because they were afraid that these brotherhoods could become centers of pro-independence movements at a time when pro-independence ideologies were popular among other segments of the population.

The Constitution of 1902 guaranteed religious freedom. This legislation dealt a deathblow to *cabildos.* Since African religions were no longer persecuted and could be practiced in the homes of believers, or virtually in any public place, the importance of *cabildos* declined. Thus, in the independent republic, their functions as religious centers and ethnic strongholds were diminished. They maintained their functions as recreational and mutual aid societies but with membership open to individuals of different ethnic extractions.

In 1909, numerous *cabildos* still existed. In 1921 Fernando Ortiz (1921a) provided a list of those that were still open, although they were registered as mutual aid societies.

The religious character and function of the *cabildos* was undeniable. These social organizations had enormous importance in the life of Africans brought to Cuba and their descendants. In the *cabildos*, something of their traditional ethos and worldview could be preserved. The slaves taught their children the language, traditions, beliefs, and rituals of their ancestors. Throughout their histories the *cabildos* were places where blacks sought meaningful social relationships and found refuge, understanding, and comfort within traditional frameworks. To blacks living in cities, *cabildos* were places where their divinities dared to come, to counsel, and to protect them in spite of the frequent intrusion of the authorities. In the *cabildos,* the African gods rejoiced and danced with their children, renewing the personal pact between them and the believers. Undoubtedly, the *cabildos* served to preserve identifiable aspects of the culture of African ethnic groups.

The impact *cabildos* had on Santería's practices is evident when one considers current initiation ceremonies. During such ceremonies the *iyawó* is seated on a throne. According to David H. Brown (2003:21): "Whereas luxuriously dressed mortal kings and queens, observed drumming from their canopied thrones in the old *cabildos*, the *orichas*,—as luxuriously dressed kings and queens—came to receive similar honors from their own canopied thrones within the *casas de ocha* by the twentieth century."

As *cabildos* lost importance, the merging process was accelerated. Cultural borrowing between Afro-Cubans of different ethnic groups was facilitated. The adoption and incorporation of European spiritualist and Catholic beliefs and practices and of other non-Yoruban African elements in a process of trans-culturation resulted in what later would be called "Santería."

As the influence of *cabildos* weakened, their religious functions were transferred to the *ilé ochas*, or house-temples, which were in the homes of priests and priestesses. It was not unusual in Hispanic America for individuals to have shrines and altars in their homes, where they placed the images of their favorite saints or paths of the Virgin Mary. Many freed black families also had altars in their homes where they worshipped— even in those cities where *cabildos* had become worship centers. This was also the case in cities and small towns where there were no *cabildos*.

From at least the beginning of the twentieth century, the homes of priests and priestesses were used for religious purposes in small towns, in the countryside, and in areas where there were no *cabildos*. Joseph Murphy (1988: 29–33) reports that even in cities where there were *cabildos*, the homes of freed blacks who were priests or priestesses were also used as temples. Presently, Santería's temples, or *casas de santo*, are still called *"cabildos."*

Cabildos were organized in cities where there were great concentrations of black people who could sustain them. In the countryside, *cabildos* were not organized. Instead, on holidays, the slaves were allowed to gather and dance in the *batey*, a central parkland area on farms and plantations, where, under the watchful eyes of their white masters they rehearsed their sacred dances. However, there is little documentation of the religious experiences of slaves in the countryside.

The following account of the town known as Carlos Rojas is offered to help compensate for gaps in the historical record. Florencio Baró was a talented percussionist, musician, and conversationalist. During several years of friendship and collaboration in musical and cultural events, Baró revealed to me stories about his hometown, his family, his life, and Santería. The stories in Florencio Baró's narrative capture the ambiance, worldview, meaning of life, and the religious beliefs, practices, and experiences of descendants of Yoruban slaves in the Cuban countryside.

The period of time recollected by Florencio Baró is the 1940s and 1950s, three generations removed from the time of slavery. Nevertheless, the basis of these stories in oral history sheds some light on the experiences of freed slave farmhands and their descendants in the area of Carlos Rojas in the province of Matanzas. This particular town is known as having being settled by Lucumíes (the name given to Yoruban people in Cuba) and their descendants. It is also a place where Santería has had old and substantial roots from colonial times. It is known to have played an important role in the foundations of Santería. Even though the Carlos Rojas experience might not be typical of the experiences of all former slave farmhands, it is representative of life in a small town in Matanzas Province.

THE COUNTRYSIDE: "THE SECRET IS IN THE HERBS"

Here, then, is the story of Florencio Baró, which has been edited for clarity.

> Carlos Rojas was a town full of mystery, as were Perico, Bolondrón, Colón, Sagua la Grande, and other towns in that region of the province of Matanzas in Cuba. Moreover, Carlos Rojas and Jovellanos had reputations for being bewitched. The mystical ambiance in Carlos Rojas was only disrupted by the expressions of nature's creatures and the epic beat of drums. This ambiance emerged from the empty lots, abandoned homes, shadowy avocado trees, ever-growing vines, and an eerie silence.
>
> During colonial times, white families had settled Carlos Rojas, then called Cimarrón. However, shortly after the abolition of slavery, my grandparents, along with many former slave families, abandoned the barracks of the sugar mill called Olimpo Baró and, searching for a place of residence and sustenance, chose this town in which to settle.
>
> Two long streets ran from north to south, the Royal Road, now called Martí, and Calixto García Street. In addition, a road ran from east to west, linking Carlos Rojas to Central Progreso. The town was organized around two neighborhoods. In the north was the neighborhood of La Solitaria [the Lonely One] where every Sunday the *yuca* drums were played. Guarajamales was to the south.
>
> There were around five thousand residents in Carlos Rojas when I was growing up, four *bodegas* [general stores], a butcher shop, a bakery, and the small central park, also called Martí. Then, there were those mysterious alleys bordering the overgrown empty lots where the red dirt nourished the coffee bushes, the pineapples, the avocados, mangoes, and sugar-apple trees.
>
> Many people worked in the two sugar mills near the town. The Carolina was located between the Olimpo Baró (which was already closed at the time when I was growing up) and the road to Cardenas. Then there

was the Santa Amalia, which was close to the town of Coliseo. Carlos Rojas was dirt poor, full of need and the needy. There was no money, but God was near. Townspeople used to say: "Each person comes with a piece of soil to walk on and function with." I was born and raised there in that town of five thousand residents, of two streets, and unpaved alleys.

People in Carlos Rojas were very religious, and most participated in both the Catholic and Afro-Cuban cults and festivities. Religion is family and is a way of life. *Santeros* in Carlos Rojas were Catholic. All of them were baptized, and when they were sick they called the priest to *santiguarse* [bless them]. When they walked by the church, they made the sign of the cross. During Holy Week the soup tureens and other symbols and receptacles of the power of the *orichas* were covered with a white cloth.[6] Everyone respected other people's beliefs.

The Catholic and Afro-Cuban religious calendars marked the rhythm of life in Carlos Rojas. The semi-official Catholic Church, located at the head of the town's central park, was the focus of everybody's attention during Christmas and Easter celebrations. It was there that Father Justo, a most beloved priest, officiated.

The difference between a priest and a *santero* is that the priest studies a lot to become a priest, while *santeros* are born with religious faculties. The priest advises according to his knowledge, with his heart, and by invoking the saints and God, but he cannot divine. *Santeros*, however, are fortune-tellers who can predict and cure.

Everybody went to church during Christmas and Holy Week and on important occasions. We all went there to get holy water. During Holy Week there was a tradition of sweeping anthills with a broom made of palm thatch. The images of the saints and the clay pots containing the *otanes* [sacred stones] of the saints were covered with white sheets.

Santeros saw the Catholic god as Olodumare. For *santeros* God is in the Catholic Church and in Santería. Before any Ocha [Yoruban religion in Cuba characterized by the cult to the *orichas*] or Palo [name given in Cuba to religious practices originally from the Congo Basin that are characterized by the cult to the spirits of the dead] ceremonies started, they had to pray to God.

At the same time, the homes of priests, priestesses, and followers of Afro-Cuban religions were the focus of attention when celebrations and drum festivals in honor of Afro-Cuban *santos* and *orichas* took place. These celebrations followed an unofficial but traditional calendar of festivities. Most of them took place on the day the Catholic calendar celebrated a saint with whom an important *oricha* was identified.[7] There were less than a dozen *casas de santo*[8] in Carlos Rojas where celebrations took place at least on a yearly basis.

In the past, *negros de nación* [slaves born in Africa] lived in Carlos Rojas. Most *santeros* in Carlos Rojas and in the neighboring towns were descendants of the religious lineage established by a Lucumí priestess and a priest born in Africa. One of them was Mamá Kele, or Ayai, a senior *santera* and godmother of many lineages who lived on the Olimpo Baró sugar plantation during the slave era. The renowned Obbadimeyi was a priest and also the godfather of many religious lineages. He lived on the Desempeño sugar plantation during the slave era.

Slavery meant long hours of hard, forced labor, but on Sundays the slaves celebrated according to their religion. In La Solitaria every Sunday they played the *tambor de yuca* [a drum of Congolese origin, which has two or three different passes or beats]. Alongside they also used the clave [Cuban percussion instrument], which consists of two eight-inch-long cylinder-shaped hardwood sticks. The sticks are beaten against each other to mark rhythm. They played the rhythms of *toque de palo*[9] [ritual music of Congolese origin].

This religion came to Cuba with some families and individuals. The Lucumíes came to Cuba in large numbers and were dispersed to all parts of Cuba, but they were concentrated in Matanzas and in Havana. In Cárdenas, I met Rafael Morgan, who spoke Lucumí very well. He claimed that when boats came from Africa to Cuba in the 1940s to load sugar, he was able to communicate with the sailors. His mother's name was Yimi and she was the daughter of one of the last slaves to be brought from Africa to Cuba. Rafael and his sister, called La Albina, learned Lucumí from their mother and their African grandmother.

In Pinar del Río this religion was hardly known; nevertheless, I went with Quique Angarica to a celebration that took place in the Orozco sugar mill. The religion is stronger in the provinces of Matanzas and in Havana than it is in Pinar del Río probably because there were larger concentrations of Lucumíes.

In Oriente there was a great Haitian influence, mixed with French culture. There they speak another language. I went to a festival in Holguín. The Haitian type of music is called rada. The drum beat was somehow similar to that in Santería, but it was not *sentado* (in tune) with the melody. They knew about the saints such as Ogún, but they called them different names.

In Oriente, the mixture of African religion and Spiritualism was stronger than in Matanzas. In Matanzas, we had everything, but each religion was practiced separately; they were not mixed with other African religious practices.[10] The Palo rituals (in which the spirits of the dead are invoked) always took place outside of the house. Everything moves because of the spirits of the dead. A *brujo* [Spanish word for witch doctor or sorcerer] is anything; it is a spirit. The spiritual *bóveda*[11] [an altar for the souls of departed family members] was inside the house; and in it we had Christ, Saint Clara, and the Seven African Powers.[12]

In Camaguey, the few people who could play Lucumí music were originally from Havana. In Sagua La Grande, Las Villas lived Nena Mongoval, who had an *asiento* of Ochún[13] [that is, she was a priestess who had been initiated in the cult of Ochún]. In Sagua lived famous *rumberos*,[14] musicians who composed and interpreted rumbas. Two such *rumberos* were Cheche Malenche and Malanga.

Many of the slaves brought from Africa, especially the priests, insisted on preserving their language, religion, and traditions. Their children, the *criollos*, learned some of those traditions while also assimilating the Spanish culture of Cuba.

I come from a family of six children, four boys and two girls. My mother's family, the Baró, came from Guantánamo. They were slaves on the coffee plantation of the Baró family. I was told that the Baró family had brought many of their slaves from Haiti after they abandoned that island when the slave revolt overthrew the colonial plantation system. My great-grandmother, Nicolasa Baró, was married to Victor Gene. Her son, my grandfather, Perfecto Baró, was married to Maria Gay. Their owner brought both of them from Guantánamo to Matanzas, where the Baró family owned the sugar mill Olimpo Baró near the town of Cimarrón, or Carlos Rojas.

The slaves who had been brought to Guantánamo from Haiti were involved in the Tumba Francesa cult and festivities. I guess it was in Matanzas where my ancestors were closely exposed to the Yoruban religion and promptly became involved in it. Thus, my grandfather's sister, Justina Baró, had an *asiento* of Ochún and was the godchild of Carolina Carrillo, who used only herbs to do the *medio asiento*[15] ceremony halfway into full initiation. She was mounted by the dead and by Ochún. She had *soperas*[16] [soup tureens] of Ochún, Changó, and also one of Babalú Ayé, which she kept outside the sanctuary room. She died the same year I was born, the *santeros* performed an *itutu* [funeral ceremony that takes place when a priest or priestess of Santería dies]. The ceremony is aimed at determining the deceased's wishes concerning the fate of his or her sacramental objects [for example, to be buried with him or her or to be disposed of in a different fashion]. At Carolina Carrillo's *itutu* her saints were not placed in her coffin. Rather, her son kept them.

While she was alive, on September 8, the day the Catholic Church celebrates the Virgin of Charity, she celebrated drum festivals in honor of her *oricha*. Long after she died, drum festivals or *bembés* continued to be celebrated in her home, the *asiento* of Ochún. I learned a song in Carlos Rojas dedicated to Ochún:

> Ochún *begua aquí Begua* Ochún, *begua aro*
> Ochún *begua aquí*
> *Iyá mi*
> *Algare*
> Ochún *begua Yeyé o*
> Ochún *begua aquí*
> *Begua aquí aro*
> Ochún *begua mi, Ki lon fon me*
> *Que te pasa a tí conmigo?* (what is wrong between you and me?)

My grandfather, whose name in Santería was Bejuco de Sabana,[17] sang in Lucumí and in Spanish. He had Naná Burukú, the serpent also known as Santa Marta, whose food cannot be touched by iron, and sang to her in Lucumí and not in Arará [the language of the Yoruban people who lived in the western part of Nigeria in the former French colony of Dahomey, nowadays the Republic of Benin].

Only one generation had passed, and all of my mother's siblings had become very involved in Santería. My aunt, Feliciana Baró, who was called Mamía, was mounted by Inle and had a Yemayá *asentada* [initiated into Yemayá's priesthood]. When she was fourteen Yemayá would mount her every evening around seven o'clock. When Yemayá mounted her, she would burst into the parlor and order all doors to be locked. After a while her father, my grandfather, took a machete to test her. He gave her a couple of *planazos* [strokes] to see if she was really possessed or not. Later on, he realized that she was, indeed, mounted by Yemayá and started singing:

> *Tu nemea cume*
> *Aboyo rija*
> Yemayá *colé tu nemea cume*
>
> *Tu nemea cume*
> Yemayá *colé* Yemayá *colon.*

Then, he patted her and raised her from the floor where she was in a deep trance.

My mother's brother, Pancho Baró, was mounted by the *oricha* Elegguá, but he never was initiated into Santería. He used to officiate in the sacrifice of four-legged animals; however, he never had to go through the *pinaldo*[18] ceremony that is currently required in order to confer the right to sacrifice four-legged animals.

When I was around twelve years old, he would take me as his assistant to hold the legs of the animals he was offering. The night before the ceremony, he would give me some herbs to bathe with and cleanse myself. He would do the same. It is important to be clean before one participates in a ceremony. For instance, the women who cooked the animals that were sacrificed would bathe with herbs and would abstain from having sexual relations the night before, otherwise the meat of the animals would be spoiled. Likewise, *batá* drummers [drum players initiated in the cult of the sacred drums, or *batá*] should also abstain from sex the night before they officiate.

My uncle sang three or four songs to Elegguá before he offered a rooster to the *oricha*. Then, he pulled the head off, and would say, "Elegguá, I am going to introduce to you so and so who is doing this offering to you so that you might open the road of opportunities to him or her." Later he used the coconut oracle to ask Elegguá if he accepted the offerings. Elegguá always said yes.

My uncle's wife, Longina Piedra, was mounted by Babalú Ayé and by Ochún. One day, when she was celebrating a drum festival in her home, four or five people were mounted by *orichas*. Around the corner lived a woman whose daughter was very sick. The people who were mounted suddenly left the house and went to a *represa* [dike] near the sugar mill and gathered herbs. They came back and asked the woman for some roasted corn, and they told her that if the corn grew her daughter would live. Then they put the herbs, corn, incense, and water on top of the girl, covered her with cotton and sang and worked for hours. When they uncovered the girl the corn had sprouted, and she was safe.

My aunt, Escolástica Baró, had *asiento* of Oyá, Santa Teresa on October 15. When she died her son kept the saint.

My mother's other siblings, Nicolasa, Ernesto, and José (Chéo), actively participated in this religion into which I was born. My mother, Francisca, who was called Yeya, was born into it too. She knew how to sing and dance to the *orichas* and knew a lot about it. Almost everything I know I learned from my family. I learned from my aunt and my uncle who killed the animals and from another uncle whom Elegguá mounted. Now that my mother has died, my youngest sister has taken her place. However, some of my uncles had nothing to do with it. But if there was a *fiesta de santo* they would go. At the time I was growing up the religion was not so structured; there was no need to get the necklaces, coconut, and so forth. In my family everybody was Catholic. The Terán family members were also Catholic and of *yesá* origin (whose Ocha festivities were so famous).[19]

On my father's side it was different. His father, Gervasio Herrera, was the son of Chinese parents, and my grandmother, Victoria Herrera, was also the daughter of Chinese parents. Victoria Herrera got divorced from Gervasio and married Daniel Gove, a black man who brought up my father. Daniel Gove and his father were *paleros*.[20] Daniel Gove was a friend of Calazán.[21]

Life in Carlos Rojas followed a pattern. On January 1, Liberina, of the Guillén family, always had a *bembé* [drum festival] to honor San Manuel, or Oduduwa. People from all over—Cárdenas, Jovellanos, and other towns—would come to join in. Everybody waited for this day with great expectation. The festivities would last two or three days. After that date, there were no important *bembés* for over five months. This period coincided with the *zafra* [sugar harvest] when all the men and women worked.

However, on February 2, the day of the Virgin of Candlemas, in Cárdenas, Jovellanos, and Matanzas they celebrated Oyá. That day women used to cut their hair, because it would grow stronger. In Carlos Rojas Oyá was associated with Saint Teresa and was honored on October 15, the day the Catholic Church celebrated Saint Teresa. Sometimes, the Dominguez family celebrated an Ocha [Santería religion] anniversary party.[22] On May 15 were the festivities of San Isidro Labrador [Oricha Oko, patron of farmers]. On Saint John's day, June 24, festivities to honor Ogún were given by the Piedra family.[23] On that day all the saints were fed.

Soon after, on July 29, the day of Saint Marta, Naná Burukú was celebrated. Matilde Aragonés and Juliana La China [two santeras] always honored Naná. Naná was fed first. The goat that was offered to her was placed under a blanket and petted for hours until it died [probably from suffocation]. Then they would shave and skin it. Later it was roasted with wood or *caña brava*[24] or it was fried in a clay pot using wooden utensils. The furnace was made with three or four stones and wood.

Naná Burukú cures and controls cancer. Her food has to be cooked with wooden utensils, because she feels an aversion to iron and it was believed that in many instances cancer spreads after a surgical operation because of contact with iron/steel.

Naná is a *santo mayor,* a highly respected, old, and prestigious *santo/ oricha.* She is a very serious lady who doesn't like to *guarachear*[25] [to have fun; to party]. She was very revered in Carlos Rojas but not as much in Cárdenas and in other areas, where she is only known as a *camino*[26] [road or manifestation] of Obatalá.

Yeguá is a similar case. She is quite well known and honored in Jovellanos, but in most other places she is perceived as a road or manifestation of Oyá. The same is the case with Olokun, who is an austere *santo mayor* that is manifested through Yemayá.

On September 8, the day of the Virgin of Charity, Justina Baró, my grandfather's sister, had a *bembé* to honor Ochún. Later, in the same month, Ines Aldereta had *asiento* of Obatalá and had a drum celebration for her *oricha* on September 24, the day of the Virgin of Mercy. She was initiated when she was seventy years old. Why did she wait so long? It was because, at that time, people did not think they needed to be initiated to work with the saints, coconuts, toasted corn, bee honey, and *manteca de corojo* [lard made of palm oil].

On October 15, the day of Saint Teresa of Jesus, Escolástica Baró celebrated her *oricha,* Oyá. On October 24, the day of San Rafael, Secundino Angarica played Palo and danced Osain, using only one foot. He called his Osain with a little bell, and his Osain talked. He never used coconuts or shells for divination; instead, his Osain, which he kept on a little table, talked to him. On October 24, they were honoring Osain and drinking firewater. Around three o'clock in the morning, a white man called Cuco, who always had a dozen women chasing him, was mounted with Changó, and then the owner of the house, Angarica, was mounted with Osain. Angarica went out of the room to the drums and started dancing. Osain dances with only one foot and uses a cane, because one of his legs is dead. Then he went running to a water tank and got a turtle that he kept inside. He hung the turtle from his ear. Then he took the turtle, which by then was wearing the green beret that Secundino had been wearing, and handed the turtle and the beret to Cuco. Cuco started bleeding from the turtle's bite. He ran and left with all the women running after him. When Secundino Angarica died, his son kept his Osain, but Osain does not talk anymore.

San Rafael was also associated with Inle, a chaste *oricha* who mounted my uncle and aunt. Inle eats fish and knows a lot about medicine. He is the *ojo del agua* [spring that comes sprouting with force from the bowels of the earth].

In November, Wito Almeral and Toscano celebrated Yemayá. Yemayá likes ducks, but she is afraid of the duck's head. So, when people are going to offer a duck to Yemayá, they have to cover its head.

Agayú Solá was honored on November 16, the day the Catholic Church celebrates the feast to Saint Christopher.

On December 4, the day of Santa Bárbara, Daniel Gómez gave a drum festival. Leandro and Carlos Peñalver also had Changó. Peñalver started celebrating on December 3 and ended on December 6 at midnight.

On December 17 Mateo Fernández, whose house was the oldest *santero* house in Carlos Rojas, honored Babalú Ayé with a drumming celebration. Also, Quique Jerónimo Angarica was a santero who had an *asiento* of San Lázaro/Babalú Ayé. He built a house, a church. He was very successful. He had important clients such as the baseball star Roberto Ortiz, the police captain of Jovellanos, administrators of the sugar mills, senators, and others. His San Lázaro brought him a lot of money, but he did not use the *orichas* well. He ended up badly.

The secrets of Santería are in the herbs. The *orichas*/saints function with herbs because herbs are powerful. With herbs you can save a life and, also, destroy the world. One washes the saints with herbs and gives them blood to give them strength. Saints eat the head and the feet of the animals, because without the head and the feet no one can go anywhere. They also eat the viscera. People eat the rest. Slaughtering took place during the early hours. For example, people would kill and clean some hens for Ochún, cutting off the wings, the head, and the feet. The heart, the liver, the gizzards, the feet, and the head would be cooked. These *iñales* were offered to the saints for a day. Then they were given to the children. Since children have no bad feelings and have clean hearts, the *iñales,* which are medicinal, were given to them. In Cárdenas, they gave the *iñales* to the children, or they threw them away. In Havana they put them in the trash can.

Many times, when there was a threat to the town, a disease or something bad, some *santeros* and *santeras* would get together to perform cleansing ceremonies. Of course they did not charge anything. They never charged for their services. They cleansed you because that was what they had to do.

There were very few people with *santo asentado* in Carlos Rojas and in Matanzas at that time. The fashion of initiating so many people started in the 1950s. In Carlos Rojas there was only one *babalao.* He was called

Pariente, and he was a friend of my Aunt Justina. In Cárdenas, there were a lot of *babalaos.* When there are contradictions in different readings of the oracles, they are the ones who say the final word. They are the ones to say what saint is going on your head before initiation. They make the *registro*[27] [divination-consultation] and tell the person which saint he or she is going to take.

The *itá* is something different. It is a consultation using the oracle of the shells, which takes place right after initiation. After initiation has taken place, the *oriaté* [a Santería priest who is an expert on the oracle of the shells, or *dilogún*] tells you what things you can and cannot do, such as taking sunbaths, bathing in the sea, eating okra or meat, drinking sodas or alcoholic beverages, and the like.

Initiation takes a while. After your godmother has taken you to the *babalao* to get the *registro* done and to tell you about your saint, you start purchasing all the stuff that is necessary; and, finally, you figure out what you are going to wear.

The *batá* [28] (three sacred drums that in Nigeria were part of Shango's cult) were not known in Carlos Rojas. People played them occasionally in Cárdenas on Sundays from two to six. If you played them afterward, it was bad for the religion. The dead would come to dance. At that time it was believed that the *batá* [the drum ensemble of the kings] should only be used during initiation for the presentation of the *iyawó* [Yoruban word meaning bride of the *oricha*]. The secret of the *batá* is the glue-like substance that is placed inside.

When I was growing up in Cuba, people did not mix up Palo and the saints, Congo and Lucumí when they had a festival. Santería was one thing, and Palo another. There were two different African currents, Lucumí and Palo. Seven Lightning, Sarabanda is the Palo equivalent of Changó, and Mamá Chola is the Palo equivalent of Ochún. They are the same gods, but each ethnic group gives them a different name. The Lucumíes work with the spirits of the dead, but people of the Palo religion work with obscure spirits to cause harm. The Lucumíes do not work with obscure souls, but they have the spirits.

The *bóveda* or altar for the spirits of the deceased family members was a fenced-in area, a small piece of the ground in the yard where offerings were given to the ancestors of the family who live in the house.[29] Ceremonies started at the *bóveda* by giving food to the dead. They were offered *ajiaco* (a Cuban countryside recipe consisting of soup made with boiled vegetables and meat). After feeding the dead, people went into the house to continue the ceremonies. Often, among the souls of the family's ancestors there would be one who had been initiated or who had served an *oricha* or *orichas.* When a young member of the family showed signs that he or she had power and religious faculties, it was known that it was because one of his or her ancestors had been very good in Santería. That departed ancestor had worshipped the *oricha* and knew how to do it. Those attributes and faculties were transmitted from generation to generation.

The *orichas* are supernatural forces; but in reality the ones that work, the ones that function, are the dead who had been initiated or had served the *orichas.* In this religion, God is first, then the *orichas,* and then the dead. The dead search for people in which they can manifest themselves. They try to find the adequate person of good heart so that they can enter that person and manifest themselves. When the heart is good, everything works right, but when the heart is evil, things do not work. Sometimes the souls of the dead make mistakes; but when they realize that the *santero* or *santera* is using the power to do harm, they abandon the body, leaving the individual alone and powerless.

When a person showed signs of having spiritual faculties, the first thing he or she did was have a spiritualist consultation. The spiritualist need not be in Santería. The spirits would function with flowers, light from candles, and perfume. Also, when people were going to be initiated in Santería, they went to see a spiritualist who would identify the spirits of departed members of the family or other spirits that accompanied them. The spirits would identify themselves, and say, "I am so and so, and when I was in the terrestrial plane, I did this and the other."

In Carlos Rojas, everybody was baptized. As I told you before, everybody, when passing in front of the church, would make the sign of the cross. Everybody went to church to get holy water. God was in the church where the priest officiated and God was in Santería: the same. The Supreme God is something out of the ordinary, set aside from the others. He is the almighty one. Without him there can be no *orichas.* Every time one wants to do something, one has to ask permission from God first, then from the earth, the sun, and the sky, then from all the different levels of souls that exist in this religion who are already dead and from all the departed members of your family who were in Santería.

The African religion is older than other religions, but does not demand or require exclusivity. For example, *santeros* were Catholic. Many attended mass regularly, and most went to church during Holy Week and Christmas. Very few went to confession, however. When people were sick they called the priest to *santiguar* [bless] them. When a *santero* was dying, people called the Catholic priest because that is what the religion prescribed at that time. Nine days after he died, a mass in the church was offered for his soul. Black followers of Santería were more tolerant than Catholics; they would not try to convert others and they would help people whether they were part of the religion or not.

Everybody wants to be the head now. This was not the case when I was growing up. People revered Taichamu, Mamá Kele, and Ayai, who, during slavery times, were the only ones to have *santo asentado* and the ones who handed this religion down to us. In this religion, Ayai is a great mother of saints. If one is going to call on someone, one calls the one in the family who died first and has more light. It is very different now. This is a testimony to the many changes that this religion has undergone in the last fifty years.

I learned to play the drums using sticks in Carlos Rojas. Later, in Cárdenas, I learned to play with my hands. I learned from the best people—Cajisote, Orestes. I also studied with the huge black man called Muñanga, with Pititi, and with Victor Lafite, a poet of rumba. I often went to the neighborhood of La Chumba and to El Guano, where Alcide Espino played. In Cárdenas they played the drums differently from the way they played them in Matanzas or Carlos Rojas. Later on I went to Holguín in Oriente Province, to a festival for Saint Lazarus, and it was more like Haitian music.

You have no idea how busy I kept while I played rumba and participated in *bembés*. I used to go with Tito Angarica. In Jovellanos I played in the home of the Terán family who were Yesá (from the region of Ilesha in Nigeria). I also played in Carlos Rojas, Perico, and Jaguey Grande. You have no idea how many of my white, linen pants were soiled while walking through the muddy roads and *trillos* [dirt paths that cut through bushes or high grass to get from one *bembé* to another].

Rumba music is not religious even though, sometimes, while playing rumba, the *orichas* and the Palo entities would be called and then the music was mixed. The Creoles were the ones who, through the rumba, introduced religious music into secular music. The young seeking acceptance and practicality made the transformation. The melodies and beats of the Congo and the Yoruba were passed to the *rumba*. In *rumba* and *guaguancó* most of the melodies are from the *orichas*. The *guaguancó* is a Cuban secular music style where the rhythms and tones from Africa and Andalusia merged.

In a *tambor* or a *bembé* [religious drum festivals], when they are playing to a saint, everyone has the right to sing to the *oricha*, to ask favors, to say whatever he or she wants to say. Pablo Reginal, what a voice he had! He was a poet in the business of the *orichas*. What conversations he had with them!

I had to leave the *rumba* because there were too many conflicts. Sometimes in a *bembé* people will sing *puyas*[30] making fun of some enemy. My grandfather and one of my uncles used to warn me: "You sing only to the *orichas* and never sing *puyas*." The singer sings to the *orichas* with the heart that helps people to get mounted or possessed by the *orichas*. For instance, to sing to Yemayá, one starts functioning with the song originally hers, by the one used to call her. One continues to move and one has a lot of songs to continue talking to her if one really knows the *fundamento* [foundation]. Creoles always sang by mixing Lucumí and Spanish rhythms and melodies.

In Cuba, to be initiated as an *olubatá*, one only needs to undergo the *medio asiento*, or halfway initiation ceremony. *Olubatalero*, drummers initiated into the cult of Añá, are authorized to play the *batá* drums. They washed their hands before they played. Many of the drums that were used had no secret. They were called *apericular*. Only the *Añá* or *batá* had a secret prepared by the *babalao*, and it was kept well. It was like a glue attached to the skin. The drums were used in the initiation ceremonies. In Carlos Rojas many people who had saints in their homes were not initiated. They celebrated drum festivals, but they did not divine. Many people in Cárdenas, who were not initiated, gave drum festivals. Those initiated went to different homes to greet the *orichas*. People would say things like "Let us greet Ochún in Carlos's house" or Elegguá in such and such a house. One would lay the prayer mat in front of the saint (as a manifestation of respect) and not in front of people.

To me, Santería and Palo were the normal things in life. Santería was gourd only, neither dishes nor soup tureens. There was nothing more sacred than to purify and cleanse yourself with a handful of corn or herbs. In Carlos Rojas I saw Santería as the normal thing in life, as part of the truth of the town where I was raised. That is the way it was in Carlos Rojas. Everything has changed here in the United States and in Cuba. Today people learn from books and from conferences. In my young days people worked with the saints to get salvation. Where is the faith now?

That is the way it was in Carlos Rojas. The most sacred act was to cleanse oneself with a handful of corn. Saints functioned on dirt floors. There was direct communication between the sky and the earth. In Carlos Rojas, people used gourds, not soup tureens for the saints. What really worked were herbs, candies, *grajea* [sprinkles], plantains, and water from the river and the sea. Herbs are for cleansing, and blood is used to give strength. That is the way it was in Carlos Rojas, a small and poor town, renowned in the 1930s and 1940s for its African roots and traditions.

These remembrances by Florencio Baró of his childhood and early adulthood partially illustrate the process of evolution of the African religions in Cuba. They also provide a unique insight into the influence of Santería in the spiritual and everyday life of an individual, his family, and the people of his town.

In Carlos Rojas religion was oriented toward securing supernatural favors for sustenance, to maintain health, and for the collective welfare. Furthermore, the Catholic Church and other Afro-Cuban religions were pervasive presences even in the nucleus of the same family. As described here Carlos Rojas was engaged in a syncretic experience, genetically, culturally, and, especially, religiously.[31]

The Baró family members, who might not have been of Yoruban descent, adopted Santería over any other religious traditions they might have brought to Carlos Rojas once they settled there. Thus, the Yoruban religion, with its well-developed ritual organization, well-trained priesthood, and complex divination system, seems to have predominated and absorbed many Afro-Cuban cults that were present on the island at the same time.

Santería's Heterogeneity

Santería derives essentially from the religion of the Yoruban people of Nigeria. During a process of adaptation in Cuba, it merged with the beliefs and practices of other African religions, while also borrowing from Spanish/Mediterranean Catholicism and European Spiritualism. Still, the predominant worldview of Santería comes from Yoruban religious practice and thought.

The most important factor underlying the heterogeneity manifested in Santería is the Yoruban religion's posture of tolerance for other religious beliefs and practices. This openness seems to be linked to basic assumptions about power in the universe and the variety of symbols and techniques utilized to communicate with and gain access to such sources of power. The ultimate goal of bringing "good" into life circumstances is not limited to one religious path only. Such a religious posture does not demand exclusivity as do, for example, Islam, Judaism, or any of the various forms of Christianity. Thus, its practitioners and followers in Cuba worshipped other deities and, concurrently, practiced other religions or absorbed some of their divinities, beliefs, and/or practices.

African priests who were brought to Cuba were deeply knowledgeable about their religion. They tried, with much success, to preserve it. Yet, several efforts to standardize Santería's practices, especially Regla de Ifá, never fully succeeded. Consequently, there is no high priest or priestly hierarchy with recognized authority to elaborate, decide, and impose strict orthodoxy or dogma. Thus, Santería as a religion is an abstraction derived from many different local groups, differing in some matters of dogma and ritual but sharing one common denominator: access to wisdom and power through worship of the *oricha/santo*.

In Cuba, frequent variations in the rituals were introduced according to a priest's personal knowledge, convictions, and the needs of his or her followers. In this process of adaptation, Yoruban religion changed. Beliefs and practices were borrowed from Catholicism, Spiritualism, and from the religions of other non-Yoruban African ethnic groups. Thus, the strength and character of the African ethnic mix in a particular region of Cuba determined the features of Santería in that area.

Santería's heterogeneity concerning dogma and rituals has African antecedents. Aside from shared worldview assumptions, a striving for both internal consistency and logico-structural integration related to external socioenvironmental circumstances, there was no uniformity in specific religious beliefs and practices among the Yoruba-speaking people. Some *orichas* were known in certain areas only. Moreover, in diverse regions, different creator gods or thunder gods were worshipped. Variations in such beliefs and practices were a reflection of the differences that existed in Nigeria from region to region. Consequently, there were variations in the religious rituals and dogma that the slaves brought to Cuba, but not in their socially constructed consciousness of "reality."

Other variations resulted from the capabilities of priests to preserve what they brought from Africa. This was the case for Creoles as well. They could preserve only as much as possible from what they were taught by their *padrinos* (godfathers).

Furthermore, the majority of African slaves and their descendants worked on plantations and lived in shared cramped quarters, or *barracones*, with slaves of diverse African ethnic groups. As a result, intermarriage between slaves of different ethnic origins led to further changes and adaptations in the religion that they or their forbears had brought from Africa. This situation is illustrated above in Baró's autobiographical account of life in Carlos Rojas.

The cities and provinces of Havana and Matanzas are considered the cradles of Santería. However, there were pronounced regional differences between the two. For instance, the religious beliefs and practices of the old Yoruban Kingdom of Oyo had a great impact in the city of Havana, where apparently many slaves from the old Oyo Empire were settled. Thus, the importance and richness of the cult of Changó, old Oyo's thunder god, is overwhelming. The preservation of its intricately embellished paraphernalia demonstrates this, as does the mandate that all initiates have to be presented to Changó's *batá* drums. In Havana the influence of the beliefs and practices of the Nigerian sacred city of

Ile Ife is also remarkable, as observed in the preservation of the cult of Ifá and the priestly hierarchy related to it.[32]

By way of contrast, in certain areas in and around the city of Matanzas, the influence of the religious practices of the Arará from the western region of Yorubaland, near the former French Dahomey, was heavily felt. In the middle of the nineteenth century Ma Monserrate Gonzalez (Obá Tero),[33] a priestess of Changó, who was probably born in Egbado, arrived in Cuba. In the 1870s she was living in Havana and collaborated closely with Timotea Albear (Latuán)an Oyo priestess of Shango. At the end of the nineteenth century she moved to the neighborhood of Simpson in Matanzas City where she presided over the *cabildo* that had been founded by Adechina, the founder of the Regla de Ifá. A few years later she initiated Ferminita Gómez (Ochabi) and founded a prestigious religious lineage.

In Matanzas, the Ilesha Yoruba subgroup was very influential, as was, characteristically, Ilesha music, and the beat of Ilesha drums, which were played with sticks rather than bare hands. Also, the cult to Naná Burukú, a divinity of Dahomian origins, was very important. In Matanzas, the *batá* drums, which were essential in Havana's festivals, did not have much preeminence. In some areas these drums were unknown. In the 1940s when Baró was growing up in the town of Carlos Rojas, in Matanzas Province, there was only one *babalao*, and there were no *batá* drums. This could mean that the ascendancy of the city of Ile Ife was not very strong; nor was the influence of Oyo.

The differences in religious practice generated problems and jealousies, especially when one compares the religious expressions of the people from the city of Havana with those from the area of Matanzas. In the words of Abelardo Hernández (June 1999), a respected senior *santero*, "The people from Havana did not want to recognize the people from the countryside or from Matanzas."

Founders of Santería

There were numerous attempts to create a common body of dogma and rituals, a *fundamento* (foundation) or a *regla* (rules) for the Yoruba, or Lucumí, practices in Cuba. During the last decades of the nineteenth century, meetings between priests and priestesses took place in Havana, Regla, Matanzas, Palmira, and other important towns. These conciliatory meetings brought about the birth of Regla de Ifá and Regla de Ocha, the two distinct expressions of Yoruban religious practices in Cuba that are popularly known as Santería. David H. Brown (2003:19–20) appropriately remarks: "I argue that two opposed fields have constituted Lucumí theory, practice, and historical process:

an 'Ifá-centric' ritual field and an 'Ocha-centric' ritual field. They are based in divergent cosmological models and structuring of ritual and oracular authority, particularly as they are embodied in the professions of the religion's two male specialists and, often, antagonists: the *babalawo* and the *oriaté*. . . . Structurally, La Regla de Ifá, with its male *babalawo* and his tutelary *oricha*, Orúla, 'feminizes' La Regla de Ocha (the collective *oricha* priests and their pantheon); the *oriaté*, in turn, must decenter the *babalawo's* authority in building his-story." The Ifá-centric position is evident in *babalao* Manolo Erice's (March 2004) words: "The *babalao* is the great father of all the secrets. The *santoral* (Ocha) gives birth. For a saint to be born, a godfather is needed [the *babalao*], the godmother is provided by Ocha."

Even though some *santeros* claim that Regla de Ifá and Regla de Ocha are two different religions, in reality the two sets of practices complement each other. Moreover, traditionally, both have been part of the same religion. Ifá is an intrinsic part of the Yoruban religion, and, in Cuba, many fundamental bases of the Regla de Ocha also came from Ifá.

Both Regla de Ocha and Regla de Ifá provide access to orichas and ancestors through which supernatural power, or *aché*, is manifested. They also have their own divination systems, priestly hierarchy, literary corpus, and rituals. However, in Cuban Santería and in Yorubaland, the Ifá divination system and the wisdom of the Ifá priest take precedence.

Yet, it is important to discuss the historical processes that culminated in the elaboration of these two rules, or *reglas*. Such analysis contributes to an appreciation of the strategic transformations and consequent Cubanization undergone by the Yoruban religion in Cuba.

REGLA DE IFÁ: FOUNDERS AND INNOVATORS

The cult to Orúnmila and the mastery of his oracles grew deep roots in Cuba, especially in the city of Havana and surrounding neighborhoods. Wilfredo Fernández Jr. (March 2003), whose father was a wealthy white man and a prestigious *babalao* initiated by Bernardo Rojas, provided the following information concerning Adechina, which corroborates statements made by Brown's informants. According to Fernández, Adechina was born in Oyo early in the nineteenth century, where he was initiated as a *babalao*. After the abolition of slavery in Cuba (1886), he went back to Africa. Later, he returned to Cuba and founded a strong Ifá lineage by initiating several *babalaos*. The most prestigious among them was Eulogio Gutierrez, who was called Tata Gaitán. In Havana Tata Gaitán was recognized as an *oba*, or king. *Oba* is also the name given to the highest-ranking *babalao*. Adechina was said to be the godfather of Bernardo Rojas, the founder of one of the most honored lineages of *babalaos* in Cuba. At that time the most important Ifá ceremonies were celebrated in the home of Bernardo Rojas in Marianao, which Fernández Jr.'s informant visited frequently in the 1950s.

According to Ezequiel Torres (October 2002) eminent priests from Ketu, brought to Cuba as slaves, were the founders of the other prominent Ifá lineages in Havana called the "Erufele Omo Ala Ketu."

Brown's informants (2003:76) claim that five African-born *babalaos* founded the roots of the *ramas* or lineages of Ifá in Cuba. They were Ño Carlos Adé Bí (Ojuani Boká), Ño Remigio Herrera Adechina (Obara Melli), Joaquin Cadiz Ifá-Omí (Ogunda Tetura), Oluguerė Kó Kó (Oyekún Melli), and Francisco Villalonga Ifá Bí (Obe Ate).

Ifá's original five Lucumí founders initiated the first two generations of Creole *babalaos* primarily in the city of Havana. They were very strict and refused to consecrate some of their trainees after they learned that they either drank excessively or were not responsible heads of households. According to Ezequiel Torres (March 2001), "The old men did not want to share their secrets. They claimed that they needed to be sure they were choosing men of irreproachable character." The frustrated apprentices retaliated. They claimed that the old men did not want to pass their secrets over to them. Consequently, they had to go to Cienfuegos and Palmira (where many religious elders resided) to get the foundations of Ogún, Osain, Oduduwa, and Olokun that are required for initiation. This controversy is called the first "war," or quarrel, among *babalaos*. It signaled the intrusion of religious practices from other parts of the island into Ifá practices in the capital city of Havana.

The founders chose candidates who were bright, literate, successful businessmen, many of a mixed racial background, who could help this society survive and thrive. The second generation (the first Creole generation), as exemplified by Bernardo Rojas and others, was outstanding. They attempted to codify Ifá, systematizing procedures such as the readings of the Letra del Año. They copied the teachings of the elders in the now famous *libretas* (notebooks) of *babalaos*—the beginning of a literary tradition. This effort failed to yield a dogmatic core for the religion, which could have prevented the heterogeneity in dogma and practices that has characterized it from the beginning.

The third (second Creole) generation of *babalaos* (during the first quarter of the twentieth century) initiated a considerable number of men. In the 1950s the number of initiated *babalaos* grew considerably. Around that time, according to Ezequiel Torres (March 2001), the second "war of *babalaos*" occurred, which was caused in part by the frustration of some *babalaos* when others initiated their sons who were homosexuals. This last era was presided by Miguel Febles Padrón, an unscrupulous and shrewd *babalao* who for over thirty years played a most prominent role in Regla de Ifá, abrogating for himself the exclusive right to prepare the *fundamentos* or foundations of Ifá: the Olofins.

REGLA DE OCHA: FOUNDERS
AND INNOVATORS

According to Miguel Ramos (2003:38–70) three priestesses were the seminal founders of Santería's religious lineages. They were also instrumental in preserving the Yoruban religion and starting the innovations necessary for this religion to adapt and expand. The first of these priestesses was Ma Monserrate Obá Tero, who was born and ordained in the cult of Shango in Egbado and was a close friend and associate of Adechina. She is credited with introducing the cult of Olokún and Oduduwa in Cuba, and to this day, her religious descendants still constitute the focus of the worship of Olokún on the island.

The second important priestess, Timotea Albear, better known by the name Latuán, was born and ordained in the worship of Shango in her native Oyo. She was a slave in the household of Col. Francisco Albear, the architect who built the aqueduct of Havana. She learned to read and write and had a great reputation as a priestess, acting as master of ceremonies or *oriaté*. In the 1870s Latuán became affiliated with the Havana *cabildo* known by its address: San José Ochenta. It probably had been founded at the end of the eighteenth century. According to Miguel Ramos (2003:45), the names of many of the *cabildo*'s founders are still recited and saluted at the onset of rituals.

The third important priestess was Efunché Ña Rosalía Abreu. She was originally from the Egbado region and was reputedly of royal lineage. As the queen of the San José Ochenta *cabildo,* she was treated like a queen by her many followers. This priestess was also the mother of Lydia Cabrera's famous informant Calixta Morales. Miguel Ramos (2003: 45) adds that by the 1870s Efunché and Latuán were collaborating very closely and had assumed the leadership of the San José Ochenta *cabildo.*

According to Natalia Bolivar Aróstegui (1994:9–10), at the close of the nineteenth century a *babalocha* called Lorenzo Samá was living in Matanzas. He moved to the small town of Regla on the outskirts of Havana where he met two prestigious priests, Tata Gaitán and Obalufadei. They demanded that he be initiated again because they did not accept the validity of Matanzas' ritual procedures. After his second initiation he chose the name Obadimelli (the king who was crowned twice). Later on, frustrated by that experience, he attempted to bring about homogeneous standards in beliefs and practices by creating the foundations of Regla de Ocha.[34]

As mentioned previously, a priestess from Nigeria called Ma Monserrate arrived in Matanzas at the end of the nineteenth century. She founded the Arará *cabildo* and a prestigious religious lineage. This lineage became the matrix of the Afro-Cuban religion called Regla Arará. The renowned priestess Ferminita Gómez later belonged to it.

David H. Brown's (2003:99) informants give a more comprehensive picture, identifying at least twelve priests and priestesses as founders of Cuba's eleven principal Ocha lineages. He lists these individuals as follows: "Efuche (Ña Rosalía, aka María Trujillo), Ainá (Ña Margarita Armenteros), Igoró (Ña Caridad Argudín), Apoto (Ña Belén González), Ma Monserrate (González), Francisca Entensa ('Palmira'), Obadimelli (Octavio Samar), José Pata de Palo (Urquiola), Los Ibeyi (the twins, Perfecto and Gumersindo), Monserrate Aisañabi, and Tía Julia Abonse."

Some of the most challenging problems that needed to be resolved were issues concerning several African practices that were neither acceptable nor functional in the new setting. For instance, according to Ezequiel Torres (March 2001) the dangerous and painful scarification of tribal and clan marks on the face and other parts of the body was discontinued. It was determined that, instead of scarification, the tribal marks would be drawn with chalk. This procedural measure is reminiscent of Saint Paul's decision to exempt non-Jewish converts to Christianity from circumcision before baptism. Another important decision was the prohibition of certain rituals associated with the worship of Oricha Oko, which included sexual intercourse and were deemed immoral in the new setting.

A third important issue reported by Ezequiel Torres (March 2001) was the problem of the *santos parados* (standing saints). This was the name given to uninitiated individuals who performed as priests. In Nigeria, a person generally inherited from his or her parents the worship of an orisha. In Cuba, in many instances, parents trained their children in religious practices and rituals. In other instances, a person inherited from a deceased relative the sacred stones, or *otanes*, which are the material receptacles of the *orichas'* power. After their initiated relative had died the heirs took over the practice as if they themselves were initiated priests. They were called *santos parados*, since the *orichas* had not been *asentados* (placed on their heads). To solve this problem, it was determined that from then on practicing priests had to be initiated. Moreover, two ceremonies were elaborated to deal with the problem: the *itutu* and the *pinaldo.* The *itutu* bids farewell to a deceased priest and disposes of his or her religious paraphernalia. The *pinaldo* enabled a practicing and knowledgeable person (a *santo parado*) to be initiated without undergoing the long and arduous initiation process. Brown's (2003:10) informants credit Efuche Ña Rosalía, a famous *iyalocha* from El Cerro, for designing the confirmatory *pinaldo* ceremony.

Other significant shifts occurred in the religion. In Africa the iyawo (the Yoruban word for bride) was brought to the presence of the religious and governmental leaders of the community. In Cuba the *iyawó* was brought to the Catholic Church.[35]

In Cuba the number of *orichas* was greatly reduced, and sometimes family and personal ties among them, unknown in Nigeria, were recognized.

In Africa priests were dedicated to the worship of one orisha, normally a local one, and during initiation, according to Cuban *santeros* described by Nicolas Angarica (1955:78), they were given Eleggua, Obatala, and the orisha they were to worship, the so called "head and foot" initiation. In Cuban Santería, the initiate receives *un juego de orichas*, or numerous orichas. Thus, the initiated is able to intercede and work with *orichas* other than the most important one that is received on the head. At first the candidates for initiation normally receive the four Warriors: Elegguá, Ogún, Ochosi, and Osún. Later on, generally during initiation, they receive the *orichas de fundamento*: Obatalá, Yemayá, Changó, and Ochún, and the principal *oricha* that is placed on the head.

There is some agreement among informants that the Cuban practice of receiving multiple *orichas* was caused by the need to train individuals in the worship practices of the *orichas* that were known. In this way they would not be forgotten and lost as had been the case with many *orichas* and rituals before. Brown's informants (2003:10) credit Efuche Ña Rosalía, Obadimelli Octavio Samar, and the Society of Santa Bárbara with restructuring, by conscious innovation, the "head and foot" initiation in favor of what Brown appropriately calls the "modern" and "pantheonized" initiatory system of Santería.

Apparently this initiatory system was the end result of survival strategies in place from the beginning of the twentieth century. Some founders of Regla de Ocha were concerned that the cult of certain *orichas* might be forgotten, because no one had been initiated in them or had been trained to carry out ceremonies associated with their worship. This was exemplified in the case of Olokun, whose cult had been very important in nineteenth-century Regla. It was disappearing however, because no one was trained to play his drums, to dance his dances, or to know how to care for the *oricha*. Thus, in many *ilé ocha*, Olokun became an avocation of Yemayá, who had usurped his status as owner of the sea. A similar case was the Dahomian divinity Naná Burukú, who ended as a *camino* of Obatalá.

In contrast, Miguel Ramos (2003: 47) supports an Oyo-centric theory that merits discussion. According to Ramos, the practice of being initiated or receiving multiple *orichas* has African antecedents. In the old Oyo Empire the Alafin, or monarch, was initiated in the cult of all the orishas that were prominent in the different regions of the empire. Ramos believes that some of the priestesses at the service of the Alafin were brought to Cuba and that they introduced this practice.

With the passage of time a number of difficulties were overcome and certain rules, or *reglas,* became more or less standard. Even though these efforts met with some success, differences still persist, and strict homogeneity in practices and doctrine has never been fully achieved.

Influence of Spanish, Mediterranean, and Catholic Beliefs and Practices in Santería

African religious beliefs, European Spiritualism, and the mystical, expressive Catholicism of Spain fused to form a uniquely Afro-Cuban religion in Santería. Santería is not the product of a messianic movement. Instead, it is for the most part the fruit of a conscious and unconscious search for equivalencies in meaning between the gods that the slaves brought from Africa and the Catholic saints of their masters.

In Brazil, a parallel process took place, and an Afro-Brazilian religious complex, the Candomblé, emerged in a form that is very similar to that of Cuban Santería. The cultural and religious elements in both Cuba and Brazil merged in a strikingly similar fashion based upon a range of associations in both the secular and religious spheres. In Cuba these associations were prompted by a search for meaningful connections to different symbols, beliefs, and behaviors in the new land. They were nourished by similarities in the worldview of the slaves brought to the Americas and that of a large majority of the island population. This worldview entailed, among other values, a deep spirituality, similar conceptions of power in the universe and religious practices related to gaining benefit from the powers of nature and supernatural entities, a respect for legitimate authority, a devotion to sacred images, and an interest in miracles.

In many instances, the Yoruban orisha was associated, in both Brazil and Cuba, with the same Catholic saint. The name applied to these spiritual beings were also the same: *santo.* The *santo* remained closer to the African god than to the Catholic saint, even though the environment fostered the loss of those attributes that were no longer tenable in the New World. Conversely, those attributes that were shared with the Catholic saint became more important. In rare instances, a characteristic of the Catholic saint that the orisha did not have in Africa is incorporated by the *oricha/santo.*

The process of change that gave birth to the *santos* was the result of the associations that the slaves made between the saints their masters wanted them to worship and the divinities they and their ancestors had worshipped all of their lives. Often, the identifications were based on superficial attributes. For example, the saint and the *oricha* could share a symbolic color or object. Generally, Obatalá is identified with the Virgin of Mercy, possibly because the color of the robe in statues and chromolithographs of the Virgin of Mercy is white.

In Nigeria white is the symbolic color for Obatalá, the *oricha* of peace, cleanliness, and purity.

In other cases the associations were based on similarities between the character, attributes, symbols, and mythology that the slave might have perceived as equivalencies between saint and orisha. Thus, in Cuba a female martyr, Santa Bárbara, is associated with Changó, the most outstanding personification of virility, womanizing, and excess. This connection might have been encouraged by Santa Bárbara's association with lightning. According to legend, her father was struck dead by lightning after he executed her in anger over her conversion to Christianity. Santa Bárbara is also associated with thunder, because she is the patron of Spanish artillery. Consequently she was very popular in colonial Cuba, where there was a considerable presence of the Spanish military and the thundering of cannons was frequent. The residents of Havana were and are informed of the time every night at 9 p.m. by the blast of a cannon from the Morro fortress. Among Cubans, including Catholics, it is said about a person who is not very religious that "He or she only remembers Santa Bárbara when it thunders." Thus, this saint thunders as does Changó, the warrior *oricha* of thunderstorms.[36] Moreover, in chromolithographs, Santa Bárbara is featured wearing a red robe, and red is Changó's symbolic color. Also, in the background of Santa Bárbara's chromolithographs there is a burning castle. According to myths, Shango, the legendary king of Oyo, once set his own palace on fire while doing magical tricks.

In some instances the association was not based on any similarity; it functioned as a disguise to fool the white masters. The use of Catholic statues and lithographs served as a cover in order to continue worshiping the orishas with little or no interference. It is possible that, in some cases, the statue of a particular saint was worshiped in the local Catholic Church and, at the urging of the masters, the worship of this saint was forced upon the slaves. Thus, the slaves "adopted" the saint as the representation of one of their orishas.

The impact of Mediterranean Catholicism on Santería was substantial. In Santería's formative years, practitioners had to be baptized, even after the republic was established and there were no pressures to do so. The appropriation of the calendar of the Catholic saints was also significant. *Orichas* are honored on the day in the Catholic calendar dedicated to the Catholic saint with whom they are associated. Even more important is the mandatory visit to the Catholic Church of the *iyawós* right after initiation. Other indicators of such influence include the use of holy water, the covering of *soperas* during Holy Week, the donning of a habit to comply with promises to Saint Lazarus or other saints, the use of images and chromolithographs. When a person dies, traditional Catholic *novenas*[37] are offered during the nine consecutive nights after the burial. All of these practices document the merging process.

Influences of European Spiritualist Beliefs and Practices in Santería

In addition to the influence of African religions other than that of the Yoruba, European Spiritualism made a significant contribution to the beliefs and practices of Santería. Allan Kardec's spiritualist teachings provided an appealing new paradigm for African- and Catholic-derived spirit beliefs already in existence in Cuba, giving them depth according to some people and a logical framework according to others.

During the nineteenth century Kardec's teachings spread wildly throughout Latin America. Kardec's ideas greatly appealed to many members of the white Creole upper and middle classes who were distrustful of the Catholic Church. The church was perceived as rigid, monarchical, and reluctant to accept scientific and democratic ideas, especially those dealing with the independence of the island from Spain. They also relished, with a mixture of expectation, hope, apprehension, guilt, and fear, the techniques espoused by Kardec to communicate with the souls of the departed. Even though the Catholic Church considered Kardec's teachings Satanic, many Cuban Catholics did (and do still) revel in them, enthused by the immediacy of supernatural phenomena and by the assumed presence of the departed ones.

Kardec's teachings proved attractive to many white Cubans of the upper Creole class, and also to those of urban and rural middle-class extraction. Later they affected all segments and racial groups on the island, contributing greatly to the emerging Afro-Cuban religions.

Lisias Nogueira Negrao (1987:260), when referring to the success of Kardec's teachings, states that "one of the reasons for its appeal was the pseudoscientific character of Kardecism. Kardecism followed the same pattern of evolution as positivism." Kardec's teachings were an intellectual and conceptual attempt to reconcile European evolutionist, positivist ideas prevalent at that time with beliefs about spiritualism and reincarnation.

Kardec's view was of the existence of a visible and an invisible world. One world is populated by incarnated spirits and the other by disembodied nonincarnated spirits. He argued that spirits go through successive stages of incarnation for the purpose of self-purification, which, ultimately, enable them to achieve eternal light (Nirvana). Nonincarnated spirits mingle in the lives of those incarnated who are akin to them, due to experiences of their present or past lives. Every individual has spiritual guides who, like teachers, influence them in the path of spiritual progress and achievement. They also have protector spirits who guard them against all types of evil. At the same time, individuals might suffer from the bad influence of *enviaciones* (lowly spirits attached to material things). These *enviaciones* might induce a person into evil and/or self-destructive acts.

Some of these beliefs have been incorporated into Santería's practices. Consequently, *santeros* deal with *enviaciones* and other spiritual problems with spiritualist prayers and the use of flowers, perfume, and candles. In many instances, Santería's believers rely on consultations with spiritualists to identify spiritual guides.

The impact of Kardec in Santería's beliefs in reincarnation has been very significant. Reincarnation among the Yoruba occurs within the framework of the patrilineal extended family since they believe that the individual is reborn over and over again within that family. With the disruption and uprooting caused by slavery, the patrilineal extended family was lost to the slaves. Thus, many *santeros* have adopted Kardec's reincarnation beliefs, which are more congruent with the Cuban situation.

Kardec was influenced by Hindu beliefs in karma. His beliefs in reincarnation are essentially different from Yoruban religious beliefs. As pointed out by Brandon (1997:88–89) reincarnation in Kardec's framework is progressive, with the soul going through different stages in successive incarnations until reaching enlightenment; in contrast, Yoruban beliefs in reincarnation are cyclical and nonprogressive.

Moreover, according to Kardec, each person has a *cuadro espiritual* (spiritual frame), a constellation of spirits that protect him or her. One of the most important is the spiritual guide, who, unlike Nigerian religious entities, normally is depicted as a member of an ethnic or professional stereotype (Congolese, gypsy, soldier, nun). Specific spiritual characteristics and powers have been ascribed to these guides who, when alive, might never have practiced Santería. At the same time, in many instances, when a person has mediumship faculties, spiritualist practices and prayers are utilized to develop these faculties.

Spiritualist and Catholic practices have been incorporated by Santería's believers as part of the rituals that are appropriate when a person dies. Besides the *novenas*, "spiritual masses" are also celebrated. During these masses, conducted by spiritualists and mediums, it is expected that the living will be able to communicate with the departed soul and assist the soul to undergo the traumatic process of accepting its new status as a nonincarnated spirit.

Influences of African, Specifically Bantu, Beliefs and Practices in Santería

Santería gained new adherents with the passing of time, and in the twentieth century, it began to spread throughout the island. In the eastern regions, where Santería was introduced quite late, the religion became more laden with Bantu features. In these areas the character of the *orichas* and the Supreme Being came to be seen as more human and vulnerable.

In the first decade of the twentieth century a *santero* named Reynerio Perez brought Santería to Oriente, the eastern province of the island. In Santiago de Cuba he founded a large lineage (Millet 2000:110–19), which was derisively called the Renegades, or the Reformers. In this eastern province, Bantu elements, spiritualist beliefs, and a generalized cult to the dead, presently called *muertería*, greatly affected Santería through a process of accommodation.

In general, the Yoruban religion in Cuba, which was more structured and organized than most African religious systems, absorbed and adapted non-Yoruban African beliefs and practices. In many cases, when non-Yoruban African divinities were "absorbed" by a powerful Yoruban orisha, they continued to be worshipped, not as separate gods, but as paths, or different manifestations, of the dominant Afro-Cuban *oricha*.

At the same time, in the past and in the present many individuals in search of protection and power were and are initiated in Santería, Palo Mayombe (Congo, Bantu), and also the secret society of the Abakwa (Calabar Bantu). This mix has brought about cross-fertilization. This is apparent when, in some versions of original Yoruban myths, the characters of orishas and of the Supreme Being change. They are portrayed as having more human weaknesses. Thus, in some myths Olodumare (the Supreme Being) is afraid of mice; in others he asks Ochún for aphrodisiac *oñí*; yet, in others, he is practically decrepit. Moreover, I have, on occasion, encountered believers who deal with the *orichas* in a fashion similar to the way *paleros*, people who are *rallados en palo*,[38] treat their *prendas*,[39] sacred objects that contain the power of the supernatural entities. They address them with disrespect, order them around, and even threaten the *orichas* with discontinuing offerings of sacrifices if they do not comply with their requests.

Chapter Summary

Santería began and has continued to grow, merge, and innovate according to the needs and tastes of the new followers. Examples of changes during the twentieth century include the following: Gourds and clay pots gave way to luxurious soup tureens of expensive China porcelain. Thrones and garments for the newly initiated *iyawós* and the altars for the *orichas* became elaborate works of art that reflect the sumptuousness of Mediterranean Catholicism and the European courts of the eighteenth century. The traditional food of the *orichas* also changed, and new delicacies were added. For example, red apples were offered to Changó and meringue desserts to Obatalá. In the face of such a multidimensional context, African practices merged with Creole culture into something essentially African but different.

4

Beliefs and Practices of Santería

Among followers of Santería, as in the case of the Yoruba in Nigeria, the belief in *aché* (supernatural power, immanent energy, universal vibration, known as ashe among the Yoruba) is of the greatest importance. It is central in the worldview of both. According to Miguel Ramos (February 2005): "*Aché* is neutral; it is manifested in catastrophes as well as in exceptionally fortunate situations. It is up to us humans to channel it in a positive or negative manner."

In Cuba *aché* is a dynamic principle, an energy, a force assumed to be immanent in humans, in all of nature, especially in untamed nature, in wild animals, and/or plant life; it is also in all fluids, such as water, the sap of plants, and blood. Some trees such as *ceiba (Ceiba pentranda)*, *siguaraya (Trichilla glabra)*, and the royal palm *(Roystunea regia)* are seen as being intrinsically sacred and as receptacles of this sacred power. This worldview is evident in the expressions of Lydia Cabrera's informants, documented in her book *El Monte* (The Wilderness) of 1954, where trees, plants, and herbs interact subjectively with humans. This perception of *aché* is also evident in Florencio Baró's description of his native town, where wild vines and weeds that grew in abandoned and empty lots filled the town's ambiance with magic, mystery, and silence.

Roots, twigs, and herbs were commonly used to treat disease and affliction. However, during the last fifty years their use has diminished, and the role of *santeros* as pharmacists has been de-emphasized. Increasingly, *santeros* have placed greater reliance on conventional medical prescriptions and treatment rather than on their traditional herbal medicine. Consequently, the wilderness in Santería has largely lost its importance as a receptacle and source of supernatural power. Moreover, Santería has been flourishing in large metropolitan areas in North America, where the wilderness is absent and natural phenomena are less threatening than in rural Cuban villages and towns. Thus, the awesome and mystical view of nature in the ambiance of Santería has weakened. *Aché*, nevertheless, is a central force in perceptions of "reality." Basic assumptions about *aché* underlie every aspect of the structure and practice of Santería.

Hierarchical Ordering of Power

In Santería, as in Nigeria, *aché* is channeled in different ways. It might be manifested in important *orichas,* in lesser *orichas,* in revered ancestors, and in consecrated objects such as images and amulets. Overall, there is a hierarchical
ordering of the categories of power. At the apex is the Supreme Being, followed
by the *orichas,* the ancestor spirits, and sacred objects. Divination is central for
accessing the power and guidance of the hierarchically ordered divinities and
supernatural entities, a matter to be discussed more fully in chapter 8.

THE SUPREME BEING

The Supreme Being, with the different names of Olodumare/Olorun/Olofin, is
the creator of the universe. He has always existed and will exist forever. He has
the high and sublime qualities of the Supreme Being in monotheistic religions.
He is omnipotent, omnipresent, omniscient, merciful, and just. He is, however,
a rather remote god who does not respond directly to human needs and takes
little interest in the affairs of this world. Even though believers respect and acknowledge his power, not much ritual attention is rendered him, and no priest
is dedicated to him or to his cult.

THE *ORICHA/SANTO*

In the manner in which Santería evolved in Cuba, the *santo* is a new divinity
born of the association of an African god, or *oricha,* a Catholic saint, and/or
another African god. In some instances, the Nigerian *oricha* did not change,
and the association was just a masquerade. In other cases, the *oricha* lost some
of its Nigerian characteristics; yet in a few instances, it assumed characteristics
specific to the saint with whom it had been associated.

   Despite their lower status in reference to the Supreme Being, the orishas/
orichas receive most of the religious attention in both Nigeria and Cuba. There
are hundreds of orishas in the pantheon of the Yoruba-speaking people. However, only a few generic gods are known throughout Yorubaland. In some cases
these generic gods are known with different names in different areas, and there
are many orishas who are only locally known. In Cuba, however, the number
of *orichas* is greatly reduced, with the most important totaling no more than
twenty.

   The most popular *orichas* in Cuba include the following: Obatalá, the *oricha*
of creation and the king of all the *orichas*; Orúnmila, who is also called "Orúla"
or "Orúnla," god of wisdom and the Ifá Oracles; Elegguá, the messenger of the
gods; Changó, the thunder god; Oyá, the owner of the meteor, the flare, and
the bad wind; Ochún, the owner of the river; Oba, the domestic goddess and
Changó's first wife; Yemayá, the goddess of the sea; Babalú Ayé, the god of the

earth and diseases; Ogún, the owner of metals and the patron of warriors and blacksmiths; *Oricha* Oko, the god of agricultural fertility and the patron of farmers; Osain, the owner of magical and medicinal herbs; Ochosi, the patron of hunters; the Ibeyi sacred twins; and Agayú Solá, the patron of porters. Part 2 of this volume provides an extensive discussion of each of these *orichas*.

THE ANCESTORS

Among the Yoruba, the cult of the ancestors of the father's family lineage had a central place. In traditional West Africa, as in many other societies, the paternal lineage is a self-perpetuating group that includes the ancestors, the living, and those yet to be born. The Yoruban belief in reincarnation within the same family lines gives this notion a cyclical and endless character. The phrase "There are no new Yoruba people" (Lowery-Palmer 1980:51) reflects the centrality of such beliefs among the Yoruba.

In Cuba, the cult of the ancestors lost importance because the slaves and their descendants were permanently severed from their African lineages without any opportunity for the extended family to reorganize. Slaves did not usually come in large family groups; and, even when they did, slavery did not respect ties beyond the nuclear family and often not even that.

Since the soil that nourishes the ancestor cult is the family, its residence, and the ancestral lands, it is understandable that the circumstances prevalent in Cuba were not conducive to its growth. Moreover, religious societies like the Gelede and the Egungun, which are primarily connected to the worship of the ancestors and play such an important role in Nigeria, did not flourish either.

Nevertheless, the cult to the dead is essential. It is commonly said that the dead come "before" the *orichas*. Instead of worshipping the ancestors of a patrilineal kinship group, the founders and departed members of an individual's religious lineage, along with that individual's spiritual protectors, are worshipped. This is evident when, at the beginning of all ceremonies, the *babanlas*, or ancestors, of the person for whom the ceremony is performed are propitiated. The ancestors of the religious lineage of the priest who is officiating, the client's protector spirits, and the dead, in general, are also addressed with prayers and songs. In this revised version of the ancestor cult, spiritualist, Palo, and *muertería* practices merged. Furthermore, a person has in his/her spiritual constellation the protective souls of the dead. Normally among them is the soul of a person who, when alive, was a protégé of the *oricha/santo* that claims the head of the individual. This dead person does not have to be related to the living initiate by either extended family or religious lineage ties. Thus, the emphasis in Santería is on personal protection and power.

In Cuba offerings are given to the souls of the dead in the yard outside of the house. The dead are offered a pig's head, a lighted cigarette, and water, which is highly important to them. According to Rigoberto Zamora (June 2004), "The dead is a fluid spirit who is offered water and perfume; while the *orichas* are spirits that are materialized in the consecrated stones and are fed blood. This is the reason that the *orichas* can be in many different places at the same time and the dead cannot be." Currently, the practice for Cuban exiles in Miami and in New York who live in apartments is to place offerings to the dead in the bathroom, which symbolically and physically connects to the earth.

SACRED OBJECTS

In Cuba, as in Nigeria, another major category of religious belief and practice includes the veneration of sacred objects, talismans, amulets, special places, and trees. The consecrated stones, or *otanes*, of the *orichas*, in which their *aché* is fixed, are extremely sacred. It is believed that the *oricha* itself is there. Also, the consecrated necklaces and bracelets of the *orichas* are considered powerful, as symbols of the *orichas* and, also, as the material receptacles of their power. Their manufacture and use is very similar on both sides of the Atlantic. The Catholic icons with which *orichas* have been associated are also revered. However, no sacrifices are offered to them as are offered to *otanes*, consecrated necklaces, and bracelets.

Despite the veneration of sacred objects, in both Nigeria and Cuba the greatest importance is given to the head. This is where the guardian spirit resides and where the *orichas* are *asentados* (seated) during initiation.

The *Orí* (Head) and the *Eledá* (Guardian Spirit)

In traditional Yoruban religion it is believed that each individual has at least three souls. There are some regional differences regarding the character and functions of these souls. According to William Bascom (1960:401):

> The first is the breath (emi) which resides in the lung and chest. In the smile of an Ife informant, this, with the nostrils, is like the blacksmith's bellows with its two orifices. The breath is man's vital force; it gives him life and makes him work. The second is the shadow (ojiji), . . . The shadow has no function during life; it does nothing but to follow the body about. The third and most important is the ancestral guardian soul (eleda, olori) which resides in the head and is associated with the individual's destiny, and with the Yoruba belief in reincarnation.
>
> One can see the shadow, and hear and feel the breath; but no one sees, hears, or feels the ancestral guardian. The breath is sustained by the food which the individual himself eats; the shadow is without substance, and requires no nourishment; but, the ancestral guardian must continually be fed through sacrifices known as "feeding the head" (ibo-(o)-ri). At

death, all three souls depart from the body (ara), and normally reach heaven eventually."

Many of Bascom's (1960:408) informants emphasize the importance of the ancestral guardian soul: "The iponri is worshipped by everyone, by kings and by the poor alike. . . . The head is more important to everyone than their own deity. It is greater than the deities who turned to stone."

Before a person is born, the ancestral guardian soul appears before Olorun to receive a new body and its destiny, or iwa, for its new life. The soul has the opportunity to choose its own destiny, including its own personality, occupation, luck, and a fixed day when it has to return to heaven.

One cannot change the date of one's death. However, if the individual has the support of the ancestral guardian soul, as well as that of the orishas, some aspects of one's path may be changed in order to fulfill a broader destiny rather than a narrower one. If the individual cannot enlist the support of the eleda (ancestral guardian spirit) and the orishas, he or she will not be able to enjoy the blessings that were part of his or her destiny and might even die before the time agreed upon. People who die before the date agreed upon with Olorun remain on earth as ghosts until the fixed and agreed-upon date arrives. People who commit suicide cannot go to heaven and cannot be reincarnated. They turn into evil spirits.

In consonance with these beliefs, a person, throughout life, consults the oracles for counsel regarding the actions to take in order to be able to fulfill his or her destiny and to enjoy the pleasantries while avoiding the misfortunes that could be part of it. Also, throughout life the individual should constantly take care of his or her ancestral guardian spirit. Bascom (1960:406) elaborates this point:
"It is the ancestral guardian . . . who takes sacrifices made to the head to heaven. The only way to sacrifice to the ancestral guardian is to sacrifice to the head, and anything that is given to the forehead or the occiput goes to the ancestral guardian soul, but is shared with the other two."

Raymond Prince has written that the Yoruba believe the Supreme God created man in two parts. One part dwells on earth, and its spiritual double, or eleda, is in heaven. Before the person is born a contract is made in heaven concerning the individual's destiny or plans for life. Then the tree of forgetfulness is embraced, and the person is born. The eleda will protect the individual if he lives on earth according to the contract or plan; otherwise, the eleda will turn against him and harm him (Prince 1964a:84–120).

According to Bascom (1960:401-410) most Yoruba associate the ancestral guardian soul with the forehead, or iwaju, the crown, or atari, and the occiput, or ipako. They believe that all three parts of the head are controlled by a single soul—that of the ancestral guardian. However, in Ile Ife some priests believe that each of the three parts of the head is associated with three different souls.

Regardless of whether there is one ancestral guardian soul or three souls, the soul(s) goes to heaven after the individual dies. The soul(s) must account for all the good and evil the person carried out on earth. In heaven the soul(s) undergoes a court trial of sorts. Good persons are released and then can be reborn; criminals and other wicked persons are held and punished. The latter are condemned to the bad heaven, orun bururu, which is described as being hot like pepper, rather than hot like fire. Sometimes it is called "the heaven of potsherds," or orun apadi, referring to something broken beyond repair. Those who are held and punished can never be restored to life through reincarnation.

Those who have been good on earth reach the good heaven (orun rere), which is also referred to as "the heaven of contentment" (orun alafia) or "the heaven of breezes" (orun afefe). There, the air is fresh and everything is good; the wrongs of earth are righted, and the multiple souls are reunited. Life there is quite similar to life on earth. People pursue their earthly occupations and remain there for a generation before being reborn. Usually they are reborn into the same lineage so they can rejoin their children and grandchildren (Bascom 1960:404).

In Cuba, probably due to the severe and complete separation of the slaves from their extended families, people are believed to be reincarnated outside of both their biological and religious families. Moreover, there is the belief in an end to the cycles of reincarnations. In this regard, the significance of the *itutu*, which is performed before burial on behalf of a deceased priest or priestess, is explained by an informant of Lydia Cabrera (1980: 344): "The Itutu is performed to facilitate detachment, it frees the soul of the initiate from the terror of the darkness of the afterlife and of new reincarnations, 'so that the person will not be reborn again, to procure once and for ever peace and rest.'"

Most practitioners of Santería do not seem to be interested in eschatological promises. There is not much emphasis on the afterlife. Among many followers of Santería the beliefs in reincarnation are blurred; and the agreement of the ancestral guardian soul with Olorun regarding the ultimate destiny of a soul in a given incarnation is forgotten. Thus, the close interrelationship between the ancestral souls, destiny, and divination has been lost.

The loss of the cult of the ancestors in Cuba significantly affected the whole system of beliefs about reincarnation, about the meaning and use of the oracle, and, in essence, it altered some of the assumptions constituting the worldview. It may be surmised that in the quest for logico-structural integration of worldview assumptions the pervasive presence of Catholic beliefs concerning heaven and hell, as well as spiritualist beliefs in reincarnation and karma, tended to fill the vacuum left by the loss of the original Yoruban conception of reincarnation involving the eleda.

Most believers of Santería believe that each person has two or more guardian *orichas* who protect them from evil. However, there is a lot of disparity among beliefs regarding the nature and names of these guardian divinities of the head. Many believe that the most important among the protector *orichas* is the one that is *asentado* (the *oricha* that a person is crowned with at the height of the initiation ceremony). Some believe that there are at least two most important protector *orichas.*

Others believe that in addition to one's protector *oricha* one has a constellation of spiritual protections. These protections are not *orichas* but spirits that are attracted to and protect a person because of affinity. One learns about this spiritual constellation by means of spiritualist consultations. In many instances these spirits might be the souls of persons who, when alive, were dedicated to the worship of an *oricha* that is not the *oricha* protecting their protégée. Or, they might be the souls of persons who, when alive, did not practice Santería, such as the spirit of a nun, an Amerindian, a Congolese, a Gypsy, or others. Clearly, this set of religious beliefs is of Allan Kardec's spiritualist extraction.

Some believers have not even heard the term *eledá.* As far back as the 1940s Lydia Cabrera's informants found it difficult to define the meaning of the word *eledá.* However, some of them came closer to defining the Nigerian concept of eleda than do most present-day informants. The following was reported to Lydia Cabrera (1954: 506): "The head commands the body. There is something godlike in it. It is sacred, because *eledá* is in it. *Eledá,* which is based or enshrined in the head, is not an *oricha.* It is the Guardian Angel, the individuals' guide and protector. Something from God, that is, a divine attribute, essence, or principle located in the center of humans' heads, or just behind the crown. *Eledá* is the owner of the head, or *ori.* He is the spiritual and divine part of the human being."

Cabrera's informants (1954: 506) also made a distinction between the *eledá* and the shadow. According to one of them: "Yes, it is the shadow that walks behind the body. It is the Angel in the head; it goes forward, faces and looks forward. One has to catch the shadow after the person has walked by; otherwise the Angel *(Eledá)* would see the danger and would defend that person if it were on good terms with it. After the shadow is taken, one can work on that person who has been left without a shadow."

These individuals clearly believed that if one does not take proper care of one's *eledá,* the *eledá* might abandon him or her, and an enemy would be able to buy it off. They believed that one has to be especially cautious when going to sleep, because at that time the *eledá* might leave the body and go roaming (Cabrera 1954: 506). Moreover, in order to harm someone, the best way to do it is to befriend his or her *eledá*:

> We do that by buying it with food, flattering it, and making it feel important so that we lure it away, so that it will abandon the head in which it is situated. The main thing is to call it by its real name. That is most important: to know the name of the Angel of the day in which the person was born, in order to be able to reach it, talk to it, and breathe on it in order to charm it. That is why no one should tell others his given name, nor the name given in Kari Ocha (the name given in Santería's initiation) or in the *nganga* (the name of the receptacle that contains the supernatural power in Palo Mayombe or the name given to the person when initiated in Palo Mayombe). To do so could be one's undoing. Those names should be left unspoken, just as in people's spoor there is "the essence of life." A person and his real name are one and the same. The name is something sacred; it should be kept concealed. (Cabrera 1954: 506)

Despite the current disparity of views regarding the soul or souls, there is no question but that in Santería it is of the greatest importance to sacrifice to the spirit that lives in the head; that is, to feed the *eledá*. Today, most believers who are familiar with the term *eledá* think that it is an *oricha*. It should be noted also that the concept of *eledá* changed in Cuba in order to make the concept understandable to white Creoles who came to practitioners of Santería for help long ago. Its meaning became Christianized, or, more precisely, Europeanized.

Presumably, the Lucumí found a degree of congruency between the *eledá* and the Catholic guardian angel and borrowed the term. Some informants say that the *eledá*/guardian angel is the *oricha* that protects the head of an individual. During a visit to Cuba in the 1940s Bascom (1950: 523) was informed that the stone is the power through which the guardian angel or saint manifests its blessings.

However, there are still many knowledgeable *santeros,* and especially *babalaos,* who have preserved the Nigerian concept of eleda. According to Manolo Erice (March 2004): "The *eledá* is a spiritual entity that is reincarnated in a person, is the protector and spiritual guide of the person, who is only known to Orúla. The *ada le yu* is the guardian angel, the *oricha* that protects that person. It is necessary that the person, through the *itá* (divination procedure that takes place at the moment of initiation), find out the route that he must follow throughout his life in order to avoid danger, disgrace, and ultimately be saved." In another interview (April 2004) he added: "La Regla de Ifá is the divine extension of the universe. Orúla is the only one that knows who the *eledá* of a person is—that spiritual entity that reincarnates in a person."

In conclusion, among most believers in Santería the *eledá*, or the guardian angel, is the product of the merging of religious concepts of different extraction—from the Yoruba, *eledá* as an ancestral spirit; from Catholicism, the guardian angel; and from European Spiritualism, the *protecciones* or protections.

Chapter Summary

The concept of ashe/*aché* is central to both the Yoruban religion and Santería.

Afro-Cubans of Yoruban ancestry experienced the severance of ties with their family lineages as well as the total society of which they had been a part. They also experienced influences as disparate as the heavy reliance on the magic of Bantu, the faith of Roman Catholicism, and the constant interaction between incarnated and nonincarnated spirits of Spiritualism.

It is understandable that Yoruban organizations connected with the cult of the ancestors did not take root in the new environment. In Nigeria, members of the Egungun societies became possessed by departed souls, which allowed the dead to communicate with their living relatives. As mentioned previously, such societies did not reorganize in Cuba. This represented the loss of a coherent conception of the afterworld, or of punishment and reward, and of the concept of *eledá* as the ancestral guardian soul. Consequently, among most practitioners of Santería, the belief in the *eledá* and the belief in reincarnation are blurred, and many don't know about the relationship of *eledá*, reincarnation, destiny, and divination.

Most followers, however, believe in the divinity of the head and the importance of *olori* (owner of the Head, the *eledá*), and they frequently engage in the complex rituals designed to take care of the head. As in Nigeria, the head must be fed frequently so that it will protect the individual. The blood of pigeons and white guinea fowl are the appropriate *olori* propitiatory sacrifices. It is also customary to refresh the head, or *orí*, with coconut water so that it will be stable. The *ko bo orí* ceremony (rogation of the head) follows a strict step-by-step ritual procedure.

In summary, the losses experienced by the Yoruban religion while adapting to Cuban reality affected the meaning and coherence of some beliefs and practices. In Nigeria, consultations with the oracles are designed to solve everyday problems, but they are used primarily as a means of finding the best way to follow the path traced in the sacred contract between the Supreme Deity and

the ancestral soul. Sacrifices are offered to facilitate the favorable opportunities that are part of that path and to avoid the obstacles and dangers that are
also part of that path. Since, among many followers of Santería, the belief in the
eledá is blurred, the eschatological focus is weakened, and the beliefs in reincarnation are primarily borrowed from Kardec's Spiritualism. Thus, divination
and magical rituals are structured in most instances to identify the conduits of
aché and to care for the material receptacles of *aché* in order to gain the power
to protect and support the individual in solving everyday problems.

Priesthood

There is no counterpart in Santería to Christian baptism or confirmation because initiation means entering into priesthood. In the past most believers were not initiated; the oracles generally did not advise devotees to go through initiation unless they showed particular signs of possessing faculties as a medium, or other similar gifts. Most people contented themselves with regularly worshiping an *oricha* or *orichas* in altars kept in their homes. They would also attend religious festivals, consult diviners, and frequently make supplications to the guardian *oricha* of their heads. Generally, they were not advised to undergo the rigorous lengthy training of initiation. In other words, they did not have a *santo asentado* (*oricha* seated on the head).

However, in the 1900s a trend began that emphasized the need for individuals who had been initiated in the worship of their guardian *oricha* to also seek the protection of various other *orichas*. Part of that trend included the position that rituals were only efficacious when they were performed by knowledgeable, professional priests. It is very possible that this trend intended to preserve the knowledge brought from Africa by certain priests by requiring that priests of an *oricha* also become knowledgeable of the rituals associated with several other *orichas*.

In the 1950s this trend toward professionalism, coupled with an interest in economic gains, resulted in the proliferation of initiations. Consequently, many individuals who were initiated lacked spiritual faculties and attributes such as communicating with the *orichas* and the spirits through trance-possession. As this trend took hold, there was a change in attitude. No longer was there an expectation that the initiated were individuals born with special gifts. Instead the view that began to predominate was that the most efficient priests were those who were most knowledgeable of esoteric rituals and procedures.

Initiation into Regla de Ocha, or Santería

Cabrera (1980: 128–234) provides a detailed step-by-step description of Santería's initiation ceremonies, but for present purposes a more condensed version is offered here. In Santería, initiation opens the road to priesthood, but not all persons who are initiated will officiate as priests. Some might be initiated because they suffer from poor health.[1] In this case, it is believed that once initiated the guardian *oricha* will help the person recover his or her health.

Others are initiated because they feel insecure and want to enlist supernatural assistance to help them cope with their existential difficulties. Still others are called to the priesthood or are moved toward it by their *oricha*. This means that that they need to be initiated into the service of the *oricha* that claims their head.

Normally, initiation does not take place until the person is an adolescent or an adult. It is common, however, for children to be born with a *santo*. This means that, even before such a child is born, the *santo* made known to the mother, through trance or consultation through the oracles, that the child belongs to him. In such cases, the child is consecrated to the *oricha* before birth or during infancy.

At other times, during ceremonies an *oricha* might possess a person, signaling that the *oricha* is calling that person to his service. If an individual is claimed in this manner, he has to be initiated as soon as possible. In rare instances, while consulting the oracle on some personal problem, an ordinary believer may be "told" that his guardian *oricha* needs to be *asentado*.

In the past, the oracle generally did not advise devotees to go through initiation unless they showed particular signs of possessing faculties as a medium or other similar gifts. But, as indicated above, a trend began in the 1950s to initiate individuals who did not have special spiritual faculties.

In Santería, initiation seals an alliance between the believer and his protector, or guardian *oricha*. The initiated assumes the responsibility for performing certain specific rituals, regularly observing certain taboos, and serving the *oricha*. The *oricha* commits himself or herself to help and protect the devotee throughout his or her terrestrial existence. The newly initiated, or *iyawós*, are a class apart.

Initiation requires a long period of apprenticeship. During this period, the novice learns the mythology and the rituals belonging to the worship of the *oricha* to which he is being committed. This intimate knowledge enables the believer to receive the visit of the divinity in his own body. On certain occasions, the *oricha* will inhabit the devotee, manifesting himself to other believers or mortals through this person, who, after initiation, is his son or daughter.

The long learning process of initiation is marked by a series of rituals that begins with the ceremony of receiving the necklaces. Neophytes receive the *collares* (consecrated necklaces) of their protector, or guardian *oricha*, and those of other *orichas*. They expect to obtain power, or *aché*, from the *orichas* by receiving, wearing, and "feeding" their necklaces. Receiving the necklaces is a necessary step in the process of initiation. However, it is not binding, which means that the person receiving the necklaces is not committed to undergo initiation in the future.

The *elekes,* or necklaces, are made of colored beads strung according to the color and the number associated with the specific *oricha* being received. Since each *oricha* may come in different *caminos* (forms, paths, or manifestations), it is important to learn through the oracles which *camino* of this particular *oricha* is protecting the person receiving the necklaces. The identification of the specific *camino,* or path, of the *oricha* is of utmost importance because it yields information concerning the personality, character, circumstances, likes, and dislikes of both the *camino* in question and the individual receiving the *oricha.* In a sense it represents the pairing of compatible personality profiles of the individual and the *oricha.* In addition, the oracle identifies the offerings preferred by the *oricha,* as well as the taboos for certain types of offerings and behavior. It also determines the order in which beads should be strung when preparing the necklace that corresponds to and symbolizes that particular manifestation of the *oricha.*

There are seven basic necklaces that correspond to the most important *orichas* in the Afro-Cuban pantheon. In most instances, only four are received at the beginning: those of Obatalá, Ochún, Yemayá, and Changó. If the *eledá* of the person is another *oricha,* that *oricha's* necklace will also be received. Later on, necklaces of other *orichas* might be received, enabling the recipient to gain access to more supernatural power.

Not all of the *orichas* have necklaces as receptacles of their power, or *aché.* The following *orichas* do own necklaces that should be received ritually by their followers: Elegguá, Oyá, Babalú Ayé, Agayú Solá, Orúnmila, and Ogún. On occasion, the oracle might advise some women to receive and wear the *idé* of Orúla. This is a bracelet of green and yellow beads worn on the left wrist; it is the receptacle of the power of Orúla.

The necklace of the Seven African Powers has the *aché* of Olofin, Obatalá, Yemayá, Changó, Ogún, Ochún, and Babalú Ayé. It is made of a large crystal bead followed by a white, a blue, a red, a yellow, a black, a green, and a brown bead in recurring order.

The necklaces are made by the *santero* or *santera* (male or female priest) who is the godfather or godmother of the person receiving them. Very strict ritual procedures are followed when stringing the beads of these sacred necklaces. Songs and prayers play a most important part. The beads should be joined together by a cotton thread, which insures that when "fed" the necklaces will absorb the powerful potions made of medicinal herbs and the blood of sacrificed animals that are offered to them. Once the necklaces are made, they are washed in the river to obtain the blessing and power of Ochún. At that time, a hen and honey are offered to Ochún. After the ritual bath, the necklaces are ready to receive the *aché* (power) of the gods and are placed in the *sopera* (soup tureen). After seven days have passed, the necklaces are ready. If the person receiving the necklaces is planning to be initiated, he should sleep on a mat in front of the *soperas* on the day before the necklaces are received. However, if the individual is not planning to be initiated, and, instead, is only going to receive the four necklaces, it is not necessary for him to sleep in the sacred presence. It is mandatory, however, that the necklaces be well fed before they are given to the neophyte.

The neophyte should be bathed with *omiero*, a sacred mixture made of twenty-one herbs, before receiving the necklaces. He is ritually washed, anointed, and blessed. After this purification rite, the initiate should be dressed completely in new, white clothes. The old and worn clothing should be thrown away. The new clothes symbolize a new life at the service of and under the protection of the *orichas*. The discarding of the old clothes symbolizes severance with the errors previously committed. The godfather or godmother then begins instructing him or her in the mysteries of the religion, the meaning of the ceremony, the duties to the saints, the caring of the necklaces, the *eledá* (guardian spirit or *oricha*), and other matters.

Afterward, the saints are asked through the cowry shells, or preferably, the coconuts, if they are pleased with the initiate. If the answer is affirmative, he receives the *elekes* (necklaces) in the following order: Obatalá, Yemayá, Ochún, and Changó. After the investiture of the necklaces, the sacred drums are sometimes played and, at this point, it is common for the person who receives the necklaces to be possessed by the saint.

For some, the ceremony of the necklaces is an end unto itself. For others, it is the starting point at which the neophyte is promised to the *oricha*. Much later, the *aleyo* (participant not yet initiated) undergoes the ceremony known as *medio asiento* (middle stage in the process of initiation) to prepare the novitiate for the great moment of initiation. In some instances the neophyte does not have to go through this ceremony in order to be initiated, but it is proper and traditional to do so.

Medio asiento is like a marriage vow. Sometimes this ceremony has to be delayed in order for the novice to save the money required for it. When it is completed, a binding contract between the neophyte and the *oricha* is established. In Matanzas, a province in Cuba, the *medio asiento* used to be the crowning point, after which the neophyte is considered an *iyawó* (person recently initiated). In Havana, however, a person is not considered initiated until after the ceremony of *asiento* (seating the *oricha* on the head).

After all the preparatory steps have been completed, then the most secret and sacred ceremony of initiation takes place. Not all the *orichas* are *asentado*. Those that are *asentado* include Obatalá, Elegguá, Changó, Ochún, Ochosi, Yemayá, Ogún, and Oyá. Other important *orichas*, such as Olokun, Agayú, and Naná Burukú, cannot be *asentados*. Instead they are received by means of a special ceremony. The explanation given is that they are too powerful to be installed on the human head. The author, however, agrees with Raul Cañizares (1999: 51), who thinks that possibly the rituals and secrets pertaining to the initiation ceremonies of these *orichas* were lost. It is also possible that priests trained in their cult were not brought to Cuba. In this regard, the cases of Olokun and Agayu are revealing. In Africa these orishas are installed on the head just like other orishas who possess the initiated during festivals and on special occasions.

Most of the rituals that are part of the initiation, or *asiento,* take place in the temple, or *ilé ocha.* The *aleyo* (uninitiated participant) stays in this temple during the seven days prior to the ceremony. In Santería's initiation there are two different procedures. In some lineages, or *ramas,* the *babalaos* participate, while others dispense with them. David H. Brown (2003: 301–4) appropriately calls them the Ifá-centric and the Ocha-centric initiations.

In the Ifá-centric initiations, a *babalao* identifies the guardian angel or *oricha de cabecera* of the initiate through Orúla, the god of divination, and by using the *ekuele.*[2] According to the *babalao* Manolo Erice (March 2004), "This is the only valid way, since Orúla is the only *oricha* that is present when the ancestor soul, or *eledá,* of a person makes a pact with Olodumare before being reincarnated."

The *babalao* also prepares and delivers the Warriors (Elegguá, Ogún, and Ochosi), the *mano* of Orúla (divining nuts), the *awofaka* (for men) and the *kofá* (for women). In addition, the *babalao* performs a reading with the *opele,* or chains, which is called the *vista;* the *opele* prescribe the protective *ebó* (sacrificial offering) that needs to be performed before initiation. Finally, according to Lydia Cabrera's informants (1974: 83–84), individuals being initiated in the cult of any of the warrior *orichas* have to be taken to the *monte,* or wilderness, by three *babalaos.*

In the Ocha-centric houses an *oriaté*[3] or the godfather or godmother of the initiate uses the dilogún, or oracle of the shells to identify the *oricha de cabecera,* or guardian angel. The initiate's *padrino* or an *oriaté* prepares and delivers the Warriors. The *oriaté* performs the *vista* and the *ebó de entrada,* and those being initiated into the service of the Warriors are taken to the *monte* by the *oriaté.* Reacting to this procedure, the *babalao* Jorge Torres (May 2004) asks: "How can they avoid using us if we are the ones who consecrate the *oriatés* and the ones who, through Orúla, can read the major *odus?*"

On the night before initiation, the candidate goes to the river accompanied by his second godmother, the *oyubbona,* where he undergoes purification rites at the hands of Ochún, the goddess of the river. Old clothing is cast off to symbolize good riddance of the misguided past life. Then, the novitiate takes a stone from the bottom of the river, which will become the *otán* (sacred stone) of Ochún. The initiate, now dressed in white garments, the color of purity, goes to the temple to rest. Once there, he receives the *ko bo orí*, the most important cleansing of the head. This ceremony is vital, because it is on the head that the *oricha* is going to be *asentado* (seated or placed).

Initiation requires the cooperation of Osain, the god. A *yerbero* (herbalist) who has received Osain and is an expert in the magical and medicinal properties of plants, roots, and herbs, is also needed. He gathers from the wilderness the herbs recommended by the *babalao*. Once the required twenty-one different herbs are gathered, the *babalao* gives them to the *iyaré* (the first godmother), of the neophyte, or *iyawó*. The herbs are then presented to Olorún, the Supreme Being. Later, they are entwined in two piles on a mat, where they are mixed. Then, the *iyalochas* shred and grind them. At this time, ritual songs, the *suyeres*, in honor of Osain and the other *orichas*, are intoned. After the herbs have been readied, they are placed in a pot that contains water from the river, from the sea, and from rain.

One by one, the *otanes* (sacred stones) of the different gods are washed and consecrated. First the *otanes* of the *orichas* that can be *asentados* are fed and later the *otanes* of the *orichas* who cannot be *asentados*. The priests dedicated to their worship learn how to deal with and make sacrifices to them. These latter *orichas* cannot incarnate in the faithful; that is, they cannot possess them through trance or dance to congratulate them.

Later, the *omiero* (sacred herbal potion) is poured into a large container. During the seven days immediately following the ceremony, the *oyubona* (experienced assistant and second godmother of the novice) will bathe the *iyawó* (initiate) with the *omiero* (sacred potion) and will make him take three sips of that water every morning. At a later date, the blood of the animals that have been used as sacrifice will be added to this blessed water.

The head of the *iyawó* (initiate) is now completely shaved and marked with yellow, green, and red chalk. He is laid on a mat where he must stay for several hours in a state of trance while the ceremony continues. The climax is reached when the *oricha* is seated on the *iyawó's* head. This occurs when certain secret ingredients are placed in a cut made in the skin of the *iyawó's* head. Normally, at this time the *iyawó* is possessed by the *oricha*.

During these final rites, the old personality of the former *aleyo* (uninitiated) dies. His head is changed. He is given a new name in religion and awakes to a new life in the service of the *oricha*. At that moment, the godparents raise the *otanes* (sacred stones) where the *aché* (power) of the *orichas* has been previously fixed. They hold them behind the head of the *iyawó* so that their power will be transmitted to him. At the end of the ceremony, the godmother, or *iyaré*, holds over the novitiate's head the stone of the *oricha* being *asentado* (seated) in order to receive the *aché* of that specific *oricha*. Then a cross is traced on the novitiate's tongue. Next, to feed the incarnated god, the novitiate eats honey, smoked fish, and the neck of a hen. When the *iyawó* returns from trance, he is already married to the god, will attend to the numerous future sacrifices of animals, and will drink blood from their heads.

Once the god is *asentado,* the *iyawó* is presented to the drums. This ceremony takes place during the daylight hours. At night, the sacred drums cannot be played. Sometimes, the presentation to the drums takes place a while after the initiation, on an occasion when, for some reason, a drum festival is offered. Under these circumstances, several *iyawós* use the celebration to be presented to the drums.

The *iyawó* salutes the drums and dances in honor of his or her *oricha*. From that moment on, he is entitled to dance at all religious festivals. After being initiated, the *iyawó* has to pay a fee to his godmother in order for her to offer a coconut and a rooster to Elegguá. He is then authorized to *levantar santo*; that is, to set up his own temple. The *iyawó* can now take to his or her home the sacramental *otanes* of the *orichas* that were formerly in the home of his godmother.

There are specific lifetime obligations between the godchild and the godparents. The godchild owes the godparents obedience and gratitude. He should treat them with the care and devotion one has for biological parents. He should take care of the *madrina* and assist her any time she needs help, caring for her when she is sick, cleaning her house, coming to her aid financially, and so forth. This bond is manifested for the first time when the newly initiated holds a drum festival; all the collections go to the godmother.

The *santos/orichas* are involved in all the problems and incidents of those initiated in their cult. The believers call their *eledá* "Babamí," which means "father," or, "Iyamí," "mother," according to their gender. Once the neophyte is consecrated to the worship of an *oricha*, he or she must take care of the *santo* and offer frequent sacrifices. Otherwise, he or she will fall into disfavor and become the object of the god's vengeance. All future happenings in life, such as diseases, illness, economic failures, and other negative events, are attributed to neglect or lack of care of the gods. Conversely, success and positive events are attributed to the favor of the *orichas.*

There are several categories of priests and priestesses in Santería. The new, or recent initiates, are called *iyawós* and are at the lowest level. The *babalochas* (males) or *iyalochas* (females) are above them. They are people who have been initiated for more than a year and have full priesthood credentials. Most important are the *italeros* and the *oriatés* who are experts in the dilogún (cowrie shell divination). They are in charge of conducting the *itá* (oracle-consultation performed on behalf of an individual at the height of the initiation ceremonies).

This oracle consultation is focused on giving individuals direction and guidance concerning the ways in which they should conduct their lives. It identifies situations that should be avoided, taboos that should be respected, and other important recommendations. *Oriatés* (knowledgeable and experienced priests) are entitled to conduct the sacrifice of four-legged animals if a *babalao* is not present. The title of *oriaté* is not obtained by specific training, but it is granted to individuals in recognition of their vast knowledge and experience. They have the role of masters of ceremony in initiation rituals, since they are the ones who shave and paint the heads of the neophyte. They seat the *oricha* in the head, and at the height of initiation they perform the *itá* divination ritual, which determines the name of the new initiates, the taboos they have to respect, and the road or path of the *oricha de cabecera* of the neophyte.

The children of Changó stand out among *santeros* and enjoy great popularity and prestige as clairvoyants. The children of Obatalá, the Creator God, follow them in importance, since Obatalá's priests have the extraordinary capacity and privilege of being possessed by any *oricha*. This preeminence is due to Obatalá's being the owner of all the heads and, therefore, the king and chief of all the *orichas*. *Oyubón* (male) and *oyubona* (female) are the titles given to those experienced *santeros* and *santeras* who assist the godfather or godmother in the ceremony of *asiento*. Seniority is very important in Santería. *Iyaré* is the title given to the most senior *iyalocha* or *santera*.

Theoretically, unbreakable ties of respect and submission bind *santeros* and *babalaos* to their godparents. However, current practices, in great part due to the uprooting experienced by Cubans within and outside the island, demonstrate that after initiation *santeros* and *santeras* enjoy great independence.

Priests in Santería perform very important functions as officiators in worship ceremonies, as medicine men, and as fortune-tellers. As priests they must care for their temples and preside over the rites that are celebrated in them. As men of medicine, they must diagnose disease and prescribe remedies to clients seeking help. Since followers of Santería believe that harmful spiritual influences and the "evil eye" can cause many ailments, the priests must also prepare magic remedies to rid their clients of whatever ails them when conditions are caused by *salación* (bad luck). Most of the remedies consist of beverages made from a concoction of herbs, weeds, leaves, and blood of the animals sacrificed to the *orichas*.

Priests prepare amulets against *salación* (bad luck) as well as love potions and all types of magical charms. Even though *santeros* know the secrets of witchcraft, sorcery, and black magic, they tend not to use these powers unless it is necessary to do so to overcome the harm against their clients introduced by an enemy's malign magic. The *santeros,* when consulted in their capacity of witch doctor, are able to diagnose the reasons for the client's misfortune caused by the workings of *brujería* (witchcraft) or *hechicería* (sorcery) by some personal enemy of the client. The priests can also show the client how to rid himself of the evil influence, but claim that they will not recommend offensive measures against the enemy. *Santeros* generally refuse to use their power for harmful purposes, although I am personally aware of known exceptions.

The priests of Ocha, or *santeros,* are also fortune-tellers who make use of several oracles, or divination instruments. The most popular oracles are the coconuts, the dilogún, or cowry shells, the board of Ifá, and the divining chains, or *ekuele.* All priests can use the coconuts and the shells, but only the *babalaos* can use the board of Ifá and the *ekuele.* These oracles are used as a means of diagnosing disease, discovering enemies that are harming the client, determining his *eledá,* and other matters related to life circumstances.

Initiation into Regla de Ifá

The most important priests in Santería are the *babalaos.* They are the children of Orúla, the god of wisdom and the oracles. The *babalaos* are preeminent prophets, for they are the only ones who can use the highest instruments of divination: The board of Ifá and the *ekuele. Babalaos* are the priests who lead initiations, funerals, and other ceremonies. They are consulted in cases of contradictory oracular messages, or whenever there is doubt about the interpretation of a prediction. They are the highest authority in all religious matters and the preservers of the true knowledge of Yoruban theology (the Ifá divination system). Orúla, their *eledá* (patron *oricha*), is the god who knows all the secrets and mysteries that were entrusted to him by Olorun, the Supreme Deity.

The dignity and office of *babalao* is reserved for heterosexual men, ideally of great moral character. However, there is no mechanism to "defrock" or "excommunicate" *babalaos* who engage in improper behavior or illicit activities.

A *santero* who can be possessed through trance by *orichas,* or *eguns,* cannot become a *babalao. Babalaos* are strict purists, and reputedly have alert and sharp minds. Normally, a person is trained as a *babalao* when, during the *itá* (the divination/consultation) that is done at the height of the initiation into the cult of any *oricha,* the divination letter, or sign, appears that advises him to become a *babalao.* The period of training involved is very long because it requires having to learn the complex Ifá divination system. This entails learning and memorizing thousands of verses, legends, and proverbs as well as knowing how to interpret them.

The ritual process for initiating *babalaos* takes a week. It emphasizes the renunciation of the former self (more than in the initiation into the cult of other *orichas*) and the emergence of a new self, or identity, at the service of Orúla. Orúla, the *eledá* (patron *oricha*) of the *babalaos,* is received during the first day of initiation. He was one of the few *orichas* present at the time of the creation of the world and is too powerful to be *asentado* (seated) in a human head.

During the initiation of *babalaos,* great attention is given to the importance of the initiate's alliance with Orúla and the *babalao's* priestly class. After being shaved and painted, the initiate is crowned with a headdress made of coconut shell, beads, and red parrot feathers. The symbols of the sixteen legendary kings of the Yoruban people are painted on a long block of cedar to signify their agreement with the initiation that is taking place and their alliance with the neophyte. Then, the five senior *babalaos* paint their symbols on the block to show their support of the initiation that is taking place. Later, two black hens are sacrificed. The feathers and the blood are used to dress twenty-one *ikínes,* or palm nuts. One *ikín* is placed on each of the twenty-one symbols (sixteen for the Yoruban kings and five that are the signatures of the senior *babalaos*). The *padrino* coats each *ikín* with a substance made of honey, cocoa butter, palm oil, and small pieces of coconut pulp. Then he calls upon *Orúla* to accept the neophyte. As the neophyte takes each *ikín* and swallows the coating, he incorporates Orúla's *aché.* The initiate then spits each of the *ikínes* into a gourd.

An Olofin[4] (a consecrated metal cylinder that contains the secrets and powers that represent the Supreme Being) has to be present during the initiation ceremony of *babalaos.* This requirement explains why, at first in the 1960s, some practitioners refused to recognize the *babalaos* who had been initiated in Miami. In their opinion, no one could be initiated in Miami because no *babalao* had been able to bring his Olofin from Cuba. At that time, if *babalaos* had tried to bring the Olofin out of Cuba, the immigration authorities would have opened it and the power of its secret would have been lost.

Raul Cañizares (1999:140) reports one version of the reason that women cannot become *babalaos:* In Yoruban mythology, a wife of Orúnla, called "Odu," was much older than her husband and felt very embarrassed by that fact, to the point that she took her own life. Orúnla went to Orun (heaven) and got her back. However, Odu asked Orúnla to keep her in a secret place, where women could not see her. Consequently, women in Nigeria are forbidden to see Odu. It is believed that any woman who gazes at Odu becomes blind. However, women can become priestesses of Ifá, because it is not required for all babalawos to see Odu.

According to Virgilio Armenteros (May 2005), in Afro-Cuban tradition Odu was lost, but some Cuban *babalaos* have recovered it from African babalawos. Among them, it is necessary to see Odu before being initiated as a *babalao,* and since women cannot see Odu they are prohibited from becoming *babalaos.* He adds that among those Cuban *babalaos* who don't have Odu, Olofin takes her place. Since women cannot see Olofin they cannot become *babalaos.* Confirming this version, the senior *santera* Silvia Eires (May 2005) explains that women cannot become Ifá priestesses because they cannot see "Oddun" (the secret and sacred symbol of Olofin, the Supreme Being). In summary, in Santería women cannot cast Ifá. In Nigeria, however, a small number of women called the Iyanifa, who are the priestesses of Orunmila, function as babalawos and can cast Ifa.

Homosexual men are also prohibited from becoming *babalaos.* One informant who wishes to remain anonymous explained that the rationale for this prohibition is that such men cannot be trusted with the secrets of sacred knowledge.[5] On this point, according to Ezequiel Torres (March 2001), a bitter struggle among *babalaos* called *la guerra de los babalaos,* ensued in the 1930s and 1940s in Cuba, when some senior *babalaos* initiated their homosexual sons.

In addition, the impact that Miguel Febles Padrón had on the history of Ifá, greatly changed the membership and practice of this religion. At the end of the 1940s, Miguel Febles Padrón, the youngest son of the prestigious *babalao* Ramón Febles Molina, took away from his older brother, Francisco Febles del Pino, the Olofin he had rightfully inherited from his father. Moreover, according to Brown (2003: 89): "He gained for himself the power to select Olofin's recipients—most often those who would pay a premium price—and 'block' the receiving of an Olofin from other sources, particularly those to whom he had already given an Olofin." For his own benefit, Febles Padrón began a trend initiating great numbers of individuals who were poorly trained and had few moral restraints.

Even though most practitioners—and even many nonpractitioners—consult a *babalao* at some point or several times in their lives, Ifá rituals are not open to the uninitiated; they are kept secret. Thus, the *babalaos,* in a sense, form a secret society.

There is a hierarchy among *babalaos.* The oldest and wisest are called *olúos.* In order to become an *olúo* one has to receive Olofin. The *olúo* who has the most seniority in a lineage is an *oba,* or king, which is the highest position in Orúla's priesthood. In 1950 only three persons enjoyed this rank in Cuba. In Africa the position of oba was inherited from father to son, but it was not so in Cuba, where the *oba* positions belonged to the most senior *olúo,* or *oluwo,* of a lineage. According to Wilfredo Fernández Jr. (June 2000), in the case of the lineage of Adechina, the legendary founder of Regla de Ifá, the *oba* was always chosen from the house or branch of Bernardo Rojas.

Rivalries and differences between *santeros* and *babalaos* often occur. Rivalries persist because some *babalaos* are perceived by *santeros* as putting on airs of superiority. For instance, *babalaos* do not allow *santeros* inside the Ifá room, where secret ceremonies take place. Consequently, *santeros* do not let *babalaos* into the room of the *santo,* or *igbodú.* Moreover, some *santeros* feel that they do not need the *babalaos.* In the past, it was the custom that four *babalaos* would "bajar a Orúla" (get Orúla to come down) to determine the tutelary *oricha* of the person being initiated. Currently, in some cult houses, the *oricha* that will be crowned on the neophyte's head is identified by the *oriaté* or by his godmother or godfather using the dilogún. Moreover, in the past, individuals who were initiated into the cult of an *oricha* could not be initiated into the cult of Ifá. This is because *babalaos* cannot have visions and cannot be mounted or possessed by *orichas* or by the spirits of the dead. During the last few years this rule has changed. As a result, some *santeros* who have undergone the ceremony of *asiento* of an *oricha* have been initiated as *babalaos.* They are called *awó* and are considered senior to all *babalaos* (Castellanos and Castellanos 1992 3:85).

According to Ezequiel Torres (February 2002) Elegguá caused the controversy between *santeros* and *babalaos* on the issue of the Warriors. It was customary for *babalaos* to prepare an Elegguá *de amasijo*[6] and the rest of the Warriors. However, as mentioned earlier, some *santeros* now claim they should prepare their godchildren's Warriors. In some cases, it seems that a compromise is being achieved. A set of the Warriors is prepared and given by the *babalaos* to the novice, who has already received a set prepared by his godmother or godfather. Thus, the person receives two sets of Warriors.

According to Ezequiel Torres (March 2002), the set from the godmother or godfather is called "the head." The Warriors from the *babalao* are called "the feet." They are constantly put to work to solve problems; while the Elegguá received from one's godparent is used only to solve the most important problems.

Chapter Summary

Since the turn of the twentieth century, there has been a powerful trend in Santería toward the need of initiates to undergo further training and to acquire further powers by receiving new *orichas.* It is also apparent that during the past fifty years a larger percentage of members have been advised of the need to be initiated than was the case in the past. This has happened in both Regla de Ocha and in Regla de Ifá.

The trend mentioned above might be the result of the ritualistic emphasis in Santería. Ritualism requires that priests learn to acquire mastery of extremely complicated procedures, to have knowledge about the diverse number of ingredients necessary to perform a ceremony, and to consecrate amulets and other religious paraphernalia. Without being absolutely correct, the ritual will not render the desired results. It will be useless and, furthermore, it could be harmful.

Controversies between *santeros* and *babalaos* have caused the *babalaos* to lose some stature and functions they formerly performed. The proliferation of Olofins that resulted from Febles Padrón's leadership in the 1960s and 1970s also undermined the prestige of the *babalao's* office. However, few deny their efficacy as keepers of the religious traditions and knowledge. Few challenge the accuracy of the advice given by Orúla through the instruments of divination that only *babalaos* can interpret.

Illness and Death

Santería's believers think that *arun,* or disease, is caused by both natural and supernatural factors. Santería does not deny the pathological effects of microorganisms as agents of infection or the debilitating effects of degenerative processes. When their clients are suffering from any ailment, *santeros* and *santeras* generally recommend that they see a physician. However, flowers, herbs, twigs, and leaves continue to be an intrinsic part of Santería. They are used for cleansing, for their demonstrated curative properties, and as complements to the doctor's prescriptions. Moreover, as Edward Norbeck points out (1974: 47): "A modern member of a tribal society may understand that small pox and diphtheria are caused by germs. To recover his health, he may then take modern medications and follow other practices of scientific medicine. But only supernaturalism can deal with one aspect of his illness, the reasons why he as an individual suffered the misfortune of contracting the disease."

The Nature, Etiology, Diagnosis, and Treatment of Diseases

Santeros consider supernatural agents as the cause of many diseases as well as factors that determine the outcomes of naturally caused illnesses. In addition, some believe that the children of each particular *oricha* show propensities toward certain ailments. For example, Obatalá's children often show a propensity for blindness, paralysis, and dementia; Ochún's for genital ailments and "bad blood"; Ogún's for nervous disorders and ailments requiring surgical interventions; Changó's for heart attacks, blindness, and hypertension; Babalú Ayé's for venereal diseases and skin and bone disorders; Agayú's for ischemia, thrombosis, and embolism; Elegguá's for accidents; and Yemayá's for intestinal disorders.

In most instances, it is necessary to consult with and to secure the assistance of the *orichas* and *eguns* (spirits of the dead) to deal successfully with illness. Diseases can result from the effect of the following supernatural agents:

- Intrusion of an object: Witchcraft may introduce an object into the body to cause sickness.
- Imitative and contagious magic: Santería's followers believe that a witch, or an enemy, can cause harm by using pictures of or objects closely as-

sociated with a person. This belief is based on the universal, magical assumption that like produces like and that anything in contact with an object or person can affect it.

- Loss of one's soul: This harm occurs when witches, paid by an enemy, buy a person's *eledá,* or guardian angel, leaving the person defenseless against injury.
- Spirit intrusion: This situation occurs when the soul of a deceased person is angered because it feels disrespected or neglected. Angry spirits, such as the soul of a person who, when alive, was very evil, or the restless soul of a person who died a violent death can cause more serious diseases. To harm a person, witches sometimes invoke these angry spirits.
- Anger of an *oricha*: Santería's followers believe that an *oricha* may feel neglected and thus turn against a person to make him or her sick or to cause harm.
- Evil eye: This belief is based on the assumption that some people have very powerful eyes. These people can harm another person just by looking at them, even when there is no intention on their part to do so.

Santeros and *paleros* use divination systems to identify the causes of diseases and the appropriate ways to treat them. In most instances, magical rituals such as offerings and sacrifices are performed to treat these conditions. The *santero's* powerful and authoritative performance is reinforced by his self-confident bearing, which reassures the client and fosters trust. The client's feeling of control is enhanced by the interaction with the *santero,* and this conveys a sense that something significant is being done to overcome the client's frustrations and impotency regarding illness.

Many *santeros* claim great ability to treat depression, obsessions, hypochondria, and phobias. Many times the advice given by the *santero* addresses a specific psychological conflict of the client and thus makes room for rationalizations and projections that defeat feelings of ambivalence, insecurity, guilt, and fear.

The Realm of the Dead

Talbot (1926:476, 477) has written of the Yoruba that when a person died, a babalawo or diviner was called to determine whether the death was natural or whether it was caused by witchcraft or ill-will on the part of an enemy. After all of the corpse's hair was shaved off, the corpse was dressed in the finest clothes. Then the corpse was buried, usually in the ground under the deceased's bedroom, and offerings were placed in the grave. Talbot describes the ceremony in greater detail:

On the seventh day, a member of the Egungun secret society, the
Egungun Image, dressed in long robes and wearing a mask, directed the
wives to a place outside of the town. This Egungun was assumed to be the
dead man. In that place the wives received a yam, which was supposed
to be the last gift of the deceased. Afterwards the wives returned weep-
ing to the compound. A few days later a small feast was prepared. Three
members of the Egungun society came to visit the family. The Egungun
who pretended to be the deceased hid in the backyard; another Egungun sat on the roof; while another one called the name of the deceased
three times in a loud voice. The one who was up on the roof repeated the
name aloud three times. Afterward, the one who was in the backyard
responded in a low voice, imitating the voice of the deceased. The following morning, the Egungun Image, representing the dead man, would
visit the deceased's old home to talk with the family and to promise to
look after them. (Talbot 1926 3:476, 477)

The Egungun society did not establish deep roots in Cuba. It is possible
that not many members knowledgeable of the rituals and functions of this
society were brought to Cuba as slaves. Also, there was in Nigeria a belief that
if the rituals were not done in a correct fashion the person officiating would
die. In Cuba, however, there were other customs regarding burial ceremonies
and burial grounds. Still, as noted previously, the overriding reason that these
societies did not become established in Cuba was an absence of the patrilineal
lineage. Other factors may have contributed to the demise of the Egungun cult
as well.

Santería's followers believe that the spirits of the dead continue to live after
death and that they inhabit the world of the living, moving around the earthly
environment even though invisible. Occasionally, they become visible to the
living, in most instances to frighten them. In order to prevent this frightening experience from happening, a series of rituals is conducted to appease the
spirit when a person dies. These beliefs and practices are similar in both Allan
Kardec's European Spiritualism and folk Catholicism. Even though the belief
in reincarnation, which was so important among the Yoruba, has lingered in
Cuba, it is not as important as it was in Nigeria. No special ritual or propitiation is connected to it, and reincarnation is not tied to the paternal lineage. It is
assumed that after successive reincarnations the soul of the person, if purified,
will go to Ara Onu to enjoy eternal peace. Moreover, Afro-Cubans believe that
Olorun, the Supreme Being, rewards good deeds and punishes wrongdoing.

However, Santería's followers do not have a clear view of the ultimate destiny of the departed. In general, there is not much concern with the afterlife

and no strong moral connection exists between earthly deeds and one's ultimate destiny. In other words, they do not share Christianity's deep concern with heaven and hell.

Santería's rituals are primarily oriented toward securing supernatural assistance to resolve interpersonal conflict, avoid disease, solve family and job-related problems and, most importantly, to avoid death for as long as possible. There is not much concern with spiritual salvation or damnation. Nevertheless, there is great fear and respect for the dead. When Santería's believers visit the cemetery or the *ceiba*, or silk-cotton tree, where it is believed the dead habitually gather, they behave with extreme respect.

In the Afro-Cuban tradition, a *novena*, as previously described, is held when a person dies. The family and friends of the deceased gather in his or her home and pray a rosary on behalf of the departed soul. Also, reflecting Catholic practices, funeral masses are offered in the Catholic Church. In addition, spiritualist masses are offered to enable communication to occur with the departed.

The spiritualist mass takes place in the home of a medium who might be a Kardecist spiritualist or a *santera* spiritualist. In the room they set up a *bóveda*, which is a table covered with a white cloth on which glasses filled with water are placed. Chairs and sitting arrangements are normally placed to form a circle. In other instances, a table is set up where the presiding and the assistant mediums sit. After the participants use cologne to rid themselves of evil influences, or currents, passages from Kardec's *Selected Prayers* (1966) are read, and the séance starts.

As the spirits possess the mediums, they are asked to identify themselves and to state the reason they have manifested themselves in the séance. Many spirits request help and prayers. Meanwhile, the most spiritually advanced come to offer advice regarding health and other worldly problems, to warn against possible dangers, and to communicate some message to the participants or their friends. At the end, closing prayers are recited, and the séance is over.

Death

In Santería, death, or Ikú, is a supernatural entity that disposes of life. Ikú lives in the cemetery, in empty bottles, in piles of trash, and usually comes out at night, searching for victims. Ikú is under the jurisdiction of Oyá, the owner of the torch (lightning), of tornadoes, bad wind, and the cemetery. If anyone, mortal or god, wants to work with death, he or she must first make a pact or alliance with Oyá. Death can be propitiated and can also be postponed by magical means. When a sick person approaches death, skillful priests can distract Ikú in those cases in which Ikú has been paid by an enemy or sent by a witch or an angry *oricha*.

Special care is taken when a priest or priestess dies. The *itutu* or "quieting down" ceremony is performed. *Santeros* gather in the house of the deceased to carry out last wishes or follow the advice of his or her *oricha*. The priests try to implement the deceased's wishes concerning disposal of the sacred stones, images of the *orichas,* and other religious paraphernalia.

The body of the deceased is dressed with the *ächó omo oricha,* the garments worn on the day of initiation. In addition, the lock of hair that was cut off on initiation day is placed inside the coffin. Then the priest who presides over these ceremonies, begins the rituals designed to sever ties with the living so that the spirit may not harm anyone. Later, Catholic masses are said, since, reputedly, masses are most pleasing to the dead.

On the first anniversary of the death of a *santero,* a ceremony called *el levantamiento del plato* (the raising of the dish) is performed. During this ceremony, an animal preferred by the *eledá,* or protector *oricha,* of the deceased, is sacrificed. At that time, the deceased is finally bidden farewell.

Chapter Summary

As already mentioned, the function of the Yoruban religion as a health service provider was one of the magnets that attracted people of non-Yoruban ancestry to Santería. This function was even more crucial in colonial Cuba, where medical services were scarce and inaccessible. Moreover, at that time medicine was not as advanced as it is at present. Later, as medical services improved and became more accessible, this religion continued to function as a complementary health delivery system by seeking supernatural support for the medical treatment involved and offering people with chronic disorders, depression, and other health problems a support system as an antidote to feelings of discomfort, despondency, and other forms of despair.

Santería's Rituals

Locus, Form, and Paraphernalia

In Nigeria, temples were erected to the orishas that were important in a specific region. In those temples priests and the oba, or local king, officiated. Family and individual shrines were kept in the homes for the specific needs of members of the family. In Cuba conditions changed dramatically. Africans were slaves; their religion did not enjoy official backing; it was denigrated—tolerated at best and persecuted at worst. Therefore, it was withdrawn from public view, its rituals and paraphernalia surviving in an ambiance of secrecy.

Temples

In Santería there are generally no buildings or temples erected specifically for worship or ceremonies. The cult centers called *ilé ocha* are mostly within the confines of the priest's home. The term comes from the Yoruban words ile (house) and osha (orisha).

In the *ilé ocha* three different parts are distinguished. The *Igbodú*, or sanctum, is the room where the secret esoteric rites are celebrated by the initiated. This part of the house cannot be used for secular, everyday purposes.[1] The *Eyá Aranla* is the big hall where the faithful meet. The *iban balo* is the court, or patio, where public ceremonies and drum festivals are held. Often during these drum festivals, when the gods are praised and asked to join in, the *orichas* come down, possess the believers, and dance with them.

In the *igbodu*, or sanctum, there are *canastilleros* (altars)[2] where the soup tureens or clay pots containing the sacred *otanes* (stones) are kept. The *otanes* serve as the foundation for the power of the *orichas.* As indicated previously, these stones are consecrated through the use of *omiero*, a powerful concoction made with twenty-one different herbs that are endowed with magical and medicinal properties. Earth from the cemetery, blood of sacrificed animals, and other ingredients are also used. The floor at the base of the altar that is covered with mats is called the *plaza.*[3] There, offerings of fruit, food, and money, and containers full of *chequeté* (a traditional beverage made of bitter orange, sugar cane syrup, and fresh coconut water) are placed.

Images

Statues and lithographs of Catholic saints associated with *orichas* are some-times used to represent them. However, no sacrifice is offered to them. Dolls dressed with the symbolic colors of the *santero's* or *santera's orichas* are also used to represent them and/or a protector spirit (the soul of a person who when alive was dedicated to the service of that *oricha*). Anthropomorphic wood-carved figurines are also used to represent the *orichas.*

Each *oricha* also "owns" specific objects as its symbols. For example, the double-bladed axe is a symbol of Changó; peacock feathers, coral ornaments, and fans are used to represent Ochún, the owner of the river; and iron objects are symbols of Ogún, the god of war and metals.

Sacred Stories or *Patakíes*[4]

Patakíes are sacred stories that narrate episodes about the origins of the world, the Supreme Being, the *orichas,* and legendary heroes and characters. They are of the greatest importance, because they carry messages regarding the char-acter, personality, attributes, vulnerabilities, and power of the *orichas.* Castel-lanos and Castellanos (1992 3:64–80) classify *patakíes* in the following cat-egories: a) cosmogonic myths, b) teogonic myths, c) anthropogonic myths, d) axiogonic myths, e) myths about religious values, f) myths with ethical teach-ing, g) myths that explain the natural world, h) myths that explain the social reality, and i) other myths and legends.

Patakíes are an important component of the *odus,* or different readings of the oracles. They convey messages concerning appropriate or inappropriate attitudes and behavior. When consulting the oracle, the diviners and the client are required to interpret the message in the story, or *pataki,* linked to a specific *odu,* and apply it to their own problem or situation. This represents the begin-ning of the diagnostic process.

Sacrifices

Sacrifice is as pivotal in Santería as it was in the religious practices of the Yo-ruba in Nigeria. The importance and meaning of sacrifice in the Yoruban reli-gion is clearly expressed by J. D. Y Peel (2000: 99):

> After divination, sacrifice. Sacrifice was at the heart of the devotional relationship in Yoruba religion: to "worship" a deity was to sacrifice (bo) to it, the generic word for sacrifice (ebo) being formed from it. Signifi-cantly one was not said to "bo" the Supreme Being, Olorun, since He was not sacrificed to. Christians and Muslims speak of their "serving"

(sin) Him. (One could also be said to sin an orisa, as well as to bo it). . . The act of sacrifice was much more central than the act of prayer, since prayers merely expressed what people wanted from their relationship with their god, whereas sacrifice actually constituted the relationship. Just as the giving of presents made and reaffirmed the civil community, so also through sacrifice did the reciprocal bonds between men and the gods become more real.

Sacrifices, or *ebó*, seal the alliance or pact between the *oricha* and the devotee. The *oricha/santo* and spirits are offered the specific cooked food, blood of animals, fruits, and other gifts that they particularly enjoy. In most instances, the offerings are meant to establish a state of communion with the supernatural entities. The believer may be soliciting or thanking the *santo* for a favor, or simply honoring an *oricha*. Also, the sacrifice is made to follow the advice of the oracles or to celebrate an important day. In these cases, the believers partake of the offerings. However, when animals are offered as scapegoats to satisfy an enraged *oricha* or to undo harm caused by witchcraft, the flesh cannot be eaten. In these cases, the carcass is disposed of according to ritual procedures.

Offerings must be made as frequently as possible so that the *orichas* will be pleased and will continue to protect the faithful. Each *oricha* favors a particular type of offering. The god of hunters, Ochosi, is most pleased when guinea hens are offered to him. Obatalá prefers land snails, and Osain, the owner of herbs, favors land turtles. The following *pataki* from a *santero*'s notebook explains the reason for animal sacrifices:

At the beginning there were very few human beings on the planet. They lived together in the same village under the leadership of a wise old man. Sometimes Olofin would come down to earth to speak to Babá Ndum, the chief, and to inquire about the whereabouts of his creatures. Everything was peace and harmony, until problems developed among the women of the village. There were old women, tired with age, who could do only a little farming, and the younger ones would have to make up for the work the old ones could not do. "These old women hardly work, and we are tired," complained the young ones. Their husbands and Babá Ndum believed that the old women were exhausted and that the young ones should do their work. This did not please the young women at all.

Early in the morning, when the rooster sang, the women would leave their homes. They carried large clay pots on their heads to fetch water from a clear stream. The village was on top of a hill close to the sun, and the stream was at the edge of that hill. The old women walked slowly, and the swift young women arrived before them. After filling their pots in the stream they jumped into the brook to swim and play. When the old women arrived, the water would be murky and muddy. The older women would plead with the younger ones, but to no avail. They would go back home and complain to their husbands. One morning, one old woman threw her pot at the head of one of the swimmers, and a fight broke out. The old women were bruised and battered. During several days similar episodes were repeated.

Babá Ndum, the warriors, and the men called a village meeting to put an end to these incidents. After much debating, they decided that the old and young women would take turns. The following day the experiment started, and the old women were allowed to go first, while the young ones were scheduled to go first the day after. To everybody's amazement, no one went to the brook that day, since no woman was willing to admit that she was old. They would let others go first, and these in turn, would not go first. Consequently, the fight started all over again.

Babá Ndum, despairing, decided to call Olofin. He climbed the highest mountain and addressed him: "Olofin, I come to you because peace and order no longer reign in my village. The women don't obey me, and the men won't listen. "Why?" asked Olofin. "Oh, Olofin, you created men, and that is very good. But you also created women, and that is not so good. One can reason with men, but no one can understand women." He told Olofín what was happening, and Olofin came down to the village without making his presence known. The following morning Olofin watched from the top of a mountain as the women started their daily routine. Afterward, he called a meeting and said, "I came here to restore order among my children. There are too many people living together, and since you have disobeyed me, peace no longer exists." The men answered, "It was not us; it was the women who disobeyed you." Olofin replied, "Men are men; women are women, and that cannot be changed. Let some of you move with your families forward, some move backward, some to the right, and some to the left."

The men anxiously asked, "Who will take the animals? They belong to all of us." Olofin said, "May each man take a male and a female of each species. What is left I will place in the wilderness."

Immediately a new fight broke out, because each person wanted to take the best animals. Olofin threatened to kill all the animals, but Babá Ndum interceded, and Olofin forgave them under one condition: "Sacrifice the animals to me, their spirits in exchange for yours." The men took out their knives and killed all the animals, the deer, the hens, and the roosters, all. With the blood of the animals a large lake was formed.

"What shall we do now for food?" they asked the Supreme Being. "Go and get your pots. Fill them with the blood and take them to the site where you will start your new village. Spill the blood in the woods nearby, and wait for the reward of your sacrifice."

They followed his orders and waited anxiously for the results. On the fourth day, at dawn, they heard the rooster's song coming from the woods. They followed the rooster's crow and came to the middle of the wilderness, where they found the forest populated with animals of all varieties.

Since that day, sacrifices are offered to the *orichas* in gratitude for the bounties received and to divert the fury of Olofin away from human beings who continue to fight among themselves. (Cros Sandoval [1975:67–68])

Music

Music and dance are an integral part of Afro-Cuban rituals. These artistic expressions play an important role in all ceremonies, as the *orichas* are likely to possess their children and come to join the faithful during ceremonies. The richness and complexity of Santería's rituals have been a magnet for new followers. Many people feel attracted to the engaging drumming, dancing, and singing that are integral parts of the ceremonies.

DRUMMING

Most of the time the drum festivals, called, *toque* or *plante de santo*, take place on Saturday afternoons. Each participant dresses in the color of his or her *oricha* and sits with the others in the form of a semi-circle. Drums are sacred because the *orichas* and the spirits of the dead speak through them. Drums represent more than simple musical instruments that mark the beat at festivals. They are the true voices of the gods and the spirits.

Drums are called *ilú*, but once they are consecrated and possess supernatural power, they are called Aña. The *olosain*, a priest consecrated to the worship of Osain, the owner of magical and medicinal herbs, is the only one with the power to consecrate drums and confer the status of Aña, the secret power and spirit that defends them from their enemies. The sacred drums are receptacles of the *oricha* Aña. They are called *batá*.[5] In Yorubaland the *bata* are the drums used by worshipers of Shango and Egungun. In Cuba the *batá* are used not only to honor Changó and the Egun, or ancestor spirits, but they are played for all of the *orichas*. Furthermore, it is required that all initiates be presented to them shortly after initiation. According to Brown (2003: 64), two African-born slaves, the master drummer Ño Filomeno García, called Atandá and Ño Juan el Cojo, known as Añabí (reputedly a *babalao* [diviner], *olosainista* [herbalist], and *oní-ilú* [master of batá drums]), made the first set of consecrated *batá* drums in Cuba in the 1830s.

The *batá* drums are as follows: a) the *konkolo,* or *omele,* is the smallest in size and plays the highest note; it belongs to Elegguá; b) the *itotele,* or *omele enku,* is medium in size and follows the rhythm marked by the largest one; it belongs to Yemayá; c) the *iyá* (mother), the largest one, belongs to Changó. When the drums are playing, the *iyá* is always placed in the middle, the *omele* to the right of the *iyá,* and the *itotele* to the left. An *osainista,* who knows how to plead to a tree to request permission, is the only person who can cut the wood used to build drums. Drums are generally made of cedar, palm, or mahogany. Each drum has two openings known as *aguo,* which are covered with skins of male goats or deer.

It is believed that drums have souls; therefore, after they are manufactured and consecrated they are given a name such as *iraguo meta,* meaning "three stars." They are propitiated with prayers and sacrifices to renew their supernatural powers and secrets. It is believed that they play and sound better when properly fed, thereby enabling better communication with the *orichas.* Also, before a festival, sacrifices need to be offered to Osain, who plays such an important role in the creation of the drums.

Drums speak to worshipers and transmit messages from the *orichas.* Drums salute and greet the arrival of priests, who are required to pay homage and to bow and kiss them respectfully. Drums are used to call the gods. Each *oricha* is greeted with his or her own specific beat. As soon as the person is mounted by an *oricha,* the god comes and bows before the sacred instruments. During the initiation ceremony, the *iyawó* (initiate) is presented to the drums and is expected to fall into a trance and be possessed by his *oricha* while dancing to the beat of the drums.

Drum festivals, or *güemileres,* are offered to an *oricha* on the feast day of the Catholic saint with whom the *oricha* is associated. Also, they are offered when the *oricha* requests it, when a petition for assistance has been granted by the *oricha,* or at any time the oracle advises. In any case, drums are always used for communication with the gods.

At the beginning of a drum festival, an *oro seco* is played. This is a series of drum solos that are not accompanied by singing or dancing. This *oro seco* is important because it is dedicated to the spirits of the dead, who are always present by the side of the *oricha* to whom the festival is offered. This *Oro* should be played before noon and, during the playing, the Oricha Aña directly talks to the dead and to the other *orichas.*

After the *oro seco,* the festival begins, following a prearranged order. As the drums are played, the *orichas* are invited to come down and join the faithful, taking possession of their children. The sacred drums can be played while there is daylight. Then they must be retired. Nighttime is when the spirits of the dead dance, and bad luck would result if the sacred drums were played then. However, if the party continues into the night, secular, or profane drums, can be played without fear of harm.

Sometimes a special drum festival is played for the dead. This drum performance, called Egungun, is part of the ceremony called *el levantamiento del plato* (raising of the dish), which is intended to bid farewell to the dead on the first anniversary of their death.

Drums are used in nearly every religious ceremony. They function in *juegos*, or suites of three. The tones and sizes of the drums are different according to the ethnic group of origin. In Cuba *batá* drums (originally from the Oyo area) were prevalent in the city of Havana. In the city of Matanzas, *arará* drums (originally from the former French Dahomey) and *yesá* drums (from the Ilesha region in Yorubaland) were played.

DANCING

Public, liturgical dances take place during the *güemilere* (drum festival). During these religious festivals dancing and singing follow the beat of the drums. The drum festivals are also called *bembés.*

The most beautiful, expressive dances and drumming of Santería's religious rituals are part of the *oro del eya aranla* liturgy. This *oro* is celebrated in the *eya aranla*, the hall in the house temple that is used to carry out festivities that include drumming, singing, and dancing. In the *oro del eya aranla*, the *orichas*, one by one, are invoked and greeted with the *batá* drums. Each god has its own particular drumbeat, or rhythm, and a distinctive song or prayer that a soloist, or *akpuon*, intones. The chorus answers and follows the soloist, while the dances, characteristic of the deity to whom the prayer is dedicated, are performed.

The first *oricha* invoked is Elegguá, the messenger of the gods. The first song, drumbeat, or prayer has to be addressed to him. Then, in a very strict order, follows Ogún, Ochosi, and Oricha Oko. The next to last drumbeat is dedicated to the *oricha* to whom the festival is offered. The closing beat, however, is always for Elegguá. After the *oro* ends, different rhythms of various *orichas* are played to entice the *orichas* to come down and dance with the faithful. These drumbeats are long and insistent and are propitious for the induction of trance.

When the god finally comes down, the *caballo* (Spanish word for "horse," which is used to mean a mounted or possessed person) is stripped of all his clothing and ornaments. He is then dressed with the robe and ornaments characteristic of the *oricha* that has possessed him or her. In addition, the instrument and symbols of his *eledá,* or protector *oricha*, are given to him so that the incarnated god can perform the pantomimic dances that are the actualization of his mythological life.

The *oro* of the *igbodu* takes place in the sanctum of the temple reserved only for the initiated. It consists of only drumming. There is no singing and dancing to this *oro* as is the case with the other ones.

The *oro* of voices also takes place in the *igbodu.* This very secret ritual occurs when a novice is initiated. As its name implies, the drums are not played; there is no dancing; there is only singing.

SINGING

The *suyeres* are the songs and prayers of the *güemilere* and are a most essential and integral part of the Afro-Cuban rituals. These recitations are the most appropriate ways to greet and invoke the gods. References to the lives, attributes, and powers of the deities are chanted. These *suyeres* are normally recited in Lucumí, the name of the liturgical or ritual language, and also the name by which this religion is popularly known.

African languages did not prevail as a means of communication in Cuban slaves' households or enclaves except in *cabildos*. Various factors account for this loss, such as the fragility of the slave family, the rarity of slaves' mating with members of their own ethnic group, and the fact that the slaves were often quartered with other slaves of different linguistic backgrounds.

Even though Yoruban words, phrases, and intonation are discernible in Lucumí, the latter is far from being a dialect of the Yoruba. It consists of remnants of Yoruban language and dialects influenced by Spanish *bozal*, a broken Spanish spoken by recently arrived or isolated African slaves. Nevertheless, Lucumí prevailed in such form as the sacred language. The *orichas* speak and are spoken to in Lucumí. *Santeros* and *santeras* need to learn it, and those who are most knowledgeable in Lucumí enjoy great prestige. However, they do not know its linguistic structure and only understand the general meaning of the prayers, songs, and invocations.

The *akpuon*, or soloist, is the person who introduces the songs of the *oro.* Elegguá is always the first to be invoked. The first and required *suyere* dedicated to this *oricha*, as recorded by Rómulo Lachatañeré (1939: 184) goes as follows:

Echú, *oh, oh, oh.*
Eleguá *a la eeeeeh* . . .
Eleguá *moforibaale,*
Eleguá *a la eeeeeh* . . .
Echú, *oh, oh, oh* . . .

The *güemilere* ends with this last *suyere* (Lachatañeré 1938: 195–96), which, like the first one, is dedicated to Eleggúa:

Coima coimani yacoima
Coima coimani yacoima
Eleguá *nita laro yo socúo*
Eh, eh! . . . *Nita laroyo socúo eh!*
Agó Eleguá *eh!*
Agó Eleguá *eh!*

Chapter Summary

Despite adverse circumstances, Afro-Cubans were successful in preserving and transmitting complex symbolic rituals, engaging ritual music and dancing, and esoteric *suyeres* (songs and prayers). These aspects of Santería attracted new followers. After attending their first ceremony, for example, some participants have confided to me how bewildered and excited they felt while experiencing these "bizarre," yet orderly rituals. Also, some expressed surprise at the unexpected confidence, based on years of extensive training, of *santeros* as compared to *curanderos*[6] and other indigenous healers, whose performances appear to be based more on improvisation and charisma. It is precisely the degree of professionalism in rituals, music, and divination that indicates that *santeros* are well-trained priests.

I am of the opinion that the extremely complicated rituals, the varied paraphernalia, and the necessity of believers to learn the sacred language, the songs, the proper steps and rhythms of the sacred dancing, the intricate meaning of all the symbolic paraphernalia, the exotic legends, the many taboos, and the richness of the symbolism—in other words the need to constantly learn how to perform and interact in this religion—is an important magnet that attracts people to it.[7] Constantly, believers refer to their religion in the following manner: "Es muy linda" (It is very beautiful).

Oracles

Oracles representing processes of divination are the means by which followers learn the wishes, recommendations, recriminations, and desires of the *orichas* and of the dead. The oracles are approached for all types of reasons. Consultation may be oriented toward identifying the cause of disease and its necessary remedies. Oracles are sought out in order to make decisions concerning significant life events such as weddings, journeys, business ventures, and love affairs. They are also consulted to learn about a person's *oricha*, whether it should be *asentado* (seated) or not, whether sacrifices should be offered, and, if needed, what particular types of sacrifice. Consultation of the oracles is very important in the lives of Santería's believers.

According to Robert F. Thompson (1976: CH5/5),

> Consider, then, the significance of divination in Yorubaland: man, in a state of anxiety, confronted by a universe of disordered energy presided over by Eshu, consults the diviner who brings him into a realm of vital confidence. Suddenly the suppliant finds the universe is actually divided into sixteen segments, the *odu*, and he is pointed in the direction of one of these segments where he finds his problem outlined with essential focus, refined and refined by further divination. I will not go as far as Frobenius and say that the divination tray is the most beautiful of the objects of West African antiquity, but I do affirm the implication, within its balanced structure, of an intellectual system that makes fate visible, as upon a screen, where man views his problems with a clarity not previously obtained.

Since oracles are so influential in the life of the worshippers, one of the most important functions of *santeros* is divination. In the capacity of diviner, the priest acts as an intermediary between the gods and human beings. The two most popular oracles are the dilogún, or oracle of the shells, and the oracle of the coconuts. These oracles can be interpreted by all *santeros,* and all of the *orichas* speak through them.

The coconut

The oracle of the coconut is also known by the name Biagué. The following *pataki* from a *santero*'s notebook narrates the story of Biagué, the first person who learned to interpret the coconuts.

Once upon a time Olofin came to this world to see how his creatures were doing. Strolling around he saw a beautiful and gracious green tree. He said to the tree: "What are you doing?"

The tree answered: "I swing with the wind, that's all."

"It is a pity," said Olofin. "Since you are so tall and beautiful, you should be doing something better. What would you like to do?"

"I don't know. I believe that the other trees already give all the fruit, wood, and nourishment necessary in the land."

"Oh," said Olofin, "I think that we can still give you something to do. Since each of the *orichas* has a fruit, which belongs to them, why not make the fruit of your pendant the only one that belongs to all the *orichas* and is used by all men? How would you like that? We will call the fruit Obí Guí Guí."

The coconut was pleased. "Thank you, Olofin, for this honor and privilege."

The following day the creator *oricha*, Obatalá, called a meeting of all the *orichas*. When they had gathered he told them: "Here is Obí Guí Guí, the coconut tree and son of Olofin, who, by order of Olofin, was created so that all *orichas* make use of it. Pieces of its fruit will have a meaning that I will teach you."

This is how the coconut became the means by which gods can find out the will of the creator.

Sometime later, a man called Biagué learned to interpret the coconut. Biagué taught his natural son Adoto how to read the meaning of the coconut. Biagué also had two adopted sons. When he died, his adoptive children took the inheritance and left Adoto completely destitute. Bitter and frustrated, Adoto held on, tenaciously and jealously, to the secret of the coconut.

Later, the chief of the village decided to settle the matter of the inheritance because public clamor was aroused by it. He asked Biagué's adopted children to bring proof of their claim and found they could bring none. Adoto was asked to consult the oracle, and the oracle pointed to Adoto as the sole heir to Biagué's estate.

Adoto was thus the first man to use the coconut for divining the wishes of the *orichas*. He, in turn, taught others to use it to search for the truth. (Cros Sandoval 1975:76)

Another *pataki* narrates the origin of the oracle of the coconut:

Eleggúa had noticed Obí was pure of heart, modest, and simple, as are the just. Olofin made his skin, his heart, and his entrails white. He was placed high on top of a frond of the palm tree. Then Obí turned very vain.

Eleggúa, the messenger of the gods and servant of Olofin, was placed at the service of Obí. Eleggúa, who sees everything and is everywhere, promptly realized that a change had taken place in Obí.

One day Obí gave a sumptuous party. He ordered Eleggúa to invite all his friends. Eleggúa knew all of them very well. He knew some that were the most important people in the world, the Akbobko, the Olorososo, the Tobi Tobi, the Omisose, the beautiful, and the clean. The poor and the ugly, the miserable, and even the deformed were also Obí's friends. Everybody was a friend of Obí, [but] Obí had turned vain and that arrogance and sick pride had changed his personality. To teach him a lesson Eleggúa decided to invite to the party not only the rich and beautiful as Obí expected, but also the pauper, the ugly, and the sick.

The night of the party arrived, and Obí, proud and full of great expectations, readied himself to welcome his guests. He was shocked when he saw the indigent mob that had come to his party. He furiously demanded:

"Who invited you to my party?"

"Eleggúa invited us on your behalf," they said.

Obí angrily reprimanded them for having dared come to his house in such poor attire. "Get out of here, all of you," he shouted.

The poor, the ugly, and the beaten of this world left Obí's house sick with shame. Eleggúa also left with them.

Time passed by. One day Olofin sent Eleggúa to this world with a message for Obí.

"I refuse to do this service for Obí," Eleggúa said. "Obí has changed. He is no longer the friend of all men. Obí is full of arrogance and has cut ties with all who suffer."

Olofin, disguised as a beggar, went to Obí's house. "Will you give me some food and shelter?" Olofin begged Obí.

"How dare you come into my presence in such rags?" Obí reprimanded Olofin.

Olofin, no longer feigning his voice, called: "Obí, Obí." Obí, surprised and ashamed, knelt before Olofin. "Please forgive me, Olofin."

Olofin replied, "Obí, you were just, and that is why I made your heart white and gave you a body worthy of your heart. Now you are full of arrogance and pride. To punish you and make you reconsider, you will keep white entrails, but you will come down from the heights to roll on the ground and become dirty. From now on you will have to serve all men and all gods." (Cros Sandoval 1975:76–78)

This story explains how the coconut became the most popular of all the oracles, intended to provide service to all men, *orichas,* and priests.

To consult the coconut oracle, the *santero* breaks a dry coconut, chooses four pieces, and rinses them in water. Using his nails he cuts off smaller segments from the four corners of the four pieces to total the ritual number of the *oricha.* For example, if Ochún, the *oricha* of the river, is being consulted, five small pieces should be taken off and placed in her soup tureen, since five is the number of Ochún. If Changó is being consulted the number of small pieces should be four.

Prayers and songs are intoned to honor Olodumare, the Supreme Being, the departed souls, the godfather and the godmother of the *santero,* and, if the client has been initiated, his godparents as well.

The *santero* next asks permission of the *orichas,* of all deceased *santeros* and *santeras,* of Biagué (the man who first learned to interpret the coconut), and, finally, the permission of the coconut. The four pieces of coconut are passed over the head, shoulders, breasts, hands, knees, and feet of the client while the priest begs the coconut to be truthful. Then, the four pieces are cast on the floor. According to the way they land, with the white, meaty side up or down, five different combinations, or figures, are formed. These combinations are the following: *alafia, otagüe, eyife, okana sode,* and *oyekun.*[1]

Alafia, which is also known by the numeral 4, is the figure formed when the four pieces fall with the white, concave side up. This combination, or figure, means happiness, well-being, health, and prosperity. Whatever question has been asked, the *alafia* answers it affirmatively. For example, if the question is, "Should I go on the trip that I have planned?" the reply of the *alafia* is "yes." However, for complete certainty, the question should be asked again. If *alafia* appears twice in a row, assurance and certainty would be the interpretation.

In some cases, when no specific question has been asked, the diviner will transmit to the client the advice and counsel of the Warrior Gods (Elegguá, Ogún, and Ochosi) and of Obatalá, Orúnla, and Babalú Ayé. They are the ones who speak through this figure or letter. *Alafia* says:

> The warrior *orichas* Elegguá, Ogún, Ochosi and Osun say that you should put them inside your house by your front door for your protection. No other *oricha* should be placed there, because that place belongs only to them.
> Obatalá advises you to make a supplication to the head with cocoa oil, candles, and pulverized eggshell to get rid of your constant headaches.

You should dress in white often, especially on Thursdays. Obatalá says that you should not eat white beans or pigeons, that you should not pay any attention to malicious gossip, because he is going to protect you.

Orúnla advises you not to gamble so much. He says that there is a standing war between Ochún and Yemayá because both of them want you for their child.

Babalú Ayé claims that you owe him something; that you are always willing to make promises that you never carry out. He wants you to offer him some dry wine, some bread, and some raw peanuts. You should put them in a gourd with water in some corner of the house. Babalú Ayé wants to protect you or some relative of yours against some infectious disease, which is threatening you. (Cros Sandoval 1975:78–79)

Otagüe, or the numeral 3, is the figure formed when, after the four pieces of coconut are cast, three fall with the white, meaty side up, and only one falls with the dry shell up. Ochún, Changó, and Yemayá speak through this combination. *Otagüe* means "It is possible." However, for the sake of certainty, the questions should be asked again. *Otagüe* says:

Ochún advises you to go see a doctor, because you are suffering from your intestines or your ovaries. You should bear in mind that you are Ochún's daughter and you cannot go to the hospital. You should also know you would not be able to solve any problem or have a happy marriage until you are initiated. She says that she is going to give you a good number to play in the lottery.

Changó says that he is your father, but that you have completely neglected him and think of him only when you need him; that is, when it thunders; that you believe you are great, but you are wrong. You are not a lucky, beautiful, black man, as you think you are, and good things in life don't grow on trees. He advises you to offer him a red rooster at his throne by the palm tree. He also advises you to freshen up your head with six of his herbs.

Yemayá advises you to be on guard, because someone wants to take your body waste to use it against you and make you sick in the stomach. She says that you should wear in her honor a particular garment made of blue and white checkered gingham. She believes that you should not threaten anyone. She also asks you to take a watermelon to the sea and offer it to her. (Cros Sandoval 1975: 79)

Eyife, or the numeral 2, is the highest letter or figure of the coconut. It is formed when two pieces of coconut fall with the meaty, white sides up and two with the dry, convex part showing. *Eyife* is an emphatic "yes." It signifies an invariable, affirmative response to any question brought before the oracle. The question should not be asked again. Elegguá, Ochosi, and Ogún speak through this letter. *Eyife* states the following:

> Elegguá says that you have to take care of him, and he will open the doors of prosperity and good luck. He requests that you offer him some candy and money and place them in one of the corners of your home. You should also offer some *ñame* (yam) (*Dioscorea alata*) to the Elegguá that you have behind your front door. Elegguá also says that the spirit of a dead person is after you and will bring you problems.
>
> Ochosi says that you should be very careful with the judicial system; you might get into problems with the authorities. He says that you should be very careful because you are the type of person who sometimes believes in the *orichas* and sometimes not; that one of these days you are going to have the proof you need. Ogún wants you to offer him a rooster so that he will open doors that are now closed to you. (Cros Sandoval 1975: 79–80)

Okana, or the numeral 1, is formed when three meaty sides of the coconut fall down and only one up. This combination says "no" to any question asked. It announces tragedy. You have to be very careful and open your ears and your eyes. Something urgent has to be done to prevent the disaster that is coming. Oba, Ikú, Oyá, and Yewá speak through the *okana*. *Okana* says:

> Oba advises you to go to a *babalao* for help and to offer her a dishpan of water with her herbs.
>
> Ikú advises you not to be afraid of the dead. You have the faculty of seeing and talking to them and you should develop those faculties.
>
> Oyá says to pay attention to your dreams. She says that you are going to be very sick, very close to death.
>
> Yewá (Yeguá) advises you not to hit children on the head, and don't let children play in your house and make noise. That will attract tragedy. She thinks that you should not let anyone touch your head because they will harm you. You should only allow a hairdresser initiated in Santería to touch your head. (Cros Sandoval 1975: 80)

Oyekun, or the numeral 0, is the figure formed when the four white sides are down. It is the worst figure of the coconuts. It announces death. The *oyekun* is dreaded, and when it is formed *santeros* light a candle to the spirits, touch their breasts, and say: "Olufina." Then, they touch the floor and say: "Mo fin kare godo godo." Oyá, Naná Burukú, Ikú, and Aganyú speak through the *oyekun*. *Oyekun* says:

Oyá Yansá says that she has been waiting for you for a long time. Once as a little child you got sick, and, also, later as an adult. Each time you escaped from her, but now she is opening the doors to the cemetery and is waiting for you. She says that you should never have been born, that you came to this world and because Ikú has always been after you, many people close to you have died.

Ikú says not to bother to go to the hospital since no physician can help you.

Naná Burukú says that you have some bad spirits hanging around you, and that is why you are a hopeless case. You should be very careful where you go at night.

Aganyú hopes that you will go to some Ocha priest, who should attempt the impossible to keep you from the disaster that is coming your way. (Cros Sandoval 1975:80)

The dilogún or oracle of the shells

The dilogún, or oracle of the shells, is very popular in Cuba and in Africa. The reason for this popularity is that the dilogún and the coconut are oracles that can be used by all *iyalochas/santeras* and *babalochas/santeros.*

The oracle of the shells, according to Wande Abimbola (1997: 94), precedes Ifá, which is the most prestigious of all oracles. However, in Cuba people believe that it is a derivative of Ifá, since, according to myths, the Dilogún is based on what the river goddess, Ochún, learned about divination while she was associated with Ifá.

In Cuba, the dilogún is more important, is more popular, and has more information than its counterpart in Nigeria. Ezequiel Torres' (March 2002) explanation is that, at first, there were not enough *babalaos* in Cuba. Thus, many responsibilities had to be delegated to the *oriatés.* According to his version, a considerable amount of the information stored in legends, stories, and anecdotes that was part of the repertory of the *babalaos'* divination systems was passed on to *santeros.* This legacy enriched the depth and scope of the repertory of the oracle of the shells, or dilogún, that is used by all *santeros*; men, women, and male homosexuals alike. *Babalao* Luisito (May 2000) and John Guerra (oso roso) (June 2001) claim that *babalaos* are very protective about the secrets of Ifá and that this story could not possibly be true.

On the other hand, according to widespread opinion and Ezequiel Torres (March 2002), a *santero* called Obadimelli, stole some of the verses, myths, and stories from the oracles of the *babalaos* and incorporated them into the dilogún. Along that line, David H. Brown's informants told him (2003: 10) that

Octavio Samar Obadimelli reconfigured the dilogún on the model of Ifá and was probably the first modern *oriaté* (2003: 12).

The *babalao* Jorge Torres (January 2005) says that *oriatés* might have taken the 16 *odus* from a *libreta de babalao* that had been circulating. He thinks that even though the information contained in the sixteen *odus* of the dilogún is very valuable, it does not compare in depth and knowledge to the 256 *odus* of Ifá. According to him Ifá contains all the knowledge of Regla de Ocha.

The dilogún is comprised of sixteen cowry shells whose bottoms or convex parts have been removed so that when they are tossed on a mat on the floor during divination they remain stable with their natural openings up or down. A one-inch-long shell called the *ayé*; a *guacalote* seed called *egue-ayo*; a small black stone, or *otá*; and a human vertebra are all used. Sixteen *odus,* or combinations, can be formed. *Santeros* can only interpret the first twelve *odus*; the last four have to be interpreted by *babalaos.*

At the beginning, the *santero* asks the client to write his name and birthday on a piece of paper. Immediately thereafter, prayers are said to Olodumare, to the *egun,* or departed souls, and to the *orichas.* Then, the priest takes the shells in his hands and blows his breath on them to give them *aché,* or supernatural power. He asks the client to do the same thing. The shells are then tossed onto a mat, and, according to how many of them fall with their natural opening side up, different signs, called letters, or *odus,* are formed. Each *odu* has a proper name and several stories full of advice that generally narrate the life or adventures of the *orichas* or some legendary heroes. The verses and stories of the *odus* contain the ethical and dogmatic foundations of the Afro-Cuban religion. The *odus'* narratives reflect the religious philosophy of Afro-Cubans and are the most reliable sources of oral traditions.[2]

The *santero* should know all the stories associated with each *odu* and should choose, among them, the one that is most relevant to the life and situation of the client. The *odus'* advice is generally conveyed in popular idiomatic expressions that have a moral content. The *odus* also prescribe to the client the way to deal with the problems confronting him or her. Usually a sacrifice is advised, or the fulfillment of some religious obligation. These *odus* are sometimes illustrated by the popular idioms or proverbs:

> *Ore odi me ta kosi ofonia guma.* (Three-days-old friend doesn't show us the bottom).
> *Guede Guede lobi ina guede lobi oromo.* (Wherever fire was born so was the rainbow born; where the crippled were born so were the not crippled).
> *Ariwo tiloguense.* (If you don't want any noise do not carry dry palm fronds).

Alagu de oni. (Double-edged knife).

Gaisoyu elede. (Don't try to be up front; the pig is the one that carries his muzzle in front of him).

Ore guma ota ku mi. (The best friend makes the worst enemy). (Cros Sandoval 1975: 82)

There are two kinds of *odus*, or letters/figures. The senior *odus* are the numbers 1, 2, 3, 4, 8, 10, 12, 13, 14, 15, and 16. The junior *odus* are the numbers 5, 6, 7, 9, and 11. The first four *odus* that are formed during the divining process are written on a piece of paper and are read to the client. The priest hands the client the small black stone and the *cascarilla*, or white eggshell composite. The client rubs them and keeps one of them in his right hand, the other one in his left hand. These objects are called *ibo-gue, aguante,* or *sujete* (to hold).

The shells are tossed several times. If the *odu* that is formed is a senior *odu*, the priest asks the client to open the left hand. If the *odu* formed is a minor one, the client is asked to open the right hand. If the chosen hand holds the *cascarilla* (white eggshell composite), it is said to carry *ire,* or good luck, and the client is told anecdotes or stories that are connected with that specific *odu* that are omens of well-being. If, instead, the hand holds the black stone, that *odu* is said to carry *osobo,* or illness, death, and other bad news. Then, the anecdotes that announce tragedy and disgrace are applicable. After the divination process has ended, the *santero* asks the *orichas,* the *eledá* (guardian spirit), and the souls of the departed whether the client should make some offerings. The first twelve *odus,* or figures, of the dilogún that are interpreted by *santeros* are provided below. These are:

OKANASORDE (1)

Okanasorde is the letter, or figure, formed when only one cowry falls with its natural opening upside. When the first throw of the cowries forms this *odu,* the shells have to be put immediately into a gourd with water, and after they are rinsed the water is thrown on the street. Once this procedure is done, the cowries are tossed again, and the *santero* asks the *odu* that is formed: "If there is noise where does it come from?" Then a piece of raw meat covered with palm oil is passed over the body, the forehead, the neck, the shoulders, the hands, and the knees of all the people who are present. Once finished, the meat is immediately cast onto the street so that a dog will take it. Elegguá, Ogún, Olofin, and Ikú speak through *okanasorde,* which says:

> Pull your ear and listen attentively. If you are not doing anything wrong, make sure you don't, since it is obvious that you intend to do it. Don't curse; and, if there is somebody sick at your home, take that person

immediately to the doctor. Be very careful, because it seems that that person is in danger.

Okanasorde recommends as *ebó*, or sacrifice, a rooster, a guinea fowl, two pigeons, bee honey, two *jutías* (rodents),[3] smoked fish, roast corn, and two coconuts. (Cros Sandoval 1975: 83)

EYIOKO (2)

Eyioko is formed when, after the cowries are tossed, only two shells fall with their natural openings up. Through *eyioko* speak the Ibeyi, Ochosi, Elegguá, Obatalá, and Changó. *Eyioko* says:

A person who is not well should leave the place where he or she is living in order to find contentment, luck, and health. Before leaving the house a supplication is made to avoid trouble with the law and secure happiness. That person has *jimaguas* (identical twins) in his family and should not trust anybody, because they are watching him to betray him. That person has to be careful, because he is hot headed, and his *eledá* is claiming him.

Eyioko recommends as *ebó* (offerings) two pigeons, a rooster, two birds, two coconuts, and two eggs. The client should also buy a small chair where he should sit and pray every day. The chair should be placed behind the front door. (Cros Sandoval 1975: 83–84)

OGUNDA (3)

Ogunda is formed when, after tossing the cowries, three shells fall with the natural openings up. Through *ogunda* speak Ogún, Ochosi, Obatalá, and Olofin, who say the following:

You intend to break somebody's skull with an iron bar, because you feel threatened and pressured by Ogún. You feel defenseless, because Ogún says that you have done something wrong and that the police might catch you. You are going to find yourself in the middle of many difficulties. Don't drink, because that makes you feel worse, and you will be more compulsive. Don't argue or fight with anybody, not even with your wife, because she will curse you, and the curse will befall you. There are three persons who are constantly fighting, because each of them believes that he or she has the right to something desired by all three. Everyone wants to give orders. Be very careful for whom you do favors, because many people are going to pay with false coins. Tears will turn into laughter, when something that was lost is found.

This letter recommends as offerings fresh fish, rubbish, and a rooster. (Cros Sandoval 1975:84)

IROSO (4)

Iroso is formed when, after tossing the sixteen cowries, four fall with their natural openings up. Olokun, Changó, Ochosi, Orúnmila, and the Ibeyi speak through this *odu*. They say:

> You have to be very careful because there is a person with a malicious tongue who has very bad intentions. This person is very nosy and likes to cause quarrels and wants to cause trouble to you and the people you love. This person never does good deeds and wants to cause you problems with the police. Do not pay any attention to this person. Be very careful with a person who is sick; the ailment might be contagious, and family or friends who catch it might die. Be very careful, because you might be robbed; or you might be tricked and lose your happiness. If you do not have any money today do not complain, since the *santos* might give you some tomorrow.
>
> The *ebó*, or offerings, prescribed by this *odu* is a chick, an arrow, a stick, three stones, lard without salt, and a *jutía* (opossum-like rodent). (Cros Sandoval 1975:84–85)

OCHE (5)

When five cowry shells fall with their natural openings up, the *odu* known as *oche* is formed. Through *oche* speak Ochún, Olofin, Orúnmila, and Elegguá. *Oche* says:

> You are the son of Ochún. You are very lucky; however, things don't go your way. All your plans fail. It seems that everything is going well, and suddenly everything is upside down. You are very unstable. Many times you are perfectly fine and, suddenly, you feel like crying. You are going to have to be initiated sooner or later. All that happens to you are trials placed in your way by the Virgin of Charity. Do not mess around. There is a person in your family who died, and you should offer a mass for his or her soul. If you have promised something to the Virgin of Charity and have not yet paid, the time is up. You are a nervous person. Rub your head with your two hands from the front to the back during the day and at night also. You have promised something to Ochún and have not kept your promise. You are going to have to offer a mass to the soul of that family member who needs it.
>
> *Oche*'s *ebó* is five fish, five hens, five pumpkins, five peanuts, and five parrot feathers. The client should take a bath with yellow flowers and make a supplication with the wooden bar that closes the front door of one's home. The client should have many things made of white cloth and

offer Elegguá a mouse and smoked fish. Then, the client should play the lottery. (Cros Sandoval 1975:86)

OBARA (6)

When six shells fall with their natural openings up, the *odu* known as *obara* is formed. Changó, Ochún, and Elegguá speak through this *odu* and say:

> You are an ill-reputed person. Your money turns to salt and water. You are a person who goes around naked and is not capable of seeing yourself. You lie constantly. Lies become true to you, and the truth becomes lies. People have to lie to you in order for you to believe them. You should not argue with anybody, especially older people. You should not help anyone pick up something from the floor because that person will advance and you will go backward. You would like to get into business, which is a good idea if you pay attention to things and make offerings. Then, things will go well. Pay attention to your wife or husband and treat her or him well. Don't wear red clothes; dress only in white.
>
> *Obara* recommends the following offerings: two roosters, sixteen pumpkins, red material, candles, coconuts, guinea fowl, and a piece of material from the dress you are wearing now. (Cros Sandoval 1975:87)

ODI (7)

Odi is the *odu* formed when seven cowries fall with their natural openings up. Yemayá, Ochún, Ogún, and Elegguá speak through *odi* and say:

> *Odi* is where the hole was opened for the first time. It is fear and death.
>
> You are a very nervous person. You don't sleep well, and you are restless in bed while sleeping, dreaming about dead people. You see them at night. If your mother is not dead, be very careful. If she gets sick, it is possible that she might die. There are three persons who are interested in you. One of them is white; the other one has white hair; and the third one is always gossiping about you. Do not pay attention to the person who advises you to get in trouble with other people. That person wants to harm you. Do not eat or drink in anybody's home. Be very careful; you might have a blood infection or problems with your eyesight. Pay attention to your dreams. You have the faculty to see your enemies while dreaming.
>
> The offerings recommended by *odi* are a gourd, a land turtle, a hen, a couple of pigeons for Echú, two ears of corn, and different kinds of beans. (Cros Sandoval 1975:87–88)

EYEUNLE (8)

When eight shells fall with the natural openings up, the *odu* is called *eyeunle*. *Obatalá* and all the other *orichas* speak through *eyeunle*. *Eyeunle* says that the head carries the body, so you should use yours.

> You are the son of Obatalá, the king of all the *orichas* and the owner of all the heads. You are a very noble person. You are too good. If people don't give you the credit you deserve, it's your own fault for being too good. If they have not stolen something from you, be very careful, they might steal something. A few nights ago you had a nightmare that worries you. You have lost your mental peace, and you are frightened. You have taken something that doesn't belong to you, maybe an object, a person, or something else. It is not yours; return it. You have no reason to curse; don't do it because it is harmful to you. If there are mice in your home, do not kill them, because they are a good influence on you. Don't let anybody influence you. You have had a hard life, and there is still a lot for you to endure. Your family and other people whom you know do not give you the credit you deserve, but in the end you will overcome all the obstacles and be triumphant. You will be what Olofin wants you to be. You were born to rule.
>
> The offerings recommended by *eyeunle* are two white pigeons, a stick the height of the client, land snails, cocoa oil or lard, two parrot's feathers, cotton, and a white cloth. (Cros Sandoval 1975:89–90)

OSA (9)

Osa is the *odu* that is formed when nine shells fall with their natural openings upward. Oyá, Aganyú, Obatalá, Ogún, Ochún, and Oba speak through this letter, or *odu*, which says:

> Your best friend is your worst enemy. There is a revolution going on in your home. There are grave problems between husband and wife, relatives, and even among people who are members of the family. These problems are so serious that you might even have to go to court. Only one person is responsible for all of this. This person wants to harm you and to bring problems to your family. Sometimes you feel weird—as if your body were full of heat with the blood rushing toward your head. You feel like getting into a fight. The *santo* says that you do not know what you are doing. You have to control yourself and to be very careful about what you eat and drink, because somebody is trying to harm you. You are thinking of moving away. Why haven't you moved already? If you feel like moving some place else, why haven't you done it yet? Be

very careful with fire, because you might get burned. Don't argue with anybody.

The offerings, or *ebó*, recommended by *osa* are two hens, a couple of pigeons, a small machete, two stones from your backyard or from in front of your door, and two *bollitos* (bread rolls). (Cros Sandoval 1975:91)

OFUN (10)

When ten shells fall with their natural openings upward, the letter or *odu* that is formed is called *ofun*. Obatalá, Ochún, and Oyá speak through *ofun* and say:

> Here is where the curse is born. The one who curses is cursed. You are very stubborn. Do not argue with your mother or your father, if they are alive. If they have died, offer masses and flowers to them. All your plans are in the air. Nothing goes well. You do not like to work hard and in this world one has to work. Do not be nosy. Do not get involved in what is not your business. You suffer from some ailment. Are you sick? There is a sick person in your home who has to leave so that good fortune can return. You have been the victim of a curse. When you gambled in the past, you usually won, but nowadays you rarely win.

Ofun recommends as offerings a rooster, a hen, and a horse's mane. (Cros Sandoval 1975:91–92)

OJUANI CHOBER (11)

Ojuani chober is the *odu*, or figure, that is formed when eleven shells fall with their natural openings upward. Elegguá, Naná Burukú, Babalú Ayé, Osain, and Oba speak through this *odu*, or figure, and say:

> Death is following you. Immediately offer it a mass. Don't stop to chat on the street corners, because somebody might be harmed and you will be blamed. You like to carry water from the sea, to overcome all types of adversities without listening to anybody's advice, and to do whatever pleases you. Offer to your *eledá* something to eat and, also, to that wandering soul that is chasing after you. Try to control your rage so that you might not do something that you are going to be sorry for the rest of your life. Do not abuse others so that you do not lose their affection, consideration, and respect. Do not take revenge on anyone, since Oyá and Elegguá say that they will protect you and will punish whoever tries to harm you. Do not argue with your enemies or with anybody else. Take good care of the Elegguá that you have in your home.

The recommended offerings are a land turtle, a razor, and white and black threads. (Cros Sandoval 1975:92)

EYILA CHEBORA (12)

Eyila chebora is the name of the *odu,* or figure, that is formed when twelve cowry shells fall with their natural openings upward. Changó, Oyá, and Yemayá speak through this *odu.* They say:

> Be very careful; somebody is trying to put you in jail. Everybody complains about you. You have many enemies. You are the child of Changó, and you owe him something. Pay him. You have been told that you are the child of another saint, and that is why you are having so many problems. You have been failing in everything. Food has been taken from your mouth. You have to take care of your father Changó. Don't play with fire.
>
> The *ebó* (offerings) recommended by *eyila chebora* are the following: a little piece of tiger's hide, a small boat, a piece or segment of rope, black-eyed beans, red cloth, and two roosters. The client should dress in white. (Cros Sandoval 1975:92)

Eyila chebora is the last *odu* that can be interpreted by *babalochas* and *iyalochas. Metanla, merinla, manula,* and *meridilogun*—figures thirteen, fourteen, fifteen, and sixteen respectively—are the *odus* that have to be interpreted only by the *babalaos.*

The *ekuele* and the board of Ifá

Among the Yoruba and also in Santería, Ifá is considered the most reliable of all the divination systems. It can only be used and interpreted by *babalaos,* who are the priests of Orúnmila, or Orúla, the god of the oracles and the voice of Olodumare. Ifá is based on 16 basic and 256 derivative figures or *odus.* These *odus* constitute an oral tradition in which the cultural history of the Yoruba, the theogony of their gods, and their popular wisdom, morality, and vital philosophy are reflected, conserved, and transmitted. The verses of the *odus* form the literary corpus that is considered by many authors the unwritten scripture, or Bible, of the Yoruba. It takes *babalaos* years of study to master Ifá and to learn the thousands of verses that are part of the 256 *odus.* J. D. Y. Peel (2000:115) believes that: "Ifa's openness to the world beyond the orisa may well go back to its origins. For it is virtually certain that Ifa derives its formal properties from the system of divination by 'sand-writing' practiced in the Islamic world, which diffused widely into Sub-Saharan Africa and so far beyond the frontiers of Islam as to seem entirely autochthonous." He adds: "Ifa was itself born, fusing a largely indigenous religious content with a new type of divining system adapted from Islamic 'sand-writing.'"

The babalawos in Nigeria and the *babalaos* in Cuba are a religious and intellectual elite. They are privileged to wear ornaments made of beads which only the *obas*, or kings, can wear. They are respected for their characteristic wisdom and are expected to lead a respectable, responsible life. Their tutelary *oricha*, Orúla, the god of wisdom, never makes a mistake. Orúla protects his children, the *babalaos*, from making errors and inviting ridicule. However, when Orúla is offended or neglected, he punishes by exposing the offending *babalao* to both mistakes and ridicule.

Babalaos should be studious and knowledgeable. Even priests and practitioners of other Afro-Cuban religions recognize the *babalaos* as religious authorities. African, Cuban, and other scholars have always been amazed that the complex Ifá divination system was preserved in Cuba almost intact. In some instances, it was preserved in a more complete fashion than in Nigeria.[4] This constitutes further evidence that individuals belonging to the highest priestly classes were brought to Cuba as slaves.

Two methods are used to obtain the *odus* in Ifá divination. One method is called the *ekuele*, which consists of chains called *opele*, in which eight shells are inserted at both ends of the chain, which are separated from each other by a single two-inch link. When the diviner tosses the chain, he holds it by the middle with his right hand and tosses it away from himself. The segment of the chain that falls to the right of the diviner forms an *odu* that is considered the masculine, and strongest, *odu*. The other half of the chain that falls to the left of the diviner forms another *odu*, which is considered the feminine, and weakest, *odu*. Thus, with a single toss of a chain two *odus* are formed with the masculine taking precedence over the feminine. According to how many half-seed shells fall with the concave or the convex side up (heads or tails), different figures, or *odus*, are formed.

The *babalao* normally has twelve chains, or *opeles*. Every morning, after greeting Olodumare, the *babalao* tosses the chains to find out which of them should be used on that day.

The other method used to consult Ifá is through the *ikínes*, or palm nuts, and the board of Ifá, or *até Ifá*. The *opon* Ifá is a wooden board that is normally round but is sometimes rectangular in shape. Generally, sixteen palm nuts, or *ikínes*, are used, sometimes seventeen. Engraved on each side of the board are the heads of the *orichas* who control the Four Corners of the world. In Yorubaland, Eshu controls the east, Shango the west, Ogun the north, and Obatala the south. In Cuba, Changó controls the east; Echú controls the west, Obatalá the north; and Oduduwa the south. This method of divination is used only on very important occasions. It means that "Orúla is brought down," and several *babalaos* are needed to interpret the advice of the *oricha*.

At the beginning of the divination process the officiating *babalao* pronounces the ritual invocations. Holding the *ikínes* in his left hand, he tries to take with his right hand as many as possible. Another way of doing it is by placing sixteen nuts, or *ikínes,* in the right hand, and opening the hand so as to allow them to sift through the open fingers. Whichever procedure is used, the result is the same. If one nut is left in the hand, the *babalao* makes two small marks on the board. If two nuts are left, the *babalao* makes only one little mark. This operation is repeated four times, resulting in a letter, or configuration, called *odu.* The *babalaos* follow a formula for recording each configuration that arises from the procedures used.

Each *odu* has its own name. For example, the *eji ogbe* is formed when, on eight occasions, two nuts remain in the left hand, which is holding them, after attempts were made to grab the sixteen nuts with the right hand; or two nuts remained in the right hand, which is holding them, when they were allowed to sift through the fingers.

There are 16 important *odus,* or configurations; each one has 16 secondary ones.[5] Thus, there is one possibility in 256 for a particular *odu* to appear. Each one of the 256 *odus* has another 16 subordinated *odus,* making a grand total of 4,096 *odus,* or configurations. *Odus* are organized into two groups. The 16 original *odus* form the first group. According to Wande Abimbola (1973: 45), "These *odus* contain the best-known and best-remembered parts of the literary corpus."

They are the following:

- *Okanran* (1) is formed when, after the fourth attempt, one, one, one, and two *ikínes* remain in the left hand. The *babalao* writes the following figure: 11−11−11− 1.
- *Oyeku* (2) is formed when, after the fourth attempt, one, one, one, and one *ikínes* remained in the left hand. The *babalao* transcribes it as 11−11−11−11.
- *Ogunda* (3) is formed when, after the fourth attempt, two, two, two, and one *ikínes* remain. This is transcribed as 1−1−1−11.
- *Irosun* (4) is formed when, after the fourth attempt, two, two, one, and one *ikínes* remain in the hand. It is transcribed 1−1−11−11.
- *Oche* (5) is formed when, after the fourth attempt, two, one, two, and one *ikínes* remain in the hand. It is transcribed 1−11−1−11.
- *Obara* (6) is formed when, after the fourth attempt, only two, one, one, and one ikínes remain. It is transcribed 1−11−11−11.
- *Odi* (7) is formed when, after the fourth attempt, only two, one, one, and two *ikínes* remain. It is transcribed as 1−11−11−1.
- *Ogbe* (8) is formed when, after the fourth attempt, two, two, two, and two *ikínes* remain. It is transcribed as 1−1−1−1.
- *Osa* (9) is formed when, after the fourth attempt, one, two, two, and two *ikínes* remain in the hand. It is transcribed as 11−1−1−1.

- *Ofun* (10) is formed when, after the fourth attempt, one, two, one, and two *ikínes* remain. It is transcribed as 11–1–11–1.
- *Owonrin* (11) is formed when, after the fourth attempt, one, one, two, and two *ikínes* remain. It is transcribed as 11–11–1–1.
- *Otrupon* (12) is formed when, after the fourth attempt, one, one, two, and one *ikínes* remain. It is transcribed as 11–11–1–11.
- *Irete* (13) is formed when, after the fourth attempt, two, two, one, and two *ikínes* remain. It is transcribed as 1–1–11–1.
- *Ika* (14) is formed when, after the fourth attempt, one, two, one, and one *ikínes* remain. It is transcribed as 11–1–11–11.
- *Iworo* (15) is formed when, after the fourth attempt, one, two, two, and one *ikínes* remain. It is transcribed as 11–1–1–11.
- *Otura* (16) is formed when, after the fourth attempt, two, one, two, and two *ikínes* remain. It is transcribed as 1–11–1–1.

The remaining 240 *odus* are called the *omo-odu*. Because they bear two names of the original sixteen *odus* combined into one, they are also called the *amulu-odu*.

Each *odu* has a considerable number of stories, or *eses*, connected to it. *Eses*, according to Abimbola (1973: 45):

> are the literary materials in prose and poetry which have been handed over from Orunmila to his children and disciples while he was on earth and which priests of Ifá have been passing down from one generation to the other for many hundreds of years.

When one *odu* is formed, the *babalao* recites all of the stories related to that figure that he knows. From the verses that the *babalao* recites, the client will choose the one that he/she thinks reflects his/her problem. The *babalao* also has to provide the practical application of the story and recommend the appropriate sacrifice to facilitate the good that is in the story or to prevent whatever evil is foretold.

The *odus* are divided into three parts. The first part consists of a saying conveyed in verse, followed by two that are an extension of the first. The first section always deals with some philosophical or theological question. The second section reveals a story about a mythological character whose life and circumstances resemble that of the client. Based on this myth, the *babalao* will prescribe an offering, and, based on the question, he will admonish or counsel the client. In cases of illness, the *babalao* will recommend the treatment the client should follow. The *babalao*, unlike the *olorishas* or *santeros*, has to follow a system of rules from which he cannot deviate; thus, the subjective element in interpretation is minimal.

The *babalaos'* prestige is augmented by the belief that Orúnmila can control death. The following *patakí,* from a *santero's* notebook refers to this belief:

> The son of a *babalao* and the son of Ikú were always arguing. One day while playing the son of the *babalao* remembered that his father warned him to be home before the moon came out.
>
> "I have to go home before the moon rises tonight," he said to Ikú.
>
> "Don't hurry," death answered. "Don't you know that today the moon is not rising at all?"
>
> "Of course it will," replied the son of the *babalao.* "It is the new moon, and it will surely rise."
>
> Since the son of Ikú did not reply, the son of the *babalao,* who loved to argue to the point of even lying to win an argument, turned around and said: "Well, I will play for a while longer, for the moon is not going to rise until three days from now."
>
> Thus, the tables were turned. The son of death insisted that the moon was rising that night; while the son of the *babalao* insisted that it would not rise until three days later. They argued and argued until they made a bet for high stakes: life itself. They parted, and when the son of the *babalao* arrived home and told his father about the argument and the bet, the father said: "My son, what have you done? Don't you know that the moon comes out every night?"
>
> The son replied, "Yes, I know. But that fool cannot win a single argument, for I am the son of a *babalao."* The *babalao* worried, thinking that his son was going to lose his life. Then he said some prayers, and placed a hide filled with oil as an offering on the hill where the moon rose every night. A dog that passed by broke the hide and the oil spilled everywhere. When the new moon slowly started to rise behind the hill, its face was soiled with the residues of the sacrifice. Dirty and ashamed, the moon hid behind a cloud and proudly decided not to rise that night. The following night, the moon started to roll around the hill in a shy stroll, but her face was soiled again. Full of shame and hurt dignity, the moon again hid and refused to rise. It was not until the third day that the moon was able to show her clean and dignified white face again.
>
> "*Maferefun* Orúnmila," forever, "whatever is implored is conceded, Orúla." (Cros Sandoval 1975:93, 94)

Chapter Summary

The role divination plays in Santería cannot be overemphasized. Santería's followers believe that by consulting the *orichas* a person will be able to learn the measures that should be taken to preserve or restore health, and to keep, regain, or acquire prosperity, affection, and everything else that makes life enjoyable.

This particular function of Santería has attracted and continues to attract new followers, especially among segments of the population, or individuals who find themselves in situations of conflict and uncertainty in their employment, family situation, and/or personal life. As has been suggested previously and will be elaborated upon in chapter 23, this sense of powerlessness or lack of control is one of the reasons that individuals in both Castro's Cuba and some marginalized people in the post-industrial society of the United States seek the oracles in search of wisdom, guidance, and magical assistance to enable them to deal more successfully with life's problems.

The oracles are a means of gaining direction and control, of being able to see more clearly a path to take, of feeling more powerful and "in charge" in order to achieve a greater sense of mastery and improved well-being in many aspects of life.

Conclusion to Part 1

Santería is the religion of the Yoruba-speaking people from southwest Nigeria that was brought to Cuba by African slaves. The nineteenth-century influx into Cuba of forced and voluntary contingents of immigrants of different cultural backgrounds triggered transculturation processes that, according to Fernando Ortiz, resulted in the rapid merging of diverse cultural traits into something uniquely new and Cuban (1970: 98).

In colonial Cuba, the processes of merging, in some instances, were nourished by similarities in the worldview that slaves brought to the island and the one prevalent in that new society. Among them were the perception of a world with a spiritually laden ambiance; a lineal, authoritarian or hierarchical order; a devotion to sacred images; and an interest in miracle seeking. In Cuba different African religions, European spiritualist beliefs and practices, Amerindian beliefs, and the mystical and emotional practices of Catholic Spain converged and fused with the Yoruban religion to form a uniquely Afro-Cuban religion.

Santería was not the result of a messianic movement but was the fruit of a conscious and unconscious search for meaningful equivalents between the gods that the slaves brought from Africa and the Catholic saints of the masters. The strain toward logico-structural integration of worldview assumptions was made easier because of congruencies linking many aspects of Yoruban belief and behavior with aspects of belief and behavior in the realm of popular piety throughout Cuba. The merging of spiritualist beliefs and practices of diverse origins was prompted by a search for supernatural assistance and counsel in a situation of harsh separation from homeland, family, and traditional ways. Efforts toward a greater sense of mastery in the face of huge cultural loss and social disorder under slavery were guided by traditional perceptions of power and order that embraced both old and new avenues of supernatural support.

The slaves in Cuba took refuge in their religions, which became the vehicles for the transmission of their languages, music, ideas, and beliefs, all meaningful within the framework of an African worldview. The African religions in Cuba were spontaneously opened to new influences and interpretations by their worshippers. The intrinsic dynamism and problem-solving flexibility of these belief systems made them popular and facilitated evolution and growth into new religious forms that were uniquely Afro-Cuban.

Processes of cultural merging have been central in Cuban history. The study of the development of Santería is a study of cultural change and merging prompted by the need to adapt to a culturally and racially heterogeneous environment. These processes of merging resulted in wide variations and even contradictions in Santería's practices and dogma, despite efforts by some priests and priestesses to create a common foundation or doctrine.

It is remarkable that in Santería's structure there is a hierarchical order similar to the one the Yoruban religion had in Nigeria. Thus, Santería's power dimension, the priesthood, the oracles, the drum festivals, the house-temple, and the rituals are hierarchically ordered.

The supernatural force, *aché*, is reflected everywhere, but in a hierarchical fashion. In descending order of importance, *aché* emanates first from the Supreme Being, then from the important *orichas* (creation, fate, wisdom), the lesser *orichas*, the ancestors, and finally from consecrated objects.

Insofar as the priesthood is concerned, the *babalaos* represent the highest authority in all religious matters. The different levels of importance among *babalaos* are determined by knowledge, experience, and training. The categories of *oba*, *olúo*, and *awó* constitute different levels of status and role based on seniority and power, with the *oba* being the most prestigious. Since only men can become *babalaos*, there is a gender differential of power that prohibits females and male homosexuals from entering the service of Orúla and enjoying the wisdom and status it entails.

Among *santeros*, the most respected are the knowledgeable *oriatés* and/or *italeros* who are specialized in rituals and oracles. A step down are the senior *santeros* and *santeras* who have parented large lineages. They are followed by the established senior *santeros,* who are called *oyubón* or *oyubona*; then by the *babalochas* and *iyalochas;* and, further down, by the recently initiated *iyawós.*

Divination is central in accessing the power and guidance of the hierarchically ordered divinities. Among the oracles, the established hierarchy begins with the board of Ifá and the *ekuele* because of their great complexity and thoroughness in embodying the truth and wisdom of the Supreme Being. These most respected oracles enrich the insight of the client with legends, myths, and stories from which diagnosis, treatment and guidance are drawn.

The oracle that is second in importance and prestige is the dilogún, which any *santero* or *santera* can use. The dilogún offers advice, conflict resolution, and therapeutic approaches in all matters and ailments. *Santeros* and *santeras* can read only the first twelve *odus* (figures through which the oracle speaks). When higher *odus* appear, the client is referred to a *babalao* to consult the highest authority of Orúla.

The least informative oracle is the Biagué, which speaks through the coconuts. It can offer simplistic advice by answering clients' questions with positive, strongly positive, dubious, negative, or strongly negative responses.

The house-temple itself reflects different levels of sanctity. The most sacred area is the *igbodu*, or sanctum, used for the recondite ceremonies normally open only to the initiated. Next, there is the large hall, or *eya aranla*, for the gathering of the faithful; and, finally, there is a patio, or *iban balo*, an open space for public ceremonies.

A hierarchical ordering is also apparent in the drum festivals, where a strict sequential order is followed. The drumming sequences, specific for each *oricha*, honor them and call them to request approval for the ceremony and, hopefully, their presence through trance-possession.

Further developments in Santería were based upon changes that occurred in Yoruban beliefs and practices related to the general functions that religion had fulfilled in Nigeria vis-à-vis Cuba, and also the ways religion functioned on behalf of the individual.

General Functions

In Nigeria, religion served as an explanatory device that, through a complex mythology, explained the origins of the universe, life, humanity, and other aspects of creation. This particular function lost importance in Cuba. African myths and accounts of the origin and descent of the gods survived unchallenged, but when they were confronted by secular or scientific explanations they began to function more as remote, beautiful, and romantic stories of legendary times. Nevertheless, knowledge of the mythology and of the legendary stories did become essential to entering the priesthood and to being well-trained in oracle reading. It also structured the behavior of believers when possessed by specific *orichas* in their numerous manifestations.

The function of African religion as an ethical and enculturation device also lost ground when confronted with Christian morality. Certain rituals that were considered immoral in the new setting were discarded, while rigid Christian morality gave way to a new "mulatto" morality that was much more accepting of the individual's frailties. This development is in consonance with the loss of stature of some gods and their subsequent humanization.

In another context, the substantial role played by the Cuban public school system, at least in the urban areas, also challenged the primary role that religion had played in Africa as a socialization device. However, the function of religion as a support system was greatly enhanced.

The early cult groups gave slaves and their descendants in Cuba a sense of identity based upon their need to be in-relation with others. The groups encouraged positive relationships and functioning between the self and others. Something of Yoruban ethos could be retained. These groups facilitated the survival of language, music, dance, literature, and traditions that were anchored in the worldview of Yoruba culture. At first the cult groups became the nuclei of cultural preservation; later, they became fictive extended families that offered emotional and economic support to their members. Thus, their function as an economic, psychological, and emotional support system grew in the absence of the Yoruban extended family and the lineage's communal way of life.

Important developments also occurred in this religion's role as a health delivery system. During the nineteenth century, when medical services were either unavailable or ineffective, people of all ethnic backgrounds, including those who labeled themselves Catholic, consulted indigenous healers on health issues. Among these practitioners there were *santeros, paleros,* spiritualists, *curanderos,* and other healers and diviners. This practice was quite common in rural areas and among members of the lower socioeconomic classes in the cities. In certain instances, some upper- and middle-class whites, when facing health, personal, or economic crises, would consult African healers and their descendants.[1] This behavior was consonant with both the spiritual orientation and pragmatic approach to problem-solving that was as characteristic of Cuban culture in the 1900s as it is today. Many clients whose health improved after consultations credited this religion with the beneficial results and eventually became sympathizers of, and in some cases initiates of, Santería.

Santería and other Afro-Cuban religious complexes and their parent religions in Nigeria, the Congo, and elsewhere in Africa utilize traditional healing to provide both physical and mental health care. This function has been central in attracting outsiders to the religion.

There is a pattern in Santería's healing culture. First, the *santero* or *santera* consults the oracles that will determine a diagnosis and treatment. Often, *orichas* who are considered to be renowned physicians, such as Osain and Erinle, need to be propitiated along with those *orichas* who own the part of the human body affected. Additionally, the *orichas* who own the magical and medicinal herbs prescribed in the treatment need to be propitiated. Generally herbs are used for teas, while sticks, branches, and roots are boiled for curative baths. If the situation warrants great concern, efforts are made to keep Ikú (death) away.

The function of Santería as a health delivery system diminished in importance as conventional medical services gradually were made available to the Cuban population.[2] Santería, however, has remained a complementary system. It often assists in the healing process by eliciting supernatural guidance for the diagnosis of illness and the prescription of treatment. As a mental health-care delivery system, Santería functions to assist in the solution of life's problems, such as resolution of family conflicts, job-related struggles, preserving or restoring health, and providing help in making decisions about weddings, journeys, business ventures, love affairs, and other matters.

Guidance in spiritual matters is, of course, another important function of

Santería. It is necessary to establish the identity of one's guardian *oricha* and to follow the priest's advice as to what rituals to follow or sacrifices to make and when to make them.

Afro-Cuban religious systems enjoy a growing following for their perceived successful manipulation of supernatural forces by magical means. Many individuals are attracted to these cults out of pursuit of mastery over situations in which they have little or no control. For example, many artists, athletes, and politicians, whose destinies depend to great extent upon the public's favor, have been especially inclined to seek supernatural assistance through magical means.

Functions for the Individual

Santería provides individuals with the means of obtaining supernatural assistance by enabling them to identify their guardian spirit, or *eledá*. Once identified, a person can establish an alliance with this spiritual entity to gain support, guidance, and protection in exchange for offerings and sacrifices. Santería also provides the individual with the means of ensuring the constant protection of one or more *orichas* in order to avoid negative circumstances and attract positive ones.

Some Santerían practices and beliefs serve to heighten the individual's self-worth. Being a receptacle for deities through trance-possession enlarges the person's sense of self. Such a "self" is empowered by being able to express or communicate the nature and will of one or more divinities. Ritual possession also provides a release of tension and reduces inhibitions, hence allowing behavior that might not be appropriate or socially acceptable in other circumstances. Also, purification and cleansing ceremonies are directed toward improving a person's sense of physical well-being by means of sacred water, magical and medicinal herbs, and the life-giving power of sacrificed animals' blood, which is offered to nourish the *orichas* one is propitiating.

Santería offers the individual access to mythology and to rituals that increase one's sense of mastery and self-esteem, while opening avenues to leadership and professional status through the priesthood. Undergoing additional rituals aimed at obtaining new powers and protection reinforces these transforming experiences. Such processes often climax with the initiation ceremony, when the initiate is born into a new life sealed by a close alliance with an *oricha* and the acceptance of a new name. This rebirth signals an individual's new identity as the protégée of a god.

Numerous rituals that follow give the individual additional knowledge, expertise, and new spheres of power and privilege. The presentation to the drums is an example. This event is propitious for possession. It also entitles the individual to dance to the beat of the sacred music.

After initiation, the individual is authorized to set up his or her own temple. The status reached is that of a priest—a professional who embarks upon a lifelong commitment to serve his or her *oricha*. This step also opens a wide avenue for self-improvement, a career ladder, and opportunities for upward mobility—from the recently initiated *iyawó* to the established *santero/babalocha* or *santera/iyalocha* to the senior *babalocha* and *iyalocha* as the founders of successful lineages.

Santería provides the believers with sources of support, feelings of belonging, and group identity. The house-temple is perceived as the home of all the people who participate in its rituals or who have been initiated by the *santero* or *santera* who presides over it. Everyone knows everyone else, the place and role of each person, and what is expected of them. Members participate in the rituals and festivities, in the ceremonies to give offerings and sacrifices to the consecrated stones, and in the preparation of the communal meals. They all participate in the Santerían ethos and share the same worldview, a common knowledge validated by the myths and sacred legends. They all participate in the festivities, drumming, dancing, and chanting—escaping from daily problems through the joy of participation, through dancing, feasting, and camaraderie. They honor the *orichas* while dancing and chanting for them to encourage their help in solving problems.

Thompson's discussion of the role of divination among the Yoruba is applicable to the Santerían experience and explains its appeal to its followers. Santería provides a hierarchical structure, an intellectual system, and a divination system "that makes fate visible, as upon a screen where man views his problems with a clarity not previously obtained" (Thompson 1976: 166–67).

Santería's cunning, capricious, and mischievous gods can provide clarification, guidance, and direction to deal with an unpredictable and chaotic world. The followers know that the *orichas*, when properly propitiated and cared for, will use every means possible to ensure the desired outcome. In summary, Santería functions generally to provide protection and help throughout life. It is a means of achieving power and mastery in all areas of the life space.

1. *Venta de Esclavos* (Sale of slaves) by Ana Mary Rodriguez, 1922. Oil on canvas. Courtesy of Roberto Ramos's Masters Collection.

2. Florencio Baró playing the drums. Photo by the author.

3. Silvia Eires (Efún Okún Lorún) and her spiritual *bóveda*. Photo by the author.

4. Norma Torrado (Egüincholá) and her godmother, Caridad
Cuesta Cuesta Oyárinú. Photo by the author.

5. *Inle, Oricha of Medicine* by Alberto del Pozo. Courtesy of the Cuban Heritage Collection of the University of Miami.

6. *Ofrendas* (Offerings) by Antonio Argudín, circa 1951. Oil on canvas. Courtesy of Roberto Ramos's Master Collection.

7. Norma Torrado (Egüin Cholá) in front of her saints. Photo by the author.

8. Oro *Wemilere.* Courtesy of Miguel "Willie" Ramos.

9. *Bembé a la Virgen de la Caridad* (Bembé in honor of the Virgin of Charity) by Manuel Mesa.
Oil on wood. Courtesy of Roberto Ramos's Master Collection.

10. The *babalao* Virgilio Armenteros (Ifá Omi). Photo by the author.

11. Elegguá by Luis Molina. Courtesy of the artist.

12. Ochún. Courtesy of the artist, Luis Molina.

13. Oba by Luis Molina. Courtesy of the artist.

14. Niurka Barrios (Olomidara and Olokun). Photo by the author.

15. *Iyalocha* Antonia "Cacha" Sánchez participating in the ritual of *ñangareo* to enter in communion with Olofin before the ceremony of *itá*. Courtesy of Miguel "Willie" Ramos.

16. The *babalao* Jorge Torres celebrating on the day of his initiation. Courtesy of Jorge Torres.

17. A *botánica*. Courtesy of Javier Echeverría, *La Letra del Año*.

18. Procession of the Virgin of Mercy, September 24, 2005. Courtesy of Oswaldo Díaz.

19. Ernesto Pichardo (Oba Irawo), a well-known *oriaté* who was instrumental in bringing Santería into the open. He won a victory against the city of Hialeah, Florida, when the U.S. Supreme Court affirmed the right to sacrifice animals in religious ceremonies.

Part 2

Santería's Transformations

The Introduction to the Pantheon

Part 2 consists of a comparison of Nigerian orishas and their counterparts existing as the best-known Afro-Cuban *orichas/santos*. As described in the introduction to this book, the basis for the comparison rests upon material collected from a variety of sources over an extended period of time. The data from such research efforts are included here and juxtaposed as the "ethnographic present" in an effort to determine similarities and differences between the orishas in Africa and their similarly known deities in Cuba. Such juxtaposition offers the reader a more direct insight into mythical content and matters of cultural stability and change.

One of the objectives of part 2 is to identify the region of origin of these *orichas*, a matter of importance concerning the influence in Cuba of particular regions of Africa. Another objective is to reveal the degree of heterogeneity reflected in the Yoruban religion; that is, the extent to which there existed in Nigeria a variety of gods with similar attributes and powers but who, in some instances, differed in gender, name, and ritual worship. The intent is to identify the changes, if any, that followed their uprooting and transplantation.

Numerous myths and legends, or *patakíes*, are included. The rich mythology of Santería, related primarily to the *odus* (letters or figures) of the oracles, and orally transmitted from *padrino* or *madrina* (godparents) to godchild, constitutes a source of information about personal characteristics and desires of the *orichas*. Such mythology is also a reflection of the worldview of the Yoruban people, Afro-Cubans of Yoruban origin, and their cultural-religious descendants: the *babalaos*, *santeros*, and *santeras*.

In this section an attempt is made to reveal the extent to which the Afro-Cuban mythology reflects changes within Cuba and in Santería, changes that strongly suggest adaptations of the Yoruban religion to a new reality, to the needs of new believers, and to the pressures of the new society.

The *patakíes* and proverbs of Santería are important diagnostic and counseling tools utilized by its practitioners. Details of their use will not be reviewed here. Instead, following the tracing of changes in mythological content, an effort will be made to accomplish several additional goals. First is the need to delineate some of the moral dimensions that inhere in the oral traditions of myths and *patakíes* (but not proverbs at this time). Second is the need to infer some of the worldview assumptions that underlie them. Third is a discussion of matters of logico-structural integration that may throw light on some of the changes, or lack thereof, in the religion identified by means of the comparison undertaken.

Ideally, each myth, or *patakí* would be analyzed along these three dimensions. However, the volume of material involved makes this an unrealistic undertaking. In a sense, it constitutes the material for a separate book. The option remaining is to outline important points of discourse related to morality, worldview assumptions, and logico-structural integration. For purposes of clarity and simplification, these points will be covered in chapter 22.

Olodamare/Oludumare, Olorun/Olorún, Olofin/Olufin

The Creator God

Olodumare/Olorun/Olofin in Africa

In the Yoruban language names have considerable character and meaning. Thus the etymology of the names by which the Deity is known helps clarify its essence.

Olodumare is a very ancient name of complex etymology. E. Bolaji Idowu (1962:30–37) thinks that the name Olodumare is formed by two words and a prefix. The prefix ol means the owner of, or the possessor of. The word odu, according to the way it is accented, has two different meanings. The two versions of odu have meanings congruent with the attributes of the Deity. According to Idowu (1962:34), the word Olodu refers to someone who is a supreme head, one who possesses the scepter of authority or one who contains the fullness of excellent attributes, one who is superlative and perfect in greatness, quality, and worth. The second word, mare, has many meanings. Combined, "The word Olodumare has always carried with it the idea of One with Whom man may enter into covenant or communion in any place and at any time, one who is supreme, superlatively great, incomparable and unsurpassable in majesty, excellent in attributes, stable, unchanging, constant and reliable" (Idowu 1962:36).

Olorun is another of the names of this Deity. The etymology is clear. The prefix ol (the owner of) is followed by the word orun (heaven). Olorun, therefore, is the owner, or lord, of heaven.

Idowu (1962:50–51) records this poem about Olorun:

Earth has a contention with Olorun:
Olorun claims to be senior;
Earth claims to be older;
On account of one emo (brown) rat.

Rain ceases and falls no more,
Yams sprout but do not develop,
The ears of corn fill, but do not ripen,
All birds in the forest are perishing;
Vulture is carrying sacrifices to heaven.

These lyrics are inspired by a myth that tells how Olorun and the earth went hunting together and caught only one rat. An argument followed about who should keep the rat. The outcome of the dispute was that Olorun was supreme over the earth.

Olofin is another name given to the Creator. It is mostly used in the liturgy but is also used in the odus (figures, letters, or verses) of the oracle of Ifa. Olofin means "the supreme sovereign." Olofin Aiye is the supreme sovereign on earth; Olofin Orun is the supreme sovereign who is in heaven.

Early researchers and scholars of the Yoruba religion did not give much importance and significance to Olodumare. They failed to realize that the subtle, complex, and spiritual essence of Olodumare is similar to that which characterizes the Supreme Being in more institutionalized religions. Farrow (1926:29) was the first author to acknowledge that the Yoruba had arrived at a very abstract concept of a Supreme Being.

The following verses, also recorded by Idowu (1962:44), make reference to Olodumare's immortality:

The Young never hear that cloth is dead:
Cloth only wears old to shreds;
The old never hear that cloth is dead:
Cloth only wears old to shreds;

The Young never hear that Olodumare is dead:
Cloth only wears old to shreds;
The old never hear that Olodumare is dead:
Cloth only wears old to shreds.

The Yoruban Supreme Deity, Olodumare, seeking immortality, was told to make a sacrifice. He had to completely cover himself with a large piece of white cloth. Once he did this, he became immortal. Olodumare is the originator of all things in heaven and on earth. He is the creator god who has existed from the beginning of all eternity. He is the author of time, of day and night.

The acts and creations of Olodumare are indeed great and admirable. One day, Orula, the god of the oracles, while admiring the wonders of nature, very serenely said to a passerby, "You who have traveled by sea and who have traveled by the lagoon, surely you perceive that the works of Olodumare are mighty?"

Olodumare speaks, acts, orders, and judges, but in all his actions he manifests himself as a unique and perfect being. His high qualities and attributes presuppose a superior essence and existence. He is an old man, but he is not decrepit. His white hair inspires respect and reverence. His authority has no boundaries, and his purity and goodness, although conceived in human terms, are of high spiritual quality. Due to his character and essence, Olodumare cannot be represented by images.

Oldumare is Alaye, the one who lives; Elemi, the owner of the spirit; Oba Airi, the invisible king who sees and judges everything and is everywhere, but who cannot be seen by anyone. The Yoruba say, "What can you do that the eyes of Olodumare cannot see?" According to P. Amaury Talbot (1926 2:29), Olodumare is often pictured as being composed of a myriad of eyes.

Olodumare is an infallible and impartial judge who controls the destiny of all men and women. It is commonly believed that the orishas punish those who transgress their laws or neglect their rituals. But Olodumare judges according to people's inner feelings and their character. Since he knows everything and sees everything, even human thoughts, he alone can judge a person's morality. Accordingly, everyone receives at the end of life what he or she deserves.

The Supreme Being is also the judge of the orishas. He moderates the disputes and solves problems that occur so frequently among them.

Nothing can be done in opposition to Olodumare's will. He orders everything that happens. He is omnipotent. He sets the universe in motion. If he desires, all life could be destroyed. One of the odus, or verses, used by the Ifa oracle called Orosun Oso, explains the status enjoyed by the Supreme Being:

> A long time ago the 1,700 divinities conspired against Olodumare's authority. They came before Him and demanded that He abandon His position. They asked Olodumare to let them rule the earth for sixteen years. The Deity accepted under the condition that they first observe a trial period of sixteen days. If everything went well after those sixteen days, He would bow to their demands. The orishas rejoiced and prepared themselves for the task. Olodumare, knowing that it was impossible to leave responsibility in the hands of the orishas, stopped the Universal machine, and everything stood still. The rivers didn't flow; rain did not fall; fruit did not ripen; everything was at the brink of disaster. The orishas tried to restore harmony, but all of their efforts were in vain. The Oracle was consulted, but it remained silent. The orishas, ashamed and defeated, recognized Olodumare as their Supreme King and begged for

forgiveness. Olodumare set the Universe in motion again, and the orishas went away singing:

Be there one thousand four hundred divinities of the home;
Be there one thousand two hundred divinities of the market-place,
Yet there is not one divinity to compare with Olodumare:
Olodumare is the King Unique.
In our recent dispute, Edumare it is who won,
Yes, Edumare. (Idowu 1962:54, 55)

The differences in the essence and the attributes of Olodumare and the orishas are of great magnitude. The Supreme Being represents a more abstract concept of nature and human qualities, while the orishas are the personification of forces of nature, and with human characteristics they are the patrons of human activities.

Idowu (1962:3) always refers to the Yoruban Supreme Being as the "Deity." He calls the orishas "gods" or "divinities" because he thinks Olodumare is more than a personification of nature or of a heavenly god. Idowu (1962:4) argues that the presence of such a sublime Deity in the otherwise animistic Yoruban pantheon might be due to the possibility that the Supreme Being revealed himself to other people besides the Jews.

In contrast, many authorities are of the opinion that African traditional religions, including the Yoruban religion, do not have a linear conception of time and, consequently, lack the notion of eternity. Furthermore, they conceive of supernatural beings as quite kin to human beings in nature, according to Jacob K. Olupona (2000: xix): "Unlike Western Christianity, which has a linear conception of time, African traditions are cyclical, repetitive, and lack the notion of eternity. . . . In addition, African tradition maintains a familiarity with the Supreme Being, and practitioners are of the view that they 'share the same advantages and disadvantages, the same rights and the same duties,' whereas Christian tradition purports an unequal relationship between God and the human beings. By conceiving of a Supreme Being as a leader in a hierarchy of beings of which one is also a part, humans see God as only a more perfect being than an order that separates the divine from the human."

Islam, too, is believed to have influenced Yoruban beliefs. According to J. D. Y. Peel Islam greatly affected Yoruban beliefs concerning not only the Supreme Being but also the orishas, destiny, and divination.

So the "traditional religion" of the Yoruba does not really present itself as a single, given, separate entity. What it designates concretely is a congeries of cultic practices, actuated by some common principles, but varying a great deal over space and over time. It was a terrain of constant questioning, contestation, and exploration, which gave much opportunity for new cults to break in, though their success in doing so permanently depended on their being able to meet existing criteria of religious need and the social rules of cultic coexistence. Two cults stood out from the rest—Islam and Ifa—which, I have suggested, may be more closely connected in their Yoruba origins than the labeling of one as part of "country fashion" and the other as a world religion may lead us to think. Islam, in the zone where it was present (albeit only as the religion of strangers and a small minority of the Yoruba), seems to have fostered significantly different conceptions of God and human destiny than those that prevailed in the zone from which it was absent." (Peel 2000:121)

Thus, as Peel contends, Yoruban theology varied regionally. In the eastern part of Yorubaland, where Islam was less important, a complex overlap of perceptions of God and the orishas developed. Moreover, in that region, the term Orisha was used for the Supreme Being, while in the central-western region the difference between the Supreme Being and the orishas was clearly distinct.

In Peel's opinion, "Orisa" is an ancient term, used throughout a broad linguistic region, to designate the Supreme Being. Its use as a generic term to designate the lesser gods is relatively recent. The term imole or umole, which is a synonym for orisa, was the old generic term for subordinate deities: "Since of all the later *orisa* is Obatala or Orisanla, the one who came closest to the attributes of the presumed original Orisa/God, it seems that Orisa became an 'overburdened' symbol and fragmented into a range of refractions or local cultic variants, the so-called white *orisa*" (Peel 2000:120).

Peel believes that as the "country fashion," or traditional Yoruban religion, confronted Islam, it underwent some changes to deal with criticism. He believes that babalawos were instrumental in recasting the religious system. As a result of these changes the concept of the Supreme Being was reworked, and distinct attributes that profoundly separated it from the orishas were ascribed to it. Moreover the Ife-derived ancient name Olodumare was used to refer to the Deity. In Peel's view, Ifa can be seen as a recasting of the *orisa* system to meet the criticism of Islam (Peel 2000:120).

In spite of the high position that Olodumare/Olorun holds in the Yoruban religion, no temples, priests, festivals, or groups of faithful are dedicated to his worship. He is a remote god who inspires feelings of admiration, reverence, and respect in every believer. But he does not elicit the sacred terror that some orishas inspire. Since he is not feared, and since he, personally, does not interfere in worldly problems, no sacrifices or specific rituals are offered and celebrated solely on his behalf. By way of contrast, sacrifices prescribed by

babalawos for Olorun are offered in the shrine of Eshu, who delivers them to
Olorun.

At the same time, Bascom (1969b:71) points out that Olorun has a very important role to play in the Yoruban system of reincarnation. Before a person
is born or reborn, his or her ancestral guardian soul goes before Olorun to
receive a new body, a new breath, and the destiny for its new life. The ancestral
soul, kneeling before Olorun, has the opportunity to choose its destiny. Olorun grants the supplicant's wishes, unless the destiny chosen is unreasonable.
Destiny includes the personality, occupation, and luck of the individual as well
as a fixed day on which the soul has to return to heaven. Bascom (1969b:79)
describes Olorun as the deity who assigns and controls the individual destinies
of mankind. Olorun can be considered as the god of Destiny. Thus, Bascom
does not see Olodumare/Olorun as being indifferent to human plight, as other
authorities have, nor as too sublime to be influenced by worldly happenings.

Among the Yoruba, Olodumare's name is invoked during all religious ceremonies and festivals. Before a sacrifice is offered to a particular orisha, his
acceptance is requested: "Olodumare gba a o," which means, "Let Olodumare
accept it." Moreover, people commend themselves to him. Before rising in the
morning and before going to sleep, the first and the last thoughts are addressed
to him.

Peter McKenzie's research on Yoruban religion during the middle of the
nineteenth century is very provocative. At that time, after the demise of the
Oyo Empire, Yorubaland was ravaged by civil wars. The vacuum of power combined with the disruptive effects of the slave trade and the civil wars caused
changes that greatly affected the life of the Yoruban people.

McKenzie's research suggests that the exclusive and dogmatic emphasis on
the monotheism of Islam and Christianity may have given Olodumare more
of a presence in the religious concerns of the Yoruba than he previously had.
McKenzie argues that Christianity and Islam were encroaching on traditional
orisha worship. McKenzie (1997:496) quotes from Robin Horton's "African
Conversion" (1971:85–108): "These and other factors such as the impact of
international trade and commerce tended towards a shift in the cosmology
towards a greater profile for the traditional and hitherto shadowy sky deity."

It is plausible that the proselytizing pressure of the two world religions,
Islam and Christianity, influenced the way the Yoruba perceived their old sky
god, resulting in their attributing to him some of the characteristics that the
Supreme Being has in these two world religions. Believers held to their religious views about orisha worship while trying consciously or unconsciously to
incorporate more awareness of Olorun. McKenzie (1997:498) quotes a woman
as saying, "Why not worship (Olorun) on the Lord's Day and the *orisa* on the
other six days?"

At the same time, McKenzie's research includes substantial evidence that, in the past, there were priests dedicated solely to Olorun's worship. Included in his study are data gathered by James White, an Egba pastor, who reported that in 1874 the king of Igbesa was committed to Olorun. McKenzie's report also included comments from another Egba catechist, Samuel Doherty, who reported that in 1878 the headman of an important compound near Abeokuta refused to make offerings to the orishas. He said he was in the habit of offering a ram to Olorun, not because he was a Muhammadan but because he knew that "God is the source of everything" (McKenzie 1997:463).

At the same time, McKenzie's (1997:497) findings point in another direction that shows the complexity of the role Olodumare plays in Yoruban religion. He adds what other informants noted: "There is not a day (goes) past in which we (olorisa) never call on the name of Olorun; but the Book people take the matter of God too much on themselves as if they only knew him."

Remnants of what, in the past, might have been a cult to Olodumare are still observable. When a child at birth is not offered to the service of some orisha, as is commonly done, the priests call these children Omo Olorun (children of Olorun).

Andrew Lang (1898) in *The Making of Religion* notes that in some religions, the one god concept coexists with polytheism, flourishing together without much dissonance or conflict. In such cases monotheism provides final explanations to the ultimate questions about existence, eschatology, and cosmology. Concurrently, and in a complementary fashion, polytheism offers understanding of supernatural forces that are influenced by human interaction. The polytheistic pantheon enables the believers to procure the support of supernatural forces to solve problems of the here and now; in other words, it responds to basic human needs.

This conceptualization reflects the situation of the religion of the Yoruba and the Lucumí with regard to Olodumare and the orishas. Olodumare is the ultimate source of the universe, the ultimate order of the universe, the creator of human beings, and the ultimate destiny of man. Olodumare represents the universal moral order. However, he is too far away, too remote to deal with each individual's problems. He cannot and will not be partial.

In contrast, the quasi-human orishas are so close to human beings, their nature is so much like ours, so familiar, that they are quasi-predictable. In a sense, they seem to invite human beings to procure their support and seem eager to deal with human needs.

The Yoruban Supreme Deity, the abstract, powerful, venerable, and excellent Being, does not seem to be capable of fulfilling human basic needs for direct and intimate contact with the supernatural. The common believer apparently needed more accessible gods who could be bargained with. Thus, it seems that with the passing of time, the worship of the high god lost strength. Therefore, Olodumare remained the powerful Supreme Being who uses his power only at special and crucial moments. The Yoruba see in him a supreme king who cannot be bothered with the small problems of daily life. The orishas as intermediaries between the Deity and man are the ones called upon to give help in daily matters and to receive sacrifices and offerings in their worship.

Paradoxically, Olofi in Yorubaland is not only the name used for the Deity in the Ifa verses but is also the name of an important orisha. According to McKenzie (1997:44, 146, 520), Olofin, or Ajayi, is an orisha and culture hero. Olofin was a son of the legendary Oduduwa, and, accompanied by the orisha Eshu, he came from the mainland (Benin) and founded Lagos. He was a great magician and created the lagoon between Iddo and Lagos. When his time of death came, he descended into the ground. A coconut grove is his shrine, and his worship is essential for the fish and crayfish of the lagoon to multiply and prosper. In Cuba Olofin is the name given to the Supreme Deity usually when he is dealing with human beings.

Olodumare/Olorún/Olofin in Cuba

As in Africa, the word Olodumare is used in Cuba in relation to the god of creation. The word Olorún is also used in this context, but etymologically it reflects some solar or heavenly connotation. Olofin, or Olofi, is the name commonly used for the Supreme Being in the *patakíes,* or legends, in which he is dealing with humans and *orichas.* These two names, however, are used interchangeably.

In Cuba as in Africa, the creator god is all-powerful. This is illustrated by the statement, "Olorún aché e" (Olorún can do anything he wants). He is omnipresent: "Olorún wa" (God is everywhere and sees everything). As in Africa, the Supreme Being in Cuba possesses the qualities of goodness, justice, and mercy in a superlative manner. He also occupies a unique place in the pantheon. He is not the first among equals, but the one well above the other *orichas.* He is called "the Father of all the other gods" and it is said that "Olorún oba tobi tobi" (God is the greatest king on earth).

When going to bed at night and when getting up in the morning, both Yoruban and Afro-Cuban believers commend themselves to him with the following words, "Olofin egua wo" (God help you rise) and "Olodumare egbeo" (May Olodumare give us a propitious day). As in Africa, in Cuba nothing concrete is asked of him. He is never "put to work"[1] on behalf of or against anyone. Afro-Cubans explain his role by saying, "He does not want to be bothered. He is tired and should not be bothered. If you have problems go to the *orichas.* That is what they are here for."

The Supreme God has no cult, no priests. He does not possess believers during festivals, because he is too powerful to possess any human head. Nevertheless, during ceremonies, when sacrifices are offered, he is mentioned first, in Cuba as well as in Africa. Thus, in the Ocha religion, or Santería, the Supreme Being's character and attributes are as sublime as in Nigeria. However, presumably because he was in many instances identified with the creator gods of other African pantheons, his image and character are more human and less sublime to some followers.

Afro-Cubans speak about the Supreme Being and his attributes in the following terms: Olofin made everything. Everything belongs to Olofín. He made the world, the saints, men, animals. Later he told them, "Now take care of yourselves as well as you are capable of," and he left. In other words, his work done, he retired. The following expressions reflect his greatness:

Our head is not large enough to understand.
Olorún is too big.
One doesn't think about Him.
He is much too great.
"Olodumare ayó bo" (Beloved God will grant us happiness).

Olodumare's importance and central position was clearly expressed by a *babalao* at a conference in Miami in 2001. He pointed out that "one needs to learn the Rules of Olodumare concerning man's relationships with the *orichas* and with the Egun to have a satisfactory life."[2]

According to the book by Cuban *babalao* Felix Espinosa and the *olúo* Amadeo Piñero (1997b:13), Olofin is the supreme vibration that created time and, by mixing an infinite number of vibrations, the universe. He also created space in order for things to have their own boundaries. Olofin felt very lonely; so by using different vibrations he created many entities to distribute in space and time. First, he created Olodumare to rule over space and Olorun to rule over energy. Later, he created Oddua, Obatalá, and Ifá, who would later become the benefactors of humanity. Then, he whistled to his right and created the major deities and then to the left to create the minor deities. According to this account, Olofin is the first entity. In Africa, the Supreme Being is known by the names Olorun and Olodumare; not by Olofin.

In some Cuban *patakíes,* Olofin is depicted as a venerable patriarch. He is an old man who farms his land and whose children, the *orichas,* constantly grieve. It is said that he lives in a house situated on top of a mountain, with difficult access. This earthly residence is merely metaphoric, since most believers acknowledge that he really dwells in the heavens.

The Supreme Being is frequently called Arubbu (old man). In Africa, he is an ancient patriarch who, in spite of his old age, has complete control of all his faculties. In Cuba, as in Africa, in most instances his advanced age garners respect. However, in some cases, despite acknowledgment of his being eternal, his old age is associated with tiredness and even decrepitude. Thus, in some Afro-Cuban *patakíes*, Olofin is depicted as a tired old man who cannot help but divide his *aché*, or power, among the *orichas*. According to a *pataki*:

> Earth was going through very hard times, very hard times indeed. The grass didn't grow, men didn't obey, rain didn't fall, and animals and men starved. Hunger and drought punished the land and sadness and desperation prevailed. "Guay guay," cried the children. "Beeh, beeh, beeh," complained the lambs. "Curse, curse, curse, curse," despaired men.
>
> The *orichas,* who were confused and bewildered by the calamity that had befallen men, beasts, and gods, decided to see Olofin. Unfortunately they could not reach him because they did not know where to find the difficult road that led to his home. So they went to see Obatalá, the king of the *orichas* and Olofin's designated representative, and asked him to take them to the Supreme Being. Obatalá, aware of the horrible conditions on earth, agreed to carry out their wishes. He led them to the Osankiriyan road. They climbed the hill and they reached Olofin's house on top of the mountain. Obatalá took the petition of the *orichas* to the Supreme Being. "We want your help" was the desperate message of the *orichas*. Twice Obatalá read the petition to Olofin and twice Olofin answered, "I am tired. I can do no more." Then the *orichas* asked Obatalá to convince Olofin to divide his power among them. Obatalá prompted Olofin to do so: "Babami, listen to our needs, please divide your power. We need your help to keep on living." The Supreme Being answered, "Obatalá, call my children. Tell them to come to my presence."
>
> They all gathered at Olofin's house for a big banquet. At sundown, when the banquet was over, Olofin arrived. The *orichas* begged him for help and the old man said, "To each I will give what is yours, whatever belongs to you." Then, he gave the thunder and fire to Changó, the lightning flash to Oyá, the sea to Yemayá, the river to Ochún, the roads of the world to Elegguá, and the medicinal and magical herbs to Osain. At the end he told Obatalá, "You are *olori*, the owner of the heads." (Cros Sandoval 1975:131)

In Cuba, even though Olodumare is the all-powerful god, immortal and perfect, he appears in numerous legends as a man of flesh and bone, a victim of old age and human ailments. The following *pataki* is an example:

> Olofin was feeling very sick. He was so tired and weak that he could not work in the fields. Each day he felt worse. He was so worried and tired that he decided to call the *orichas* to see if they could help him. Each *oricha* prepared a medicinal potion, but they failed to help Olofin. He was getting weaker by the day; he could hardly get up from bed. He

complained: "I have so many powerful children and they cannot help me."

Elegguá, the mischievous child, was at that time living in poverty. He ate nothing but trash. When Elegguá found out about Olofin's ailment, he told his mother, "Mother take me to Taita Olofin. I am sure that I can prepare a remedy that will cure his ailments." The woman took Elegguá to Olofin, who told him: "All of my children have tried to make me well; let us see if the youngest one has enough ingenuity and knowledge to prepare the medicine that will cure me."

Elegguá examined Olofin and then went to the wilderness. He asked permission from all the sticks, woods, and plants that he needed. "With your permission," he said, while he pulled them, "I need your power." He paid them tribute, and took only what he needed to prepare a potion. He took the medicine to Olofin.

The old man made grimaces while slowly drinking the powerful beverage. Pretty soon the medicine started to work and the old creator god felt better. His tired face grew healthier; his cramped legs stretched more easily; his weak voice made echoes. Olofin was so grateful that he told Elegguá, "Come close to me. Elegguá, I want to thank you. Ask for anything that you want."

Elegguá who had always lived in poverty, who knew the high and the low, the beautiful and the ugly, the sublime and the corrupt, immediately answered. "I want the right to be the first of the *orichas* to be fed." Olofin, smiling, responded, "From now on you will be the first to eat of all the sacrifices. Nobody will eat before you do." Elegguá added, "I also want to be placed by the front door so I will be greeted before anyone else." The old man answered, "That is the way it will be. Take this key; you will be the owner of the roads, and the messenger of all the *orichas*."

Elegguá, the child with an old man's face, smiled and sucked his cigar while his eyes shone under the *guano* (palm-frond) hat. (Cros Sandoval 1975:108–9)

In some Cuban *patakíes* the Supreme Being is portrayed as a vulnerable being suffering from old age and ailments and having embarrassing panic attacks.

The *orichas* were jealous of the power of the old god. They thought they didn't need him. One day they decided, "Let us band together and overthrow Olofin. The old man is no longer capable of satisfying our needs." None of the *orichas*, however, was capable of preparing a plan. One voice was heard: "I have an idea. We all know how very fearful Olofin is of mice. Let us place some mice in his home. They will scare him out of his wits. He will be forced to leave and then we will divide his power among us."

Elegguá, the owner of destiny, who, as usual was posted at the door, heard everything. His mischievous eyes shone and, without saying a word, he rushed to Olofin's house. He sat at the door as a sentinel and waited. When the rebellious *orichas* arrived, they rushed the mice into the house. Olofin, all shaken up at the sight of mice, trembled with fear and confusion. Right at that moment, Elegguá jumped after the mice and ate them. Olofin, full of gratitude, asked Elegguá, "Tell me Elegguá, what can I do for you?" Then he added, "I know you. I concede to you the right to do whatever you please." (Cros Sandoval 1975:109–10)

In these legends the Supreme Being loses stature in favor of an *oricha*. In some *cabildos* (house-temples), the Yoruban Supreme Deity was identified with creator gods of other African ethnic groups, who, in many instances, lacked the sublime attributes: the omnipotence and transcendence that characterize the Yoruban Supreme Being. Even though Olodumare was associated with the Christian Supreme Being, this identification did not reinforce the elevated and abstract characteristics.

Another important point for consideration is that the Hebrew-Christian dualistic dichotomy of good and evil is alien to West African belief systems. Among the Yoruba supernatural power is not associated with morality or natural law. It is neutral but when activated can be used for good or evil. Thus, amoral power does not necessarily have to work against the Creator but alongside him. The *patakíes* introduced above attempt to explain why the cunning Elegguá, the god of the unpredictable, has so much power and influence. Elegguá, in his malevolence and greed, is by no means a power opposite the Supreme Being. He is not the equivalent of the Christian devil, as many observers once thought. In Cuba, Christian influences might have contributed to other noncongruent conceptualizations of good and evil.

Santería's followers assessed Catholic beliefs from their own point of reference. The Yoruban Supreme Being in Cuba (Olodumare/Olorún/Olofin) became identified with the Christian God, as God Almighty, the Holy Spirit and Jesus Christ. The reasons for the identification are evident. However, such identification did not function to sustain Yoruban images of the Supreme Being and the expression of that deity's power through lesser gods. Presumably, since the slave society lacked the wide and extended hierarchy that was the basis of African monarchies, it may have been very difficult for Santería's devotees to conceive of the *orichas* as administrators of the power of the Supreme Being. In line with the ethos of Cuban Creole society, a great deal more emphasis was placed on the characters, powers, and preferences of specific *orichas* in the search for a good life.

The influence of religious forms and legends from other African nations that had a less transcendental and abstract concept of the creator god, also, may have contributed to humanizing the Supreme Being at the expense of his stature and power. In the *patakíes* already mentioned, Olofin's senility is the rationalization Afro-Cubans made of the atomization of divine power. To them, the Catholic religion's Supreme Being was remote, but below him there was a myriad of accessible saints who, in exchange for offerings and sacrifices, aided the believers. In this regard, there was congruence between Yoruban conceptualizations and those of Santería's believers.

In chapter 14 a review is provided of the changes in character that the mischievous god of destiny, Elegguá, experienced on Cuban soil, especially in his relationships with the Supreme Being. It is important to emphasize nevertheless that, in spite of what the above *patakíes* imply, most believers of Santería still firmly maintain that Olodumare/Olorún/Olofin is an omnipotent god.

Chapter Summary

It might have been difficult for Afro-Cubans to assume that the great power and autonomy the *orichas* enjoy was due to their being only ministers or administrators of the Supreme Being. The conditions on the island were very different from those in Yorubaland, where traditional divine kingships constituted the basis of a well-established hierarchical order, an order on which a balance of power was based upon practical local autonomy. It is possible that in some cult-houses in Cuba, especially due to Bantu influence, the assumed decrepitude and weariness of the Supreme Being was perceived as the reason that the *orichas* enjoyed such power and autonomy. In Africa the celestial court mirrored the earthly hierarchical order where a range of administrative levels were endowed with different attributes and power. In Cuba, the celestial court mirrored a different ethos despite congruencies along a substantial number of social parameters. It is my opinion that Olodumare is possibly gaining stature due to a greater understanding among many believers of his role in Yoruban religion, where the complexity of the power hierarchies in African earthly and celestial courts is so different from the supremacy of the Christian god.

The Origin of Good and Evil

Like most people, Santería's believers wonder about the reasons for paradoxical situations and experiences in life, especially the presence of horror and pain in a world created by an essentially good supernatural being. The following *pataki* intends to explain why the earth's sick arrogance brought rage and punishment by heaven and led to the beginning of evil on earth:

At the beginning Heaven and Earth had an argument. Earth claimed she was older and more powerful than her brother was: "I am the basis of everything. Without me, Heaven would fall apart since it would have no support. Everything would be smoke. I create, nourish, and support all living things. I own everything. Everything originates from and returns to me. My power knows no limits." She kept repeating: "I am solid, solid. Heaven is emptiness; it has no substance. Can Heaven's possessions be compared to mine? What does it own but clouds, smoke, and light? I am worthier than he is. He ought to revere me and make me *moforibale* (honor me)."

Oba Olorún did not reply. Severely and in a threatening manner, he signaled Heaven to move away. "Learn your lesson," Heaven said while moving away. "Your punishment is going to be as great as your arrogant pride." Iroko,[1] the silk-cotton tree, worried, meditated in the great silence that followed after Heaven moved away. Iroko's roots sank deep in Earth's bowels, and its arms extended high into Heaven. Iroko's sensitive heart trembled with fright, knowing that the great harmony that existed between Heaven and Earth had been destroyed, and that all earthly creatures would suffer terrible calamities.

Until then, Heaven had ruled over the seasons with tender care, in such a manner that heat and cold were tempered. Neither storms nor drought had punished Earth. Life had been happy, and death was painless. Sickness and tragedy were unknown. Death was clean and merciful since diseases did not exist.

Men enjoyed long life, and old age did not bring physical handicap but only a desire to rest while silence moved slowly through the veins, delightfully aiming at the heart. Death brought infinite happiness. The end was like a beautiful sunset, as the eyes would slowly close and darkness would slowly set in. Since goodness belonged to the world, the dying person would smile at the thought of the great feast his body would give to the numberless worms that would devour him; the fun that birds would have plucking his eyes turned into seeds. In his dreams, the fraternal beasts would graze in his hair, which was turned into tender and juicy grass. And most of all, he would delight in marveling at the thought of the nourishment his bones would give to plants and tubercles, which his children and brothers would eat.

Nature had not yet set a bad example. There were no poisonous plants, no evil witches. No one thought of harming anybody. Nobody had to control the power of the evil forces that later emerged from pain and misery.

Everything belonged to everybody, and no one had to rule, conquer, or claim ownership of anything. The human heart was pure. Heaven and Earth were one. Heaven had not yet sent a single destructive lightning bolt. Celestial forces had not yet destroyed the woods, nor had the sun mercilessly punished Earth. The sea was infinite, calm, and serene and had not yet begotten any furious winds. No one was frightened or intimidated by the power of the sea. Mice were the greatest friends of cats; the poison of the scorpion was a drop of the sweetest honey. Monsters had benign, candid souls, and hyenas and pigeons shared the same beautiful soul.

Ugliness came later, when the time for suffering arrived. This change brought tears to the eyes of Iroko, the tree beloved by both Heaven and Earth. Iroko filled with deep mourning for what he knew was being lost. His tears filled Earth and his sadness, manifested in light, airy flowers, scattered its pain over Earth. This sadness, never felt before, flew on the wings of the wind and permeated the souls of men and beasts and everything alive. At sunset, the cry of the owl was heard, a deep disconcerting scream, a new lament in the silence of a different sunset. Iroko extended his arms in a protective gesture that encompassed all the sadness and suffering of the world.

That night was different from all previous nights—an alien night during which, for the first time, fear and anguish appeared, penetrating dreams and engendering Illondo (Evil), giving new cruel shapes, characteristics, and forms to the paws of darkness. Fear entered men's dreams, and unhappiness and anxiety became part of their lives.

In the morning that followed that terrible night, men, beasts, and all living creatures, dumbfounded, asked themselves the reason for this confusion and anxiety. They were unable to give meaning to their despair, since words had not been created to convey those feelings. The voices that were heard were absurd and menacing, filling the wind and the water's rush. The day was born full of hardship. The sun mercilessly devoured life; clear, sweet waters were slowly drying up. Iroko would tell the creatures who came to look for protection under its arms: "Let us make a rogation for our mother Earth who has so offended Heaven." But nobody understood what the silk-cotton tree was saying since no one knew the meaning of the word offend. Earth was secretly drying up. The sun, obeying Heaven's orders, did not desire to burn her all at once with excessive heat or light, but to slowly dry up her waters. Until then, the waters of Earth had been sweet, harmless, clear, filled with qualities that made them drinkable. However, since their mouths were opened to the sun, they ascended to Heaven where they were held in an abyss.

Earth was feeling in her bowels the effects of the rage of her brother, Heaven. Earth suffered such bitter thirst that she begged quietly: "Brother, my entrails are drying up. Please send me a little bit of water."

Heaven, instead of alleviating the atrocious thirst of his sister, covered her with white fire and later blew her burned body with a hot wind that savagely worsened her pain. Earth and all of its creatures suffered the horrible torments of fire, thirst, and hunger.

The suffering of her creatures was more painful to Earth than her own suffering. Earth humbly asked for forgiveness on behalf of those innocent creatures, the burned-out grass, and the dying trees. Pain has made them forget the last vivid memory of past happiness.

All happiness was now remote, incredible. Curse and disgrace were born. Ugliness entered the world. Suddenly, words became instruments of evil. Even the peace of the dead was disturbed. Those who passed away were no longer able to rest in the beauty and peace of the never-ending sweet night.

The martyrdom of her children cut deeper into her pain than her own suffering. Earth humbled herself to the Sky, asking forgiveness for the brown and burnt grass, for the dying trees, for the scorched plants.

"Forgive me," begged Earth. But Heaven mercilessly kept the waters away. Earth was a fruitless dust bowl and little by little nearly all the animals died. Men, thin as skeletons, roamed Earth with no water or food for sustenance. They continued to dig in the wounded body of Earth looking for water and the strength to devour those who lay helplessly on the bare rocks. All vegetation had disappeared, and only one tree remained, miraculously green and healthy, amid the arid Earth.

Iroko, who had always worshipped Heaven, was the only alive and healthy creature in all the Earth. The dead looked for refuge under its shade. The spirits of Iroko constantly spoke to Heaven trying to save Earth and her creatures. Iroko, who was the favorite son of both Heaven and Earth, with its powerful branches embraced those who had survived Olorún's punishment and sought refuge under its shade. Iroko gave instructions to those who could penetrate the secrets hidden in its roots. When they learned about the magnitude of the offense, they humbled and purified themselves at the foot of the tree, making supplications and sacrifices.

Thus, the few patches of grass that were still green, the four-legged animals, the birds who had survived, and the men who were still alive and had become clairvoyant through the secrets of the silk-cotton tree, consummated the first sacrifice for the sake of Earth. The offerings were sent to Heaven using the lightest of all birds, the *tomeguín* [Cuban grass quit],[2] which they believed would be the most able to reach the great heights of Heaven. The little bird took off, but he could not reach his destiny. On the way he became the victim of great fatigue and could not go on. The *pitirre* [giant king bird][3] was then chosen because of his courage and daring. Yet he had no better luck. Other birds were also chosen for the mission, but their wings either broke or their hearts failed.

Then *ara kolé* (the vulture), said: "I am going to take the supplications to Heaven since I am sure that I will be the only one able to reach the other shore." Everyone looked down at the somber and repulsive bird. Then the intrepid kestrel, a great flier, took off and was soon out of sight. A very short distance from his destiny the fast kestrel collapsed, and Earth lost, again, one of its best messengers.

Everyone then wondered if that heavy and dumb bird that fed on carrion would be able to carry out the mission. That ill-smelling scavenger was their last resource. *Ara kolé* took off, carrying Earth's last hopes even though no one really trusted in the success of his mission. Ara Kolé flew tirelessly during days and nights. Serenely, he flew to the other side of the firmament, where he delivered Earth's message and deposited her offerings.

"Heaven, Earth has sent me to ask your forgiveness. The creatures and children of Earth ask your pardon. They are your slaves and from deep inside their hearts they beg you to forgive them. Lord, Earth has died. All of us are dying. Hens, roosters, pigeons, lambs, dogs, cats; they have all died. Men are dying, too. Please forgive us."

Heeding his plea, Heaven turned his eyes to Earth, which he had for so long ignored. He took an intense look and saw her naked death. He took another look and saw how those dying dutifully revered him. Heaven accepted the offerings and said to *ara kolé*: "I forgive Earth." At that same moment the creatures on Earth saw the clouds rushing in from the Four Corners of the sky, and they heard the croak of the liquid frogs that came from the clouds or had been resurrected from the dust. Noisily, the water began to roar in the abyss where it had been kept, and it rushed down like great cascades until it reached the thirsty Earth.

Ara kolé flew days and nights, in the great spatial desert running away from the deluge, which threatened to drown him. As he was reaching Earth it almost overtook him in its untamed gush over the thirsty land. The incessant rains formed a great lake.

Thanks to Iroko the creatures were saved from the deluge. Earth quenched its thirst and covered its nakedness with new green foliage, while incessantly thanking Heaven. However, Earth never knew again the happy days of the beginning of creation. Heaven never again gave much attention, care, or affection to Earth and became indifferent to her many calamities and woes. Everybody knows how life has been since then. (Cros Sandoval 1975:109–10)

This *pataki* has great importance in understanding the Yoruban worldview and the worldview of followers of Santería. It reveals very clearly the meaning of "good" in the Supreme Being's "heart" and the creation of the world. It points to the need for coolness, balance, and tranquility in all of creation—both heaven and earth. It specifies the great harm triggered by the assumption of illegitimate authority, and it identifies the nature of "evil" that is engendered by such disordered relationships. Finally, it underlines a fundamental assumption about the presence of both good and evil in all aspects of life on earth. There is also the implication that these characteristics of power in the world will require constant attention and care. Many other inferences could be made but, aside from pointing out the positive and negative in all realms of life as a consequence of failure to acquiesce to legitimate authority, these will remain for interested readers to ferret out at their leisure.

11

Orishas/Orichas

The Yoruba make a distinction between the supernatural nature of the orishas versus the human nature of deified ancestors. When asked what an orisha is, they will frequently respond, "An orisha is someone who came from heaven." The following Afro-Cuban myth explains how these supernatural forces were created:

> In the beginning Olodumare visited this planet and there was no earth, no trees, nothing but flaming rocks. For many centuries the fire flared, and the vapor produced by the flames accumulated a nebula so heavy in space that it could not hold itself up. This was so because it was the will of Olofin, and he discharged this vapor, already transformed into water over the flames.
>
> In areas where the flames were more destructive and the rocks were more heavily burned, great depressions were formed. This is where the great oceans appeared, where all the Yemayás of the sea were born, from Okute to Olokun. Afterward the fire in this planet was no more, and now it is in heaven according to Olodumare's will, illuminating the sun Aganyú, and all things created.
>
> After many days the ash left by the ignited rocks accumulated in the highest areas and the muddy mass formed was Oricha Oko. This muddy mass brought epidemics and putrefaction, and Babalú Ayé was formed. As a just consequence Osain was created, along with all the medicinal herbs and bushes of the planet. In the highest areas, mountains, or Oke, were created, which only Olofin can destroy. From Oke volcanoes were born, which produce *metralla* (munitions) used by Ogún and all strong *orichas*. (Cros Sandoval 1975:119)

The orishas are the lesser divinities of the Yoruban pantheon. They are immortal beings and generally the personification of the forces of nature and the patrons of human activities and professions. Often the Yoruba will say that the orishas are people who were turned into stone or who disappeared into the bowels of the earth. These comments refer to archaeological materials found in the sacred city of Ile Ife, where the statuettes made of wood, bronze, and terra cotta are considered relics of the gods.

Pierre Verger (1954:13) notes that, in reality, an orisha is a force of nature, something of supernatural aspect, a powerful phenomenon that has been assigned to the care of a human being in a determined place. This first person who was initiated in the cult of an orisha is an alashe (guardian, or owner of supernatural power, or ashe). The orisha establishes with the alashe a relationship of interdependence. In order to preserve its force, the sacred power, or ashe, of the orisha needs the offerings and sacrifices of the alashe. Conversely, the orisha protects the alashe to the same degree that the latter makes the prescribed sacrifices and offerings. The power of the orisha is fixed normally in a material object, frequently a stone. This object is given to the alashe by the orisha to signify that he or she accepts the pact.

Several earthly elements, such as a diversity of dirt, leaves, and animal bones are used in the process of fixing the force. After being fixed to objects consecrated to him or her, the orisha remains incorporeal and immaterial, but his/her force has been tamed. The alashe is then capable of invoking the orisha by means of formulas known only to the alashe.

According to Verger (1954:14), eventually the first alashe becomes an orisha. After his or her death, the descendants continue to celebrate the rites and ceremonies that the alashe practiced while alive, intimately associating their ancestor and the god. Later on, after a process of ancestor deification, the first alashe, now transmuted into an orisha, will serve as liaison between the living and the power of the orisha. Moreover, rituals, dances, and songs to the orisha might incorporate reference to the passions, wars, and great deeds of the mythical ancestor. Thus, the orisha is assigned human passions and personality.

Robin Horton also focuses on the double aspect of the orisha as partly a nature spirit and also a deified ancestor:

"In this way, an orisa that started its career as a force of nature, pure and simple, will come to acquire a strong overlay of deified human individuality" Horton (1983:63).

This belief has been preserved in Cuba. An informant of Lydia Cabrera (1980:344) told her: "The dead are as sacred as the *orichas*, since before being *orichas* they were men; they died and they became saints. It is a fact that from the dead the *santo* was born."

The fact that a mythical ancestor is identified with the orisha it served does not detract from the superhuman character of the god. The Yoruba clearly distinguish between the supernatural nature of the orisha and the human nature of their revered ancestors. Yet, revered ancestors receive worship in measures appropriate to their wisdom and character. There are several etymological interpretations of the word orisha. According to James Johnson (1899:34), Ifa, the oracle god, ordered some of the first inhabitants to go in search of the wisdom he had spread around the world. Those who found it were hence called awon to orisha, that is, "the ones who were successful." They were worshipped after death. R. E. Dennett (1910:12) believes the word means "the sanctified who left," while M. L. Epega (1935:6) thinks that the word orisha is derived from the practice of sinking a clay kettle in the dirt to mark the chapel of a god.

Orisha worship is open to everyone. It often takes place in public ceremonies in the temples or chapels dedicated to each or a few of the gods. The leading celebrants are priests exclusively dedicated to the worship of a specific orisha. The faithful also usually have chapels in their homes, where they worship their orishas in private.

People ordinarily worship several orishas as children, including the adopted orishas of their father, mother, or both. In most of the cases studied by Bascom (1969b:77), the family seems to be the nucleus of the worship of an orisha. This tradition does not mean that the worship of a specific orisha is always tied to a particular family.

Children might abandon the worship of the orishas of their parents due to personal reasons or because the oracle has so advised. Moreover, a person might worship an orisha who was never worshipped by his or her parents or grandparents. Often a priest indicates that an unborn child has to worship a particular orisha. Others may have to render service to a certain god all their lives because, at birth, some signs were observed that identified them with that divinity.

Commonly an orisha is worshipped by the inhabitants of the neighborhood of a city, by the whole city, or by a district formed by several towns and cities. Even though there are gods who are revered throughout Yorubaland, many gods are known only in a particular village or district. Moreover, in Yorubaland, different generic gods are worshipped regionally. For instance, in the area around Oyo, the thunder god was Shango; in Ile Ife it was Oramfe; in Sabe it was Aira.

Many Cuban scholars argue that a large number of slaves were brought from the region of Oyo to Cuba, which would explain why Changó is the undisputed thunder god in Afro-Cuban Santería. Moreover, the complex paraphernalia related to his worship has been preserved, and some rituals specifically related to his cult are now part of the worship of all *orichas*. A similar situation is the case of Oshun, who, in Nigeria, is one of many river goddesses. She is worshipped in Ilesha, especially around the area of Oshogbo. In other regions, however, she is not as well known. In Cuba, she became the sole owner of all rivers, brooks, and springs, while, Oya and Oba, two other fluvial divinities in Yorubaland that are spouses of powerful Shango, are worshipped by Afro-Cubans but not as fluvial divinities. Oyá is admired for her courage and determination and because she owns the destructive flare (lightning) as well as the keys of the dreaded cemetery. Conversely, Oba elicits respect, sympathy, and compassion for her selflessness, for being a model for devout housewives.

According to some oral traditions, there were 401 orishas in the Yoruban pantheon. However, if local demons and supernatural beings are included, the number changes to thousands. In Cuba, the number of *orichas* was greatly reduced from hundreds, or even thousands, to a mere twenty. In Cuba, only the generic divinities known throughout Yorubaland, such as the generic gods of thunder, the sea, fluvial waters, metals, herbs, and diseases and epidemics, took root; the local gods of lagoons, hills, streams, and brooks failed to do so.

In most instances, the pervasive Yorubaland divinities were identified with local Yoruban orishas as well as with non-Yoruban African gods who shared similar attributes and characteristics. Through this process, the generic Yoruban orisha absorbed the minor or local orishas, as well as non-Yoruban gods. Thus, Yoruban local gods were forgotten in Cuba or, if worshipped, lost their identity and became known as *caminos* (paths or different manifestations) of the generic gods. Thus, Obatalá, the Yoruban creator god, and "viceroy" of Olodumare on earth, is an *oricha* in Cuba, with many *caminos*, or manifestations. In Cuba *Obatalá* assimilated creator gods known in only certain regions of Yorubaland as well as creator gods of other African pantheons. For example, Obalufon, the Yoruban god of peace and speech, is worshipped in Cuba as one of the many *caminos* of Obatalá, the peace-loving god who sculpted the human body. Naná Burukú, the great creator goddess of Dahomey, is a *camino* of Obatalá in some areas of Cuba.

Many *caminos* of the Afro-Cuban divinities reflect the diverse local expressions of the worship of a god in Yorubaland, where localism prevailed over religious uniformity and homogeneity. For example, Ayágguna is one of the *caminos* of Obatalá in Cuba, whereas in Yorubaland Ayagguna is the name given to Obatala in the regions of Ketou and Sabe. This process had African antecedents. According to Percy Amaury Talbot (1926 2:29): "The deities assume different forms, names, and attributes—or perhaps it might be said with more accuracy that different aspects come into prominence—in successive ages."

The processes of change reached the point where kinship ties, unrecognized in Nigeria, intimately related members of the Afro-Cuban heavenly court. In some Cuban *patakís*, Changó, the thunder god, is the illegitimate son of Obatalá and Agayú Solá, the patron of porters. In these same *patakís*, however, Obatalá appears manifested in a *camino* as a strong female. In still other *patakís*, Obatalá who, this time, is manifested as an old man, is the father of Changó. Obatalá and his wife Yemmu had four other sons: Orúla, the god of the oracle; the warrior Ogún; the messenger Elegguá; and Babalú Ayé, the god of plagues. Changó's godfather is Osain, the owner of all magical medicinal herbs. In this fashion, the gods appear related to each other as if they were members of one great family whose problems, worries, and actions affect the entire world.

The merging process also strengthened some gods at the expense of the attributes, character, and mythology of others. Eleggúa, the restless messenger of the gods, the greatest assistant of Orúla, also assumes in Cuba the important role that Ogún, the god of war, had in Africa; that is, Eleggúa in Cuba opens the door to contact between gods and men. Ochún, the Afro-Cuban goddess of the river, likewise usurps the place of Aje Saluga, a most propitiated Yoruban god who is the owner of cowrie shells and, consequently, riches and money.

The Afro-Cuban religion had to make some concessions to the New World environment. Thus, Oricha Oko, the popular Yoruban god of horticulture, associated with the fertility of domesticated roots, lost importance in Cuba, where his worship and cult practices were perceived as lewd, lascivious, and obscene. It is also possible that Oricha Oko lost in Cuba because slaves would not care to worship him to encourage the fertility of the master's crops. Moreover, many slaves were involved with the planting and processing of sugar cane, coffee, and tobacco, which were not crops associated with Oricha Oko in Africa.

Most importantly, the *orichas* were also identified with Catholic saints. Blacks, in the search for congruencies and logico-structural integration of worldview assumptions, understood Catholicism in their own way, interpreting it according to their own religious meanings. To them the worship of saints was nothing more than the white man's equivalent of Yoruban polytheism. Consequently, the Catholic influence did not reinforce monotheism or the position and importance of Olodumare, who remained as remote as he had been in Africa. Since the processes of syncretism and transculturation included the association with Catholic saints, the Afro-Cuban *oricha/santo* that emerged from this fusion was essentially an African divinity, who, due to Christian influence, sometimes assumed new attributes and characteristics. For example, Babalú Ayé, the god of smallpox in Yorubaland, once identified with Saint Lazarus, lost some of his terrifying and awe-inspiring characteristics and assumed instead those of a pitiful and merciful healer.

In chapters 12 through 21 a comparison is made between the character and worship of the principal orishas in Yorubaland and the *orichas* in Cuba. The intent is to delineate some of the changes and modifications in character, status, and attributes that Yoruban orishas experienced as a result of adaptive and transculturative processes in Cuba.

12

Obatala/Obatalá and Oduduwa/Odudua

Creator Gods

Obatala in Africa

Obatala, or Orishanla, is the oldest and most important orisha in the Yoruba pantheon. He is one of the few gods that is known to all Yoruba-speaking people and their neighbors. He is the king of the orishas and is credited with playing a decisive role in the creation of the world and human beings.

Obatala is, without a doubt, a very ancient divinity. According to oral traditions and myths, he is the son of Olodumare. Contradictory stories, however, claim that he was born in Igbo and was the monarch in Iranje. This would categorize him as a deified ancestor and not a heavenly god. Nevertheless, no myth or oral tradition associates him with any historical figure. In other words, he is not a deified hero like Shango. Indeed, these very traditions narrate how Obatala, who was a heavenly god, was ordered by the Supreme Deity to come down to live on earth.

Obatala is the "viceroy" of Olodumare, whose attributes are revealed to mortals through Obatala. Consequently, Obatala is called Alabalese, which is Olodumare's title meaning "the proponent who carries the scepter." According to one myth, Obatala came to earth by order of the Supreme Deity. Olodumare gave him odu, the attribute of supreme authority, so that his mandates would be obeyed by all, including the other orishas. Obatala, thus, is the viceregent and permanent delegate of Olodumare on earth. He is the most ancient of all the orishas, a sort of dean and chief of all the gods.

As legend tells us, the creation of the earth took four days. The fifth day was for rest and for the worship of the Supreme Being. According to the myth, when Olodumare created the world, the planet was nothing but a swamp. The orishas had to use spider webs to climb down. One day, Olodumare decided to create solid land. He called Obatala and gave him a land-snail shell that held some dry dirt, a five-fingered chicken, and a pigeon.

Obatala came to earth in search of the appropriate place to accomplish the task assigned to him. Once he found the right spot, he spilled the dirt and let the chicken and pigeon loose. The fowl, with their feet, scattered the dirt in all directions, thus covering a large part of the swamp. The place chosen by Obatala was Ife, where the city of Ile Ife, the cradle of humanity and the home of the Yoruban people, was founded. Pleased with Obatala's accomplishments, Olodumare sent him to embellish the planet. This time Obatala came with Orunmila, the god of wisdom and divination. The two orishas brought trees, among them the palm tree. They also brought several human beings with their leader, Oreluere, whom Olodumare had created to populate the earth.

Olodumare kept for himself the power of giving life to human beings, but he entrusted Obatala with the task of sculpting and molding from clay the physical human form. Obatala is called Eleda (the maker). Pregnant women usually make offerings to him in the hope that they will have healthy children. After the offering is given, the priest says, "Ki Orisha ya na re ko ni o," which means, "Let Orishanla make for us a good work of art." If, instead, a child is born with physical imperfections, it is assumed that Obatala's rage or oversight caused it, and that child has to commit to the cult of Obatala. Albinos, very specifically, are considered children of Obatala. They are called Eri Orisha (the devotees of the orisha).

The name Obatala is a contraction of the phrase "Oba ti o nla," meaning "the great king." There is yet another etymological interpretation: "oba ti ala" means "the king who dresses in white." White is the color of purity, one of the attributes of this orisha, who always dresses in white. Obatala, the god of purity, is the manifestation of Olodumare's ethical and moral principles and the embodiment of these qualities. Immaculate whiteness, the symbol of purity and holiness, symbolizes this god who, consequently, demands high moral conduct from human beings. Two words, orisha (god) and nla (great), form the word Orishanla, one of the names given to Obatala. The Yoruba envision this god as a kind, venerable, reasonable, respectable, and authoritarian old man, always dressed in white.

Obatala is the fun fun white orisha par excellence. The fun fun orishas (Obatala, Osanyin, Orisha Oko) always dress in white, cannot eat food cooked with palm oil and are associated with tranquility. The temples of Obatala are painted white; his emblems are kept in white receptacles; and white is the color of the beads of the necklaces that symbolize his power. His priests and priestesses must always be dressed in white, and they can eat only white food, cooked with "shea" butter made from the seeds of the shea tree. Their food must never be cooked with the red oil of the palm tree.

The water in Obatala's temples must be changed daily by a virgin or an old lady of good moral reputation. These women fetch the water from a clean spring very early in the morning to ensure its purity. As mentioned above,

Obatala demands exemplary moral behavior from his followers. It is frequently said that their lives must be "as clear as water gathered very early in the morning from a fresh spring."

Land snails belong to Obatala. According to Thompson, the Yoruba say, "Snail fluid is the thing we use to cool Obatala when he is angry, to make him patient, for the snail itself is the patient animal." Thompson explains (1976: CH16/1), "The fluid of the snail is called the 'water of the calm' (omiero), an exalted purity exciting man to be beautiful and strong. It is a positive vitality. It is patience brought to bear against darkness and hate."

Whereas Olodumare, the Supreme Being, never takes iconic form, Obatala is represented by anthropomorphic images made of wood and stone. In Ile Ife ancient images of Obatala are still revered. In some of them, Obatala, or Sky, and his wife Yemowo are portrayed. In other parts of Yorubaland, Obatala, or Sky, is married to Oduduwa, or Earth.

Obatala is Adimula, the orisha of security. He is the trustworthy god who always respects agreements and is faithful to duty. He is also Obata Arugbo, the ancient father king of the orishas. At times he is called Ibikeji Edumare, "the deputy of Olodumare," because the orishas frequently ask him to intercede on their behalf before Olodumare. Obatala's importance is such that the Oni (king) of Ile Ife, the spiritual head of the Yoruba, has to be presented to Obatala on the day of his coronation to receive from Obatala the scepter of authority that makes him a divine ruler.

Obatala is also the god of peace and order and the protector of the doors of the city. Images of Obatala as a knight with a spear, attended by a serpent, a turtle, a fish, or a leopard, are often placed at the entrances of towns. Throughout Yorubaland, Obatala's cult and attributes are very similar. However, he is known by several different names. In Ifon, he is called Olufon; in Owe, Orisharowu; in Oba, Orisha Oloba; and in Ijay, Orisha Ijaye. In Ketou, he is called Ayagguna; in Ejigbo, Oshagiyan. In Ile Ife, Obatala is worshipped under different names in the three neighborhoods, or districts: Orisha Ideta, Orisha Akire, and Orisha Ijugbe. According to Thompson (1979:CH16/1), the music played for Obatala in festivals has some unique characteristics: "There is ease, space, and flow to the phrasing of the drums for Obatala: force with relaxation. Obatala music is a journey to the cool, guided not by fire but by rippling meter, lucid as water jeweled by the wind."

Obatalá in Cuba

In Cuba, as in Africa, Obatalá is the *oricha* of creation, the chief of all the *orichas* and the most influential assistant of Olodumare, the Supreme Being.

Afro-Cuban oral traditions claim that, in the beginning, there were sixteen Obatalás who met at Iran Yé, the land of good luck and the highest and hottest point in the area where all matter was solidified. These traditions show very close resemblance to the Yoruban creation myth.

In another very well-known Afro-Cuban *pataki*, Obatalá is the son of Olodumare, who came down to earth to rule in Olodumare's name. An informant of Lydia Cabrera (1954:307) specifies that Babá, a male Obatalá, and his wife Yemmu, a female Obatalá, came down from heaven, trembling with fear, to do good and to establish order and respect.

Obatalá is Olori, the owner of heads. The word head stands for holiness, saintliness, and divinity. Every human being has "a head," or *ori*, an *oricha* who is his guardian angel. As described previously, at the end of the ceremony of initiation into this religion, the person's guardian angel is fixed on his head. Thereafter, the initiated enjoys the privilege, or power, of being possessed by his protector divinity. Obatalá may act on behalf of a person who, for whatever reason, may have caused the displeasure of his protector *oricha*. The *orichas* respect him and usually behave very well in his presence.

In Africa and in Cuba, Obatalá is the sculptor of the human form. Olofi made man without a head; Oduduwa made the head with only one eye; Obatalá Iba Ibo, however, gave human beings their other eye, their mouth, words, and language. When creation was complete, Olodumare breathed into man until his heart started to beat "fuque fuque." For this reason, in Cuba and Africa, Obatalá is called Alamorere (the one who works with the best clay).

Obatalá has multiple manifestations, or *caminos*. In some myths he is a male warrior, in others an old man, and yet in others an old lady or even a young woman. This variety of persona is caused by Cuba's absorption of local cults of Obatalá from different areas of Nigeria as well as various creator divinities from diverse areas of Yorubaland and other African regions.

In numerous *patakís* collected by Rómulo Lachatañeré (1938: 38–59, 132–34, 145–51), Obatalá, manifest as a goddess, is a vigorous woman in the prime of life. She alone knows the road that leads to the residence of Olodumare. She is so influential that she persuaded the Deity to meet with the *orichas* and grant each one part of his power. Obatalá was given power over all other deities. Thus, she is called the "owner of the heads." Obatalá is the agent of the Deity on earth, and as such is the arbitrator of restrictions and concessions to the *orichas* in the cult houses.

Obatalá is called Baba Arugbo (the old father). In some cult homes he is perceived as a white-haired, respectable, and venerable old man with sideburns. He resides in a palace with sixteen windows, situated on top of a mountain.

According to yet another version, Olofin is the Supreme Being and Olodumare is the combination of the sixteen original Obatalá *oruns*, which formed Olorún, the sun. In another Afro-Cuban myth recorded by Teodoro Díaz Fabelo (1956:164), also known in Yorubaland, Obatalá and Oduduwa are the two great halves of a gourd, which form a sphere. The top half depicts Obatalá as heaven and the bottom part depicts Oduduwa as earth. In Santería, Obatalá's children have to be consecrated to Oduduwa, who is considered the guide of all Obatalás. Obatalá is known for his great healing powers. He is the owner of hospitals, and, together with Ochosi, owns prisons and jails. He is the *oricha* of purity and owns all "white" parts of humans: thoughts, dreams, and the head.

As mentioned previously, the paths (*caminos*, or manifestations) of this god are numerous. Most people believe that there are sixteen Obatalás; while others think there are twenty-four. Lydia Cabrera recorded information about many of the different *caminos* of Obatalá (1954:308–14). In my Ph.D. dissertation (1966), I theorized that many of the paths or *caminos* are regional manifestations of the cult of Obatalá. Andrew Apter (1992:30) believes that "most of Obatala's local names are in fact modified place-names and kingship titles from areas that fell to Oyo." In Apter's opinion the Oyo Empire fostered the worship of Obatala as a compromise and amendment gesture between the conqueror and the conquered. He thinks (1992:31) that the festivals to Obatala that were celebrated annually in areas under Oyo's suzerainty dignified Oyo overrule for the victors as well as the vanquished, diminishing Ile Ife's political status while validating its ritual primacy.

In Cuba, no temples were built specifically to Obatalá, though like other *orichas* he is worshiped in sanctuaries in priests' homes. Rooms dedicated to his worship are painted white. Obatalá is represented either by images or lithographs of Catholic saints with whom the *oricha* has been associated. His consecrated stone, or *otán,* is white, and it is called *oke.* This stone is carefully kept in a white soup bowl that is decorated with white beads. Inside the soup bowl, this god's attributes are placed: a serpent of white metal, eight or sixteen land snails, and cocoa lard (obtained from the cocoa fruit). These symbols must be covered with cotton, because Obatalá is a very sensitive and clean god.

Obatalá's priests are called *olo Obatalá.* The word *olo* is used to designate all priests. The priests, priestesses, and children of Obatalá are called *ochabi.* They enjoy the extraordinary privilege of being possessed by all other *orichas,* as their *eledá* is the "owner of all heads."

The necklace of this *oricha* is made of white beads, the color of purity. Moreover, Obatalá's flag is white, and the color ivory is used to represent him. The tusk of an elephant is also his symbol. In Cuba, as in Africa, albinos belong to this *oricha* and should be consecrated to his cult. The cotton flower is another symbol of Obatalá. The following legend, a part of the Afro-Cuban oral tradition, is recorded in a *santero's* notebook: "The cotton tree flower tenderly covers Obatalá with a cape. This honor provoked the terrible envy of Eiye the birds. They disrespected and slandered the tree. They also asked the sun and the moon to burn it and dry it with fire and ice. The cotton tree gently suffered and, close to extinction, it pleaded to Obatalá. Obatalá was moved by the innocence of the cotton tree. In the eyes of Obatalá, birds became despicable and perverse connivers. To punish their evil ways, Obatalá commanded their eyes to swell any time they touched the buttons of the cotton tree, which from that moment on, were equipped with thorns."

In Cuba, the fruit known as *zapote (achras nill)* belongs to Obatalá and is one of his favorite foods. The following *pataki* from oral tradition was recorded in a *santero*'s notebook: "Obatalá knew that the Supreme Being loved to eat *zapotes*. She hoped to gather and give some as presents to obtain merits. Although she had to go through numerous and unpleasant incidents, she was finally able to get the *zapotes* and offer them to the Deity."

A white, edible tubercle known as *ñame* (yam; *Alata dioscorea*) belongs to this *oricha*. Land snails, whose bodies are covered with a liquid that represents coolness and are believed to lack blood, belong to this *oricha* and are Obatalá's favorite meal. Obatalá is offered white fowl, pigeons, white canaries, and white female goats. He enjoys *kamanaku,* a white paste made of ground rice; *tamales* made with black-eyed peas without salt; and meringues. According to legend, Obatalá cannot eat salt because one day Babalú Ayé, the god of plagues who once lived in the wilderness, came to Obatalá's house when everyone had finished eating. Only Obatalá's portion was left, and she gave it to Babalú Ayé. Afterward, when Obatalá went to the kitchen to cook, she realized that there was no salt. Since that day this *oricha* eats without salt. Obatalá cannot eat land crabs or white beans either and, as in Africa, liquor is taboo for her Cuban children.

The half moon, a serpent, and a full moon are symbols of this *oricha.* The *opa* is Obatalá's baton and the *opaye* is his/her scepter. Silver bells are used to call Obatalá, and silver bracelets are given as offerings. Number eight is Obatalá's number, and eight herbs are used to wash this *oricha*'s necklaces. Thursday *(yoba)* is dedicated to this *oricha.*

During drum festivals Obatalá's dances vary according to the different manifestations, or *caminos,* of the god. As Obalufón, Obatalá is a bent little old lady who dances with great elegance and cadence. Obamoro is a decrepit old man who falls on the floor and cannot dance. Naná Burukú trembles and drools and can hardly dance. Ayágguna is a handsome warrior who dances vigorously with warlike movements while carrying a sword. Ochalufón is also a warrior who dances with vigor. Obanlá does not dance. Instead she speaks softly and foretells the future. People embrace her with fondness in greeting. Yeguá very rarely dances or possesses the believer, but when she does she is dressed in a pink robe with a crown of cowry shells. She is especially shy in the presence of men. Instead of dancing, she rotates her arms as if unraveling yarn.

Obatalá's children always dress in white. When Obatalá possesses them in a warrior manifestation, a wide red stripe is placed across their chests. Obamoro is exceptional among Obatalás because sometimes he is dressed in purple. The choice of color may account for his association with Jesus of Nazareth, who is represented wearing a purple garment on the day of his crucifixion.

Obatalá is one of the most important *orichas* of Afro-Cuban Santería despite the contradictions in many of the traditions regarding this god. Since the Supreme Being in both Nigeria and Cuba has no priests dedicated to his worship, the power and influence of Obatalá gained importance. In Afro-Cuban Santería, in some instances, Obatalá is associated with the Catholic Supreme Being. In Cuba, as in Africa, Obatalá is considered the *oricha* of creation, the chief of all the gods, and the most influential helper of the Deity.

In Cuba, Yoruban people converged from very different regions and knew the *oricha* Obatalá by different names. Moreover, myths referring to his character, origin, and attributes varied from region to region in Africa. In Cuba these diverse regional traditions were merged under the worship of Obatalá, and regional differences in names and characteristics were perceived as different manifestations of this *oricha.* The merging of the cults of other non-Yoruban African creator gods with the cult of Obatalá further complicated this situation. The differences in characteristics and attributes of the merging elements were perceived as different manifestations of this god.

The most important *caminos,* or paths, of Obatalá in Cuba are included in Appendix A.

Oduduwa in Africa

The worship of Oduduwa is widespread throughout Yorubaland. Etymological interpretations of the name Oduduwa vary. Some scholars believe that the word derives from dudu (black) and the substantive iwa (existence). Oduduwa would thus mean "the black one." Others speculate that the name Oduduwa is derived from odu (figure, supreme chief, scepter) and the element da wa (one who exists by himself). Oduduwa would then mean "the chief who exists by himself." Other scholars believe that the name Oduduwa is derived from the adjectival clause o ti da iwa (the chief who created human beings).

In Nigeria, traditions and myths about the character and gender of Oduduwa are often contradictory. In some regions, Oduduwa is a creator goddess of high moral attributes, while in other places the rituals of the goddess Oduduwa involve lascivious behavior and practices. In yet other regions, Oduduwa is a masculine divinity.

The contradictions about the gender, character, and behavior of this god are due in part to its great antiquity. In the oldest myths, Oduduwa is a creator goddess, older than Obatala and a contemporary of Olodumare. Oduduwa is depicted as a breast-feeding mother who represents the feminine principle, the fertile creator mother of the Yoruba. In some liturgical songs Oduduwa is invoked as Iyá Imale (the mother of the gods). In other myths, Oduduwa and her husband Obatala are the creator couple who form the gourd or planet. Oduduwa is called Iyá Agbe (the mother of the gourd) and shares with her husband Obatala the attributes of purity and order. In contrast, in the coastal city of Ado, Oduduwa, far from being the embodiment of purity and order, is a licentious and passionate goddess probably associated with fertility. In some regions, Oduduwa usurps the attributes and power of Obatala; in other areas he shares them. However, in Porto, Dahomey, the two divinities are one androgynous god—Oduduwa.

More recent traditions portray Oduduwa as a masculine divinity. In Ile Ife, Oduduwa is married to Olokun, the goddess of the waters. They form the creator couple: earth and water. Moreover, in the regions where Oduduwa is a masculine divinity, he is associated with the legendary hero, Ile Ife's first king. There, Oduduwa is represented on horseback, leading his people. These myths are known in Ile Ife and the regions under its influence.

Oduduwa is the name of the legendary leader of the invaders who, coming from the north, conquered the city and territory of Ile Ife. They subjugated the aboriginal population and eventually organized a vast kingdom that dominated and influenced large areas of Nigeria. According to some traditions, Oduduwa's sixteen children formed the first sixteen kingdoms. According to other traditions, the descendants of Oduduwa's seven children formed the first seven tribes of the Yoruban nation. Thus, most of the local kings of Nigeria legitimize their authority by claiming direct descent from the legendary Oduduwa.

E. B. Idowu (1962: 22–29) says that when Oduduwa and his warriors arrived at Ile Ife, Obatala was the creator god of the local population. The invaders' creator goddess was Oduduwa. Great conflicts developed between conquerors and vanquished. The invaders refused to pay homage to Oreluere, the vanquished king. Oreluere, seeking revenge, poisoned the daughter of the leader of the invaders, who desperately tried to save her, but to no avail. Finally, Oduduwa asked Oreluere for help. Oreluere demanded as retribution sheep and fowl, and when Oduduwa complied his daughter recovered.

After the leader of the invaders died, Oduduwa was worshipped as just another ancestor. He probably had a different name; but after death, apotheosis, and consequent deification, he came to be worshipped by the name of the goddess Oduduwa, whose cult he had tried in vain to impose on the original population in Ile Ife. Later, his cult took on the characteristics of orisha worship.

In a contrasting story from Ile Ife's traditions, Obatala, the orisha of peace and purity, fought a long war against a strong adversary, which was contrary to Obatala's character and personality. Who was this adversary? It is probably Oduduwa, the goddess of the invaders of Ile Ife. Consequently, the cult of Obatala is characterized by ceremonies in which battles are enacted. Moreover, the image of Obatala, revered in Ideta, a neighborhood of Ile Ife, depicts him holding the head of an enemy in his own hands.

Idowu (1962: 22–29) makes reference to a myth in which Oramfe, the god of thunder, following urgent orders from Olodumare, had to come down from heaven to earth to suppress a civil war. It is possible that the myth originated during that period.

Three years before Idowu's work, Ulli Beier (1959: 15) also pointed out that Obatala was the creator god of the original people of Ile Ife, who were conquered by the invaders, who later adopted him as their deity. In Beier's opinion this greatly affected Obatala's character, who conquers through patience and wisdom, abhorring violence.

Later on, in Ile Ife, new generations emerged that belonged to the two conflicting worlds. Local women conceived children fathered by the invader's warriors. These children were exposed to the traditions of the conquerors and their creator goddess, Oduduwa, as well as those of Ile Ife's residents and their creator god, Obatala. After a few generations, the religious beliefs of conquerors and conquered merged. Thus, a creator god emerged with the attributes and name of the goddess of the conquerors, those of their legendary human leader, and also those of the creator god of the vanquished.

The political and religious ascendancy of Ile Ife propelled this cult. In many areas around Ile Ife individuals who distinguish themselves as examples of civic virtues are called omo Oduduwa (children of Oduduwa). This tradition became known in a large area of Nigeria, and it evolved into an official, civic, national, and patriotic cult. For instance, in Ibadan, in the center of Yorubaland, there is a nationalistic society called The Society of the Children of Oduduwa, whose members recognize Oduduwa as the founder of the Yoruban people. This society's aims are more political than religious. According to Idowu (1962: 22), ancient myths were revised to accommodate the new views contained in the Obatala and Oduduwa myths. In the original version, Obatala creates the solid earth during his first trip to the planet, casting a handful of dirt on the place where Ile Ife was erected and letting a chicken spread the dirt over the primeval oceans. On his second journey, Obatala brought palm trees and other plants that Olodumare ordered to be planted. In these myths Oduduwa is not even mentioned.

In the revised version, Oduduwa usurps Obatala's place as creator of the earth at the price of great contradictions. Thus, according to the revised myths, after Olodumare gave instructions to Obatala to create dry earth, on the way down to the planet Obatala felt very thirsty and drank the only thing he found, palm wine. He drank excessively and fell into a drunken stupor, failing to return to Olodumare. The Supreme Deity, worried, sent Oduduwa to fetch him. When Oduduwa found Obatala sleeping, instead of waking him up, he took the bag containing the instruments of creation and carried out Olodumare's command. Oduduwa selected a place to put the dirt, which later was scattered by the chicken and pigeon. In this place the city of Ile Ife was later founded. Olodumare, satisfied, gave Oduduwa credit for creating the solid earth.

One can see the inconsistencies of the revised version. Since there was no solid earth, how could palm trees grow, thus making available the wine that intoxicated Obatala? Even in Ile Ife, the source of these revised versions, it is believed that, although Oduduwa is the creator of the solid earth, Olodumare had to send Obatala to establish order, since Oduduwa was not respected.

It is my view that the "jostling" of elements in this myth reflects the process of striving for logico-structural integration of images to fit changed understandings or historical circumstances.

Oduduwa's priests enjoy great respect and influence. They wear white clothing and ornaments, as do the priests of Obatala. Oduduwa prefers palm wine and sheep as offerings. Many pregnant women offer sacrifices to Oduduwa as they do to Obatala. In Nigeria there are many temples dedicated to the cult of this orisha. In Ile Ife, where he is associated with the royal house, his worship is a civic duty. In the temple dedicated to Oduduwa in Igbo Ora, there are several images of this god. In one of these, Oduduwa is represented as a goddess, breast-feeding her child. In another image the statue has two faces.

Oduduwa in Cuba

It is very likely that slaves from different areas of Nigeria brought the cult of Oduduwa to Cuba. Diverse places of origin might be the reason that Oduduwa is considered a male *oricha* in some cult houses; a female in others; and in still others, a divine power projected into the life of a legendary king. Many, however, consider Oduduwa to be a manifestation of Obatalá.

In a *pataki* known both in Cuba and in Africa, the universe is a giant gourd. The top half is the sky where Obatalá dwells. The lower half is the earth, the residence of Oduduwa (Cabrera 1971:392). Egungun ghosts wander between the two halves. Many followers of Santería think that Oduduwa is the goddess of the underworld, of the spirits of the dead.

In other *patakís*, which are derivations of myths known in Africa, Oduduwa takes Obatalá's role as sculptor of the human figure. According to these myths,

Olofín gave instructions to Oduduwa to make human beings' heads with only one eye. Obatalá Iba Ibo (a manifestation of Obatalá) then completes the physical outline of the body.

Among some believers, Oduduwa is the oldest Obatalá, who, with his wife Odduaremu, parented sixteen Obatalás. In many cult houses he is considered the guide of all Obatalás. In such situations the children of Obatalá have to be consecrated to Oduduwa.

In a *pataki* recorded by Lachatañeré (1938:40, 41), Oduduwa is a child/god who crosses the river on the shoulders of the powerful boatman, Agayú Solá. Oduduwa rewarded his carrier, Agayú Solá, by making him the owner of the river. In parts of Africa, Oduduwa is a goddess who breast-feeds her child. It is quite possible that Afro-Cubans associated Oduduwa with the image of the Virgin with the child Jesus. However, in those cult houses where the masculine character of Oduduwa is predominant, the identification is with the child instead of the Virgin. This myth seems to be an Afro-Cuban adaptation of the myth of Saint Christopher and baby Jesus, which predates Christianity. The original myth, which dates back to ancient Egypt, makes reference to a god that assisted the baby Osiris cross the Nile.

Oduduwa represents justice, truth, righteousness, immaculate essence, purity, and intelligence. Since these attributes are also characteristic of Obatalá, Oduduwa in Cuba is generally considered to be the most earnest manifestation of Obatalá.

In some cult houses, Oduduwa is perceived as a warrior on horseback carrying a machete, which may be reminiscent of the African leader who carried his men to victory in Ile Ife. In other households, Oduduwa is a male Obatalá who lives in the *iroko*, the silk-cotton tree. Oduduwa is considered the supreme concept of god, probably due to his omnipotence, omnipresence, and omniscience, the same characteristics of the Supreme Being. He knows and sees everything with his one eye. Oduduwa is also a great prophet. He works with Orúnmila, and together they represent the concept of firmness and certainty in prophecies.

The stones and images consecrated to Oduduwa are very powerful. It is believed that they are the basis for security in life, firmness of character, health, and intelligence possessed by their owners.

In Cuba Oduduwa also represents the dual principle of life and death. There is an image of Oduduwa in a temple in Igbo Ora that has two faces: one looks toward life and the other toward death. Nevertheless, the symbolism of this representation is quite obscure in Africa, especially when compared with Cuban renditions of Oduduwa, where such duality is rare or nonexistent.

In the past, in Santería Oduduwa was represented by lithographs of the Catholic saints with whom he/she had been identified. This *oricha* is also represented by the Osun of the *babalaos.* Osun is an *oricha* that protects the *babalaos.* It is the source of accuracy in their prophecies, and is represented by a little rooster or pigeon made of metal. Impure acts cannot take place in its presence since it is so delicate that any rudeness or noise would unsettle it. If harm should come to this Osun, it would be considered a catastrophic sign for its owner.

Oduduwa's power resides in his sixteen *otanes,* or sacred stones. These stones must be gathered on hills and roads and are consecrated in a long and complicated ceremony. Very few people can possess these stones; only those of whom the oracle approves may do so. Following consecration, the stones are placed in a soup bowl, or *goricha,* and are wrapped in pieces of cotton, as Oduduwa is very sensitive and pure. This soup bowl, containing the stones, has to be placed in a very high place.

Oduduwa's necklace is constructed of sixteen beads made of mother of pearl followed by eight coral beads. White, which in Nigeria represents purity, is the color of both Oduduwa and Obatalá. Oduduwa is also associated with ivory, pigeons, white horses, and deer. He shares with Obatalá the *iruke,* or baton of command, and Thursday *(yoba)* is the day dedicated to him and to Obatalá. Even though he owns thirty-six shells, he does not speak through them. Instead, the hand of Ifá, a bracelet, or *koide,* that is received by those consecrated to his worship, is the instrument used by Oduduwa to communicate with his followers.

Oduduwa loves to eat white roosters. Goats, washed with an African soap made with ashes and weeds, are also offered to him. He also likes to eat bulls, cows, and elephants. Even though it is impossible for Afro-Cubans to sacrifice elephants to these gods, this animal is still associated with him in Cuba. He also enjoys land snails and white hens. Most of the sacrifices offered to this divinity are similar to those offered to Obatalá, and in every temple of Obatalá, Oduduwa is also worshipped.

In the sequence of liturgical dance known as *oro del eya aranla* (the *oro* that takes place in the hall of the *ilé ocha*), after the three drumbeats dedicated to Obatalá an additional beat is offered in honor of Oduduwa. However, Oduduwa does not possess the initiated, because he is too powerful and awesome to be received by a human being. Oduduwa's high attributes of purity, goodness, justice, and truth may be the reasons that many believers use lithographs of Jesus Christ to represent him. Sometimes, Saint Emanuel, who is honored on January 1, also represents this *oricha.*

13

Orunmila/Orúnmila, Orunla/Orúnla, Orula/Orúla

God of Wisdom and the Oracle

Orunmila/Orunla/Orula in Africa

Everyone worships Orunmila, the god of wisdom and the oracles. In times of crisis, all benefit from his great wisdom and powerful influence over destiny. He mediates between men and Olodumare, because the Supreme Being lets men know his will and desires through the oracles. According to E. B. Idowu (1962: 75), the name Orunmila derives from the phrase Orun-l-o-mo-a-ti-la (Only heaven knows the means of salvation), or Orun-mo-ola (Only heaven can effect deliverance). Other authorities think the name Orunmila derives from the phrase Orun-mo-ola (Only heaven can give judgment). These interpretations seem to indicate that the most important function of the god of wisdom, oracles, and destiny is to save human souls. As such, Orunmila/Orunla/Orula's role is larger than merely helping human beings with the daily and less transcendental problems of everyday life. William Fagg (1982:25) states the following: "We may go further and say it is in sympathy with the Yoruba cosmological concept of an essentially square world founded on the number four and more especially on its multiple, sixteen—a system which can be endlessly illustrated from Yoruba art and myth, from the birds on the beaded crowns of the Yoruba Obas, and above all from the Odu of Ifá divination in which the order of the universe is both defined and applied to daily life."

Orunmila, one of the first orishas created by Olodumare, has the privilege of knowing the origin of all things, including gods. He has a special relationship with the Supreme Being, who is always referred to in the Ifa divination system as Olodumare. According to most myths, Olodumare sent Orunmila to the world to accompany, counsel, and aid Obatala during his second voyage, when human beings, trees, and plants were brought to earth. Many myths claim that Olodumare sent Orunmila to organize things and oversee experiences such as pregnancies, births, child-care, the use of medical and magical herbs, and other similar matters.

In one myth, Orunmila came to this planet and traveled through many lands before settling down in Ile Ife. In his journeys, Orunmila went to the land of the Ekiti, the Ado, and Ilesha. His worship was established everywhere he visited (Idowu 1962: 66). Thus, other people besides the Yoruba learned his divination system. When he arrived in Ile Ife, he decided to stay there, though he made it known that he belonged to the entire world. Since he is a linguist who knows every language in the world, he can be consulted by anyone anywhere.

Orunmila lived in Ile Ife for a long time. Later, he lived in different regions of Yorubaland until he settled, according to Wanda Abimbola (1997:5), possibly in Ado-Ekiti. Abimbola (1973:42) also thinks that accounts of the later life of Orunmila can be found in Iwori Meji, the third odu of the oracle of Ifa. As reflected in that odu, Orunmila never had children until later in life, when he had eight sons. One of these sons insulted Orunmila, who left earth and went to heaven. After Orunmila's departure all kinds of catastrophes began to occur: rain refused to fall, women could not bear their children alive, corn and beans would not ripen. The sons of Orunmila were persuaded by the people to beg their father to come back to earth. Instead of coming back, Orunmila gave his sons the sixteen palm nuts of divination by Ifa, representing all the power and wisdom of Olodumare that had been received upon his creation by the Supreme Being.

In many ways, Orunmila guides the destiny of humans and gods. He is present at the time human beings are created and their destiny sealed. Orunmila knows the future. He also has the power to prescribe the remedies and sacrifices necessary to avoid any catastrophe forecast by him. His name Eleri (the witness or lawyer of destiny) refers to this ability. Orunmila mediates between men and Olodumare, since Olodumare, through the oracle, reveals his will and desires. Orunmila is the most suitable orisha to decide if a plea to avoid disgrace needs to be taken to Olodumare. He personifies destiny and hope, since destiny is neither blind nor unavoidable. Orunmila's wise advice and brokerage with Olodumare can alter one's destiny. He represents support, certainty, comfort, and the solution to life's problems and uncertainties. He is commonly called Okibitiri a-pa-ojo-iku-da (the great changer who alters the date of death).

In another myth, Olodumare was worried about the problems of governing the world. The orishas offered their suggestions. Orunmila's opinion was that Olodumare should send a delegate to the planet as his representative so that men could come to him for comfort and guidance. Olodumare promptly accepted Orunmila's reasoning and chose him as his deputy in charge of wise and divine counsel, while retaining Obatala as the deputy for administrative affairs and for the maintenance of order and morality.

Orunmila is a great physician. Through the oracle, Orunmila medicates and heals. His priests, the babalawos, must be knowledgeable about remedies and medications that consist primarily of infusions of herbs. Babalawos claim that Orunmila is the oldest brother of Osain, the owner of medicinal herbs.

"Orula," a word that is a contraction of "Orunmila," is also a name given to this god. Sometimes he is known by the name Ifa. However, in oral traditions, Orula is a heavenly god who was sent to this planet by Olodumare to carry out missions of great importance. Ifa is a famous diviner, who, after death, was deified and became identified with Orula, the god that he had served all his life. These beliefs led to the assumption that, even though Orunmila is the god of wisdom and destiny, the name of Ifa is mostly associated with the oracle. Ifa is, in reality, the intermediary between humans and Orunmila, the real owner of the oracle.

A. B. Ellis (1894: 58) refers to a myth concerning the origin of the Ifa cult. In those early days there were very few human beings in the world to sacrifice to the orishas. Gods and humans were in very precarious situations. Ifa tried fishing to satisfy his hunger, but the results were disheartening. He consulted Elegba (Elegguá), who told him to ask Orungan, the leader of men, for sixteen nuts from his palm trees. Elegba would teach Ifa how to foretell the future by using the sixteen nuts. Humanity and the hungry gods would benefit extraordinarily from this knowledge. Elegba established one condition, which was that the best offerings would be for him. Ifa agreed, and asked Orungan for the nuts. Elegba then taught Ifa the art of divining, and Ifa taught Orungan, who became the first babalawo.

In a myth collected by Oyesile Keribo (1906: 38–40), Ifa is not a god who inhabits the planet, but a human being deified after death. In this myth, Ifa is a native of Itase, a region near Ile Ife. His parents were very poor. Nobody knew them, and people thought he had no parents. Ifa despised manual labor and begged in order to eat. He wanted to improve his situation and asked a wise old man for counsel. The old man taught him the art of divining. Ifa became a famous babalawo known all over the region. The original sixteen odus correspond to the sixteen stories that the wise man taught Ifa. After his death, Ifa was deified.

J. Olumide Lucas (1948:74) quotes the following myth published by Feyisara Sopein in the *Nigerian Chronicle* of March 12, 1909:

> Ifa was born at Ife, the cradle of the Yoruba people. He was a skillful medical man, who had an extensive practice and was an eminently skilful [*sic*] diviner. After he had become famous he founded a town called Ipetu and became king of the place. . . . People from every part of the Yoruba country flocked to him. . . . Out of these, we are told, he chose only sixteen men. . . . The names of these apprentices are said to be identical with

the names of the sixteen divinatory signs called *Odus*, and the order of precedence among them, which was probably based upon priority of appointment, is said to be still preserved in the present order of the *Odus*.

All the orishas are friends of Ifa, but none is as close as Eshu. A story about their friendship is reported by Robert F. Thompson (1976: CH4/3), who describes a story in which Echu tells Ifa that on the day of his death he would find out who his real friend is, since many people who came to his home to eat his food were not real friends:

> It happened that one day Ifa decided to find out who his real friend was among these people. He had to test them. So he told his sons to tell these people, when they came to his house, that he was dead. And he got a white cloth to cover himself, like a corpse. An hour later, he asked his sons to keen in a loud voice that Ifa had perished from this earth.
>
> As soon as the deities heard this cry they started to rush to the house of Ifa. Some started an agitation against the properties of Ifa, about which piece of property went to whom, others came to take what money remained of the estate of Ifa.
>
> On that day Eshu was shaving his head. As he was shaving, he heard the voices of the sons of Ifa, lamenting that their father had passed away. Eshu said: "What a sudden death! Come to my friend." He left his hair unfinished and ran, the tears streaming from his face, to the house of Ifa. Ifa opened his eyes and looked at Eshu and said, "You are my real friend. You will be my friend forevermore. I have seen you arrive with your hair unfinished. Henceforth, this tuft will remain on your head as the sign of friendship which is genuine." And the tuft came to be called "ere" which means "ore" (friend).

Even though, in some instances, it seems that there is conflict between these gods, everyone acknowledges that Orunmila and Eshu are closely linked and that Eshu is in charge of punishing the person who ignores Orunmila's advice. In a legend collected by Pierre Verger (1954: 169), Orunmila gives his divination powers to Ifa instead of Eshu, who claimed them. Orunmila feeds Eshu and when Eshu is not satisfied he turns against Orunmila and hinders his mandates and work.

The Yoruba have implicit faith in Orunmila, as they know that without his help nothing is possible. His mandates are undisputed; his counsel followed with reverence.

Orunmila's priests are called babalawos (father of the man who works with secrets). They are the best-organized, wisest, and most coherent priestly body in Yorubaland. They have to undergo rigorous training that takes from three to seven years.

Normally, a boy of the age of ten starts training as a babalawo. At that time he becomes an apprentice under a master priest. He lives in his master's home and does many household chores and errands for his master. At first, the training is informal. The apprentice watches the master priest during divination and becomes familiar with the paraphernalia needed for divination. After three or four years have elapsed, more formalized training begins, when the apprentice learns to use the ikines (divinatory nuts), the opeles (divinatory necklaces), and other instruments used in divination.

The babalawos have to master all the knowledge related to the cult of Orunmila, which constitutes the most systematic philosophy of Yoruban experience; that is, its ethos and morality within the framework of basic worldview assumptions. According to Wande Abimbola (1973: 48), the training of a babalawo does not end with his initiation. It continues while he attends the meetings of babalawos in the area where he lives. This continuous training results in babalawos becoming specialized in different areas of Ifa, such as medicine, magic, poetry, and the like.

Many enter this profession because it brings prestige and economic rewards. The divination system around which this worship revolves is very complicated. The babalawos are expected to know how to prescribe and use magical and medicinal herbs, and they have to be experts in everything concerning myths, sacred music, and rituals.

Orunmila's priests are organized into three ranks. The oba, who is the senior oluwo in a lineage, has the highest standing. The oluwo is the dean, respected and obeyed by all. The odofin is the oluwo's deputy and second in importance. The ajibona assists the oluwo and the odofin. The aro holds third place in rank and serves as deputy when the oluwo and odofin are absent. The asare-pawo is the messenger who prepares the meeting of babalawos. The arewo is the assistant to the asare-pawo.

The priestesses of Orula are also organized by hierarchical ranking. The most important is the apetebi, who, supposedly, is the wife of the god. The rank of apetebi is usually given to the wife of a senior babalawo.

Babalawos have to shave all hair from their bodies. In Yorubaland they wear white clothing, except in Ile Ife where they wear light blue. A bracelet made of palm fibers or of white, blue, and red beads is a mark of their office. The babalawo carries the iruke, a whip made from the tail of a horse or a cow, which is a symbol of authority. Babalawos also carry a carved wood scepter with a round handle. Sometimes it is made of iron and shaped like an iruke.

Orunmila's shrines are in the houses of the babalawos. The sixteen palm nuts used for divining, which are his emblems, are kept in covered earthenware containers on a small altar in the room dedicated to the god. Frequently, the image of Eshu, his assistant, is also placed on this altar. Cowry shells and carved pieces of ivory are placed on Orunmila's altar. Orunmila's favorite foods are rats, goats, fowl, pigs, and yam loaf. He is also very fond of palm wine.

In summary, the worship of Orunmila, as evidenced by the extent of its influence throughout Yorubaland and among neighboring territories, was very important in the daily life of the Yoruban people centuries before their initial contact with Europeans in the fifteenth century. Everyone, regardless of social position, sought Orunmila's comfort and advice for a dual purpose: to be spared from adverse fortune and to preserve favorable circumstances. His priests, the babalawos, constituted a very powerful and influential class in the life and affairs of their fellow citizens. Currently, despite the in-roads of Christianity, Islam, and secular modern culture, great numbers of Yoruba still consult the oracle and follow its advice. Presumably, their assumptions regarding the nature of power and causality in the world support and may even "require" such actions.

Orunmila is the orisha who publicly declared his desire to serve the entire world. Thus, the worship of this orisha has extended, without noticeable change, to regions beyond the areas inhabited by Yoruba-speaking people. The oracle of Ifa is known by the Ijaw, the Ibo, the Popo, the Ekiti, the Ekoi, the Iyala, and by most of the inhabitants of southern Nigeria.

From an observer's point of view, this suggests congruencies or cultural borrowing based upon a "shared consciousness of the world" (Lowery-Palmer 1980:40) that is so widespread in West Africa.

Orúnmila/Orúnla/Orúla in Cuba

The reason that the cult of Orunmila was transplanted so accurately in Cuba was the presence of priests knowledgeable in his worship who arrived in slave cargos. Subsequently, shortly after the abolition of slavery, one or more priests skillfully organized and trained others in the secrets of his cult.

In Cuba the god of the oracle is known under the names of Orúnmila, Orúnla, and Orúla. Orúnmila, in Cuba, was associated with other African gods, such as Nsambia Munalembe of the Congo, who is also called Cuatro Vientos. It is not surprising that even though some of the legends associated with this *oricha* seem to be derived from African gods of other than Yoruban origin, the character and worship of Orúnmila in Cuba have been faithfully preserved. Key factors ensuring such an outcome may have been the following: sufficient numbers of priests, the rigidity inherent in the training and use of the instruments of divination, and the role of Echú as the enforcer of Orúnmila's advice.

In Cuba the priests of this *oricha* organized the same priestly structure dedicated to his worship as in Nigeria. The *babalaos,* as they are called in Cuba, are the wisest, most intelligent, and knowledgeable priests, as well as the most conservative in religious matters and traditions. The presence in Cuba of this priestly class guaranteed great orthodoxy in ritual, divination, and practice. In Afro-Cuban Santería, the priesthood of Orúnmila has flourished and *babalaos* continue to carry the religious tradition. This is in contrast to the situation in Brazil, where the Yoruban religion has also thrived but where other factors may have intervened. In Brazil, the followers of Orúnmila and the interpreters of the oracle of Ifá have never been very important.

According to many *patakís,* Orúnmila was a deaf-mute as a child. When he reached sixteen years of age, Olodumare gave him a spanking for each year of his life. After each spanking, Orúnmila recited an *odu,* or figure of the oracle. From this recitation the first sixteen letters of the oracle of the shells, or dilogún, originated. After the first whipping, Orúnmila said, "Eyiobe Meyi," which in Cuba is rendered "Eyi Ogbe" (the Yoruban name of the first letter of the oracle).

Another myth offers further insight into the nature of Orúnmila in Cuba:

Orúnmila is a sixteen-year-old boy endowed with extraordinary telepathic powers. His reputation was so great that even the powerful Obatalá came to seek advice about a trip that he was going to make. Orúnmila advised him, "Do not take the trip until you have made *ebó* with three dry coconuts. Postpone the journey for some other day." Obatalá went on the trip that same day in spite of Orúnmila's advice. The trip was a complete disaster, which ended with Obatalá's being put in jail. Obatalá's own son mistakenly charged him with being a thief. When the situation was cleared and Obatalá's son tried to kill the guard responsible for the incident, Obatalá told him: "Son, do not punish the guard. It is my own fault for not having paid attention to Orúnmila. (Cros Sandoval 1975:157)

This story is also known in Brazil and Nigeria. In the Nigerian version Orunmila advises Obatala against making a trip to visit Shango. Obatala went on the trip and on three occasions Eshu soiled his white garments. After cleaning himself in the river he continued his journey. On his way he found Shango's horse and took it to bring it to its owner. Later the servants of Shango accused him of stealing the horse. Shango apologized and gave him all sorts of presents. Obatala, who is opposed to retaliation and violence, returned to Ile Ife.

In Apter's view (1992:28) this myth reflects the rivalry between the gods of Ile Ife, Obatala and Orunmila, and Shango of Oyo. Eshu, the trickster, is the personification of adverse destiny, but Eshu is the messenger of Orunmila and in charge of making sure that the counsel of the oracle god is obeyed. This myth demonstrates that Orúnmila in Cuba, as in Africa, is not just the advisor of men but also of the *orichas*. The most powerful Obatalá has said about Orúnmila that those who disregard his advice deserve the worst punishment.

In another series of myths collected by Lydia Cabrera (1954: 240–42) Orúnmila is the son of Obatalá and Yemmu. He was born after his brother Ogún forced his mother into an incestuous relationship. After that incident, Obatalá swore not to have any more male children. When Orunmila was born Obatalá was furious and took him away from home. He buried his body up to the neck by a silk cotton tree.

The following *pataki* is rather similar to the one recorded by Cabrera:

> Then Orúla was born; and Obatalá, without saying a word, took him far away. When he came to a silk-cotton tree he dug a hole in the ground and buried Orúla up to his neck. Elegguá, who had followed them, told Yemmu. Yemmu took food to him every day. Afterward Obatalá forgot all about it, and some time later another strong boy, Changó, was born. Obatalá took the beautiful child in his arms and took pity on him. He decided that his eldest daughter, Dadá, who lived away from home, would take care of him.
>
> Four years later, Dadá took Changó to see his father and mother. Obatalá was very happy, but Yemmu was sad because she remembered her unfortunate son Orúla. Changó was all dressed in red, and Obatalá sat him on his lap. Changó asked Obatalá, "Why is mother crying? Why is she so sad?" Obatalá told him, "Some day I will tell you the whole story." From that moment, Obatalá asked that Changó be brought to his presence every day.
>
> Obatalá would sit Changó on his lap and tell him the story about Ogún. Changó grew up with a great hatred in his heart for Ogún. When Changó became a man, he had a fierce temper and liked to quarrel at all times. He went to his godfather, Osain, the owner of magical herbs, and asked him for weapons. Osain gave him a little gourd: "Hang this in a corner of your house, and every day, after you dip your fingers in it, make the sign of the cross with them on your tongue." This is why, when Changó answers your greeting, fire and smoke come out of his mouth. This is also why, when it thunders, we call upon Changó. The flame is the lightning, and the thunder is his voice. He is as great as his roar.
>
> Time passed and things started to go wrong. Obatalá didn't know what to do. One day, when Changó was visiting, Obatalá confided his problems to him. Elegguá asked Changó to talk to Obatalá about Orúla. Changó said, "Father, I have always obeyed you and I have always given you good counsel." Obatalá agreed. Changó added, "Before I was born,

you buried Orúla." Obatalá lamented having been so unfair to Orúla, and he blamed himself for the bad luck and the terrible moments they were going through. He wanted to punish himself and do penance.

Elegguá told him it was unnecessary for him to do this, and added, "One day, as I was passing by a silk-cotton tree, I found a man buried to his neck. This man is a great diviner and I suspect that he is your son Orúla."

Obatalá went to see Orúla and asked his forgiveness. After they embraced, Obatalá asked Orúla to return home, but Orúla declined because the silk-cotton tree furnished him with the shells and twigs he needed to make his prophecies. Obatalá made a deal with the silk-cotton tree. He took a piece of wood from it and made a board for Orúla. Since then, Orúla has become a renowned diviner.

Obatalá told Orúla, "You are a diviner, and from now on, any diviner will have to consult you." (Cros Sandoval 1975:157–58)

In another *pataki* recorded by Rómulo Lachatañeré (1938: 130–42), Orúnmila is forced by Olodumare to go into the domain of the owner of the woods, the dreaded Ogún. Orúnmila in this *pataki* is a weak old man, and he falls into one of the many traps that Ogún uses to protect his territories. Three young women—Ochún, Obatalá and Yemayá—who, luckily, were passing by, rescued him.

This legend probably is not of Yoruban origin, since the calamities that happened to Orúnmila are not congruent with the character of the powerful Yoruban god of wisdom and of divination.

In some houses of worship, it is believed that Changó was the original god of divination. However, he got bored with the respectable and sedentary life of a *babalao* and gave his brother Orúnmila the *ate Ifá,* the board of divination, in exchange for drums and music. In Nigeria, there is no reference to Orúnmila being the owner of music and drums and later becoming the oracle divinity.

In *patakís* where Orúnmila and Olodumare participate, Orúnmila is an old man who is the counselor and steward of the Supreme Being. One such Afro-Cuban *pataki* explains how Orúnmila became the owner of the oracles:

> The Supreme God, Olofin, decided to give Orúnla the divination instruments. However, he had doubts concerning Orúnla's ability to deal with them wisely. Olofin called Changó, the thunder god, and asked him to bring Orúnla to his presence. Olofin then took several kernels of roasted corn and planted them in the ground, and some corn seeds, which he planted a few feet to the right of the roasted corn.
>
> Elegguá, who sees everything, saw what Olofin had done and decided to warn Orúnla. When Orúnla came to see Olofin, Elegguá had already

told him all he had seen. Then the Supreme Being told Orúnla: "In this world . . ."

Orúnla didn't even let him finish the statement. He said, "Babamí, the corn that you planted on your left side is not going to grow because it was roasted corn; the corn you planted on your right side will grow and will reproduce because you planted fresh corn."

Olofin, now convinced of Orúnla's wisdom, was totally satisfied with his decision to make Orúnla the greatest of all soothsayers and the owner of the divination instruments. (Cros Sandoval 1975:93)

Orúnmila has identical attributes in Cuba and in Africa. He is the god of wisdom and oracles, who knows all the secrets of life and living. Olofin revealed to him all the mysteries. Only the *babalaos* can use the two supreme divining instruments through which Orúnmila speaks with absolute wisdom.

Orúnmila is considered a great physician, and his priests are very knowledgeable about the healing powers of plants and herbs. Orúnmila owns one of the four winds, along with Oyá, Elegguá, and Obatalá. The power of Orúnmila is such that, when he claims a person to his service, even if that person has already been consecrated to the worship of another *oricha*, he must also serve Orúnmila. Even Obatalá's children have to worship Orúnmila when he claims them.

The role of Orúla in Cuba and in Africa is very consistent. He is the wise, just, and knowledgeable counselor consulted by everyone. His commands are obeyed, because even though he is not vindictive or wicked, he does punish by causing dementia in those who offend him or disregard his commands.

Orúnmila molds destiny and is held responsible for the good or bad luck that an individual may enjoy in this world. A common expression is "Ire elese Orúnmila" (the good luck that Orúnmila grants). Orúnmila's opinions must be accepted without question, since he is the embodiment of order, justice, legality, and firmness. According to a *pataki* Orúnmila's power is of such magnitude that he can postpone death:

One day, a very desperate woman came to consult Orúnmila. "Orúnmila, Ikú is hovering over my house. Please help me so that he will not take my only child. During the last few days my boy has had a fever, and I have heard and seen Ikú prowling about, waiting to sneak in and take my boy." Orúnmila answered, "*Omordé* (woman), go to the market with four baskets and fill them up with okra. Then bring them to your house where I will be waiting. I will take care of everything."

The old diviner went to the woman's house and made an *ebó* (sacrifice) for the boy. When the woman arrived, he took the okra and spilled it all over the floor until it looked like a green carpet. When Death walked in with firm steps, its bony feet stamped the okra pods. Death slipped, stumbled, and fell down. Completely bruised, humiliated, and frightened, he ran out of the house screaming "guí, guí, guí." (Cros Sandoval 1975:156)

Generally, lithographs of Saint Francis of Assisi are used to represent Orúnmila, as well as little anthropomorphic wooden statues. The hand of Orúnmila, a symbol of this god, is made with thirty-two *ikínes*, or seeds. It is given to the *babalaos* when consecrated. They also receive, for protection, the Osun of Oduduwa, a metal rod with a small rooster on the top.

Orúla's necklace is made of sixteen alternating green and yellow beads. The *kofá* and the *irdé* (bracelets made of green and yellow beads) belong to Orúla. They are given to men and women respectively for protection. Orúnmila also owns the board, or *até Ifá*, used for divination.

Orúnmila cannot possess believers because his power is too great. In the religious festivals of the *oro del eya aranla*, the eighteenth drumbeat is dedicated to him. Since he cannot possess the faithful, the priestesses of Ochún dance. The movements are sober with little pantomime. In festivals in which only drums are played, the fifteenth drumbeat is dedicated to him.

Orúnmila's priests are the *babalaos*. His priesthood is closed to women and male homosexuals. In Cuba, women receive the *kofá*, which is equivalent to the *awofaka*, or *mano de Orúla* (hand of Orúla, or divining nuts), that men receive as part of the preliminary initiation into the secrets of Ifá. However, when men receive the *awofaka* they are given sixteen *ikínes*, the full set of divination palm nuts. When women receive the *kofá* they are given only one divining nut. Moreover, they cannot proceed to become *babalaos* as their male counterparts do after receiving the *awofaka*.

Ideally only men of great integrity and character can become *babalaos* and thus be in such close proximity to the powers and wisdom of Olofin, the Supreme Being. The discriminatory posture that prohibits women and gay men from becoming *babalaos* has been the source of considerable controversy. Undoubtedly this posture in the cult of Orúnmila has political overtones. In the Yoruban and Cuban worldview men take precedence over women in both secular and sacred realms. Their higher status implies greater power. Greater power in the religious sphere is marked by greater secrecy, responsibility, and privilege.

Babalaos normally dress in white, carry the *iruke* or horse-tail symbol of authority, and wear the bracelet, or *idé*, made of woven fibers. In Cuba Orúnmila enjoys the sacrifices traditionally offered to him in Africa: pigeons, goats, lambs, and rats.

In both Africa and Cuba, the highest ranked status is that of the *oba,* or king. The second rank in Cuba is the *olúo,* which is the counterpart of the oluwo of Nigeria. The *awó,* considered the greatest of all diviners, is known in Nigeria as the Awon ti-a-te-nifa. In Nigeria, babalawos' wives are considered priestesses of Orunmila. In Cuba, the priestesses of Orúnmila's wife Ochún, are considered wives of Orúnmila and have knowledge of some of his secrets. When they are married to a *babalao,* they become his assistant and are called *apestebi.*

Chapter Summary

The great prestige that *babalaos* enjoy in all religious matters has given them an important role as preservers of the religious and cultural traditions of the Yoruba. However, despite the evident structuring that exists in the priestly class, each *babalao* acts with great independence. This has prevented the emergence of an orthodox dogma, which would have remedied some of the contradictions that are present in Santería.

As indicated previously some *santeros* and *santeras* avoid using *babalaos* in certain rituals, thereby dispensing with their knowledge and services. In the past, the Warriors were given to believers exclusively by *babalaos.* Currently some godparents prepare them for their godchildren. Moreover, the fact that the dilogún, which is consulted by all *santeros,* displays such richness and complexity in Cuba is also evidence of the preeminence of *santeros,* even in divination. Presumably, observable tension within the structure and practice of Santería is linked to the need to bring religious behavior into line with changed socioenvironmental circumstances and changing worldview assumptions regarding the degrees of independence allowed to meet clients' needs.

Overall, however, to Afro-Cubans in Santería and their followers, the supernatural is magical. In its realm, everything is possible, analysis is irreverent, and worship gives access to power.

14

Elegbara/Elegguá, Eshu/Echú

Messenger of the Gods

Elegbara/Eshu in Africa

Elegbara, Obatala, and Orunmila are the most revered orishas in Yorubaland. However, the essence and character of Elegbara is rather complex and difficult to understand from the point of view of Judeo-Christian morality. Elegbara, the messenger of gods, is acknowledged as a powerful orisha who carries offerings of human beings to the gods and whose support is indispensable in fulfilling one's life and destiny as well as surviving and succeeding. At the same time, Elegbara is a trickster who, when manifested as Eshu, enjoys indulging in antisocial and destructive behavior.

The specific name of the god, Elegbara, Elegba, or Elegguá, means "the one that saves." It also means "the one that grabs or hits with a stick." This god always carries a stick to strike his enemies, and this aspect of character is clearly revealed when manifested as Eshu. There are many different etymological interpretations of the name Eshu. The name apparently derives from the word shu (to cast out, to evacuate). It also means "to be" or "to become dark." According to J. Olumide Lucas (1948:56), some people believe Eshu represents darkness, a reference to his supposed diabolical character.

Some scholars have considered Eshu an African version of the devil. S. S. Farrow (1926:85) claims that Eshu is the devil, the prince of darkness, and for Samuel Johnson (1921:28), Eshu is the personification of evil, a true Satan. To them Eshu signifies the opposite of Olodumare. Thus, he is a god of negative force, essentially opposed to the Supreme Being. Many authors like these were missionaries who believed that Eshu was the Yoruban version of the devil.

This view could be the result of past treatises on the subject written by clergymen who, influenced by their own Christian beliefs, thought they had discovered in this god the Yoruban counterpart of the devil. However, E. B. Idowu states that this Christian view of Eshu as the devil is not correct. Even though Idowu was also a Christian priest, his opinion (1962:80) was that the identification of Eshu with the Christian devil is not valid. He believed that the fear and respect men and orishas have for Eshu is not because he is the devil, but because of the role assigned to him as messenger of the gods. He has the power of life and death over them. Prosperity and catastrophe depend on the reports that Eshu gives to Olodumare. In other words, Eshu is the messenger of and for the Deity; thus he can control the destiny of men and the actions of gods.

Eshu is not a malignant power opposed to the creator god. On the contrary, he is one of Olodumare's most efficient collaborators. According to Geoffrey Parrinder (1961:26), "Eshu is demoniac, but not diabolic," and he is not essentially evil. This whole problem stems from the fact that this god is full of contradictions, as are human beings. He is a malicious divinity who relishes the numerous tricks he plays on gods and men, but he is not essentially evil. He is a trickster, a tramp, a dangerous character but not absolutely perverse. This god of mischief enjoys causing embarrassing and violent situations. He likes to alienate human beings and to hinder their actions.

Even though Eshu is respected for fear of his malice, it is undeniable that he also inspires awe and admiration in his followers. His might, the swiftness of his actions, and his unique power of ubiquity, which enables him to be in several places at once, make him an extremely dangerous and resourceful god.

Divinities with characteristics similar to these are frequently found in the pantheons of West Africa. In Dahomey, the counterpart of Eshu is known as Legba.

Eshu is a most indispensable god. Without him, nothing would be possible. With his favor, the most difficult enterprises are solved satisfactorily. For this reason, everyone wants to propitiate him. However, it is very difficult to please him, because Eshu is unpredictable, versatile, and elusive. He is called by two hundred different names. The Yoruba call him the indulgent child from heaven, the one whose greatness is manifested everywhere, and the one who breaks into a thousand fragments that can never be reassembled.

Eshu is as cruel, generous, unexpected, fast, powerful, treacherous, and capricious as chance or destiny can be. Cuban scholars disagreed with early African scholars, many of whom were clergymen, because they saw Eshu as the personification of chance or luck. Paul Mercier, referring to Legba, Eshu's counterpart in Dahomey, concurs with the Cuban scholars' assessment of Eshu. Mercier says that Legba "introduces in destiny the element of chance or luck" (C. D. Forde 1954:333). He adds: "Each individual has a Legba—as he has a destiny—, and he must propitiate it so that it will not be adverse."

A great number of myths corroborate the qualities of Eshu's character: his cruelty and malevolence. In such myths, Eshu is a trickster. According to oral traditions there was once a man with two wives (Idowu 1962:82). He loved and cared very much for both of them, and all three of them lived a happy and harmonious life together. The family was considered an example of conjugal happiness. Eshu, aware of this, became very angry and decided to put an end to their joy. The following day, disguised as a merchant, he went to the market. When one of the wives passed by, he showed her a beautiful hat that he, himself, had made. The woman bought the hat for her husband as a present. The husband showed such signs of appreciation that the other wife became jealous. The following day, the second wife went to the market, where Eshu offered her a hat even more beautiful than the first one. This woman also took the hat to the husband, who, acting again without much tact, manifested great enthusiasm. Each day, one of the wives would go to the market, and Eshu would offer her a hat that surpassed in beauty and quality the one sold on the previous day to the other wife. The rivalry between the wives was reaching a climax when Eshu decided to disappear. The wife whose turn it was to go to the market place that day felt very sad when she realized she could not outdo her opponent. When she reached the house she was so upset that the catastrophe that Eshu had planned immediately took place, and the joyful and harmonious household was no longer.

Oral tradition (source unknown) also narrates the story of a one-time king who, for some time, had been estranged from his wife. One day Eshu went to see the queen and told her that if she could cut a small lock from the king's hair, he would prepare such a powerful charm that the king would immediately return her affection. The queen, delighted with Eshu, agreed to do so that same night. Eshu then went to visit the crown prince, who lived in a nearby palace, and told him, "Your father is going to war tomorrow and he wishes to see you and your soldiers today." As a last trick, Eshu went before the king and told him that his wife was very jealous and that she was going to attempt to kill him that night. The king so warned went to bed and pretended to sleep. When his wife walked in with a knife in her hand, the king, convinced that she had come to kill him, tried to disarm her. At that precise moment, the crown prince arrived and, seeing his father wrestling with his mother, immediately thought that he was trying to kill her. The king, in contrast, assumed that his heir, with his guards, was trying to make him the victim of a plot. The king called his own soldiers, and a bloody massacre ensued. If the happy husband with the two wives and the powerful king had taken care of Eshu as he deserves and commands, these catastrophes would not have occurred.

Eshu is considered an ambiguous divinity. He can either be malevolent or benevolent. This is true of other orishas as well; however, Eshu is far more capricious than any of the other gods. In a sense, the worship of Elegbara epitomizes efforts to control the uncontrollable. In general people tend to blame him for all misfortunes that befall them. When a person behaves badly, people say that Eshu has forced the bad action. When a very evil person is being talked about, it is remarked that he or she is a worthy child of Eshu, or omo Eshu. It is also common to use Eshu against an enemy. When such use of Eshu is made, great care should be exercised. Eshu is a capricious god, prone to fits of temper toward whoever tries to use him.

To use Eshu against an enemy, the person must bow in front of his image and offer him palm oil, Eshu's favorite food. He then must say, "Eshu, here I bring you palm oil, which I know you like a lot. I also bring you palm nut oil, given to me by so and so (the enemy), who asked me to give it to you in his name. I don't dare offer it to you because I know that you cannot take this food, but I'm giving it to you in the name of the person who sent it to me." Then, the person pours the palm nut oil on top of Eshu and awaits the god's revenge at this offense.

Eshu is so powerful that all gods fear and respect him. It is said that at one time the mighty and vain thunder-god Shango was bragging that no orisha could beat him. Eshu immediately challenged him by asking, "Are you also referring to me?" Shango answered apologetically, "You know very well that does not include you." Eshu, indeed, enjoys a unique status. He has power over all other gods, because their luck depends on the information he carries to Olodumare. A frequent comment is that "Eshu ota orisha," which means that Eshu's followers render him tribute not only to protect themselves from his malevolence but, also, to enjoy his protection. His followers call him "baba," or father. They admire his ability to come speedily at the call of his children.

Eshu is Olodumare's "inspector general" of the orishas and their cults. He is the orisha who informs the Deity about things that are happening in the world and what men are doing. Eshu is the inspector of worship ceremonies and sacrifices. He must ensure that everything is carried out in a proper manner. Eshu is also the messenger of Olodumare and the orishas. He is the guardian of the temples, the cities, and the homes.

It is precisely in the last of these functions that his services are most appreciated. In spite of his great capacity for evil, shrines dedicated to his worship are frequently found at the entrance of homes. Many believers think that Eshu is a great guardian and that when one takes care of him with respect he will protect zealously the homes commended to him. He will allow only good influences to enter the house. He will close the door to death and other misfortunes.

Eshu's possession of the precious power of ubiquity facilitates his innumerable activities. He owns a stick, ogo, which permits him to travel long distances at great speed. He can also move objects from one place to another with the use of this stick.

This orisha plays a most important role in divination. According to one myth, Eshu taught Orunmila the system of divination that uses palm nuts. There is a close relationship between Orunmila and Eshu. This god of wisdom is capable of knowing the Deity's desires and of communicating them to men through the oracle. When Orunmila's advice is not heeded, Eshu is responsible for punishing the transgressor. In exchange for this service, Orunmila feeds Eshu. If Eshu is not satisfied with the offerings he receives, he uses all of his power to hamper Orunmila's work.

According to another myth (Idowu 1962:81), one day all the gods went before Olodumare to complain about Orunmila. Olodumare listened to their grievances and then called Eshu. Eshu sided with Orunmila, and Olodumare exonerated Orunmila of all charges.

A stone slab nailed to the ground in a reclining position is commonly used to represent Eshu. At other times, he is represented by anthropomorphic figures made of wood or clay. Many times these images have a knife in one hand and a stick in the other. This god is frequently depicted naked, sitting on his feet, with flexed knees and crossed arms. The necklace of Eshu is made of red and black beads. A clay kettle, placed upside-down with a hole in the bottom, is often used as a symbol for him.

Eshu also has the dual purpose of acting as a path to the gods when their advice is needed. In cases such as this, a virgin or an old lady who is no longer sexually active, acts as medium. Chapels and shrines dedicated to this orisha are found in many places that, on the one hand, seem vulnerable to negative powers and, on the other hand, seem to offer promise of favorable powers and events. These include shrines at crossroads, at the entrances of villages and towns, near the doors of houses, anywhere the potential for harm is perceived to exist or where there may be potential paths for a better future.

This orisha is one of the few gods in West Africa who, at one time, was propitiated with human sacrifices. Now the sacrifices generally offered to him are roosters, male goats, dogs, sheep, and palm oil. Since Eshu is the messenger of the gods, and because of the fear his malevolence inspires, he must be propitiated before any other god. Any time a sacrifice is offered to a god, the first part must be offered to Eshu. His portion must be set aside and offered first. After he has been fed, the other god may receive the offerings. Eshu is not a negative power. Eshu is, rather, an amoral power who, due to his ambiguous and sometimes cruel character, likes to cause problems and invite tragedies. He is a vindictive god ever ready to destroy those who offend him. Yet, the mighty power and efficiency of this god can also be used for positive ends.

Eshu is a wild and untamed power, feared and respected by all. In spite of his volatility and malevolence, Eshu has to be propitiated because of his mighty power and great efficiency. Parrinder (1961: 56) reports that the image of Eshu, placed at the entrances of towns and houses, functions as a fierce dog. The dog is not expected to bite the hand that feeds him but is there to protect those who care for him. In summary, Eshu is generous and cruel, powerful and capricious, and as unpredictable as chance itself.

Elegguá/Echú in Cuba

Afro-Cubans make a distinction between Elegguá and Echú. To Afro-Cubans, Elegguá is the *oricha* who protects the entrance to houses, and he controls every road and corner of the world. According to a *pataki*:

> Once upon a time, there was an *oba* (king) called Okuboro. Okuboro was married to Echú Añagui. The royal couple had a son called Elegguá. One day, when the prince was a young man, he set forth on a walk with his royal court. Suddenly, he stopped at the crossroads, advanced cautiously a few steps, and stopped again. Three times he took a few steps and abruptly stopped. The courtesans were bewildered. Finally, he made a final stop in front of an object, which was lying on the ground at his feet. The object had two sparkling eyes. To the amazement of his court, the prince picked up a dry coconut from the ground.
>
> This young mischievous boy who meddled in everyone's affairs, who was afraid of nothing, this capricious person who could be either your best friend or your worst enemy, this capricious prince, was awed and reverent in the presence of a small dry coconut. Elegguá took the coconut home and told his parents about the vision he had. Nobody believed or paid any attention to his story. Elegguá then cast the coconut behind the front door of the palace, where it remained hidden.
>
> One day, a great party was held at the royal house. A light coming from the coconut, which was lying on the ground in the room behind a closed door, bewildered the guests. They were horrified at such an unusual spectacle. Three days later Elegguá died. During his funeral, the coconut shone with such an intense light that everyone feared and respected it.
>
> A long time after the death of the prince, the people of the kingdom met with desperate times. The *agua* (the elders) gathered together and decided that the ill fortune befalling them was due to the state of abandonment in which they had left the miraculous coconut. They decided to render it homage, but on getting close to it saw that insects had eaten it. They discussed the poor qualities of the coconut as an object of worship and decided they should worship it but in the form of an *otán*, a stone. From that moment on, they placed an *otán* in a corner of the house, behind a door, as is done nowadays.

This is the story of the birth of the saint, Elegguá. It reflects the meaning of "Ikú *lori* Ocha," (the dead give birth to saints). If there were no ghosts, no dead, there would be no saints. If the prince had not died, the coconut would not have been worshipped as a stone that does not rot. That is why, in Santería, stones are used as objects of worship, not only for Elegguá but also for other saints as well. (Cros Sandoval 1975:168)

Elegguá is the messenger of Olodumare and the *orichas.* Moreover, he is closely related to all the other gods. He is a close friend of Ochún and Ogún, a companion to Changó, and a keeper of Orúnmila. Elegguá, Changó, Obatalá, and Oduduwa are the four cardinal points of the Ifá board. Orúnmila, Obatalá, Oyá, and Echú rule over the Four Winds (from the north, south, east, and west). Ogún, Ochosi, and Elegguá are the inseparable warrior comrades.

Elegguá, as doorman of Orúnmila, has great power over the tools of divination. If he is not propitiated as he deserves, he closes the way to propitiatory gods and opens it to destructive powers such as Ikú (death). As Elegguá is the owner of the key to the cemetery, he is considered to have dealings with the dead, a trait that adds to the fear he inspires. To a certain extent, he is a troublesome god. His favor has to be sought at any price or the door to happiness and hope inevitably will be closed. A *pataki* from a *santero*'s notebook explains how Elegguá became the doorman of Orúnmila:

> The original owner of the board of Ifá was Changó, who gave Orúnmila the highest divination instruments in exchange for the ownership of the drums. Changó placed as a condition that Elegguá, a close friend of his, would be the doorman of Orúnmila, who would have to feed him. Orúnmila agreed and, henceforth, became a very wealthy and prestigious *babalao.* He forgot to feed Elegguá, though; and Elegguá, dying from starvation, decided to take revenge.
>
> One day, as clients came to consult Orúnmila, Elegguá stood in every corner of the town, in the fields, and at the crossroads, and sent them all back home saying, "Go back. Orúnmila cannot see you for he has gone on a trip." Day after day, the frustrated clients went back to their homes. The wealth and prestige of Orúnmila decreased substantially. Orúnmila became concerned and went to see Changó, who advised him to treat his doorman with the consideration and respect owed him. Orúnmila complied, and since then, Elegguá has been Orúnmila's best ally.

Elegguá is also a great diviner. Orúnmila, in exchange for his services, gave Elegguá the dilogún (oracle of the shells) to use in divination. In Yorubaland, it is Elegguá himself who gives the divining board tray to Orúnmila, and it is he who taught him how to use it. Another characteristic of Elegguá is his healing power. At one time, when Olodumare was very sick, the only *oricha* who could minister to him was Elegguá. Olofin, gratefully, gave him the right to perform any trick he desired. He was also granted the privilege of eating before all other *orichas.* In another myth Elegguá was made the owner of the roads in exchange for a service rendered to Obatalá:

> Olofin had promised the *orichas* that he would reward the one who would bring him some pigeons he longed for by making that *oricha* the king of them all. These pigeons had a lot of *aché.*
>
> Both Obatalá and Agayú wanted to be the owners, or kings, of all the heads. Agayú scattered snakes in the path that led to the tree where the pigeons slept. Then he climbed a nearby tree to wait for the best moment to catch the pigeons. In one of her female manifestations Obatalá was afraid of snakes, so she was not able to get to the pigeons. She went to Changó for help, but the brave *oricha* was also scared of snakes. Changó advised Obatalá to seek the assistance of the shrewd Elegguá.
>
> Elegguá cast smoked fish, corn, and *jutías* (rodents) in the path. The snakes became so distracted with all the food that Elegguá was able to reach the tree where Agayú was hiding. Once there, Elegguá offered Agayú alcohol, inviting him to have a good time. Agayú got drunk, and Changó grabbed the pigeons and gave them to Obatalá.
>
> Olofin rewarded Obatalá by making her the owner of the heads, and Elegguá became the owner of the roads. (Cros Sandoval 1975:169)

In another *pataki:*

> Olofin called all the *orichas* and asked them to bring him "the best and the worst of this world." Each brought an object, which they thought met the requirements. Olofin did not agree with their selection and told them they had failed.
>
> Then, Elegguá arrived carrying a tongue. Olofin was very pleased and told him: "Elegguá, you are very shrewd. You have guessed right. A tongue, according to the use it is given, can do more good or more harm than anything else in the world." (Cros Sandoval 1975:169–70)

In many *patakíes* Elegguá is characterized as a trickster. The following story, also known in Brazil and in Nigeria, illustrates this aspect of his personality:

> There were two friends who were so close that the people of the town commented on the devotion and respect they felt for each other. One day, Elegguá decided to destroy this beautiful friendship. He painted half of his body with white paint and the other half with black paint. Then he started walking down the road that separated the fields in which the two friends labored. In this fashion each man could only see one side of

him. One man would see a white man; the other one would see a black man. Later on, when they met and talked about the stranger, a terrible argument ensued. It turned so bitter that the two old friends became the worst of enemies; exactly what Elegguá had intended. (Cros Sandoval 1975:170)

Those who claim they have seen Elegguá believe him to be a child with the face of an old man. He seems always to be wearing a hat made of palm leaves and pants and shirts in large white and black checks, reminiscent of a clown but symbolic of both good and evil. He constantly smokes cigars. Elegguá is a mischievous and capricious boy who uses his power with complete disregard to mores and morals. He is astute, fickle, and quite dangerous. His amoral behavior enforces in his followers respect and obedience. His behavior is not emulated, however. Instead, it may function to ensure greater caution in daily living. There is no escaping the eyes and ears of Elegguá and his potential for disruptive behavior.

Elegguá is everywhere and interferes with everything, manifesting himself in the most varied ways. He can be the highest and, at the same time, the lowest, a prince or a pauper, an adolescent or a senile old man. This god adopts any disguise in order to make his presence known and his power felt.

As previously mentioned, most *santeros* make a distinction between Elegguá and Echú. They consider Echú and Elegguá as two different manifestations of the same god. They argue that Elegguá is less destructive than Echú, and can be *asentado*, whereas Echú cannot be. They also emphasize the fact that Elegguá is the first *oricha* that *santeros* have to receive, while Echú is not a very desirable *oricha* in times of need.

Elegguá has many *caminos,* or paths. Some informants list as many as fifty-one Elegguás and seven Echús. Some think there are twenty-one; others hold that there are many more. This discrepancy is understandable. This god has at least two hundred different names in Nigeria. The better-known and most common manifestations of Elegguá and Echú, with their characteristic personalities and attributes, are included in Appendix B.

When an *omo Elegguá*, a priest of Elegguá, is mounted by this *oricha*, he is dressed with very tight pants, a short jacket, and a cap decorated with red and black beads, shells, and dangling bells. Similar attire is worn in Brazil by those possessed by Elegguá.

Elegguá occupies a unique place in the Afro-Cuban pantheon. He is the indispensable *oricha* who can do away with the life and plans of gods and men. At festivals, the first drumbeat is dedicated to him; in sacrifices, he eats of all the offerings before anyone else does. This god of fate, fortune, and roads is so important that nearly every believer has one Elegguá in his home for protection. His omnipresence, his constant activity, his swiftness of reward and revenge, and his interference in all human and divine affairs make him feared and respected by all.

Followers of Santería believe destiny can be changed. Therefore, Elegguá represents hope as well as hopelessness for them.

Elegguá's priests are attracted to his service because, notwithstanding his fickleness and the danger he represents, they consider him to be very powerful and able to do much for those who believe in him. His priests are called Echúbiyi which means "the child or son of Echú." An *omo Elegguá* (priest of Elegguá) is quite aware of the care his worship requires. His followers believe that he was once so angry at his *omo* (priests) that he burned them all in a huge bonfire.

Elegguá's shrines that are placed behind front doors or in the yards are small houses in which his *otán*, or stone, is placed, together with a doll representing him. His stones are almost always pyramidal in shape and are placed on a base commonly made of metal.

All *babalochas* (priests) and *iyalochas* (priestesses) are qualified to consecrate an Elegguá. Some *babalaos* make these *otanes* (consecrated stones) with cement, using three cowry shells to mark the eyes and mouth; others make them of clay in the shape of a pillar, as they were made in Yorubaland.

All Elegguás are hollow inside to receive the power or magical load. The powerful Elegguá de amasijo (icon shaped as a cone) is prepared after previously consulting the tutelary *oricha* of the client.

Lydia Cabrera (1954: 88) gives an excellent description of how to prepare the Elegguás. According to her, one takes a handful of dirt from among the following places: a crossroad, a *bibijagua* (fire-ant) nest, a church, a marketplace, a courthouse, a hospital, a prison, a bakery shop, and other places. Three herbs and seven pieces of different twigs that belong to this *oricha* are also needed. The head of a land turtle, likewise, is needed. Additional required objects or ingredients include a twig from Osain, a stone from an empty lot, magic powders, or *afoche* made by the *babalao*, and twenty-nine different coins that have been obtained as change from seven different purchases of groceries. *Omiero*, or the sacred liquid made with herbs and the blood of sacrificed animals, is also needed, as well as *corojo* oil (oil made from royal palm nuts), cooking wine, honey, and a little piece of charcoal. These different things are mixed in wet cement, and the resulting mixture is modeled into the face of the *oricha*. Later, this image is buried at a crossroads or "four winds" (a place facing all directions; the cardinal points) to ensure that the power of the *oricha* will infuse it. Elegguá's favorite foods and animals are offered to him as sacrifice. Their owners then take the Elegguá de amasijo home to protect the threshold of the house.

Elegguá is one of the few *orichas* represented by anthropomorphic statuettes called *ereres*. These *ereres* are small figures that are very popular and are
made by the believers themselves. Another symbol of this god is the cross,
representing the crossroads of the world. Elegguá appears in many ways as a
playful child; therefore, kites, marbles, and tops belong to him. A dry coconut
often represents Elegguá, as was requested by him in a previously described
myth.

Elegguá's necklace is made in patterns of three red beads followed by three
black beads, then, three sequences of one red bead followed by a black one.
Black is associated with him and with destruction and death. Red is associated
with passionate, fierce power.

Monday (*yo awo*) is the divining day dedicated to Elegguá, Ochosi, and Oricha Oko. On that same day, Elegguá's consecrated stone must be fed.

The *garabato*, a crooked stick half a yard long ending in a hook, is one of
Elegguá's belongings. According to Fernando Ortiz (1985b:300) this stick is a
remnant of a phallic symbol. The basis for this assumption is that Elegguá has
a phallic character in some places in Nigeria and in Dahomey, as well as in
Haitian Voodoo (Vodun) as Legba.

Among Afro-Cubans, Elegguá also has a phallic character. In the past in
Cuba when he possessed one of his children, the possessed individual often
simulated sexual intercourse. When informants made comments about this
characteristic of Elegguá, they said, "Here he is not allowed to do his indecent
things anymore." Even though in Nigeria he is represented with a great phal-
lus, it seems that the *garabato* (crooked stick) itself has an additional function.
Pierre Verger (1954:183) claims that this stick, which in Africa is called *ogo*,
enables Elegguá, the messenger of the gods, to travel anywhere.

Elegguá is a glutton. He likes to eat young goats and black and red speckled
chickens. He also enjoys white guinea fowls, monkeys, sheep, bulls, and deer.
He is addicted to alcohol and can be bribed in exchange for liquor.

Elegguá must occupy the leading position in all things, including drum festivals. In all ritual drum festivals, the first beats are dedicated to him. In the *oro
del eya aranla* liturgy, three drumbeats are dedicated to him, and the lyrics are
sung in Lucumí. When he possesses one of his children, he stands at his usual
place behind the door and never stops moving and jumping and making faces,
exactly as a mischievous child would do. Sometimes, he will move lasciviously,
with one hand on his lower belly and the other one holding his buttocks. At
other times, he will hold one hand at the other hand's wrist, moving it rapidly
up and down in a gesture allegorical of sexual intercourse.

This *oricha* has been associated with several Catholic saints, depending on
the particular *camino* involved. One of Lydia Cabrera's (1954:94) informants
considered Echú to be Saint Bartholomew. This linkage was probably based

upon the informant's interpretation of chromolithographs representing the massacre of Protestants ordered by a French monarch, which occurred in the sixteenth century on an August 24 (the day of Saint Bartholomew). In this lithograph Saint Bartholomew is depicted holding a knife and, in Africa, Eshu likewise holds a knife in his hand. Saint Bartholomew is also seen by Afro-Cubans as the saint who changed from the role of victim to that of perpetrator.

Echú Beleke is associated with the Holy Child and the Good Shepherd of Atocha; Echú Lagguana with the Lonely Soul of Purgatory. According to Lachatañeré (1942b:88), this association might be due to the fact that the Lonely Soul of Purgatory asks for frequent masses and prayers, just as Eleggúa is always requesting offerings in exchange for his favors. A more logical supposition might be that the association was based on the ambiguous character of both the Lonely Soul of Purgatory and Eleggúa. Both are neither good nor evil and, although the Lonely Soul is in a period of trial and Eleggúa is not, both can be swayed toward good or evil. It is also possible that this association resulted from Eleggúa's involvement with the dead and his capacity as messenger of the gods.

Chapter Summary

In Cuba Eleggúa possesses the same attributes as in Africa, but Afro-Cubans also consider him the *oricha* who opens all roads. Ogún, the god of metals, plays this role in Africa, but in Cuba this pioneer divinity forfeits this function to Eleggúa, who assumes it as part of his duties as messenger of the gods. In many myths, the African Ogun holds this power but, in practice, he does not use it because he is more interested in wars and adventures. In Cuba Eleggúa, who is linked to destiny and associated with divination, replaces Ogún as the divinity that opens the roads. Eleggúa lives in the wilderness; so a stone from the wilderness is used by *santeros* as his foundation.

Eleggúa is a trickster but not a devil. Eleggúa was never a devil for the Yoruba or the Lucumí. He represents capricious and cruel chance. This moral ambivalence might have made his association with a specific Catholic saint difficult, since no Catholic saint is amoral.

Eleggúa is an *oricha* who brags about the tricks he likes to play on people, but he also helps them. In contrast, Echú, a manifestation of Eleggúa, is nobody's friend: he is an evil spirit.

The difference that Afro-Cubans established between Eleggúa and Echú might be a concession to the new environment. Although all recognize them as the same *oricha*, Afro-Cubans, confronted with Christian beliefs, may have endowed Echú with the negative qualities of a devil and Eleggúa with those endowments befitting a guardian divinity. Faced with a belief system that includes the concept of a devil, Afro-Cubans may have incorporated it into their own beliefs by making a more specific distinction between the different manifestations of the same divinity. If this interpretation is correct, the concept of logico-structural integration in a changed social environment once again helps us to understand specific processes of cultural change.

Shango/Changó

God of Thunder and Fire

Shango in Africa

Along the equatorial coast of West Africa powerful thunderstorms and torna-does are some of the most dramatic and impressive manifestations of nature. Shango, the Yoruban thunder god, spitting fire from his mouth and riding his white horse, Esinle, roars as he gallops through the heavens while using the lightning rod as a warning of his mighty power and of his righteous punish-ments. His swift and powerful display of wrath is feared and respected by all. Everybody wants to propitiate this powerful god.

There are differences and even contradictions in the way believers perceive Shango's character and personality and in the way he is worshipped. These dif-ferences are due to the fact that Shango's name is both the name of a Yoruban thunder god and that of a historical character who was the fourth Alafin, or ruler, of the powerful Oyo Empire.[1]

According to Samuel Johnson (1921: 43), the name of the original thunder god of Oyo was Jakuta. After the powerful Alafin Shango died, the Oyo royal dynasty moved to deify him. Thus, he was rendered cult, not just as a royal ancestor but as a heavenly god, or orisha. Once deified, Shango acquired the characteristics, attributes, and powers of Jakuta, the very ancient and revered god of thunder and lightning.

Subsequently, contradictions emerged between the moral teachings that Shango's priests offered and the character and moral behavior of the historical Alafin of Oyo, Shango. While the teachings of the god Shango/Jakuta pro-hibited his followers from stealing, lying, poisoning, and cheating, the alafin of Oyo had often indulged in these behaviors and never repented. Thus, the ethical basis of Shango's worship was part of the original worship of the former thunder god, Jakuta, who was absorbed and displaced by Shango.

The contradictions about Shango's character and personality led Leo Fro-benius (1913: 210) to believe that there were two historical characters called

Shango. Frobenius' thesis was based on the existence of different versions regarding Shango's place of birth and also the place of origin of his family. Some authorities claim that Shango was originally from Nupe. Others, including Frobenius, believe that he was born in Borgu. According to Frobenius, a historical character from Borgu called Shango, is the source of the ethical basis of the cult of the orisha of thunder. With the passing of time, when the cult of Borgu's Shango and that of the Alafin of Oyo named Shango merged, two very different experiences, characters, and personalities also merged.

This interpretation by Frobenius is questionable. Nevertheless, the confusion regarding Shango's origin is caused by the fact that his name is linked to many different regions, such as Nupe, Ile Ife, and Oyo. It seems that his parents, as well as his legitimate wife, were originally from different regions, which helps to explain his association with diverse areas.

E. Bolaji Idowu (1962:89–95), who has studied Shango's origins in great depth, came to the conclusion that Shango, a king of Oyo who was deified after death, usurped the personality and attributes of the solar god Jakuta. The name Jakuta means "the one who throws stones of fire" or "the one who fights with stones." These titles make reference to the stones of fire (lightning) that the thunder god throws to earth. Jakuta was the personification of the rage of the Supreme Being, Olodumare, who uses lightning and thunder against wickedness and evil.

Apparently members of the ruling family of Oyo, who were interested in encouraging the worship of its illustrious ancestor, directed their efforts and resources to spreading the cult of Shango as a god of thunder by identifying him with Jakuta. To this day, the name Jakuta is associated with Shango. Many believe that Jakuta was Shango's father, while others believe he was his son.

In Cuba and Brazil, Shango is also known by the name of Jakuta. If Shango had not usurped the personality and power of Jakuta, he would have been known only as one of the many glorious ancestors of the royal family of Oyo, an ancestor worshipped and revered only by his descendants and subjects. The identification with Jakuta gave Shango larger dimensions, turning him into a generic god revered all over Yorubaland and even beyond its frontiers. There is little doubt that the inclusion of Shango in the Yoruban pantheon was primarily due to the ambitious and imperialistic political dreams of the Oyo dynasty.

Saburi O. Biobaku (1957:8) believes that the supreme priest of Shango and the delegates of the Alafin in Egba territory served the political and economic interests of the Alafin. Biobaku establishes a similarity between the worship of Shango in the territory subjugated by the Oyo, or under their influence, and the worship of the emperor in Rome. Both were official cults under the auspices of the rulers, with purely political aims in mind. For example, the priests of Shango used the respect the Yoruban people had for the thunder god to persuade them to pay high tribute to the Alafin. Notably, when the people of Egba freed themselves from the rule of Oyo, Shango's most important priests were massacred.

In Ile Ife, the thunder god is Oramfe, who, as is the case with Jakuta/Shango, hurls the stone axes that produce lightning. In Ile Ife, Shango could not replace the local thunder god. Thus, Shango and Oramfe are known as two different gods. Oramfe, as Jakuta, is a heavenly god who came down to earth only once when Olodumare, who was afraid of a catastrophe, sent him to settle a dangerous dispute between Obatala and Oduduwa. Oramfe made his voice heard, and the contending parties agreed to make a pact.

Even though Oramfe and Jakuta are known as two different orishas, they share the characteristics of a pure solar divinity and personify the same concept: the righteous wrath of the Supreme Being, Olodumare. Worshippers address them by looking at and calling to the sky. Both Oramfe and Jakuta's favorite offering is orogbo, or bitter kola nuts. None of these gods is represented by anthropomorphic images.

Political exiles from Oyo introduced the worship of Shango into Ile Ife at a relatively recent date. These immigrants settled in nearby Modukeke and worshipped Shango in private. Since they had no political power in Ile Ife, they were unable to erect temples or shrines to Shango.

The myths and stories about Shango, the legendary fourth king of Oyo, are sometimes contradictory. Often there are several versions of the same episode. The reason for such redundancy is that the ruling family of Oyo apparently edited, at their convenience, the adventures and anecdotes regarding their illustrious ancestor whom they had turned into a god.

The series of myths called "Iwa Kika Ekerin" give a comprehensive account of Shango's life. According to this series, Shango ruled Oyo more than three hundred years ago. He was a powerful witch doctor, a formidable warrior, and a great hunter. He also owned powerful "jujus" that gave him control of lightning and thunder and enabled him to exhale fire and smoke through his nostrils and mouth, provoking horror in his enemies. In spite of his wisdom, Shango was a cruel and tyrannical king, who used his supernatural powers to frighten his subjects and to conquer new lands from his fearful neighbors.

Shango was a jealous ruler and allowed no person to be better known than he was. However, two of his generals, Timi and Gbona, enjoyed great reputations. Shango became very envious of them and decided to destroy them. He provoked a duel between them, which resulted in the death of one of the contestants. The survivor was ordered to lead a risky military maneuver that had been set up as a trap. His subjects knew the horrible treason and cruelties of Shango. They were so enraged that they forced him and members of his family into exile. The distraught exiled king wandered in the jungle until one day he hanged himself from an ayan tree.[2] Only his legitimate wife, Oya, who had been his most intimate companion during his war adventures, had remained at his side.

When Shango hanged himself, Oya, in despair, left for the northern part of the region, where her numerous tears formed the river that carries her name, Odo Oya (Niger). Meanwhile, some travelers who were crossing through the jungle saw the body of Shango hanging from the tree, and, when they returned to Oyo, they spread the news of the death of the king. They told everybody, "Oba so" (The king hanged himself).

Shango's opponents, free at last from their feared and ferocious enemy, persecuted his followers in efforts to eliminate the influence of Shango's powerful family. At the same time, Shango's followers skillfully put together a plan to save their lives and their future. They obtained a potion that had the power to attract lightning, and they used it to produce severe thunderstorms in the area around Oyo. Then they spread the rumor that Shango, the powerful witch doctor and king, was in heaven and that from there he was punishing his enemies.

After the first thunderstorm passed, they went to the streets screaming, "Oba ko so" (The king has not hanged himself). They added, "The king is angry with us; he has turned into a god and has ascended to heaven and from there he punishes us with lightning." Then they demanded that the inhabitants of Oyo bring bulls, male sheep, and palm oil to offer to Shango and obtain his pardon.

Oyo's ruling family circulated a different account of this story, which exalted the divine character of Shango. According to this version, two of Shango's wives constantly quarreled and provoked dissatisfaction among the courtesans. Moreover, many subjects complained that Shango was a tyrant. Shango was annoyed by these complaints. One day he mounted his horse and rode into the jungle. Everybody anxiously expected his return, but stubbornly the king remained in the wilderness, paying no attention to his kingdom. Then, rumors started circulating about Shango hanging himself, having committed suicide. Finally a group of courtesans went to the woods looking for him, but all they found was his horse.

Sorrowfully looking among the trees and brushes they shouted aloud, "Where are you, King? Have you hung yourself?" From the distance the voice of Shango thundered, "No, I have not hung myself." The subjects pleaded for his return, claiming they needed him. Shango answered that since there had been so many complaints about him, he never wanted to return to the palace, but that he would rule from heaven. Then, using a chain that ascended from the ayan tree, he climbed into heaven; and from heaven, he rules over his subjects. In heaven he became the hurler of stone axes, the lord of tempests, who destroys houses, burns trees, and kills men.

These myths illustrate how the long process of deification of Shango began. They also provide a description of the way in which the worship of Shango as the god of lightning spread throughout Yorubaland.

The cult of Shango is the most elaborate in the Yoruban religion. The richness of the myths and stories associated with Shango is reflected in complicated and elaborate rituals and dances that are laden with symbolism. Shango's priests are organized into several ranks and are very influential. The highest dignitary, the magba, exercises great authority over the rest of the priests.

Until almost the first quarter of the nineteenth century Shango's priests in Nigeria enjoyed certain privileges that their counterparts in Cuba and Brazil never had. For example, when a house was struck by lightning, the owner had to seek a priest of Shango to determine what propitiatory offering should be given to intercede with and obtain the favor of Shango. Moreover, in precolonial Nigeria all properties of the victims of lightning passed into the hands of Shango's priests.

In Africa there are numerous temples dedicated to Shango, especially in Oyo. Altars in his honor are frequently built outside homes. These altars are called "tree of thunder" and consist of a fork-shaped rod. Neolithic stone axes are placed around it.

The worship of Shango requires numerous and complicated paraphernalia. The oshe (double ax) is his most characteristic weapon. During his festivals, this god possesses the believers and then dances. His dances are virile and warrior-like while the dancer carries his sword and his oshe.

Neolithic polished stone axes, which are archaeological relics of a culture prior to the Yoruba, are associated with Shango in Nigeria. Throughout western equatorial Africa, they are considered symbols of this god. It is believed that Shango hurls them from the heavens to produce lightning. Thus, Shango's priests travel to the areas that have been stricken by severe lightning storms in search of these stones. The offerings that Shango enjoys the most are male goats, fowl, kola nuts, and dried fish.

In summary, before the deification of the fourth Alafin of the Oyo Empire in the sixteenth century, Jakuta and Oramfe were the names by which the thunder god was known in different areas of Yorubaland. Both Jakuta and Oramfe were essentially the personification of the same principle, the rage of Olodumare, and were worshipped in a similar fashion.

After Shango, the fourth Alafin of Oyo, died, he was deified and identified with Jakuta, the local thunder god. Shango later usurped the attributes of Jakuta in the areas where Jakuta was the god of thunder, and even the name Jakuta was used as an appellation for Shango. In this way a new religious com-

plex—a cult to the orisha Shango—emerged, in which the ethical basis of a solar divinity merged with the historical realities, weaknesses, and vulnerabilities
of a deified ancestor.

By way of contrast, in the territories where the influence of Ile Ife was predominant and Oramfe was the thunder god, the royal family of Oyo had limited power. In those regions, Shango could not replace Oramfe, the solar god.
In those areas, Shango and Oramfe are considered two different thunder gods,
whose followers come from different social classes and family lineages.

Changó in Cuba

In Cuba, Jakuta is a name used to invoke Changó, while the name Oramfe is
totally unknown among Afro-Cubans. Presumably, slaves originally from Oyo
or from regions where the Jakuta-Shango religious complex was thoroughly
integrated, introduced the worship of the thunder god in Cuba. This presuppo-
sition is supported by the central place that the cult to Changó has in Santería.
It is also supported by the way in which the esoteric mysteries, the passionate,
emotion-filled rituals, and the symbolic paraphernalia that Changó's worship
requires were preserved.

The popularity of Changó in Cuba is also great because he absorbed other
African thunder gods. One of Lydia Cabreras's informants, Aliprete, who expressed himself in *bozal* and was involved in the search for meaningful equivalents and/or logical consistency in his religion, told his own version of the story
of Changó: "Changó nació en Takua,[3] arranca di, mete en tierra Sabalú;[4] mete
en tierra Dajomí;[5] en Dajomí ñame Jebioso. Arranca di Dajomi, cae en Congo
. . . Changó camina pa la panma, y ese son rey de Cuba." [Changó was born in
Takua, leaves it and gets into Sabalú land, gets into Dahomey land; in Dahomey
he is called Jebioso. He leaves Dahomey, falls into the Congo . . . Changó walks
towards the royal palm tree, jumps to the top or crest, and he becomes the king
of Cuba] (Cabrera 1954: 229). This story implies that throughout West Africa
there is a widespread cult to thunder gods and that Changó rides high in status
and power in Cuba.

The most popular *oricha* in Afro-Cuban Santería is Changó. In the adaptation process that the religion of the Yoruba underwent in Cuba, Changó was
also identified with thunder gods of other African ethnic groups and assumed
some of their characteristics and attributes. Also, in Cuba, Changó is part of
the lives and adventures of all the other important orichas. This is due to the
fact that the number of *orichas* in Santería, as compared to those known in
Yorubaland, was greatly reduced, and also to the fact that Afro-Cuban *orichas*
became perceived as being closely related to each other by family ties. These
kinship ties, in most instances, were not recognized in Africa.

In some *cabildos,* Changó is the son of Obatalá, the creator god, the foster child of Yemayá, the owner of the ocean, and the brother and enemy of Ogún, the god of metals. Moreover, he is also the brother of the oracle god, Orúla, and of Babalú Ayé, the owner of diseases. He is married to the domestic goddess Oba, to Oyá, the goddess of the flare, and to Ochún, the goddess of the river, with whom he fathered the Ibeyi, or sacred twins. His godfather is Osain, the owner of magical herbs, and his closest friend is Elegguá, the mischievous divinity. The belief of Afro-Cubans that the board of Ifá belonged to Changó and that he is associated with all aspects of Santería provides strong support for the view that people from Oyo had strong influence in Cuba.

The cultural processes that took place in Cuba greatly humanized the personality of Changó. This god of thunder, fire, and lightning also owns the sacred drums to which all initiates have to be presented. Changó enjoys dancing, drumming, and every manifestation of fun and merriment. In the new environment, Changó is a loud-mouthed extrovert, a libertine who is always chasing after women. In many ways, he exemplifies the typical Cuban *chuchero* of the 1950s, a streetwise witty character, culturally a descendant of the nineteenth-century *Curro* who, with his sensual swaying and peppery talk, enlivened the streets of Havana.

When a man is loud, quarrelsome, and a lover of parties and women, Afro-Cubans claim that he is the son of Changó and that his behavior takes after his supernatural father. Thus, Changó has come to symbolize the less sterling but more exuberant and pleasurable qualities of masculinity among Afro-Cubans. However, this boastful and passionate *guarachero,* a lover of parties and fun, can also be violent because of his implacable temper. His power and attributes attract admiration and popularity and far outweigh the feelings of fear and awe that his rage elicited in Africa. He is the genuine representative of Afro-Cuban masculine virility, a god of freedom, a great diviner, and the glorious victor in all battles.

In the following *pataki,*[6] Changó is the son of Obatalá and Agayú Solá:

> Obatalá, a powerful woman, wanted to cross a river and recruited the services of the boatman Agayú Solá. Once they crossed the river, Agayú Solá demanded payment. Obatalá, instead of paying, offered her body to him. Many months later Changó was born in Obatalá's white *ilé* (house).
>
> When Changó was old enough to speak, he would constantly ask for his father. Obatalá always refused to answer, but one day, tired of his insistence, she told him his father's name. Changó immediately went to see Agayú Solá. Agayú, who felt humiliated by Obatalá's arrogance, was full of resentment. He mistreated the child and beat him up.

Changó seemed delighted by the way Agayú treated him, since he didn't know how fathers behaved toward their sons. This further angered Agayú to the point that he threw Changó into the fire. Two good women passing by ran, horrified, to intercede for Changó before Olofin. Olofin gave the woman named Oyá the lightning flare that she used to set the woods on fire, scaring off the enraged Agayú, who took refuge on top of a tree. The other woman, Ochún, rescued the boy from the fire. She was amazed when she realized that Changó had not been harmed. They went back to see Olofin, who made Changó the owner of fire, gave Oyá the lightning flash, and told Ochún: "I will attend to you another day; today I have granted too much *aché.*"

Changó went back to his mother's *ilé* and told her what had happened. However, he spoke very favorably about his father, saying that he had given him the ownership of fire. Obatalá, who knew that the power to grant *aché* belongs solely to Olofin, severely punished Changó for lying. Thus, their close relationship ended.

Changó, in spite of his tender age, started to go to *güemileres* (drum festivals, parties) to play drums, dance, and drink sugar cane alcohol. One day, nosing around his mother's house, he found one of her most valuable talismans. He took it to the *güemilere.* When Obatalá came home she realized the talisman was missing. She became so angry that she picked up Changó in her arms and said, "You want to ruin me, but before you do I will kill you." She threw him down from the top of the mountain where her house was built.

Yemayá, the goddess of the sea [who in this myth is portrayed as an ordinary village woman], saw the sky turn black and a ball of fire descend from the heavens. She opened her skirt to catch the falling object and saw it was a young boy. Yemayá asked him, "Young boy, who are you?" Changó answered, "I am Changó. My mother, Obatalá, threw me out of heaven."

From then on, Yemayá took care of Changó and became his foster mother. Yemayá was delighted with Changó, whom, she thought, was a present from Olofin. She did everything in her power to please him, but Changó treated her badly, making her the target of his hurt pride.

One day he asked her to go to Obatalá's house and bring him the *ekuele* board. The poor woman took the terrible road of Osanquiriñán that goes to Obatalá's home. Finally, out of breath and completely exhausted, she reached the top of the mountain. There she found Changó with the board on his lap. Changó had ascended the difficult mountain road with the swiftness of lightning. He insulted her for being slow and inefficient. He then turned his back on her, leaving her, fainted, on the ground. Later, when Obatalá found Yemayá, she punished her for having dared to enter her house.

Forty days later, Obatalá told Yemayá: "This is the *ekuele*; give it to Changó in my name. You will be doing him a great favor." Yemayá brought the *ekuele* to Changó, who became the most prestigious and wealthy diviner in all the territory. Some time later, annoyed and bored with the responsibilities and eager for a life of adventures, he gave the *ekuele* to Orúla in exchange for drumming and dancing. (Cros Sandoval 1975:185–86)

The following *patakí* is well known among believers of Santería:

The oracle of the *ekuele* belonged to Changó who, tired of the sedentary life he was leading and anxious for adventures and war, decided: "I am tired of being a diviner. I will give the *ekuele* to someone else."

He called on an old and wise man named Orúnmila and told him, "I am bored with this life. Please accept the *ekuele* and carry on my services. But, the profit you make you must share with my friend Elegguá."

Orúnmila learned to toss the *ekuele* chains and became a prestigious *babalao.* From all corners of the world people would come to consult him, and he became richer and more powerful every day. However, he forgot his promise to Changó and did not share his profits with Elegguá.

"Give me what is due to me," Elegguá would tell him every night.

"Don't bother me. I will settle things with you some day," answered Orúnmila.

Elegguá, hurt, hungry, and feeling cheated, decided: "I am going to make that old rascal pay for the harm and injustice he is doing me."

The following morning all the Elegguás stood around the paths that led to Orúnmila's house. Every time a client approached they would tell him, "Go away; Orúnmila is sick today. "Don't bother to go see the old *babalao.* He is not working today."

Orúnmila's clients, disappointed, stayed away, and the prestigious *babalao* soon fell into a desperate situation. Elegguá, pretending he had not noticed the problems Orúnmila was confronting, would go to him every night to ask for his share. When Orúnmila finally told him he no longer had any clients, Elegguá said to him, "Why don't you call Changó and ask him to inquire with the *ekuele* what is behind your bad luck."

Orúnmila, in desperation, decided to do so. When Changó arrived Orúnmila asked for a consultation.

"What is the matter with you? Have you forgotten how to use the *ekuele*?" Changó asked him impatiently.

"I have lost my *aché;* my power is gone," said Orúnmila.

"Pay Elegguá his due and don't bother me with this nonsense," Changó said and left.

From that moment on Orúnmila was able to work successfully with the *ekuele.* He made a point to keep his promise to Changó and reward Elegguá handsomely. This is why Elegguá is always the first *oricha* to be propitiated. (Cros Sandoval 1975:94–95)

According to another *pataki,* Changó is the son of an old Obatalá Iba Ibo, and his wife Yembó (Yemmu). This couple had other sons: Ogún, Ochosi, Elegguá, Orúla, and Babalú Ayé. In this *pataki,* when Iba Ibo found out that the oldest son, Ogún, had committed incest with his mother, he rejected his other sons. This rejection is the reason Changó was raised by his half sister Dadá, who is also called Obañeñe. When Changó grew up, he took revenge on Ogún by taking his wife Oyá, the feared owner of lightning and of the cemetery. The two brothers became bitter enemies after that incident.

In Africa, Oya is considered the first and legitimate wife of Shango, but, in Cuba, Oyá is the second wife. In Cuba, Oba, the domestic goddess and the good wife who would sacrifice anything to please her husband, is the first wife. In Cuba, the third wife is Ochún, the voluptuous goddess of love. This passionate woman is Changó's favorite. During festivals, if Changó is in an ugly mood, his three wives and his foster mother, Yemayá, are invoked so they can calm him down. Shango's sacred tree in Africa is the ayan. Since this tree does not grow in Cuba, the royal palm tree is perceived as Changó's throne. The heart of this tree is a natural lightning rod targeted by Oyá's firestones. Reportedly, when she is enraged by Changó's infidelities, she punishes the royal palm trees because, perched from their tops, Changó can advantageously look out for beautiful women. If one catches his attention, he descends as a thunderbolt to dance his seductive and sensual rhythms before her. Also, from there, Changó keeps a watchful eye on his enemies and thunders in moments of rage.

The royal palm is Changó's throne and place of refuge. The children of Changó place their foreheads against its trunk to talk to Changó and receive his counsel. They believe that the tree holds Changó's entrails. The palm is the pedestal of Changó *obakoso.* It is so identified with him that many believe it is the god himself. Changó is also associated with rain since, in the tropics, rain is nearly always accompanied by thunder and lightning. Also, Changó's three wives, Oyá, Ochún, and Oba, are fluvial divinities in Africa. Thus, when sacrifices and offerings are made to Changó and Oyá requesting rain, they are placed by the royal palm.

Changó presents himself in various *caminos* or characterizations. These paths represent different aspects of the life of the legendary Alafin Shangó.

They also represent the myths, adventures, attributes, and titles of the thunder gods of other African ethnic groups that were associated with and assimilated with him. Changó is also called Kago, Oluoso, Changó Ladde, and Changó Lari. The Arará people from Dahomey call him Jebioso, the name of their thunder god. People from the Congo call him Nsasi; in Regla de Palo he is called Sarabanda and also Seven Lightning; and, in the territory of Ilesha, he is known as Alado.

Changó's priests, *oni* Changó, are greatly respected since they are considered to be gifted diviners, a power they posses from birth. In the past, it was believed that they were born with a cross on their tongues. Their hair could not be cut until they were twelve years old, since it was believed that cutting it would make them lose their clairvoyance. In Cuba, Bamboché is the name of the servant who runs Changó's errands, and some of Chango's priests are called Bamboché.

In Cuba, lithographs and icons of Saint Barbara, the Catholic saint with whom Changó has been identified, nearly always represent him. However, he is one of the few *orichas* still represented by wooden images of African inspiration. These crudely carved anthropomorphic figures are called *arere.* The figurines carry a sword in one hand and an ax in the other. They wear on their heads an ornament, which resembles either the double-headed ax or tongues of flaming fire. This is a departure from Nigerian ways, where no anthropomorphic figures are made to represent Shango.

In Cuba, as well as in Africa, believers think Changó lives in the Alafi Ile Lodi, a sumptuous castle on top of the clouds. From this palace he sends thunder and lightning. A toy soldier inside a castle also represents this god. On Afro-Cuban altars, a soldier on horseback is sometimes used to represent him, since Changó's horse, Esinle, is his inseparable companion. In western equatorial Africa, only noblemen owned horses.

The sword is one of Changó's symbols. Saint Bárbara's sword is worn as a protective amulet by Catholic devotees of this saint who do not practice Santería as well as by followers of Santería. Many are not aware that some of the powers attributed to it are based on the association of Saint Barbara with Changó. This mingling of Catholic and Santerían beliefs is one of the ways that Santería influenced and permeated the religious concepts and preoccupation of great sections of the Cuban society who worshipped Saint Barbara and attributed to her powers based on Changó's attributes.

Changó's most characteristic symbol and weapon, however, is the double-headed ax, or *oche.* It is decorated with the red and white colors of Changó. In Africa, the oshe is made from the wood of the sacred ayan tree. In Cuba, it is made of wood from the royal palm tree. The handle usually represents a human figure carrying fire on his head. The edge is the flame. These images are supposed to represent a ceremony called *ejere*. In the past, during *ejere* ceremonies, Changó's initiates carried on their heads a vessel filled with lighted charcoals that had several holes in the bottom. These *iyawós* could not give any indication that the fire bothered them because it would mean either that they were simulating trance or that they were not worthy children of Changó. Afro-Cubans report that this ordeal was part of the initiation rites that Changó's children had to endure during the nineteenth century. This ritual is no longer practiced. According to Florencio Baró,[7] in the 1940s in Carlos Rojas Changó's children used to put their hands in the flames of the fire without showing any signs of pain or harm.

Changó's necklace, or *eleke*, is threaded with six red beads followed by six white ones; then six sequences of one red bead followed by a white one. This order is repeated to complete the necklace. Originally, this *eleke* was made of red beads only, but Changó's mother, Obatalá Yemmu, inserted the white beads in order to cool Changó. Inasmuch as Changó's rage is uncontrollable, and his head is very hot, it is not surprising that his mother would try to calm him down.

When Changó speaks through the oracle of *dilogún* (cowry shells), the priests pour cold water on the sixteen shells to cool them. Then they warn the client to be careful of fire, to take good care of his or her head by refreshing it often, and to calm down any impetuousness that could lead to trouble.

The three *batá* drums belong to Changó. The *pilón de asiento*,[8] an artifact in the shape of a pestle, also belongs to Changó. People are initiated in Ocha by the *pilón de asiento*. Later, they are presented to Aña, the Changó of the drums. These requirements demonstrate how Changó grew in relevance and stature in Cuba as compared to Nigeria. In Nigeria he does not participate in the ceremonies of initiation to the cult of other orishas. The fact that he does in Cuba demonstrates again the great contribution and influence that people from Oyo had at the inception of Santería.

Changó's color is red because this color expresses life, activity, strength, and blood to the Yoruba. Although the number four has no relation to Shango in Africa, it is Changó's number in Cuba. December 4 is the day Catholics celebrate the feast of Saint Barbara, the Catholic saint associated with Changó. Changó has a reputation for being a glutton. According to myths, when he returns from his numerous wars, he is ravenously hungry and impatiently demands food. His wife Oba prepares for him his favorite dish, *amalá*, from cornmeal and lamb. He also likes to eat male goats. He likes to offer food to the guests, but later he demands exorbitant payment for it.

In *güemileres* (drum festivals), when Changó possesses one of his children, a short jacket and red-and-white-striped trousers are used to dress him. The possessed person, while dancing, charges forward by doing three somersaults approaching the drums. These movements are the reason Changó is called "el toro de la loma" (the bull of the hill) in Cuba. In Nigeria, he is compared with the male goat that charges when least expected.

His children, the *omo Changó*, do not wear caps on their heads as is the custom with other *orichas*. Since Changó is an oba, a king, they wear a crown, which, like Saint Barbara's, resembles a fortified castle or citadel.

Most of Changó's dances are warlike, especially when the possessed devotee is in the *camino* of a warrior. Changó moves with the speed of lightning. While dancing, an *omo Changó*, carrying the double-headed ax and the wooden sword, enacts adventures and episodes of his life through the use of mime and dance. The priests, when possessed by Changó, perform a dance in which a crucial battle is fought with an imaginary enemy. These bold, masculine dances are impressive expressions of great daring and courage. The dancer opens his eyes with exaggeration and sticks out his tongue, an indication that he is on fire.

In other *caminos*, Changó dances voluptuously, moving his pelvis as in sexual intercourse. He brags that he is the incarnation of male virility. Yet, at other times, he appears in a very effeminate manifestation. The latter is reminiscent of an embarrassing mythological episode in which he was forced to wear Oyá's wig in order to escape the enemy.

Changó has been identified with Santa Bárbara, the Catholic martyr patron of Spanish artillery and of storms. According to the Catholic Church, Saint Barbara was born in Nicodemia at the beginning of the third century. She was well educated and belonged to an upper-class family. She converted to Christianity, and her father tried to persuade her to abandon Christ. She refused. Frustrated and angry, he personally beheaded her at a site on a nearby hilltop. Barbara faced her executioner by kneeling and thanking the Lord for opening paradise to her. Shortly after her death, a terrible storm began and her father was struck dead by lightning.

The association of Changó and Saint Barbara seems contradictory considering the virile character of Changó and the chastity of the Catholic martyr. In this regard, *santeros* claim that Changó sometimes disguises himself as a woman. In relation to this gender issue, there are some precedents from Nigeria. In Dahomey the thunder god, Jebioso, is manifested as a complete family of gods, including male and female appearances and characteristics.

Nevertheless, there are many similarities between the attributes and symbols of Saint Barbara and Changó. As indicated previously, statues and chromolithographs show Saint Barbara wearing a crown and a red cape. Conversely, Changó is a crowned king, and his symbolic color is red. Saint Barbara, the patron of holy wars, carries a long sword, while Changó is a great warrior who uses a wooden sword. In addition, in the background of Saint Barbara's lithographs there is a castle on fire, and Changó, the legendary king of Oyo, reportedly set his own palace in flames while practicing magic one day. Furthermore, it is believed that Changó lives in a sumptuous palace in heaven that is surrounded by fire. Thus, in the case of Saint Barbara and Changó the identification is so close that Saint Barbara sometimes is depicted on horseback, influenced in all probability by the history of Shango the legendary king of Oyo.

Appendix C provides a list that identifies some of the best known manifestations of Changó in Cuba.

Oshun/Ochún, Oya/Oyá, and Oba/Oba

Fluvial Goddesses

Three important fluvial goddesses in Yoruban religion—Oya, Oshun, and Oba—are Shango's wives. They, too, are associated with atmospheric phenomena. Oba is associated with wild clouds, Oshun with gathering darkness, and Oya with tornados (McKenzie 1997: 32). In Cuba Oyá and Oba lose their fluvial character to the benefit of Ochún. However, Oyá's ownership of the cemetery and the lightning flash warrant this goddess's important position. In the case of Oba, her sweet and unselfish disposition and her domestic virtues earn the admiration and sympathy of believers.

Oshun in Africa

According to oral traditions (Verger 1954: 186), the legendary King Laro was roaming around with his subjects in search of a site for his city when he came upon the river Oshun. Some days later, the king's daughters, who were swimming in the river, disappeared in its depths. After a while, they finally resurfaced and spoke of a river goddess who had treated them with care. To show his gratitude, King Laro asked his people to offer sacrifices to the goddess. Fish, which are the messengers of the goddess, accepted the offerings. One of them gave the king a pumpkin that Oshun had sent as proof of her desire to seal a pact with King Laro and his people.

King Laro then adopted the name Ataojo, a contraction of "A tewo Gba Aja" (the one that took the fish with his hands). Then, he said, "Oshun Gbo" (Oshun is in her fullest maturity, her abundant waters will never fail us). In that very place the city of Oshogbo was founded. Every year the current king, or Ataojo,[1] of the area, comes to the river carrying in his hands a great crown ornamented with pearls. He and his family offer sacrifices to the river goddess in the same place where Laro sealed his pact with Oshun.

Although the Oshun River runs in the eastern part of Yoruban territory, the goddess is known and revered in many places far from its margins. Thus, in the distant city of Abeokuta her worship is quite important. This large sphere of influence is partly due to the fact that the river Oshun is the largest river in the vicinity of Ile Ife, the sacred city of the Yoruba.

Moreover, Oshun is associated with important generic gods, and through them she became known in many areas of Yorubaland. Thus, according to widespread oral traditions, Oshun is Shango's second wife. After Shango died, Oshun and his two other important wives, Oya and Oba, cried so hard that they were transformed into rivers. Oshun was very special to Shango because she has a gay temperament and vast knowledge of the art of love. Shango preferred her above other wives and women.

Oshun's temple is located near the royal palace in Oshogbo. Inside the temple there is an image of Oshun with very large eyes and ears that enable her to see all that goes on and to hear the prayers addressed to her. She brandishes a sword to defend her children. River stones are placed on her altars to symbolize the waters of the rivers. Copper bracelets and necklaces made of amber beads are also placed on her altars, since copper and amber are associated with her.

Ochún in Cuba

Ochún is the most revered female *oricha* in Cuba, and her cult enjoys the greatest popularity. Many of her followers associate her with La Virgen de la Caridad del Cobre, the patron Virgin of Cuba. She is a pampered goddess, loved by all for her joyous disposition, her inclination toward lovers, and her miraculous powers. Ochún has an important role in the creation of the human fetus in the uterus. She and Yemayá preside over the human embryo; then Obatalá comes to sculpt the human body and to grant it the *aché* of speech.

Numerous *patakís* tell of her adventures, qualities, and power. Ochún is one of the *orichas* who gained higher status in Cuba than in Africa. This was primarily due to the fact that, in the creolization process, she replaced and assumed the power and attributes of other African fluvial divinities.

Ochún, in Cuba, is acknowledged as the only fluvial divinity, although African myths were preserved in which the fluvial character of several other goddesses is expressed. Thus, according to a popular myth, Ochún is one of the principal wives of Changó, the powerful king of Oyo who possessed special talismans. One day, he was playing with them and unwittingly provoked a terrible storm. During the dreadful tempest, lightning struck the palace and destroyed it. The wives and children of the king died during this catastrophe. Changó, full of rage, struck the floor with force and was converted into an *oricha*. His principal wives, Oyá, Ochún, and Oba, became the goddesses of the rivers named after them.

In Cuba, Ochún is considered the legitimate wife of Orúla, the god of oracles, although she is not considered his wife in Nigeria. However, in some areas of Yorubaland she is known as the companion of Ifa, Orúla's most famous babalawo whose name, sometimes, is used to call Orúla.

A *pataki* describes Ochún's character and the nature of her relationship with Orúla:

> Ochún was the most beautiful young woman in her town. All the men wanted to marry her, but she was not interested in any of them. One day her mother publicly announced that she would give her in marriage to the one who learned her real name. An old *babalao*, Orúla, sent his mischievous messenger, Elegguá, to find out. Elegguá . . . spent many days around Ochún's . . . home until one morning he heard her mother call her Ochún. He immediately reported back to Orúla, who was able to claim her in marriage.
>
> Orúla . . . loved and pampered Ochún, but differences ensued. Ochún was full of life; she loved parties, dances, and every pleasure that life offered. Men desired her. Since she was not satisfied by Orúla, who was much older, she was constantly unfaithful to him. She even went so far as to prostitute herself with Ogún Areré, the rude owner of metals, in exchange for gold. (Cros Sandoval 1975:197–98)

In another *pataki* the relationship between Orúla and Ochún is further explained.

> Orúla, the rich and esteemed *babalao*, was married to a young, sensuous girl named Ochún. He lived with his wife in a big house that could be reached by all the roads that crossed Yorubaland. Many clients went to see him, looking for the counsel and help that only Orúla . . . could give them. Orúla was very generous with Ochún, and he always satisfied her every whim, but Orúla was old and was not able to give her the sexual satisfaction that she desired. Ochún . . . would constantly implore him to engage in *ondokó* (to make love to her).
>
> Orúla worried, suspecting that his wife was going to satisfy her sexual desires somewhere else. His suspicions proved true when Ochún met the cruel and ferocious Ogún Areré, the owner of metals and the patron of wars. Ogún was very rich, and his domains were vast. He would rape women and then, once satiated, would throw them from his realm. One day Ochún entered the part of the woods where he lived, hoping to be raped by him. She covered her body with an aphrodisiac, *oñí* (honey) and danced completely naked around him. Ogún frantically tried to grab her, screaming, "Woman, come to me," but Ochún, laughing and

making fun of him, would gracefully slip away. When they finally came together, a violent copulation ensued. Ogún, charmed by the exquisite pleasure Ochún ... gave him, delighted her with presents and begged her to "come and visit me every day."

While consulting the oracle, Orúla realized that his wife had made him a cuckold. He went to the market place and bought some parrots to take home to spy on Ochún. When Ochún came home from Ogún's place, the parrots started murmuring: "Ochún ... is adulterous. Ochún ... makes *ondokó* (sex) with Ogún Areré." Ochún then began to feed the parrots delicious morsels made of *otí* (liquor) and *oñí* (honey) and quietly told them, "Omeye lepe lepe" (children of my eyes, keep quiet). When Orúla returned that night the parrots told him, "Ochún is most virtuous; she has not gone out." And Ochún ... told Orúla, "What a good man you are. You are always giving me nice presents."

One day Orúla returned to the house earlier than usual only to find the parrots fast asleep. Orúla realized that they were drunk from the liquor Ochún gave them every day. Perhaps this time, she had given them so much that Orúla could not wake them up. Orúla wondered, "What is the matter with my poor darlings?" They could not move. When Orúla ... and Ochún went to bed that night neither of them could do anything or had any desire since both of them were worried. The following morning Orúla told Ochún, "Go to the market place and get me some *oguegué.*" When she left for the market, he put *epo* (smoked fish) on the parrots' beak, knowing that this would force them to tell the truth. When Ochún returned, he told her not to feed them, because he had already done so. Nevertheless, Ochún fed the parrots again, and told them: "Omeye lepe lepe." Then she went to the secret meeting place with Ogún Areré. When she returned that night, the parrots screamed: "Orúla, Ochún is adulterous; she sleeps with Ogún Areré." (Cros Sandoval 1975:198–99)

In another *pataki*, more attributes of Ochún are mentioned, and we find the reason that the daughters of Ochún wear a yellow robe as fulfillment of a vow or promise to her.

Ochún was a beautiful woman who liked to go to *güelimeres* to dance to the beat of sacred drums. The young men of the territory were deeply in love with her, but she treated them with contempt. One day Changó was playing the drums when Ochún arrived at the *güemilere,* or drum festival. "Drummer, come with me to my house," said Ochún. "I am busy," replied Changó disdainfully. Every night Ochún ... would go to the *güemilere* and use all her arts of attraction on Changó ... until finally he fell in love with her. From that day they became perfect lovers. The fruits of their illicit love affair were the Ibeyi, the sacred twins.

Later, when Changó was miserable, involved in all types of difficulties, rejected, and forgotten by everyone, Ochún, who was separated from him, went back to him. She sacrificed her life and possessions for him. He was her true love. Changó . . . was so very poor that Ochún had only one dress. Since she constantly had to wash it, it lost its original color and turned light yellow. (Cros Sandoval 1975:197)

In many *ilé ochas* (cult houses), Ochún is perceived as a black woman *de pasa* (with kinky hair). In others, she is a young and voluptuous mulatto with long hair, because her sister Yemayá gave Ochún her own straight hair. Ochún was born in the mountains next to a spring. She is the owner of the waters of the rivers, the fountains, springs, and sweet waters. In fact, she is the owner of everything that is sweet. As a young girl she used to enjoy dancing naked in the spring, her beautiful body covered with the powerful aphrodisiac *oñí* (honey). The amber-like liquid made her flesh shine in the moonlight.

Ochún is the goddess and patroness of love. In Yorubaland, Oshun is Shango's favorite lover; in Cuba, Ochún is the epitome of the female lover who is always asked for counsel in romantic matters. Some Afro-Cubans say, with malice, that all the daughters of Yeyé (the nickname of Ochún) like other women's husbands.

In Cuba, Ochún is the owner of money,[2] as the following *pataki* illustrates:

Ochún had a beautiful patch of pumpkins that grew so large they were the amazement and the envy of all the villagers. Ochún was a very good farmer. She proudly and fondly gave the pumpkins all of her care, which made them so very happy. At one time, one of the pumpkins grew so large and healthy that it stood out from the rest. When Ochún saw it she began to pay more attention to it than to the others. The others became jealous and began to conspire against it. One night they beat it up saying: "You rascal, you have stolen the affection of our owner. We will kill you." "Guí guí," the pumpkin cried.

Hearing the noise, Ochún came out of the house and the pumpkin told her, "Give me refuge in your house. They are trying to kill me."

Ochún brought the pumpkin into the house and put it in bed to sleep with her and Orúla. During the night Orúla was annoyed and told the pumpkin, "Sleep on the floor. I cannot sleep with you in bed." The pumpkin was not happy with Orúla, but Ochún protected it and punished the other pumpkins for having tried to harm it.

At that time Orúla was making so much money that he hid it in a secret place. The pumpkin would watch him, take the money from the secret hiding place, and put it in her bosom after he left the house. The pumpkin, naturally, got fatter and fatter.

One day while Ochún was caressing the pumpkin, she heard the tinkle of money and asked the pumpkin, "What is that sound?"

"I take Orúla's money from him and save it for you." Ochún was very grateful.

One day Echú came to the house disgusted with Orúla . . . for not having paid him his dues as guardian of the door. He said, "I am going to destroy that old man, and also his marriage."

The pumpkin made a deal with Echú, gave him a bottle of alcohol, and told him, "Have no mercy on Orúla, but don't do any harm to my owner. She is very kind to me, and I am her bank."

From that moment on Echú began pouring evil potions in every corner of the house to cause bad luck to Orúla. The old man consulted the divining board, but he could not understand the messages he received.

One day, the pumpkin asked Echú, "How far are you going with your revenge?"

Knowing that Echú was not going to leave the old man alone, she fed Echú more and more alcohol to encourage him to continue with the diabolical revenge. One day Ochún found Echú . . . lying on the floor, drunk.

"What are you doing here?" she asked. Echú replied, "Your pumpkin can give you the answer." Ochún . . . asked the pumpkin, but she learned nothing.

That day Orúla was so weak and sad that Ochún . . . thought he was dying. In desperation she decided to take revenge on the pumpkin. The pumpkin started to run and scream, "You have fattened me up with Orúla's money and now you are trying to kill me."

Ochún . . . finally caught up with the pumpkin and, with a knife, she cut it in two. The gold spilled at the feet of Orúla who, full of happiness, recovered completely and told Ochún, "Yalodde,[3] you are the owner of *awo* (money)." (Cros Sandoval 1975: 199–200)

Even though Ochún is the owner of money in Cuba, in Africa wealth belongs to Aje Saluga. This god is the patron of merchants, and his symbol or emblem is the cowry shell. In Nigeria people frequently greet each other by saying "Aye," which is a wish for good fortune. In Cuba, the word Ayé continues to have its original meaning, and it is one of the substantives used to designate money. However, Ayé Saluga is unknown in the Afro-Cuban religion.

It seems that this god of wealth was linked very closely to his material manifestation in Africa, the cowry shell. The monetary system in colonial Cuba was completely different, and shells were not used for money. Moreover, slaves were generally not traders. Thus, the cult of this *oricha* did not take root, and Ochún assumed the ownership of money.

Many believe this identification was due to Ochún's early association with gold, since, in Cuba, the precious metal was found in some springs and rivers. Also, since amber-like yellow is the color of this goddess, her association with gold was strengthened, making her the ruler of all money.

It seems very likely, however, that Ochún became the goddess of money not through her association with gold but with copper. The characteristic color of both metals is associated with Ochún, but most ornaments and objects offered to her in Nigeria are made of copper. For this reason, it is possible that, in Cuba, she was identified with the Virgin of Charity.

According to Levi Marrero (1975 3:48), this Catholic Virgin was brought to Cuba by Captain Francisco Sanchez de Moya, who was in charge of the copper mines of El Cobre in the eastern part of the island by the year 1599. Sanchez de Moya was devoted to the Virgin of Charity, the patron saint of his native town of Illesca, Toledo. According to Levi Marrero (1975 3:266–67) by 1609 he had built a small chapel on a hill on top of the mine. A hermit took care of the small shrine, dispensing religious services to the slaves who worked the mines every evening. The Virgin of Charity came to be known in Cuba as the Virgin of El Cobre (copper), after the name of the small town that grew around the mine.

Historical religious traditions indicate that in 1627 the Virgin appeared to three fishermen who were capsized during a storm in the Bay of Nipe in the northeastern region of Cuba not far from the copper mines. This miraculous event, as depicted on lithographs, shows Our Lady of Charity floating over the waters while blessing the fishermen, who, kneeling in the sinking boat, invoke her protection. It might very well be that the linkage of Ochún and the Virgin of Charity stems from her association with water. Even more important might be her association with copper, as explained above.

Furthermore, in all probability, most coins that slaves handled were made of copper. Money to them very likely meant the *perras gordas* and *chicas* (small change coins).[4] Thus Ochún, the Virgin of Copper, rules over money.

There is another reflection of Ochún's association with money through her relationship with copper. During the first decades of the twentieth century in Cuba, U.S. pennies were offered to her. At that time, Cuban pennies, two-cent coins, and nickels were made of a nickel alloy; all other coins were made of silver. Since no Cuban coins were made of copper, Afro-Cubans had to resort to U.S. currency that circulated freely in the country to use as offerings to Ochún. The U.S. pennies took the place of the *perras gordas* and *chicas*, the small change coins of colonial times.

Ochún is also the ruler of the dilogún oracle. According to different myths, Orúla gave his wife the oracle of the dilogún and the techniques of the twelve minor *odús*. He kept for himself the power of interpreting the major ones. Ochún taught the other *orichas* the use of this divining instrument. In Yorubaland, Oshun is considered the collaborator, messenger, and assistant of Orula.

Since clients constantly came to consult her, she asked Orula for the power of divination. Orula gave her the power of divining with six shells on the condition that the answers had to be given by Eshu, to whom the power of divining really belonged.

In Santería, statues and chromolithographs of La Virgen de la Caridad del Cobre represent Ochún. Dolls resembling a black woman wearing a yellow gingham dress also represent her. The *aura tiñosa* (buzzard) is considered a sacred bird and Ochún's messenger. Sometimes a gourd ornamented with this bird's feathers symbolizes Ochún. When Ochún, after taking possession of a believer, comes down and dances at the *güemileres* (drum festivals), she acts as a coquette, using a fan made with the feathers of this bird or of the *abeyemi* (peacock).

The sacred stones, or *otanes*, of Ochún, where her power resides, have to be gathered at dawn from the bottom of the river. After they are consecrated they are kept in clay pots, or *tinajas*, and nowadays in porcelain soup tureens. Currently, in Santería, as indicated previously, soup tureens made of expensive china are used to keep the *otanes* of the *orichas*. Presumably, Ochún keeps the secrets of her magic and her money in a pumpkin hidden in the river. Pumpkins symbolize the lower abdomen and belong to Ochún. Anyone who suffers from problems in that area of the body should refrain from eating pumpkins.

Yellow is Ochún's color. Thus, her distinctive necklace, the oba eleke Ochún, is made of strands of five amber beads followed by five golden yellow ones. Also, a sequence of one amber bead, followed by a golden one, is threaded five consecutive times. These sequences are repeated until the necklace is completed. Often, five coral beads are incorporated into her necklace. Her followers favor the *iyon eleke*, which is totally made of coral beads.

Some traditions indicate that Yemayá gave her sister Ochún straight hair, coral, and money. Other traditions state that Ochún gave her straight hair to Yemayá in exchange for colorful cloth.

Offerings to Ochún are made on altars dedicated to her in the homes of her devotees. However, she most prefers to have her offerings given to her at rivers. Her favorite food is *adalú*, which is made of black-eyed beans seasoned with saffron. She also enjoys hens, fish, pigeons, mutton, and *odans* (castrated goats). This goddess of sweetness always finds honey on her altar, which she uses to prepare her famous *oñi* (aphrodisiac honey).

Five is Ochún's number. Sacrifices to her and payments made to her priests should be in this number or be divisible by five. For example, payment for a consultation with a priest of Ochún could very well be five dollars and fifty-five cents. Her day is Saturday (*yokefa*). It is the day dedicated to Ochún in both Cuba and Brazil and is the day most propitious for love.

Ochún is fond of dancing and loves to possess the participants in drum festivals, or *güemileres*. When she comes to the *güemileres* she rocks with laughter while her followers greet her with joy: "Yeyé Kari" or "Yeyéé" (the sweet and lovely one). They also say to her, "Yeyé *ome ti bare*" (Holy mother, your child begs you). To pamper her they call her Ochún *sekese efiguereme* (the beautiful one who is in the river, who brings happiness and protection, and whom everyone loves). Her dances are the most beautiful among those that are part of the *oro del eya aranla* sequence that calls the *orichas*. The seventeenth drumbeat is played to honor her. The dancers reenact episodes that bring to life myths related to her. The majority of the drumbeats dedicated to Ochún are from Yesá (Ilesha) territory. Afro-Cubans claim that Ochún is originally from that area.

Fernando Ortiz (1985b:348) called the first dance dedicated to Ochún during the *oro del eya aranla* sequence the "Dance of the Springs." The dancer calls the water on both sides of the shallow river so as to make the river full again. The next dance is the "Bath of Ochún." The dancer teasingly plays with the water and combs her hair while looking with delight at her reflection in the crystal clear waters of the river. Later, the goddess, adorned with golden bracelets and necklaces, performs a dance, which incites lovemaking. The possessed dancer wears a yellow robe with little balls hanging from it. The robe is tied around the waist with a wide belt that has a rhomboid ornament in front.

In some *ilé ochas*, people claim that the daughters and sons of Ochún cannot escape from getting wet during drum festivals, because when Ochún possesses a devotee, she likes to cool herself and the public with water. In many dances she imitates the movements of oars and the rapid vertigo of the whirlpool. On other occasions, she mimics the chores of a woman embroidering, grinding grain with a pestle, and busily engaged in domestic tasks. At other times her dances are full of voluptuousness. She moves with sensual contortions while asking for her aphrodisiac, *oñí*, to cover her naked body so that it glistens like gold among the mountain springs. Ochún is an *oricha* with many *caminos*, or manifestations. Each *camino* has its corresponding pantomime and dance. The best-known manifestations are included in Appendix D.

Oya in Africa

In Yoruba mythology, when Shango hanged himself from the ayan tree, Oya, one of his wives, cried so hard that she turned into the Niger, the large river that runs north and east of Yorubaland. Oya, however, is more than a localized fluvial divinity. She is worshipped throughout Yorubaland as Shango's wife; also, she is associated with atmospheric phenomena, as he is.

Yoruba people see Oya as a fierce and courageous warrior who accompanies her husband, the thunder god, on his frequent war excursions. She is "Obirin t' o t' ori ogun da rungon si" (the woman who grows a beard to go to war). Her face is so terrible that no one dares look at her. However, Oya is tall, distinguished, and even graceful. According to myth, Oya won Shango's love with her good looks and energetic personality. He chose her from among sixteen other goddesses.

Oya, the goddess of the Niger, also presides over storms and the strong winds that precede them. She is "efukele ti' da gi l'-oke" (the rushing wind that tears down trees). She is also known by the name of Yansan, and she is the only orisha who has the power to control the ancestral spirits, or egun. At times, she possesses one of the Egungun, who visits the family of the deceased. As an Egungun she acts and speaks just like the dead. In this capacity she and the other Egungun counsel and admonish the living.

Among all the Egungun, Oya Egungun is the most dreaded. This Egungun wears a mask that gives it a frightening appearance. This image may explain why Afro-Cubans claim that Oyá should not be looked at directly in the face.

In oral traditions, Oya is Shango's first wife. She is a daring woman with a fiery temperament. One day Shango sent her to Bariba territory to deliver his talismans. These talismans had such power that if anyone touched them and then put a finger in his mouth, he would have Shango's power of producing fire and smoke through the mouth and nostrils. Shango told Oya not to touch them but, against his advice, she did. From that moment on, she was able to share the power of her husband. When Shango learned what she had done, he was enraged because he had wanted to be the only one to possess this power.

Oya is worshipped in various parts of Yorubaland. In Lokoro, near Portonovo, there is a temple consecrated to the exclusive worship of this orisha. On the altar, Oya is symbolized with eight little heads representing the mouths of the Niger near the delta. Interestingly, Lokoro is quite distant from the Niger and its delta.

The spear is Oya's symbol as is a metal object shaped like lightning or an electric charge. When Oya possesses a devotee, she carries in her hand a saber and an iruke (horse-tail), a symbol of authority.

This goddess seems to embody a feminine ideal foreign to the Yoruban ethos. Among the Yoruba, women were not part of the army, as was common in other ethnic groups of western Africa. In Dahomey, for example, tradition indicates that a large part of the royal army was formed by women, who were greatly feared for their brutality and fierceness. Oya originated in the northern Yoruban territory, but it is possible that in that area, as in Dahomey, women were part of the royal cavalry. Even though Yoruban cultural patterns, generally, are not congruent with a goddess who typically engages in activities limited to males, it is possible that the influence of Dahomey endowed Oya with the characteristics of an intrepid and violent warrior.

Oyá in Cuba

In Africa, Oya is the goddess of the river Niger; however, in Cuba, she is not considered a fluvial divinity. To Afro-Cubans she is the goddess of storms and winds. As in Africa, together with her husband she is associated with atmospheric phenomena such as lightning and tornados. She is very much dreaded and respected in Cuba because she is also associated with death.

In Cuba, unlike in Africa, Oyá is not Changó's first wife but his second one. She is a tall, slender woman, full of passion and violence. When angered, she can be even more dangerous than Changó. Changó married Oyá in gratitude for the many services she bravely rendered him during his many wars. Oyá enjoys war as much as she loves her husband and is responsible for starting many wars between Changó and Ogún. Hence, when a storm is forming, the first thing to be seen is Oyá's lightning, followed later by Changó's thunder and Ogún's metallic noises. According to a *pataki*:

> At one time Changó was in serious trouble because his many enemies were hunting him down to hang him. He went to Oyá's house seeking refuge but found his official concubine's home completely surrounded by his enemies. He was very frightened, for there was no way out.
>
> "My horse has just left, and I have also lost my spirit. I am completely trapped. There is no way out. Neither thunder nor courage will free me from my enemies," Changó said.
>
> "I will lend you my braids and my clothing so you can escape from this situation you have got yourself into," responded Oyá.
>
> "Omordé (woman), I will reward your courage and help. I am indebted to you forever."
>
> Then Oyá cut her braids and put them on Changó. She dressed him in her clothes. Then she told everybody that she was going for a walk. Changó and Oyá were more or less the same size. Thus, when he came out dressed like her, acting in the dignified manner peculiar to her, saluting everyone ceremoniously without saying a word, Changó's enemies took him for her and saluted back. This allowed Changó to escape. When all danger was over, Oyá herself went out, and Changó's enemies were so bewildered they wondered what was going on. Then they realized Changó had escaped from their hands dressed in Oyá's clothing and wearing her braids.
>
> Changó, recovered from his fright, later returned to face his enemies, and triumphed over them. (Cros Sandoval 1975:207–8)

Oyá is the bad wind, the tornado and the lightning. When she moves her petticoats, she produces the strong whirlpool motion that Afro-Cubans call *afefeyike.*"[5] This violent, domineering, and jealous woman does not allow any-one to outshine her. This characteristic of her personality may explain why, in Cuba, mirrors are covered during storms. It is believed that Oyá does not want other women to decorate themselves because Changó might see them and fall in love with them. Thus, it is claimed that Oyá's lightning will destroy houses by shattering mirrors that reflect the beauty of women.

Another myth portrays Oyá as a jealous woman who strikes the royal palm tree because Changó likes to climb there to look for other women:

> Changó used to climb the royal palm to communicate in sign language to women with whom he had secret affairs. One day Oyá found out and climbed to the top of the tree to wait for Changó. Changó, knowing that Oyá was suspicious, did not say a word, but did not climb the tree that day. The following morning he decided to act.
>
> "I am going to fill the palm tree with lizards and scare Oyá out of her wits."
>
> That afternoon when Oyá tried to climb the tree, lizards of all sizes and colors came to greet her. Oyá didn't know what to do, and, amazed and frightened, she struck and burned down the palm tree with her lightning. Since that day these trees are the favorite targets of this jealous goddess. (Cros Sandoval 1975:208)

Oyá is the owner of the *ilé yansá* (the cemetery). Many believers think she inhabits the cemetery. Others claim she lives by the *iroko* (the silk-cotton tree) where the souls of the dead reside. When a person passes away a common ex-pression is *"Okwo chon chon ilé Yansa"* (He died; he took the road of Yansá).

Oyá governs death, an attribute that makes her powerful and dreaded. Most of her worship is related to death. When the spirit of a dead person who has been properly attended continues to bother the living, appearing before them and mingling in their affairs, it is necessary to call Oyá to remove him. In such cases a lighted candle is passed close to the inside walls of the house while prayers are said to Oyá asking for help. When an *omoricha* (priest) or an *iyalocha* (priestess) is buried, songs are dedicated to Oyá to encourage her to pamper that soul to prevent it from haunting the living.

Changó is afraid of ghosts, and Oyá often sends Ikú to his house to scare him when he is misbehaving. Changó has no choice but to behave. According to the following *pataki*:

> At the time when Changó and Ochún were enjoying the height of their romance, Ochún threw a big party. She and Changó danced and enjoyed themselves to their hearts' delight. Oyá, infuriated with jealousy and spite, sent Ikú to Ochún's house. Ikú knocked; Changó answered the

door and saw the horrible skeleton making grimaces at him. The brave warrior, trembling with fear, left the house hurriedly. Ochún was very angry, and the guests were completely bewildered. Ochún, humiliated and frustrated, thought, "I can always outwit Oyá and Ikú."

The following week Ochún prepared another big party and she invited Changó. He told her, "Some other time, woman. I want no problems."

She then went to the market and bought several baskets of okra. She spilled the okra around the house. Then she asked a drummer to play while she danced and stamped on every okra pod. When Changó and the guests arrived she led them safely into the house. When the party was at its peak, Ikú, ordered by Oyá, came to spoil the fun. But when Ikú tried to knock at the door he began to slip until he finally fell down and broke his crown. He disappeared screaming: "Guí . . . guí . . . guí." (Cros Sandoval 1975:209)

Oyá, Orúla, Obatalá, and Elegguá share rule over the Four Winds. Oyá's priestesses are called *Iyá mi taide*, or *Toki*. The day they are initiated they wear the *acho pupa*, a robe of red material with a skirt usually made of dried palm fronds. Oyá's initiates frequently go before the *iroko* to make the vow that they will wear her habit: the *acho dodo*, made of an iridescent material (she is the rainbow). Reputedly, in the past Oyá's children, when possessed by the goddess, were capable of sitting on an open hearth or on top of a boiling kettle without getting burned.

Oyá is represented with images and lithographs of the Virgin of Candelaria. She became associated with this Catholic divinity because of the Virgin's name, which is derived from the noun *candela*, or fire. There is little doubt that Oyá, as lightning, is linked to *candela*, fire.

In other *ilé ochas*, Oyá is associated with Saint Teresa of Jesus. In Brazil, Oyá is identified with Santa Bárbara, who, in Cuba, is identified with Changó. This identification might be due to the fact that Santa Bárbara is also associated with atmospheric disturbances. In addition, the silk-cotton tree is the symbol of this goddess since, under the shade of this tree, the souls of the dead gather to rest.

Oyá has many different necklaces. Sometimes her necklace is made of black and white beads. Another one of her necklaces is made of brown beads with blue and white stripes. Yet at other times Oyá's necklace is made of purple beads with black and white stripes. The beads in her necklaces are strung in sequences of nine, sometimes mixing one of each color. At other times they consist of brown and white beads in cadences of nine. The *achere*, or gourd, which is used to invoke her, is painted red.

During funeral rites or in cases when a person is seriously ill, Oyá is called with a rattle made of pods of the poinciana tree. She owns a crown with nine points from which hang a pike, an *ochosi*, a flash of lightning, a scythe, a shovel, a hoe, a rake, and an ax. She also wears nine copper bracelets. Oyá rules over Fridays (the day of hope) together with her husband Changó.

Oyá likes to eat cooked food and pigeons. *Guenguere*, a paste made of lima beans, is one of her favorite dishes. *Adalú*, a paste made of black-eyed peas seasoned with saffron, is offered to her at the cemetery. She also enjoys *ekro*, a porridge made of fermented corn meal. When she is manifested as Yansa Oriri, she demands that her children not eat lamb, which she reserves for her husband, Changó.

When Oyá possesses one of her children in *güemileres* (drum festivals) they are dressed in a costume made of flowered cretonne material. A multicolored ribbon is tied around the forehead. Since Oyá is as swift and violent as lightning, her dances manifest impetuosity and bravery.

Oba in Africa

Oba is the fluvial divinity who owns the main river that runs through the eastern part of Yorubaland. She is a relatively minor orisha in the Yoruban pantheon. Oba and her husband, Shango, are among the orishas that sprang from Yemaya's body. Her worship has spread to territories far from the margins of the river because of her association with her husband, Shango. Oba, nonetheless, does not share the great character and power of Oya and Oshun, Shango's other wives. Thus, without Shango she would be merely a local fluvial divinity.

In oral traditions, Oba, Shango's third wife, knew he had a predilection for his second wife, the voluptuous and coquettish Oshun. Oba, wanting desperately to capture his affection and attention, asked Oshun for the secret to attracting him. Oshun astutely told her that men have to be won through their stomachs, so successful wives should cook well. Later, Oshun invited Oba to her house to teach her how to prepare Shango's favorite soup.

Oshun wore a handkerchief around her head while she prepared the soup with two mushrooms floating on it. Oshun told Oba that for Shango's sake she had cut off her ears and put them in the soup, since they were required ingredients. Oba took the mushrooms to be Oshun's ears. Shango arrived just a short while later, drank the soup, and complimented Oshun for her culinary expertise.

The following day Oba cut off one of her ears and prepared the same soup for Shango. On seeing her mutilated head, Shango rejected the soup in horror. In despair, Oba went to see Oshun and found her with both ears in place. The two women had a violent fight, and Shango, in a mad rage, began exhaling smoke and fire through mouth and nostrils until Oba and Oshun were both turned into rivers.

The river Oba is a tributary of the river Oshun. The waters near the confluence of these two rivers are always very rough, and when they meet the waters collide with great violence. Yoruban people claim they still remember the incident that turned Oba and Oshun into rivers. Consequently, Oba's name should never be pronounced in Oshun's presence; neither should the name of Oshun be pronounced in Oba's presence.

Oba in Cuba

In Cuba, Oba lost her character as a fluvial divinity. Ochún has taken over the ownership of all fresh waters at the expense of two former fluvial divinities of Nigeria, Oya and Oba.

The worship of Oba in Cuba is intimately related to that of her husband, Changó. Among Afro-Cubans she is Changó's first and most important wife, the original status that Oya had in Nigeria. Thus, change enhanced the character and prestige of Oba, whose tragic predicament endears her to believers. An Afro-Cuban version of the African myth provides evidence of this:

> Oba, Changó's first and legitimate wife, followed him everywhere the non-ending struggle against the powerful Ogún took him. Changó hardly had any time for his faithful wife, but she would, nevertheless, care for him with infinite devotion and patience. She would feed and counsel him at night when he came home, exhausted, from his many war adventures. She would sing tender songs to him with her sad and melancholic voice to calm his impatient and impetuous heart.

> Every night Changó would come back from his battles, and every night Oba would ready for him his favorite dish of *amalá*, made of corn meal, okra, and lamb. Day after day, Oba would roam the markets trying to find the ingredients necessary for her husband's supper, while he was away in his never ending wars, taking for granted her sacrifice and loyalty.

> One day, Oba roamed markets and fields in search of lamb, but found none. That evening, knowing that Changó was about to arrive and she had not finished supper, in desperation she cut off her ears and put them in the gruel. Courageously, she covered her mutilated head with a turban.

> When Changó arrived she served him his supper and listened to his tales of victory. Changó asked her, "Why are you wearing that dark turban at home? Don't you know that I don't like it?" Oba did not answer.

Changó, furious, took the turban off her head. When he saw how disfigured she was he said, "Woman, without ears, I can't love you anymore."

Oba, in complete despair, left the house and went into the deepest part of the forest. Screaming like a wounded bird she cried, "I am a woman without ears. I am no longer beautiful." Changó followed her, but he was too late and could not prevent her suicide.

On stormy nights, one can hear a shy, whistling cry. This is Oba lamenting her lost beauty, desperately pleading to Changó to give her back his love. (Cros Sandoval 1975:211–12)

Oba is the goddess of the home; she is the good wife who makes any sacrifice for her husband. Changó is very fond of her and respects her very much. Her children pray to her and ask her to calm Changó when he is enraged. They know he respects her and is responsive to her counsel. Afro-Cubans describe this relationship by stating, "Changó Oba *o mague alada yina*," (Oba is the most esteemed wife of Prince Changó). Afro-Cubans address her with devotion and affection. She symbolizes marital devotion and dedication. Her sacrifice for love is always remembered with respect and tenderness.

Oba cannot be *asentada*. She cannot possess the believers. However, dances and drumbeats are always offered in her honor at every liturgical festival. Oba rules with her husband, Changó, over *yima* (Friday), the day of hope. Her necklace is the color of lilac. She has become identified with Santa Rita and Santa Catalina de Siena. In some *cabildos* she has also been identified with the Virgin of El Carmen.

Olokun/Olokun and Yemonja/Yemayá

Gods of the Sea

Olokun in Africa

Olokun rules over the waters of the ocean. In the past, he must have been one of the most important divinities of the Yoruban pantheon. Evidence of his ancient preeminence is found in archaeological sites in Ile Ife, Benin, and in literary sources. Leo Frobenius' (1913) investigations and excavations at Ebo-Olokun, a religious center near Ile Ife, yielded a bronze bust of Olokun that is one of the finest pieces of Yoruban craftsmanship.

The name Olokun is composed of the particle *ol*, an abbreviation of the word *oni* (owner of), and *okun* (the sea). Olokun is the owner of the sea. He rules over the sea and all the creatures in it. This powerful divinity dresses in black and resides in a huge palace at the bottom of the ocean. In a myth recorded by Ellis (1894: 71) Olokun was once infuriated with humanity because human beings had neglected him. He decided to destroy the earth with a great flood. He had already done away with hundreds of human beings when Obatala interceded on behalf of the survivors. Obatala forced Olokun back into his palace and tied him up with seven iron chains. Olokun remained tied until he promised to abandon his plan of destruction.

This myth, with slight changes, is also known in Cuba. It seems that in Cuba Olokun is a very ancient divinity who, originally, was linked to the act of creation. He/she is popular among fishermen and boatmen and other people who live by the sea. In some areas of Yorubaland, Olokun is considered a masculine divinity. In other areas, Olokun is a creator goddess. In Ile Ife, the sacred city of the Yoruba, which is distant from the coast, Olokun is perceived as the water and as the wife of Oduduwa, the earth. Together they form the creation couple. The Ilesha people, who live inland, also worship this orisha who, they believe, lives in a sacred mountain.

In coastal Nigeria, Olokun's priests used to dress in black or very dark blue garments.[1] Fishermen and men of the sea offer him all types of sacrifices to avoid his terrible rage, the violent storms, for which he is greatly feared. Many ritual banquets are offered in his honor. In these feasts, excessive amounts of food are intentionally prepared so that leftovers remain in abundance. Once the banquet is over, the leftovers are thrown into the sea to the songs and cries of joy of the participants, who also go into the sea to swim and honor Olokun.

As indicated previously, Olokun is a god who, in the past, required human sacrifices. Olokun's worship must have been essential and widespread for this orisha to be so well known in both Africa and in Cuba.

Olokun in Cuba

At the end of the nineteenth century and the beginning of the twentieth, the cult of Olokun in Cuba was quite important. It was differentiated from that of Yemayá. The *babalao* Hermes Varela claims that Olokun is associated with Tum, the god of the ocean and the soul of the abyss in ancient Egyptian mythology (Brown 2003:337).

In parts of Yorubaland the Gelede secret society flourished. It was known for its dealings and practices of witchcraft. There is an illustration of a Gelede mask in Fernando Ortiz's earliest book (1906:119). According to Ortiz, at the end of the nineteenth century the Gelede society in Cuba offered a pig to Olokun in the midst of the sea and afterward celebrated the dance of Olokun. The Gelede society, however, did not flourish in Cuba for long.

Fernando Ortiz (1951:347) also reports that Matilde Zayas, a freed female slave originally from Egbado, organized a great festival to Olokun every year in Regla, a town across the bay from the capital city of Havana. Zayas commissioned a wood-carver of Yoruban origin brought to Cuba as a slave to sculpt a mask of Olokun. Lydia Cabrera reports (1980:27) that that mask, after several years, was found in the city of Matanzas in the house of Ferminita Gómez. This supports Miguel Ramos's report that Má Monserrate Obá Tero left Havana and moved to Matanzas after she had some problems with Timotea Albear Latuan. It is possible that she took the Olokun mask to Matanzas, where she initiated Ferminita Gómez and introduced the cult of Olokun. Moreover, the legendary *santero* Reynerio Perez used to sacrifice to Olokun the god of the sea, on the surface of the open Caribbean Sea, in the area above the great Bartlett oceanic depression in the southern part of the province of Oriente. The *otán* of Olokun is kept in a *tinajón* (large pottery vessel) containing seawater. Olokun owns seven goblet-shaped drums that are used to communicate with him (Cabrera 1980: 27).

Yemonja in Africa

Yemonja is the goddess of water, wetlands, and the river Ogun. Her name is derived from the phrase "Yeye omo, eja," where "Yeye" means "mother," "eja" means "fish," and "omo" means "species." Yemonja is the mother of fish. Yemonja is also considered the mother of most of the Yoruban gods.

According to one well-known myth (Lucas 1948:98), Yemonja and Agayu were the only children of the creator couple, Oduduwa and Obatala.

> There being no other persons to marry, Aganju and Yemonja married one another and had a son named *Orungan*.[2]
>
> Orungan is said to have committed incest with his mother. She fled from him in horror, but was hotly pursued by her wicked son, until she fell backward to the ground owing to exhaustion. Streams of water began to pour forth from her body, and these eventually united to form a lagoon.
>
> From her body the following deities emanated: *Olosa* (the lagoon goddess), *Olokun* (god of the sea), *Dada* (the god of vegetables), *Sango* (god of lightning), *Ogun* (god of iron and war), *Oya* (goddess of the river Niger), *Osun* (goddess of the river Osun), *Oba* (goddess of the river Oba), *Orisa Oko* (god of agriculture), *Ososi* (Oshosi, god of hunters), *Oke* (god of mountains), *Aje Saluga* (god of wealth), *Sopono* (god of small pox), *Orun* (the sun-god), *Osu* (Oshu, the moon-goddess). The origin of several of the well-known Yoruba deities is thus traced to Obatala and Oduduwa.

Yemonja personifies fertile motherhood. Yemonja's creativity is different; she is the fertile goddess who, without the intervention of any masculine element or principle, is capable of reproducing. Truly, no life can exist without water; that is, Yemonja is vital to all.

Yemonja, therefore, is the mother of most of the orishas known throughout Yorubaland, with the exception of Obatala, Oduduwa, Orunmila, and Elegbara. These four are direct agents of the Supreme Being and were not begotten by Yemonja.

Yemonja's worship is very important in the city of Abeokuta, where it is believed that she inhabits the river Ogun. In the temples dedicated to her worship in Abeokuta, she is represented by anthropomorphic wooden images depicting a woman with very large breasts and the swollen womb of pregnancy.

Yemayá in Cuba

In Cuba, as in Africa, Yemayá is considered a powerful divinity. Her cult is especially strong in western Cuba, where she is associated with the Virgin de

Regla, who had and continues to have a great following among Catholics, and whose church is in the town of Regla, bordering the eastern shore of the harbor of the capital city of Havana. The processions in honor of this Virgin were once frequented by a multitude who, conscious or not of the identification of the Virgin with Yemayá, came to offer prayers and request miracles. Many popular songs described the merits of this miraculous black Virgin.

Most Afro-Cubans believe that Yemayá was originally from Abeokuta. Yemayá is *obini adu adu* (a very dark-skinned woman). She is a tall, graceful, and haughty woman. According to tradition, she once wore her hair in long braids. Later, she gave her braids to her sister Ochún. In Cuba, as in Africa, she rules over the sea and all its creatures. She preserved her maternal character in the New World, but the Yoruban myth about the creation of the orishas from Yemonja's womb is unknown in Cuba. However, a *patakí* that is similar to an African myth has been recorded in a *santero's* notebook: "Yemayá was married to Ogún, the powerful warrior. Ogún spent his life fighting, and Yemayá, distraught, decided to put an end to all wars. She went to Olokun (the bottom of the sea) and stirred the waters until a great deluge was formed. The catastrophe was of such proportions that Obatalá had to tie up Olokun to restore normalcy to the planet." (Cros Sandoval 1975:218)

In the Yoruban version of this myth, Olokun, who, in some *ilé ochas* in Cuba is considered a path of Yemayá, causes the flood without Yemayá's intervention.

Another popular *patakí*, recorded in a notebook of a *santero*, explains why Yemayá was given the ownership of the sea: "Obatalá ordered Yemayá, Ogún's wife, to search for some shoes for Olofin. Eleggúa placed obstacles in her way, but Ogún, who was walking ahead of Yemayá, dismantled all the traps. After overcoming many hazards Yemayá was able to obtain the shoes. To reward her, Olofin made her the owner of the sea and all its creatures."

In another *patakí,* which seems to be an Afro-Cuban version of the Yoruban myth in which Yemaya's son Orungan attempts to rape her, Yemayá is the foster-mother of Changó. According to this Afro-Cuban myth:

> Young Changó was the child born of a fortuitous sexual encounter between Obatalá and Agayú Solá. Obatalá didn't care for Changó and, infuriated, threw him from her house. Yemayá, a very powerful and strong woman, took over the rearing of this extraordinary child. Changó grew up to be a powerful warrior, a successful fortune-teller, and a popular drummer. Yemayá cared for him with tenderness. When Changó rested in bed, she would lie next to him and nestle close to him with her body, full of maternal love.
>
> One day, during their daily nap, Yemayá woke up full of sexual desires. Impelled by them she made advances to the unsuspecting Changó. Hor-

rified, he repudiated her saying: "Iyá. . . mi, I am ashamed of you." He ran away from the house to escape her advances. Yemayá would not resign herself to lose the pleasure that such a lover could give her and ran after him. Changó had reached his refuge on top of the royal palm tree. Yemayá continued her siege. "Leave me alone, disgraceful woman," he cried. Yemayá would not leave him alone and embraced the trunk of the palm tree while she mimicked the sexual act.

"Obiní, I am going to give you such pleasure as you have never experienced before."

Angry and intrigued, Changó descended from the palm tree and embraced her. They rolled on the fresh ground and rocked in slow, deliberate movements, as Changó possessed her against nature. (Abridged from Cros Sandoval 1975:219)

In a similar *pataki* from a *santero*'s notebook:

Changó arrived one day in Yemayá's domain. He did not know that she was his mother. He found her very attractive and started making romantic advances. Some time later, at a drum festival, Yemayá pretended that she, also, was in love with him and asked him to go to her house with her. Pointing toward the sea she told him, "That vast blue space that you see far beyond is my house." Changó anxiously asked, "Do we have to go there? I don't know how to swim. Nevertheless, if you take me I will go." They walked to the edge of the shore and Yemayá jumped in her boat and asked Changó to step in.

The coastline faded away and Changó worriedly said, "I cannot see the coast anymore." Yemayá dove into the sea all the way to the bottom. As she disappeared from sight, a big wave turned over the boat, throwing Changó into the ocean. He held to the boat, desperately struggling to keep from drowning. Yemayá returned to the surface, laughing, while she watched Changó's antics as he screamed for help.

Obatalá then arrived, stamping on a snake, and said to Yemayá, "*Adyacua omodukue Onisaggo*" (Don't let your son die). Changó could hold to the boat no longer. Yemayá held him above the water saying, "I am going to save you, but from now on, respect your *iyá* (mother)."

"*Confiedeno iyá mi*" (I didn't know you were my mother). Yemayá retrieved the boat and helped Changó get into it.

Looking at the two goddesses, Changó then asked, "Which of you two brought me into this world?" Yemayá answered him, "Obatalá gave birth to you, and I took care of you." . . . Changó and Yemayá embraced each other. (Cros Sandoval 1975: 219–20)

This story explains why, during *batá* festivals, when these two goddesses come down, boastful Changó, who claims no one is higher than he except Olodumare, humbly bows in front of his two mothers and treats them with great deference and respect. When he is in an ugly mood, these two goddesses are called to calm him.

Yemayá is usually represented in Cuba by Catholic chromolithographs of the Virgin of Regla, and sometimes she is represented by wood-carved images. The sexual characteristics of these are not as accentuated as in the statues made of her in Nigeria. An anchor, a key, a half moon, and a mermaid also represent Yemayá, as do black dolls wearing dresses made of white and blue checkered gingham material.

Aro (blue), the color of the water of the sea, belongs to Yemayá and Olokun. Olokun's necklace is made of deep blue and coral beads. Yemayá's number is seven. Her necklace is made of seven white or crystal beads followed by seven blue ones, then seven sequences of a blue bead followed by a white one. Yemayá's *otán* (sacred stone) is kept in a clay kettle; Olokun's *otán* is a rock from the sea.

Yemayá rules on Saturdays along with Ochún. Yemayá likes to eat ducks, and Lydia Cabrera (1957:57) mentions the following prayer, which is addressed to her when the sacrifice is offered to her: "*Awoyo tolo be ya mi kueye adufa*" (My lady, to worship you I am going to offer you a duck). These sacrifices should be made in a lagoon. In Nigeria, according to Talbot (1926 2:88), the orisha Olossa is the wife of Olokun and is the deity of the Ossa lagoon near Lagos. She is the giver of fish and shares some qualities that, in Cuba, pertain to Yemayá.

Yemayá enjoys lamb, fish, pigeons, and watermelon. Her favorite dish is *ekru* (tamales made with black-eyed beans died with indigo). She also likes desserts made of coconut and corn.

When Yemayá comes down to the *güemileres,* or drum festivals, she wears a tight-fitting dress with a belt and rhomboid-shaped front piece. Yemayá is a very haughty, slender, and graceful woman. When she possesses a believer, the person exudes poise and elegance. Although she is very proud and distinguished-looking, she is always happy, because, as Fernando Ortiz (1951:247) remarks, "In the African Olympus, virtue, wisdom and *sandunga* (charm, wit) are not incompatible."

The initiated, when possessed by Yemayá, laugh loudly while daintily fanning themselves. Her dances mimic the movements of the waves in the ocean. Sometimes the dancer pretends that she is swimming; at other times she runs quickly toward her sister Ochún, who is waiting by the shore. The dancers of the choir turn around rapidly like the whirlpools that form at sea during tropical storms. The best known *caminos* of Yemayá are listed in Appendix E.

Shopono/Babalú Ayé

God of Diseases and Plagues

Shopono in Africa

Shopono is a most dreaded manifestation of the wrath of Olodumare. He commands such fear and respect that it is considered dangerous to address him by his real name for fear of retaliation. It is believed that smallpox, leprosy, and other horrible sexually transmitted and skin diseases are punishments he inflicts on those who offend him.

There are a number of contradictions regarding the personality and place of origin of this orisha. Shopono carries the title king of Nupe, and there are speculations that he might be indigenous to that territory, which is located north of Yorubaland. However, some Nigerian and Cuban traditions suggest that the cult of Shopono originated in French Dahomey (currently the Republic of Benin). In Ketou and Abeokuta, Shopono is considered to be the son of Nana Buruku, the creator goddess of Dahomey.

Paul Mercier (1959: 316) is one who concurs with traditions from Dahomey that point to Savalou (an area in Dahomey close to Yorubaland) as the birthplace of Sakpata (the orisha in the pantheon of Dahomey that has the same character, personality, and attributes of Shopono). Pierre Verger's view (1954: 184) is that Kpein Vedji, which is in Dahomey and close to Savalou, is the cradle of Shopono's cult. One way or another, Shopono is closely associated with Sakpata. However, it is not clear whether the worship of the orisha of disease and plagues first originated in Dahomey and was spread from there to the Yoruban people; or originated somewhere else and, from its place of origin, spread both to Yorubaland and to Dahomey.

There are also some contradictions regarding the character and the personality of Shopono. It is possible that Shopono was originally a dangerous divinity, respected, pampered, and flattered by believers because of fear of punishment.

A. B. Ellis (1894: 73) records a myth that describes the character and attributes of Shopono, also known as Shankpanna or Shakpana. In this myth, Shopono is an old lame man with a wooden leg, who limps as he walks with the aid of a cane. One day, when the orishas were having a party at Obatala's palace, Shopono tried to join in the dance but, due to his deformity, stumbled and fell down. The orishas burst out laughing, and Shopono, in revenge, tried to infect them with smallpox. Fortunately Obatala came to their rescue and drove Shopono away. From that day onward Shopono was forbidden to associate with other gods. He became an outcast, and since then, he has lived in desolate and uninhabited tracts of the country.

Shopono is called Ile Gbona (hot earth) since it is believed that when he is angry the earth turns hot, causing serious diseases. He is also called "destruction at noon," since his rage is strongest during the hottest hours of the day.

According to E. Bolaji Idowu (1962: 97), it is believed that Shopono walks the streets at midday when the sun is hottest, dressed in a scarlet robe. His presence is the reason people avoid walking on the streets dressed in bright colors at midday. They fear that Shopono, thinking they are making fun of him, will take revenge. In fact, people were said to be so fearful of this sensitive and vengeful god that when they wanted to say "Ile Gbona" (the ground is hot), they would say just the opposite, "Ile Tutu" (the ground is cold).

Shopono is the king of the world and the earth, where man resides and grows his food. Originally, he was called Oba-lu-aiye (king, lord of the earth), the name by which Shopono is still known in Ife and in Igana. He is also called Olode (the owner of the open spaces and the environment).

Shopono is an ambiguous divinity. On the one hand, he is praised as god of the earth who cares for and nourishes the seeds. On the other hand, it is commonly accepted that Shopono uses infectious potions to punish people who have offended him. Thus, during the dry season when epidemics flourish, abundant sacrifices are offered to him. Shopono is propitiated to avoid the terrifying manifestations of his anger and rage: smallpox, leprosy, and other infectious diseases. Moreover, his will is accepted with resignation and even with outward signs of happiness. Even survivors and relatives of victims of his curse show signs of happiness to further avoid his wrath. He is called Alapadupe (the one who kills and is thanked for it).

Paradoxically, many titles by which he is addressed proclaim his just character. He is called A-ru-mo-l-ogun-ika-danu (the one who throws poisons away). Some sources claim that he is not evil, that, instead, he is opposed to the use of poisons and only uses them against transgressors. However, other sources argue that he wants poisons to be thrown away because he does not want any competition.

It seems that, in the past, Shopono's cult had an ethical basis. Even today, when festivities are held in his honor, his very influential priests admonish and counsel the believers to lead a moral life to avoid incurring Shopono's displeasure.

Unfortunately, it seems that some of his priests' behaviors have not always been exemplary. Allegedly, some of them, when called to care for the victims of the diseases caused by the god, have made use of their knowledge to infect people they wanted to harm. In addition, others have been accused of disseminating these diseases for profit. Numerous stories are told in Nigeria of priests using their knowledge to spread the illnesses they were supposed to cure. These stories might have further tainted the character of Shopono.

Among the Yoruba, it was customary for Shopono's priests to dispose of the bodies and personal possessions of the victims. This custom was based upon sound sanitary practices. The priests of Shopono would bury the bodies of the victims of contagious diseases in the countryside far from the family compounds located in towns and villages. In the absence of the priests, the relatives would, instead, bury the bodies in the backyard, inside the compounds. Unfortunately, many unscrupulous priests demanded as payment the possessions of the victims, plus a high fee for burial services. Consequently, it was to their advantage to spread the disease, using potions derived from the ulcers of the corpses. Relatives who refused to pay the fee requested were threatened and, whenever possible, infected.

There is evidence of this in the literature. For example, many years ago, several smallpox epidemics ravaged the area around Lagos. J. Olumide Lucas (1948: 113) reports that Dr. Oguntola Sapara, a Yoruban physician, joined Shopono's worship groups and discovered that the priests prepared an infectious potion, which they used to spread the disease. The consequent scandal reached such proportions that the British government forbade the worship of Shopono in its protectorate.

Thus, from both a medical point of view and also from a moral standpoint, the worship of this god became a negative force in the life of the Yoruban people. The fear that this orisha inspired had demoralizing effects on the residents of the community.

J. Olumide Lucas (1948:112) cites an oral tradition published by Feyisara Sopein under the pen name Adesola in the *Nigerian Chronicle* of February 25, 1910: "One tradition states that Shokponna (smallpox) was a very wicked boy who often excited great commotions in his town. On one occasion when he had beaten to death several of his townspeople, he was taken by his parents and sold to a native doctor, who taught him the use of very bad and poisonous drugs." This recent myth seems to echo the actions of Shopono's priests.

Interestingly, in Cuba Babalú Ayé is known as a very merciful god in contrast to the view in Nigeria of his role as expressing the wrath of Olodumare. It is possible that the association of this orisha and its cult with antisocial behavior occurred after the slave traffic ended.

Shopono's priests do not belong to a specific clan, as do the priests of other orishas. However, the children of his initiates generally follow in their fathers' footsteps. These priests wear beautiful, colored robes and silver jewels, and smoke pipes. During festivals, they sing spicy songs, which are the delight of the public, and they brag about the power and the strength of their god. Vigorous movements characterize the dances of his priests.

Temples and chapels dedicated to this god are generally found in the bush away from the towns. Such practice reflects the dangerous character of this orisha as well as his agricultural connection.

Shopono's walking stick is one of his symbols. Generally the face of the god or of a person suffering from a high fever is carved into the handle.

Shopono is the owner of the shashara, a small broom made from the fibers of the palm tree and decorated with shells. This little broom is used to sweep away bad things. Shopono also owns the gourds that contain the remedies for the diseases he causes and, reputedly, might also contain the potions that cause those diseases.

In essence, if Shopono had always been such a terrible divinity, and his priests had always been dedicated to such dubious practices, it is doubtful that they would have been assigned the care of the stricken. It is also difficult to believe that festivals to this god would have attracted such large numbers of the faithful, as they normally had, unless they were motivated by extraordinary fear and, therefore, respect.

Currently, Shopono continues to be a very well-known and respected divinity, even though the importance of his worship suffered heavily after the British government forbade it in 1917. In Dahomey, this god is still one of the most important. His festivals attract large crowds hoping to see the beauty of the colorful and energetic dances, which are still performed to propitiate him.

Babalú Ayé in Cuba

Babalú Ayé, the Cuban *oricha* who is the equivalent of Shopono, became associated with the Catholic Saint Lazarus. Saint Lazarus, "the man with the crutches," as he is commonly known, is one of the most revered Catholic saints in Cuba. He has many followers in the eastern part of the island, especially in the city of Santiago de Cuba. In the western region of Cuba, Saint Lazarus is also well loved, especially in the town of El Rincón, in the province of Havana, where there is a chapel dedicated to him at the site of a hospital for lepers. On December 17, the feast day of the saint, numerous processions were held in his honor in many towns, and especially in El Rincón. Saint Lazarus was and is still popular because, reputedly, he is the miraculous healer of dreadful diseases.

As mentioned previously, Oba-lou-Aiye or Baba-lu-aiye were the names by which Shopono was known in Ile Ife; and Babalú Ayé is the name by which the *oricha* of diseases is known in both Cuba and Brazil. Thus, it is possible that the worship of the god of epidemics was brought to Cuba by people originally from Ile Ife.

In Cuban Santería, as expressed in the following myth, Babalú Ayé is Changó's brother. This kinship tie is recognized in Nigeria. According to a myth:

> On an occasion when Changó was predicting the future in front of a large audience, a crippled leper came and asked him "Why don't you say something to me? Don't you want to predict my future?"
>
> Changó answered him, "My father has told me that in this land I have a brother and a half-brother who are older than I. You are the half-brother. Listen to me carefully. I could not live where I was born. Today I am called Oni Changó, but I live in foreign lands. Your future and your good luck are far away from here. Turn your back and leave. Cross the wilderness, and you will find lands where you will be king."
>
> The man asked, "How am I going to travel in this miserable state?"
>
> That man was Babalú Ayé.
>
> Changó told Ogún, his other brother, who was standing there with his two enormous dogs, "Give the dogs to this man." Then, he rapidly took the dogs and gave them to Babalú Ayé.
>
> Ogún later claimed his dogs, but since then a great hatred grew between Changó and Ogún. (Cros Sandoval 1975:228)

According to this *pataki*, Changó, the great fortune-teller, advised his brother Babalú Ayé to go to Dahomey where he would rule as king. As predicted, Babalú Ayé was accepted as king in Dahomey. There he fostered the worship of his brother Changó, under the name Jebioso.

Some Afro-Cubans are aware that in Dahomey the thunder god, with characteristics and attributes identical to those of Changó, is called Jebioso. Other informants say that Changó brought Babalú Ayé from Dahomey to Yorubaland.

Insignificant details of the theogony and genealogy of Yoruban gods were preserved with fidelity in the religious memory of Afro-Cubans. In addition, in Cuba, minor details about the *orichas* have been cherished and preserved, while many negative aspects of the gods have been forgotten.

There are two explanations for Babalú Ayé's lack of the terrifying personality in Cuba for which Shopono, his equivalent, is known in Nigeria. The first explanation is that the negative incidents that were associated with the priests of Shopono took place after the slave trade with Cuba had ceased.

The second explanation is the identification of Babalú Ayé with Saint Lazarus, a character from one of Jesus' parables. According to Juan J. Sosa (1994:6), in 1681 a sanitarium for the care of lepers was founded in the town of El Rincón, near the city of Havana. In 1854 the order of nuns of the Daughters of Charity became responsible for its administration. A chapel dedicated to Saint Lazarus was built next to the hospital. This saint was portrayed in statues and chromolithographs as a leper, walking painfully with the aid of crutches, assisted by two dogs. The saint worshipped at this shrine gained a large following. He was perceived as a saint of great compassion for people who were suffering as he himself had suffered. He also had the reputation for having great healing powers.

The chapel of Saint Lazarus became almost something of a national shrine in Cuba. Every December 17, the day the Catholic Church honors Saint Lazarus, thousands of pilgrims, Catholics, *santeros*, and other faithful used to flock to this shrine.

In the 1960s the Catholic Church declared that the Saint Lazarus worshipped in Cuba and in many other countries was not a real saint or person. According to the Catholic Church, the real Lazarus had lived in the village of Bethany with his sisters Martha and Mary, who were close friends of Christ. When Lazarus died, Christ prayed to his Father on his behalf. After Christ resurrected him, Lazarus committed his life to spreading the good news of Christ. Following Christ's death, Lazarus, running away from persecution, settled in Marseilles, where he later became a bishop. He has had a following in the Catholic Church as a miraculous saint. His tomb in Marseilles is a place of pilgrimage for devout French Catholics, who revere him as the bishop of Marseilles.

The statue, or image, that is widely worshipped in Cuba is not the semblance of the Lazarus of Bethany. Instead, it is the image of a beggar covered with sores, assisted by crutches and by dogs that lick his wounds. This image, worshipped by thousands, represents a character in one of Christ's parables, as narrated in chapter 16 of the Gospel of Saint Luke. In this story, Dives, a rich man, abused poor Lazarus. The parable ends when both men die and Lazarus goes to live with the Lord while Dives is punished for all eternity.

Father Juan Sosa (1994:17) has researched the issue of the various images of Saint Lazarus. He came to the conclusion that the source of the confusion is that the military order of hospitaler-knights of Saint Lazarus of Jerusalem took as its patron the fictitious Lazarus, "full of sores," of the parable, instead of Lazarus, Christ's disciple. Later on, "One suspects that this military order supported or was transformed into a community of servants dedicated to the care of the sick, particularly those suffering from the plague or from leprosy, a reality which echoes the physical condition of the Lazarus depicted by Luke's gospel" (Sosa 1994:17).

Presumably, in the search for meaningful similarities, this Lazarus of the parable, who suffers from skin ulcers and who has a reputation for being miraculous, compassionate, and sympathetic to those suffering from painful ailments, was associated with Babalú Ayé, the *oricha* that, as Shopono in Nigeria, causes and cures plagues.

The Catholic Church's declaration brought confusion and consternation among Catholics who were devoted to "Saint Lazarus." It also did the same among Santería's adherents who were devoted to Babalú Ayé/Saint Lazarus.

It is possible that the identification of Babalú Ayé with the suffering, compassionate, and miraculous character of the parable in the Gospel of Saint Luke had a positive influence on Babalú Ayé's character. To Afro-Cubans, Babalú Ayé is a sick old man, *cañengo y jorobeteado* (decrepit and deformed). He walks with the help of crutches, guided by two dogs, just as Saint Lazarus did. He suffers from syphilis or leprosy and is also associated with smallpox and gangrene.

Smallpox was eradicated by the end of the nineteenth century, hence Babalú Ayé, the god of infectious skin diseases, became associated, also, with leprosy and syphilis, which, in Cuba had yet to be eradicated. Even though Babalú Ayé punishes through these diseases, he is also the miraculous *oricha* who cures them. The ambiguity of his personality in Cuba is tilted toward the positive, as he is regarded more as a miraculous healer than as a vindictive *oricha*. Nevertheless, a guarded attitude surrounds him.

Silvia Eires (January 20, 2005) recounts that once she was preparing to do a ritual for Babalú Ayé and the *babalao* warned her that she should throw some raw dry corn on the floor to distract Azo (disease), which was coming. Later, following the advice of the *babalao,* she picked up the corn and disposed of it in the wilderness.

Babalú Ayé enjoys the pleasure of cohabiting with all women. Rómulo Lachatañeré (1939:196) refers to a *pataki* that explains how Babalú Ayé received this power from the hands of Olofin. Babalú Ayé, who was very fond of women, made constant use of this *aché*. He is presented as a libertine who behaves as the traditional gigolo, living off women. The following *pataki* from a *santero's* notebook so describes him:

> The day Olofin divided his *aché* among his sons and daughters he gave the river to Ochún, the thunder to Changó, and the lightning to Oyá. He was running out of grants to give away when he asked his son Babalú Ayé, "What power would you like to possess?"

Babalú Ayé, who was a libertine, a party lover, and a gigolo, replied without hesitation, "Babá, I want to have the power to cohabit with all the women."

Olofin had no choice but to grant Babalú Ayé his request, since he had already given his word. However, Olofin warned him, "On Holy Thursdays you will have to restrain your sexual impulses and practice abstinence."

Time passed by and, despite Olofin's warning, Babalú Ayé made use of his power with no limitations. So, on Good Thursday he used his *aché* as usual. The following morning he woke up and saw with horror that his whole body was covered with terrible ulcers. Olofin punished his imprudence and disobedience and infected him with syphilis. He died a few days later after much pain and suffering. His death brought great consternation. Women could not console themselves to living without him. They cried and lamented their terrible loss.

Ochún, the beautiful goddess of love and sensuality, decided to put into effect a daring plan. Since she was the owner of the aphrodisiac *oñí*, she decided to go to Olofin's palace and scatter an abundant amount of *oñí*. The old man woke up the following morning a victim of sensual temptations he had not felt for quite some time. He did not realize that the strange feelings he was experiencing were caused by Ochún's *oñí*. When he finally figured this out, he asked that Ochún be brought to his presence. He told her, "Ochún, I order you to give me more of your *oñí*."

Ochún cunningly replied, "I will be more than happy to give *oñí* to you, but you will have to do something in return."

Olofin was so delighted with the new sensations that he immediately replied, "Anything you want will be granted to you."

Ochún then requested, "Olofin, restore back to life that most committed of lovers, the great libertine Babalú Ayé, so that the women of this world will continue to enjoy his many abilities and services."

This is how Babalú Ayé was brought back to life to the delight of all the women. (Cros Sandoval 1975:229–30)

This *pataki* has elements that are undoubtedly Afro-Cuban and that, according to some *santeros*, are of Bantu influence. In Africa, Shopono does not have the power to cohabit with all women. It seems that this Cuban myth served to explain this *oricha*'s association with syphilis, a disease with which he was not associated in Africa.

Babalú Ayé, Elegguá, Oyá, and Orúla each own respectively one of the Four

Winds. Babalú Ayé is a *santo muertero* (hangs around with the dead). He likes to do business with the dead, and he is the driver of Oyá's wagon. In Africa his priests were, and still are, in charge of burying the victims of infectious diseases. In Cuba, he is Oyá's driver and transports the bones of the dead. However, in Cuba, Babalú Ayé lost his power as sovereign of the earth.

The priests of Babalú Ayé in colonial Cuba did not organize the secret society their counterparts had in Nigeria. They did not have the privilege of burying and inheriting the possessions of victims of plagues.

Images and lithographs of Saint Lazarus represent Babalú Ayé. Crutches are also his symbol. His stone, or *otán*, is kept in an *apoto* (a clay kettle). His symbolic color is purple, based on his association with Saint Lazarus, the real Catholic Saint Lazarus who was a bishop.

Afro-Cubans of Arará, or Dahomian descent, keep his *otanes* in a completely closed kettle. His necklace is generally made of black and sometimes white beads with blue stripes. The *charará*, a little broom made of palm brushes, belongs to him, and in Cuba, as in Nigeria, it is used to sweep away all evil influences. Babalú Ayé also carries the *bilaba*, called the *ja* by people of Dahomian ancestry. It is a whip made of *corojo* (royal palm) twigs tied with a piece of leather. It is used to scare evil away and to protect the neophyte during the presentation to the drums. Dancers use it when honoring this *oricha*.

Babalú Ayé's followers usually wear a habit made of burlap. They wear these coarse clothes in gratitude for the many favors they have received from him. Dogs, or *aya*, are his guides and also belong to him. Wednesday is the day of the week over which he rules. Mosquitoes and flies are his messengers.

This *oricha* enjoys eating pigeons and hens, and he likes to be offered tobacco and *orí* (coconut oil). He claims that coconut oil sharpens the intelligence. He also enjoys stale bread, a glass of water, milk, and dry cooking wine as well as nuts, especially peanuts. His food is offered to him anywhere in the house.

In religious festivals, drumbeats of Dahomian origin are often played to honor Babalú Ayé. In the *oro del eya aranla* (ritual sequence of chanting, dancing, and drumming that takes place in a large room or patio and is opened to the public), the sixth drumbeat is dedicated to him. When this *oricha* mounts, or possesses, one of the believers, that person will be dressed with garments made of burlap or a plaid material. This *oricha* manifests himself as a very sick person suffering from a high fever and pain from many wounds. He speaks with a lisp and can hardly walk. He brandishes the *bilaba* (fly whisk) to scare flies away from the ulcers and to chase evil spirits away.

The dancers in the chorus imitate him, bending over as if they were feeble old men limping painfully. The possessed tend to be people who are sick, especially those who suffer from skin diseases.[1] In the past such people in Cuba would clean their ulcers by rubbing them with a piece of raw meat that was later offered to the *oricha*.

The title most frequently given to Babalú Ayé is that of Konfieddeno Kofidenu (merciful and clement).[2] This title could be interpreted as a form of flattery since, even in Africa, the followers of Shopono express gratitude to him to avoid being subjects of his rage and vengeance. However, this does not seem to be the case in Cuba, where believers, showing pity and sorrow for him, call him Kole Baye (the one who is rotting away and has no strength). During *güemileres* (drum festivals) this *oricha* inspires believers to sing songs expressing pain and compassion that they genuinely feel.

The most well-known *caminos* of this *oricha* are discussed in Appendix F.

19

Ogun/Ogún

God of Metals and War

Ogun in Africa

For many centuries in West Africa, the mining, processing, and manufacturing of iron and steel have been of vital importance. Therefore, Ogun, the god of metals, has enjoyed great popularity and prestige. He is the patron of blacksmiths, soldiers, hunters, butchers, and anyone who uses iron tools. Ogun is a ferocious god who craves wars, adventures, and the lonely life of a hunter. He has a terrible personality, being cruel, bloodthirsty, and rude. Yet, he is not evil; he is just and righteous.

Ogun is the pioneer divinity who opens the way to all other divinities. This role, precisely, is his most important one. In a metaphoric sense, he is seen as the god who opens a path with his machete or "opens the road" to other divinities in their contacts with mankind. He makes communication possible between gods and men. In this respect, his role is even more important than that of Elegbara, the messenger of the gods. At the entrance of temples in Ile Ife and in other areas of Nigeria, his symbol occupies a place of eminence, signifying that, without his intervention, no one can reach the other gods.

Ogun is the sculptor god who assists Obatala in molding the human form. As the owner of metals, he is in charge of circumcision, scarification that creates the symbols of the clans and tribes, and other procedures necessary in the restoration of health. Moreover, without his iron knife, sacrifices of four-legged animals cannot be made. Ogun presides when oaths are taken. A testimony given in his name is held so sacred that, on many occasions, the British government accepted it as valid in the courts of justice in its Nigerian colony (1900–60), where perjury was considered a crime punishable by death. It is strongly believed that this god punishes those who use his name in vain.

Oral traditions (Idowu 1962:85) reveal that Ogun is a powerful and ancient god who played an important role during the first incursions of the orishas onto this planet. When the world was created, it was a great swamp. Ogun and the other gods managed to climb down to earth using a giant spider web as a ladder. When the solid part of the planet was next created, Ogun and other gods prepared to take up the positions that Olodumare had assigned them. When they were on their way, they were prevented from arriving at their respective positions by a heavy thicket. Obatala tried to open a clearing with his machete. But, since the machete was made of lead, it bent. Ogun, the only god who owned an iron knife, made the other gods promise him a reward if he could get them through. Then he cut through the thicket, enabling them to continue on their way. His intervention made it possible for the orishas to come to earth.

Once in Ile Ife, the orishas rewarded him for his services with the only crown they had. They also gave him the title of Osin-Immale (chief among the divinities). Based on his ability to cut a path through the thicket, he has a place of eminence. There is an understanding that, without him, it is not possible to communicate with the other orishas.

Oral traditions (Idowu 1962:86) relate that when the gods settled down in Ile Ife, Ogun, who loved warfare, conquests, adventure, and hunting, and did not like a sedentary life, went to the mountain called Ori-Oke. There, he lived as a lonely and savage hunter until one day, tired of being alone, he decided to return. When he left Ori-Oke, he was surrounded by fire, and his clothes were full of blood. He made new clothes for himself with the fronds of the palm tree. Dressed in this attire, he entered the city of Ile Ife, where he was proclaimed king.

In some myths (Verger 1954:179) Ogun was the son of Oduduwa, the first legendary king of Ile Ife. Ogun was a brutal and bloodthirsty warrior, who conquered the city of Ire, expelled the king, and put his own son in his place. He then went back to Ile Ife. Later on, he returned to Ire while a ceremony was taking place, during which people could not speak to each other. Ogun, hungry and thirsty, was enraged when no one responded to his questions and requests. Using his machete, Ogun went on a murderous rampage. Then, his son arrived and explained the reason for his subjects' silence. Ogun was deeply ashamed of his ill-fated bad temper.

In some myths Ogun was closely related to Oraniyan. In some accounts he was the son; in others the brother; in still others the father of Oraniyan (Barnes 1997:58). In one myth (Verger 1954:178–79), Ogun took a very beautiful woman as prisoner in a battle. Oduduwa, Ogun's father, seized her without knowing of Ogun's desire. Sometime later she had a son, named Oraniyan. His body was half white, like Oduduwa, and half black, like Ogun, because both Ogun and Oduduwa had fathered him. Since Oduduwa didn't know that the captive belonged to Ogun, he harshly scolded Ogun for having sex with the object of his own desire.

In Nigeria, blacksmiths and ironsmiths were once very important. Therefore, Ogun, the patron of these artisans, enjoyed an influential and important following and worship. Blacksmiths in West Africa were part of a powerful caste. They were so respected and appreciated by the community that the chiefs of the blacksmith's caste had the right to attend all the meetings of the village council. Ogun, the patron of blacksmiths, and also of soldiers, fishermen, hunters, and other artisans who use iron tools, enjoyed special devotion by the members of these economic classes. His worship, however, was also open to all clans and tribes.

Although Ogun is worshipped throughout Yoruban territory, his importance is greatest in Ire, Ilesha, Ondo, and Ileoko. In Ilesha his cult exhibits the characteristics of a civic or national worship. In Dahomey, a god of similar characteristics is known by the name of Gou.

Since Ogun is a wandering divinity who enjoys the power of ubiquity, his chapels are often found on roads and in open places. These sanctuaries consist of three or four sticks placed in the ground in vertical position and tied together, forming the frame of a door. This frame is covered with palm fronds, which are symbols of this god. Every blacksmith has a small chapel dedicated to Ogun that is normally situated in a high place in a corner and holds the orisha's emblems.

Tools and objects made of iron represent Ogun. Soldiers and blacksmiths regard their spears and anvils as sacred. Ogun's priests wear iron bracelets on their left arm as symbols of authority. Also, fronds of palm thatch and marigwos (a type of palm) are emblems of this god, who dresses with them. Such fronds are placed at the entrance of homes and at crossroads to signal Ogun's guardianship. Therefore, Ogun, like Eleggua, is a tutelary god.

The peregun plant *(Dracaena Frafra ves)* belongs to Ogun and is also his emblem. A piece of stone and the tail and the tusk of elephants are also used as his symbols. The number seven is associated with Ogun, and seven iron rods symbolize him.

In the past, at very critical times, such as during wars, human sacrifices were offered to Ogun. The victim usually was a slave purchased with public funds.

Dogs are Ogun's sacred animals. Blacksmiths, hunters, and soldiers used to sacrifice a dog to Ogun each year. Ogun enjoys eating roasted yams, kola nuts, white beans, and palm wine. Hunters returning from a successful excursion often offer him the lower jaw of the skull of the prey. Soldiers used to offer to him the skulls of their enemies.

The worship of Ogun lost some importance with the arrival of the Europeans and the establishment of a new economic system. The importance of local blacksmiths diminished considerably. Moreover, at the end of the nineteenth century, Ogun suffered another setback as the endemic civil wars between competing chiefdoms and kingdoms dwindled. Soldiers and blacksmiths lost importance. Nevertheless, Ogun still held some prestige, and his worship was renewed to meet the needs of the times. At present, he is the patron of motorists and cyclists. Also, he continues to be the patron of all those who use tools and objects made of iron and steel.

In remote rural areas of West Africa, Ogun continues to be the powerful god whose assistance is sought whenever a risky enterprise requires his support for it to be crowned with success. In regions to the north of the coastal zone, where hunting is still important, Ogun continues to enjoy prestige. However, Islam, Christianity, and a growing popular skepticism threaten the prestige and influence of this god in Nigeria.

Ogún in Cuba

Ogún's worship established deep roots in Cuba by the end of the nineteenth century, even though the Yoruban slaves who were brought to the island did not labor as soldiers or blacksmiths. Such laborers in Nigeria constituted a large part of his following, since he is the patron of those professions. However, in Cuba this *oricha* remained indispensable because he owns the knives and machetes that are used in such essential tasks as sacrificing four-legged animals and harvesting sugar cane.

In Cuba, Ogún is a powerful warrior who longs for adventures, hunting, and war. As in Nigeria, he lives the life of a lonely and ruthless hermit in the middle of the wilderness. He nearly always wears a tiger skin trimmed with shells over one of his shoulders. This bloodthirsty and cruel divinity enjoys mischief and punishes those who antagonize him by making them victims of bloody accidents.

Ogún has many personalities. At times, he manifests himself as a coarse farmer; at other times, he is a hunter; more often, he is a brutal warrior; and often, still, he is a powerful blacksmith. In Cuba, he is likewise the god of iron and metals, as well as the ruler of the thicket and the wilderness. He is closely related to hunters and to Ochosi, their patron *oricha.*

Ogún and Elegguá have the power of ubiquity. Echú Aguanilebbe, a manifestation of Elegguá, is Ogún's inseparable companion, whose job entails sacrificing dogs to quench Ogún's thirst. Since these two *orichas* share numerous characteristics, Elegguá in Cuba has usurped many attributes that Ogún formerly had in Africa. Ogún, Ochosi, and Elegguá are inseparable warrior *orichas* who hide in corners to provoke accidents and quarrels.

Ogún and Changó are constantly fighting. Neither is ever victorious over the other. They are eternal rivals. The following *pataki* describes the reasons for the rivalry.

Ogún was the son of Obatalá Ibaibo and his wife, Yembo, who lived with their children Elegguá, Ogún, Ochosi, and Osún. Their daughter Dadá did not live with them.

When Obatalá went to work the fields, he left Osun in charge of the family. Every day when he returned, he would inquire about the incidents of the day.

Ogún was the hardest worker and was obeyed by his siblings. Ogún fell in love with his mother, Yembo, and knowing that the ever-watchful Elegguá could spoil his plans, he began to mistreat him, giving him less and less food every day. Elegguá kept an eye on Ogún, preventing him from getting close to their mother. He confided his concerns to Osún. Exasperated, Ogún threw Elegguá out of the house. However, Elegguá hung around the house watching everything from all Four Corners (cross-roads).

At that time, Ogún started feeding Osún four sacks of corn a day to keep him happy. Every day he would feed Osún and close the door to prevent Osún from watching him approach his mother with his evil intentions.

One day Elegguá waited for Obatalá to return from the fields. When Obatalá saw Elegguá he asked him, "What is the matter, son?"

"I haven't eaten in many days, because Ogún threw me out of the house." Then, Elegguá told him everything.

"How come Osún hasn't informed me of this?"

"Because Ogún feeds him so much that he falls asleep."

"Impossible," replied Obatalá. "Osún can never go to sleep."

Elegguá advised his father to return early from work the following day.

Obatalá was so sad that night that he could not sleep well, being delirious with nightmares. The following morning he set out to work as usual, but instead of leaving he hid behind some mangroves and watched Osún go to sleep while Ogún closed the door of the house. Obatalá, who was filled with sorrow, cried and had to use a cane made of mangrove to help him walk to the house because his strength failed him. Slowly, he approached the door and knocked with the cane.

"Do you see, Ogún?" said Yembo. "What need had I to get into all this trouble? What can I do now? I will open the door."

Realizing that Yembo was not to be blamed, Ogún said, "No, mother. I am a man. I will open the door."

When he saw Obatalá standing and raising his hand to curse him,

Ogún said, "No, father, don't speak; don't curse me. I will curse myself. While I live and while the world exists, I will work day and night without rest."

Later, Obatalá entered the house and called to Yembo. Ogún then said, "My mother is innocent; don't blame her."

Obatalá told Ogún to leave the house forever, reprimanded Osún harshly and declared, "From now on Elegguá will be the guardian. Elegguá will never go hungry. If he doesn't eat, no one else will eat in this house." He then added, "From now on, to go in and out of that door everyone will have to reckon with you. Therefore, only you will allow goodness and evil." He said to Yembo, "I am not going to blame you, but if we have another male child, I will kill it myself."

Yembo cried, but didn't say anything.

Ogún left. From that time he became Ogún Alguedé, the blacksmith. Later, Orúnmila was born, and Obatalá buried him up to his neck. Orúnmila survived because Elegguá fed him. When Changó was born Obatalá spared him but sent him to live with his sister Dadá. Many years later, Changó took revenge and stole Ogún's wife Oyá-Yansá. From that moment on a bloody rivalry began between these two powerful divinities. (Cros Sandoval 1975:132–34)

In another *pataki*, the relationship between Ogún and Changó is described further:

Changó could not forget what Ogún had done to their mother, Yembo. One day, Changó dressed up in his warrior garment and went to Ogún's domain. Ogún's wife, Oyá, immediately fell in love with him, and Changó carried her away to avenge his father, Obatalá. Changó took Oyá to Dadá's house.

Dadá was Changó's sister, who had raised him. Changó loved and respected her as a mother. When Ogún found out, he went after Changó and won a bitter battle.

Oyá was dissatisfied with the outcome of the fight. She was also intrigued, because every morning before leaving his home Changó would put his fingers inside a little gourd that Osain, his godfather, had given him. Then with his fingers, he would make the sign of the cross over his tongue.

One day, after Changó left, Oyá placed her fingers inside the gourd and made the sign of the cross with them over her tongue. Later on, when she talked to Dadá, fire and smoke exhaled from her mouth. Oyá and Dadá, afraid of Changó's rage when he found out that his secret was discovered, tried to hide by burying themselves under a royal palm tree. When

Changó came home, he noticed that the women were missing and that the little gourd was not in the place where he had left it. He went out to search for the women, who were hiding under the palm tree. He bitterly scolded them for discovering and making use of his precious secret.

Oyá responded to him, "You should declare war on Ogún instead of scolding us."

Ogún was very well prepared for the battle, but Changó and Oyá were also ready for it. Changó, with his thunder, and Oyá with her lightning, defeated Ogún, who had no choice but to hide in the wilderness. At that time a bloody rivalry between these powerful gods began. (Cros Sandoval 1975:239)

Another *pataki* tells about their wars and the less than honorable behavior of Changó.

One day Changó and Ogún met by chance in the fields and decided to renew their unending war. Changó cunningly told Ogún, "There is no hurry, comrade. Drink your fire water, and I will wait for you."

Ogún, who loves alcohol, drank more than was prudent, and then Changó incited him to fight. Ogún, completely drunk, suffered a tremendous defeat. From that day he has never forgiven Changó for tricking him. (Cros Sandoval 1975:239)

In another *pataki* Ogún makes Changó the victim of trickery:

Ogún came to see Changó and offered him a truce, claiming, "I am tired of so much fighting."

Changó accepted the truce: "I knew my strength and ability would make me victorious."

This statement naturally led to another argument. In the midst of the heated discussion Ogún proposed a contest. The winner would be the one who collected more shells on the beach in one day. Changó accepted.

Ogún went to see Ikú, since he knew how fearful courageous Changó was of death. Ogún offered Ikú a great reward if, on the following day, he would go to the beach and give Changó the scare of his life.

The following morning Ogún and Changó went to the beach to gather the shells. Changó calmly collected shells, bragging of his abilities. Just then, Ikú appeared, giving Changó a hard kick. Changó, terrified, ran away to his house.

That night Ogún went to see him, throwing at his face the two sacks of shells he had gathered. Ashamed, Changó had no other choice but to recognize Ogún's victory. (Cros Sandoval 1975:239)

The rivalry between these two *orichas* is so intense that whenever they meet a fight ensues. In the *igbodu*, or sanctuary, they are kept in separate places; otherwise they would fight. Moreover, during the drum festivals these two *orichas* can never take possession of the believers at the same time, because if they came down together fighting would break out.

In another *pataki* Ogún is depicted as a coarse farmer:

Ogún, the owner of wilderness, forbade entrance to his domain because he wanted all the benefits for himself. He placed deadly traps on all the roads. These traps would capture and kill all that dared to ignore his warnings. Ogún, who was very cruel, enjoyed watching the agony of the victims of his traps.

One day Olofin ordered Orúla to go to the wilderness and take Ogún's *obí*, which he needed to prepare a powerful potion. Orúla knew the dangers involved in this enterprise but had no choice but to comply with Olofin's orders. The following day, supplied with provisions, he set out to accomplish his mission. He was hopeful that, since he had a slight build, he might be able to slip through the traps. Unfortunately, luck was not on his side, and soon he fell to the bottom of a deep hole. There, he sadly awaited death with resignation.

The following day, three young women from a nearby town, Obatalá, Yemayá, and Ochún, entered the forest. They were terribly frightened by the sight of the skeletons of Ogún's victims. As they hurried away they suddenly heard weak cries of pain: "Guí, guí, guí."

They walked toward the place the cries came from and, looking down into the deep hole, they saw the weak and feeble body of Orúla. The three young women managed to rescue the old man. Once they got him out of the hole they took him to Olofin.

Olofin brought the beautiful Ochún back to the wilderness to settle matters with the cruel Ogún. Ochún, the goddess of love and feminine charms, entered the forest calling loudly, "Ogún . . . Ogún."

In a mad fit of rage, Ogún went after her with his machete. Ochún offered her body and told him, "Take me and you will know what pleasure is all about." Ogún could not resist Ochún.

Later, Ochún offered him alcohol and got him drunk. Then, Ochún went to his hiding place and took all his belongings. From that moment on, Ogún allowed free passage and ready access to his domains, because he was convinced that all his precautions had been fruitless. (Cros Sandoval 1975:240)

The priests and children of Ogún are called ogún *bi*, ogún *beleko*, and ogún bara. They have the exclusive right to kill four-legged animals.

Most ceremonies to honor Ogún are held in the open fields or by the silk-cotton tree. The ceremony of his *asiento* should take place in an open field, but, if this is not possible, a courtyard of a *cabildo* will do. For the ceremonies *santeros* or *santeras* have to build a hut with the twigs and fronds of trees that belong to him. Altars dedicated to Ogún simulate green palm fronds. Ogún is a *montuno* (hick, country) god and should be revered as such.

Ogún is generally represented by lithographs of Saint Peter, the porter of the heavens, with whom he is associated in most *cabildos*. This identification appears to be based upon the image of Saint Peter holding the keys to heaven. Since all iron objects are considered symbols of the *oricha*, and Ogún is considered a pioneer divinity that opens the roads of other gods with his machete in the wilderness, the association of Ogún and Saint Peter is quite understandable. However, in some areas of Cuba, as in Carlos Rojas, he is associated with Saint John.

Lydia Cabrera (1971:25) reports that at the beginning of the twentieth century, in Palenque, formerly a suburb of Havana near the town of Lisa, a great celebration took place every year to honor this god. Ogún was represented by an iron rod stuck in the ground and covered with the vines of the *ñame (Dioscorea alata)*, an edible tubercle, which, in Nigeria, is considered his favorite food.

As in Africa, the ritual dress of Ogún is made of *marigwo* (palm fronds). An iron chain with seven iron charms symbolizes Ogún. The charms are an arrow, an anvil, a pick, an ax, a machete, a hammer, and a key. In Cuba, as in Nigeria, the number seven belongs to this god. Seven pieces of iron are used to symbolize him, and his priests wear a metal chain called a *chabá*, as a bracelet. Sometimes his necklace is made of sequences of seven light brown beads followed by seven black ones and then alternating a brown and a black one. At other times it is made of purple and green beads.

The children, or priests, of Ogún do not have to make *pinaldo* (a required ritual that entitles initiates to kill four-legged animals). Instead they receive a chain with twenty-one tools that confers the authority to sacrifice four-legged animals. All tools and instruments made of iron—even airplanes—are symbols of this god.

The color black, or *dudú*, which implies evil and death, is associated with Ogún; so in funeral rites his masks are used. In Cuba and in Brazil this divinity rules over *martes* (Tuesday), the day of war. As such, Ogún is a bloodthirsty divinity who enjoys drinking blood. His favorite animal is a dog, but *eledde* (pigs), lambs, red roosters, and *jutías* (a Cuban variety of opossum) are also offered to him. On very special occasions, bulls are sacrificed to him under the shade of the silk-cotton tree. However, bulls are very expensive and rarely sacrificed. Ogún is a drunkard, and *otireke* (sugar cane alcohol) is his favorite drink.

During rituals when Ogún possesses a follower, that person is dressed with a small purple jacket, pants tight at the knee, and a sash made of palm fibers. This *marigwo* (sash) is used as protection against evil. When he "comes down," the faithful salute him shouting, "Ogún *kabu kabu*" (Ogún is very great).

The dancer possessed by Ogún generally pantomimes battle scenes by carrying a machete and acting as if he were fighting. At other times, the dancer imitates a farmer who opens a path through the wilderness or a blacksmith working tirelessly in his shop. When possessed, the children of Ogún are capable of drinking a whole bottle of hard liquor in a few seconds. If during his visit a dog enters the temple, Ogún will fall on him to drink his blood. Ogún's children display certain psychological affinities with him. They are very independent and don't like to be ordered around. They are expected to be successful merchants and artisans.

Ogún's worship is very important in Santería. However, in Cuba, Ogún lost to Eleggúa what was one of his most important functions, that of opening the roads to other divinities in their communication with humans. It seems that Ogún, neither in Nigeria nor Cuba, utilized to the utmost the powers he enjoyed as mediator between gods and men. He was more interested in wars than in spiritual matters.

In the most ancient Yoruban myths, reference is made to Ogún's lack of interest in sacred matters. When the gods arrived in Ile Ife and crowned him king, Ogún preferred the life of the lonely hunter to the role of leader of his fellow gods. It is possible that the turbulent history of the Yoruban people in some ways emphasized Ogún's character as a warrior at the expense of his other attributes. This may have been especially true after the fall of the Oyo Empire when the Yoruba became the victims of civil wars and slave raiders.

Nevertheless, among Santería's followers, the belief is preserved that Ogún is the pioneer divinity who permits the other gods to enter the earthly realm. In many *ilé ocha*, Ogún "is the one who clears the roads." The dances in his honor reenact a farmer opening a path through the thicket with a machete. A *patakí* narrates how, during a journey, Ogún walks ahead of Babalú Ayé and Changó, and opens the way for them. This function as the *oricha* who opens the way might be the reason that, in so many *ilé ochas*, Ogún is associated with Saint Peter, the Catholic saint who opens the doors to heaven.

In this regard it is natural for Eleggúa, the messenger of the gods, to take over the functions that Ogún relinquished. One possibility in understanding this loss of status is to question whether it might have been caused by the absence, in Cuba, of large black professional classes, which represented the bulk of his following in Africa.

Ogún has many *caminos* (roads), or paths, which correspond to different aspects of his personality. The most important are shown in Appendix G.

Osanyin/Osain

The Owner of Magical and Medicinal Herbs

Osanyin in Africa

The people of equatorial Africa greatly depended upon their knowledge of the medicinal and supernatural powers of plants. Among the Yoruba, every plant contains ashe, a power that can be either beneficial or harmful. The ashe of some plants and herbs can cure, grant courage, longevity, luck, and fertility, and even attract lovers. The ashe of other plants and herbs can, instead, bring disgrace and harm. To the Yoruba, herbs and plants are so important that an indigenous taxonomical system emerged as a result of observation and experimentation through countless generations. Hundreds of herbs have been incorporated into this system, even though they cannot be cultivated and must be gathered in the wild.

The qualities and attributes of plants depend on the will of Osanyin, the orisha who is the owner of the wilderness. Osanyin does not concern himself with domestic plants or vegetables. He is not a horticultural divinity; he is the owner of weeds, bushes, vines, and roots that are found in the countryside and the woods. In order for plants and herbs to render their full power, Osanyin has to be propitiated.[1] Osanyin's myths are not filled with heroic deeds as is the case with those of other orishas. According to Fagg (1982: 197): "Osanyin works quietly and secretly. His is the hidden power of the mind, of inquiry and thought. Thus, his priests are skilled in the therapeutic powers of various leaves and are extraordinarily adept in treating emotional and mental disorders. Along, with the priests of Ifa, the priests of Osanyin rank among the intelligentsia of traditional Yoruba society."

The power of plants, or ashe, is used not only by mortals but also by the orishas. Even though each orisha possesses a certain number of plants, Osanyin, as owner of all wild plants, must be respected by the other orishas to whom the power of certain plants has been distributed, in addition to being propitiated by humans.

Grass, flowers, and bushes are used to make potions that are utilized in purification rites. Plants are so sacred that only the priests consecrated to the orishas of certain plants can shred or crush them. During the ceremony of maceration, the priests sing ritual songs celebrating the powers of each plant and of the orisha who owns it.

Since nothing is possible without the power that resides in plants, the purification, initiation, and propitiation rites cannot be carried out without Osanyin's sanction. For this reason he occupies a unique and high position in the Yoruban religion.

Osanyin's worship is present in every region of Yorubaland. His priests, the Olosanyins, are greatly respected as physicians. They are in charge of collecting the herbs, roots, vines, and leaves necessary for various healing rituals and ceremonies. When collecting the plants in the woods, the Olosanyins must be in a state of total purity. They must abstain from sexual intercourse the night before gathering herbs. Very early in the morning they go into the bush. If they happen to meet someone on the way, they must refrain from speaking. Once in the bush, they make their supplications and offerings of money so that Osanyin will not render the herbs powerless.

Osanyin is a rustic god, a little man, constantly smoking a pipe and hobbling with only one leg. He is frequently represented by the figure of a small bird perched on an iron rod. In sanctuaries, these images are often placed near the Osun of the babalawo (a metal rod crowned by a small rooster, which is the protection of babalawos) to ensure Osanyin's cooperation in the divining process.

Osain in Cuba

In Cuba, as in Africa, the *oricha* of medicinal and magical herbs and plants occupies a place of prominence. Around this indispensable god revolve all the rituals that are so fundamental to the Afro-Cuban religion. Afro-Cubans claim that, without Osain, no remedy is possible; no medicine is available; no hope can be fulfilled; and no magic can be performed. All *orichas* are herbalists, but Osain is the undisputed master of the herbs, the medicine man, the botanist, the protector and benefactor of all. Osain, or Osanyin, has no other manifestations, no ancestry, no siblings, no progeny, and he belongs to all Lucumíes. He originally came from the Ijesha country, from the land of the Oyo, the land of the Ijebu and the Egbado.

As in Africa, Osain in Cuba is perceived to live in the wilderness. In Osain reside the spirits of the savanna, the woods, and the bush. It is said that he has no father or mother and that he sprang to life from the earth, as plants do. He has only a right foot and a left arm. He walks with a hop or by leaps and bounds. Osain has one huge ear that hears nothing and a little one that is so sensitive he can hear even the footsteps of insects. Likewise, he has only one eye.

Osain is as good a hunter as Ochosi. With his one arm he handles efficiently the bow and arrow and the rifle. With his one leg he swiftly runs in the woods. One legend explains that Osain lost an arm and a leg after hunting down a deer protected by Olofin. Another myth claims that Changó, in one of his fits of rage, mutilated him.

> Changó and Oyá had agreed to rob Osain of his secret powers. Oyá visited him and asked him for some of his magical herbs. In return she gave him a cigar and a gourd full of alcohol. Osain drank and became infatuated with Oyá and tried to make love to her. They began to argue and fight and Changó came to her rescue. Ogún, who was nearby, sided with Osain. Changó threw a lightning rod at Osain and broke his arm. When Osain tried to hide, Changó threw another rod and tore off his leg. As Osain looked back to see if Changó was pursuing him, Changó threw another lightning bolt, which burned his eye. Ogún then turned into a lightning rod and stopped the rays Changó was throwing, but it was too late. Osain had already become a total wreck. (Cros Sandoval 1975:247)

The following *pataki* gives another account of the reason Osain was disfigured:

> What really happened is that Osain made Orúla's life impossible by constantly working witchcraft against him. Orúla had never bothered Osain, so he couldn't think of him as his enemy. Tired of such annoyance, one day he asked Changó for help. Changó told him to prepare twelve cotton wicks to find out who was his enemy. While Orúla was at home preparing Changó's . . . prescription, Osain was in the woods gathering herbs to do sorcery. As soon as Orúla began to light the wicks, lightning started to fall in the woods, striking Osain and crippling him for life. (Cros Sandoval 1975:247)

In the last two *patakíes* Osain was involved in a quarrel with Changó. However, there is wide agreement that Osain never engages in war with any of the *orichas*. All of them need him, and even though he favors Changó, his godchild, he serves all of the *orichas* equally. These patakíes might have been influenced by non-Yoruban elements.

Osain is a chaste god. This is the reason that his priests do not marry. Osain likes to smoke cigars, and he approaches people on the streets at night to ask them for a light. Most of all, Osain is a great physician who knows the curative qualities of plants that are to be used in the preparation of talismans and for healing. This god knows everything about witchcraft and magic, more than any other oricha. He is very closely linked to Ochosi, the god of hunters, and he and Changó own the sacred drums.

Oral tradition tells us that, originally, Osain was the sole owner of all herbs and plants as well as the only *oricha* who knew their secrets. He kept his secret herbs in a gourd hung from a tree. One day Changó requested Oyá's assistance to carry out a plan to rob Osain of his secrets. Oyá unleashed a strong wind, which broke open the gourd holding Osain's herbs. Blown by the wind, the herbs were dispersed all over the land so that the happy *orichas* were able to distribute them among themselves.

Osain is also Changó's godfather, as illustrated by the following myth:

> One day, when Changó was strolling in the wilderness, he heard the cries and sighs of a person asking for help. Startled, he looked around and found a man lying on the ground, severely wounded. The man had lost his left leg and an arm. He had a large wound, bleeding profusely, over his left eye; Changó took care of the man, curing him with medicinal plants. When the man finally woke up, he asked Changó: "Who are you? What are you doing in the wilderness?"
>
> Changó replied, "I am Changó. I was lost and couldn't find my way out of this vast wilderness."
>
> The man told Changó that he lived in the untamed jungle and that he usually lived on top of a tree. He must have fallen asleep and fallen down. He thanked Changó for helping him.
>
> "I am grateful to you. Many men come to the wilderness to take what they need, but they never help or respect me. My name is Osain, and I am the owner of the woods and of all wild plants. Oludumare gave me this power, and, from now on, I am going to protect you. Make your tools, weapons, and instruments out of wood, because wood belongs to me and iron and metals belong to Ogún, your enemy. Take the gourd in which you keep the medicine you used to cure me, and every morning, before you leave your house, wet your fingers with the herbs you have in it and make the sign of the cross on your tongue."
>
> This is why, when Changó speaks, fire and smoke come out of his mouth. (Cros Sandoval 1975:248)

Osain's priests, the *osainistas,* have great knowledge of wild plants and their properties. They know how to handle them and how to address them. Some plants are easily frightened; others are shy and like to be treated with courtesy and respect. The *osainista* must know the proper prayer to use in requesting plants' permission before pulling them from the earth. He must know the way to their hearts, and how to pamper them so that they will be in sight and not hide from him. Most of all, the *osainista* must know what tributes have to be paid to Osain to ensure that the plants will yield their full power when used.

There is a large diversity of prescriptions that were part of African-derived Cuban pharmacology. In addition, many popular remedies based upon Spanish and aboriginal Amerindian pharmacology were available. Among them were teas made of boiled guava leaves and of green banana peels that were used to stop diarrhea, while teas made of boiled peony roots were prescribed for pneumonia. A tea made of boiled seaweeds was prescribed to strengthen the blood, and teas made of boiled Cedar bark, parsley roots, and cinnamon were used to induce abortions. *Saco saco* weeds obtained by the seashore were used to counter witchcraft. The water in which eggplant peels were soaked was prescribed for diabetes. *Albahaca* (basil) was popularly used in Cuba in spiritualist practices to cleanse away bad influences, but it was not used in Santería's rituals.

Osain is a god that cannot be *asentado*, and the *osainista* does not need to be initiated. However, if Ifá advises (through divination) that he should be, then the *osainista* may receive either Changó or Ochún.

Osain, like most *orichas*, has his own stone, or *otán*. The stone of Osain is chosen from among wild forests, from rivers, or from the hills. This stone, together with two others, is placed inside a clay kettle. The power of these stones is prodigious, but some priests of Osain, instead, own a consecrated and powerful object in which the power of the *oricha* is fixed. This sacred object is called an *osain*, as is the *oricha*. They are highly esteemed by Santería's followers. Those who own an *osain* claim that it speaks to them in a low, nasal voice.

A priest who has Osain and is a son of Changó can make an *osain*. Only men can make and prepare such a powerful object. Women can only possess an *osain* after menopause, and even then their *osain* is considered to be less powerful. It is incomplete because they cannot make a new one or give theirs to anyone else.

An *osain* is made with a large dry gourd. Its inside is scraped out and cleaned with an *omiero* (sacred potion resulting from the rinse water from several medicinal herbs that is mixed with the blood of sacrificed animals). To prepare Osain's *omiero*, sixteen different herbs and the blood of a land turtle are necessary. When the gourd is clean, it is taken to a silk-cotton tree, where Changó is offered a red rooster. Then, the practitioners ask permission of the silk-cotton tree to bury the gourd under its roots. If permission is granted, the gourd is left there for nine days. Next the gourd is taken to a crossroads to offer Elegguá a white chick, pieces of candy, toasted corn, honey, a smoked rat, and twenty-one cents, thereby to obtain his blessings and power. There, the gourd is buried for another six days. Afterward, finally, it is ready to receive the ingredients that give it its power, the so-called secrets of Osain.

The ingredients are two small deer horns, dirt from the wilderness, seven sticks, seven vines, seven of the herbs belonging to Osaín, toasted corn, and the feet, tail, and head of a land turtle. In addition, sixteen small *otanes* from the soup tureens of Changó, Ochún, and Eleggúa are included, plus sixteen shells that had previously received the *aché* of an *osainista*. The gourd may also require the eyes and tongue of a black rooster and the feathers of an African parrot.

After this concoction is made, the gourd is carried to the same silk-cotton tree where the entire process began. A hole is dug next to the tree, where alcohol, honey, and the blood of a land turtle are poured over it. The *osain* is kept buried for twenty-one days to complete the process. Then it is ready to be carried home. This gourd, which is the body of Osain, is placed in a glass, clay, or wooden soup bowl and is kept completely sealed so that insects, which are also owned by Osaín, will not eat it. *Osains* can also be made inside the shell of a land turtle.

When a *yerbero* (an expert in knowledge of wild grasses, leaves, twigs, and vines) goes into the woods looking for plants, he pays tribute to Osain. This god likes sugar cane, alcohol, coins, and tobacco. Land turtles, black roosters, black Guinea fowl, goats, seeds, flowers, and grass are also offered to him. Osain does not come down in *güemileres*, or drum festivals. An informant of Lydia Cabrera (1954:100) says that Osain can possess no one because the wilderness is too strong and powerful for anyone to receive it on his or her head. However, some dances are dedicated to his honor.

Some believers of Santería associate Osain with Saint Joseph. It is possible that this association is based on the fact that in most lithographs Saint Joseph appears carrying a small bunch of flowers. Others have identified him with Saint Sylvester. Since in Spanish the word *silvestre* means "wild," this association is quite logical, and lithographs of Saint Sylvester are sometimes used to represent Osain.

Osain continues to occupy a unique and high position in Cuban Santería. Several Afro-Cuban *patakíes* attempt to explain his physical handicaps, which do not prevent great physical feats on his part. Possibly another Cuban elaboration is his kinship tie with Changó as well as his tempestuous relationship with him, in spite of his reputation as being a benevolent *oricha*. Moreover, his priests in Cuba do not enjoy the high esteem they had in Nigeria, where they were respected as part of the intelligentsia. This might be due to greater dependence on physicians' medicines than on their pharmacopoeia.

21

Oshosi/Ochosi, Orisha Oko/Oricha Oko, Ibeji/Ibeyi, Aganju/Agayú

Minor Gods of Hunting, Horticulture, the Sacred Twins, the Porter God, and Minor Orishas Also Known in Cuba

Oshosi in Africa

In the predominantly agricultural society of precolonial Yorubaland, Oshosi, the god of hunters, enjoyed great popularity. Verger (1954: 182) identifies three important functions provided by Oshosi in former Yoruban society: 1) Oshosi was responsible for making hunting fruitful and providing food; 2) Oshosi was closely related to Osanyin, the orisha of medicinal leaves, since both operated in the wilderness; and 3) Oshosi, in a sense, led hunters to locate appropriate places to establish new farms and settlements. Moreover, elephant hunters enjoyed a prominent place in Yoruban society because of the high price bestowed upon ivory. Consequently, the patron of these pioneer hunters would naturally be the object of worship early in the life of new communities.

According to tradition, Ijebu Ode is the place of origin of Oshosi, although he is known throughout Yorubaland, especially wherever hunting is popular. Among the Fon of Dahomey, the god Agbe shares with Oshosi similar attributes and characteristics.

Oshosi is perceived as a skillful hunter who lives in the wilderness. There is a close relationship between Oshosi and Osanyin, since hunters are always in Osanyin's domains and are also quite knowledgeable about herbs and medicinal plants. Oshosi wears the monkey-skin cap that hunters use as a symbol of their profession.

Oshosi, as their patron, protects and assists hunters by leading animals to the traps. Without his collaboration, the efforts of the hunters would not be successful. Hunters who displease him are always victims of serious accidents.

Oshosi's necklace is made of green beads, and his symbols are the stretched bow, iron-tipped arrows, and anthropomorphic dolls representing a hunter with bows and arrows.

Ochosi in Cuba

Although in Cuba and Brazil the African slaves were not engaged in the activities that Oshosi patronized in Africa, his worship survived. In Cuba, Ochosi is a hunter, physician, and diviner. He lives in *el monte* (the wilderness) and is, alongside Ogún and Elegguá, one of the Warrior *orichas*. He owns the jails, even though in Africa he was not related to jails. It is quite possible that, in Cuba, he became associated with prisons because of the similarity between the prison bars and the hunter's traps. Prison bars were more real in the lives of the slaves than forest traps, which were uncommon in Cuba.

According to the following *pataki* Ochosi is a skillful hunter:

> One day, Olofin asked Orúla to bring him an *akuaro* (a quail). Orúla tried to excuse himself, for he thought it was going to be very difficult to catch one of these birds alive. Olofin insisted, and Orúla had no choice but to go out in search of the bird. He went from town to town asking, "Who is the best hunter around here?"
>
> "Ochosi of Mata is the best among all hunters," everybody answered him.
>
> Ochosi, who lived with his mother, was a great hunter. He would go out to hunt and in two hours he would be back with enough game to last him for days. He would then party and enjoy himself until it was time again to get new supplies.
>
> Orúla went to Ochosi and asked him to get him the quail for Olofin. Ochosi complied and asked him to return the next day. Early that morning, Ochosi went in search of the quail; and, as soon as he had trapped it he took it back to the house and put it in a cage.
>
> Ochosi's mother, who was very hungry and was out of supplies, ate the bird, unaware that the bird was for Olofin. When Ochosi returned and found the cage empty he angrily asked his mother, "What happened to the quail?"
>
> "I don't know anything about the bird," she answered.
>
> Ochosi, disgusted, asked Orúla to come the following day, when he would have another quail ready for him. Next morning Ochosi gave Orúla the promised bird. As a reward for his services, Olofin named Ochosi king of hunters. Ochosi then asked Olofin a very special favor. "Olofin, I want the arrow that I am about to shoot to find its way into the heart of the person who stole the first quail I caught."
>
> Olofin granted his request, and when Ochosi shot his arrow it went through his mother's heart, killing her. In despair, the hunter gave up his profession.[1] (Cros Sandoval 1975:252–53)

Another *pataki* tells a different story:

Orúla, following Olofin's orders had forbidden Ochosi to hunt on Holy Thursday. Ochosi, disregarding Olofin's advice, entered the wilderness in search of prey. Just at that moment a beautiful animal appeared before him. Ochosi took careful aim and, as he was about to shoot, the animal took human form. Ochosi, astonished, recognized Oduduwa, the god of creation. Ochosi was totally paralyzed before the strange vision and could not hunt anymore.[2] (Cros Sandoval 1975:253)

Ochosi is closely related to Ogún. A *pataki* from Castellanos and Castellanos (1992 3:36), explains the reason for this relationship:

Even though Ogún owned a machete, he was always awfully hungry. With the machete he cleared the bushes; consequently the prey ran away, having been alerted by the noise. He could not hunt. Ochosi was a great hunter, but the thicket did not allow him to go and chase the animals. Hunger also tormented him. He consulted with Orúnla, who advised him to climb on top of a hill and drop an offering. That is exactly what Ochosi did, with such good or bad luck that the offering fell on top of Ogún. "You have annoyed me," said Ogún. Ochosi apologized and then they became confidants discussing the problems they had. Ogún . . . came up with the following idea: "Man, I clear the thicket and cannot shoot, and you shoot well and cannot cross the thicket. From now on I will clear the path and you will kill."

Myths where Ochosi renounces his profession as hunter are known in Cuba but unknown in Africa. It is curious that, in the first myth, Ochosi is presented as a successful but lazy hunter who pursued the pleasures of life and would only hunt when needing provisions. It is possible that these legends reflect Santería's believers' attempts to explain in theological and ethical terms why hunting ceased to be important in their lives.

In reality, hunting ceased to be important in Cuba because slaves in a plantation economy were expected and forced to work as laborers in the fields or sugar-processing factories. They were not permitted to make a living by hunting. In the eyes of Afro-Cubans, moreover, the leisure time that hunters in Nigeria enjoyed between expeditions was unreal. In their situation as slaves on a plantation there was little or no leisure time. In contrast, the domestic slaves in the cities, who had some free time, had no opportunity for hunting.

Ochosi is a rustic *oricha* who has to be *asentado* in open spaces. He owns a necklace made of red, black, or deep purple beads, and his emblem is the *chafá*, a bracelet made of metal. Prisons and the bow and arrow are symbols of this god who rules on Tuesdays together with Ogún. He favors pigeons, Guinea hens, and sheep for offerings. When he comes down in *güemileres*, or drum festivals, he gives a loud scream at the top of his lungs to scare prey into flight. He dresses in a purple jacket and pants and wears a cap and bag of tiger skin. His dances simulate the shooting of arrows.

Undoubtedly Ochosi lost importance in Cuba because hunting as a profession lost importance. At the same time, his association with prisons gave him greater relevance. Unfortunately prisons figured prominently in the lives of slaves and, to a lesser degree, among the underprivileged classes in Cuba. This, in a sense, points to the external pressures this religion was experiencing in the Cuban situation. It is noteworthy that according to some Afro-Cuban *patakíes* both Ochosi and Babalú Ayé are punished for inappropriate behavior on Holy Thursday. In the case of Oricha Oko pressures were strong to curtail some of the fertility rituals associated with his worship, which were considered lewd. Afro-Cubans would say, "Oricha Oko cannot dance. No one is going to put up with his indecencies." Moreover, the Afro-Cuban myth about Oricha Oko's humiliation and shame caused by his illicit relationship with Yemayá may have been an attempt to explain the great loss of importance and stature suffered by this *oricha* in Cuba as compared to his importance in Nigeria. Logical consistency may have required modification in mythology to better match altered conditions of life in Cuba.

Orisha Oko in Africa

Orisha Oko is the god of horticulture and farming. He is associated with the fertility of the farms and enjoyed great importance throughout Yorubaland. He is the patron of the farming activities that were so important in the eminently agricultural society of pre-colonial Yorubaland. Many persons who were engaged in field labor offered him sacrifices to win his favors.

He is one of the orishas of whiteness, as are Obatala and Osanyin. Orisha Oko is also in charge of settling disputes between divinities and of judging ordinary persons accused of crimes. J. Olumide Lucas (1948:110) informs us that when there is a controversy between two women who accuse each other of black magic, both suspects are taken to his temple to settle the argument. Each woman has to give a white gourd to Orisha Oko's priests. Then, they remain in the temple for three days. Afterward, the priest invokes the god and opens the gourds. The gourd belonging to the innocent woman will have remained white. The guilty woman's gourd will have turned black. At times she would then be executed by a beating with an iron bar called a polo that has to be purchased by the innocent party, who normally pays a high price for it. Immediately thereafter, the innocent woman is declared wife of Orisha Oko.

Orisha Oko is a phallic god whose cult is centered on fertility, as is usually the case with agricultural divinities. On the days of the new moon, women render worship to this orisha, and each year at harvest time a festival is held in his honor. When the crops are gathered, the first and choicest fruits are offered to him before transporting the rest to the marketplace.

This occasion is one of great festivity in which the whole community participates. Large numbers of fresh yams are cooked. The first ones are offered to the orisha. The participants consume some, and the remaining yams are given to the poor and dispossessed. As in most celebrations of this kind, large quantities of palm wine are consumed, and sexual license is allowed.

The priesthood of Orisha Oko is strictly hereditary. Once the iron emblem of this god enters a family, it remains there forever. It is a very high honor to have a member of the family dedicated to this god. The cost of the initiation ceremony is so high that only members of very important families can be priests of this orisha. Orisha Oko's priests formed a powerful and influential secret society. They wore on their heads a vertical insignia painted in white and red. His priests officiated in the numerous chapels dedicated to his worship.

Bees, which represent happiness and strength, are the messengers of this god. Orisha Oko likes all types of food, but dry meats, yams (edible roots, *Dioscorea alata*), beans, and land snails are his favorites.

Oricha Oko in Cuba

Oricha Oko, the god of fertility, of the farms, and of edible root-crops, is a minor divinity in the Afro-Cuban pantheon. In colonial times the worship of this god in Cuba was very important, although his worship dwindled rapidly in the cities. An informant of Lydia Cabrera (1971:495) says:

> Oko, San Isidro Labrador, the owner of all edible tubercles, was very revered in Havana in colonial times, especially by women, nowadays in Matanzas and the countryside. . . . Orisha Oko, or Osako, as many elderly called him, who is the one that makes sure that the land is fructiferous, has been neglected in the city of Havana. They don't pay homage to him as in the past.

This divinity of *aratakos* and *araokos* (farmers) took refuge in an environment more suitable to his worship—the countryside. Afro-Cubans are prone to say "Oko *bi aye* Oricha Oko *afefe ku oko bi aye oma lara*" (the earth that belongs to Oricha Oko gives forth everything, it gives birth, and it eats everything it produces). Ultimately even cadavers are given to Oricha Oko to devour.

In Cuba, as in Africa, Oricha Oko is the judge of the other *orichas*. According to tradition, even Oba once went before him to make a judicial claim against Changó. However, unlike the situation in Africa, this god has no jurisdiction over human disputes or lawsuits in Cuba.

The following *pataki* describes how Oricha Oko lost his role as judge of human disputes:

> Obatalá was the owner of vast yam plantations. She was the only person in possession of the secrets of planting yam seeds so yams would grow big and wholesome. Everybody envied her knowledge, but she kept it to herself and proudly displayed the fruits of her power. One day, Obatalá was forced to hire a farmer to care for her many plantations. Fearful that, through him, everyone would learn her secret, Obatalá carefully selected the person to whom she was going to entrust her beloved yams. After much consideration, Obatalá chose . . . Oricha Oko, a serious, responsible, and chaste farmer. She thought to herself: "A man who has no sexual relations with women will not be easily seduced and should be more discreet than those who run around from one love affair to the other." Her choice proved to be effective, for the yams grew bigger and healthier and reproduced better that ever.
>
> At that time Changó wanted the powerful Obatalá to give him the ownership of drums and dancing. She constantly refused his requests. Yemayá, Changó's mother, one day conceived a very ingenious plan. She thought that if she stole Obatalá's secret of the yams, she might be willing to give Changó the drums. Yemayá went to chaste Oricha Oko and seduced him: "Take me. I have come for you." The shy young man was so impressed with the woman who introduced him to the pleasures of love that he gave her the secrets he had so far staunchly protected.
>
> Yemayá then went to see Obatalá and offered to give her back the secrets in exchange for the drums. Obatalá accepted, and Changó was made the owner of the drums.
>
> Oricha Oko, ashamed of his weakness, took refuge in the wilderness and lost his position as judge in matters of conflict among human beings. (Cros Sandoval 1975:256)

As in Africa, the worship of Oricha Oko in Cuba is hereditary. It is transmitted from mother to daughter. In Cuba, as in Nigeria, the majority of his priests are women. Sterile women make sacrifices to this god, hoping to become fertile.

Oricha Oko is represented, for obvious reasons, by lithographs of Saint Isidro the Tiller, the Catholic patron of farmers. He is also represented by a plow pulled by oxen. The plow and oxen are Afro-Cuban symbols exclusively, since, traditionally, Yoruban farmers did not use the plow or oxen until colonial times. Yams, which in Yorubaland are one of the staple foods, are also one of the symbols of this god in Cuba.

Oricha Oko's necklace is made of lilac-colored beads. The *achere*, a gourd used for calling this god, is painted with longitudinal lines of dark red and white colors. Oricha Oko rules on *yo awo* (Mondays); the day of divination. Many claim that he likes to be on top of the tile roofs and that he converses with eagles and vultures.

This rustic *oricha* does not come down in drum festivals, or *güemileres.* When they play a drumbeat in his honor, the believers perform dances that lack the lewd pantomimes, which, in Africa, were appropriate to a god of horticulture and fertility.

In Cuba, the worship of this *oricha* has lost the importance it had in Nigeria. This might seem surprising since the majority of slaves brought to Cuba worked in the fields. Further analysis, however, suggests that Afro-Cubans may have neglected his worship because of a lack of motivation. As they did not personally benefit from their work in the fields, the power of this god would only improve their masters' lot and not their own. Also the change from a simple horticultural society to a more complex agricultural economy of market crops such as sugar cane, coffee, and tobacco contributed to the eclipse of a god who was intimately connected with subsistence farming.

Another important reason seems to be that his worship was linked to fertility rites that were totally unacceptable in the new environment. Moreover, in Africa, the worship of Orisha Oko was centered on the annual festival of the ñame (yam). As this crop was not important to the plantation owners, it lost some importance in Cuba among the slaves. Furthermore, the slaves had to abandon the ritual fertility practices associated with this god. His meaning and significance were diminished. Thus, in drum festivals, or *güemileres*, the dances dedicated to Oricha Oko lack a specific pantomime, probably because in Africa they were allegorical of the sexual act. When these dances were forbidden in Cuba, the *oricha* was left without the symbolic pantomimes and the choreography characteristic of his worship. Oricha Oko doesn't possess believers during drum festivals.

The Ibeji in Africa

In some societies, the birth of twins is generally accepted as an unnatural event. In equatorial Africa, some tribes welcome twins with great delight, while others consider their birth a bad omen. In the past, when a double birth occurred among the Arebo of Guinea, the mother was put to death together with the children because they were considered a danger to the community. However, in other parts of Guinea and Nigeria, the birth of twins was and is received with great happiness.

The Arebo people of Lagos told Robert F. Thompson (1976 CH13/2) that, in the past, it was believed that only the poor and wicked were the progenitors of twins, who, therefore, had to be put to death at birth. Then, many children of the region of Ajashe began to die, and people consulted the Ifa oracle to understand why. The oracle commanded the people to stop killing the twins and to start honoring them. Thereafter, the mothers of twins began to worship twins every five days and to dance in their honor. The spectators gave them considerable gifts of money. In this way, having twins became associated with prosperity for the family, good fortune, and a reason for rejoicing.

According to the Arebo, this tradition is the foundation of the cult of twins among the Yoruba. However, Fagg reports (1982: 80) that the cult of the Twins is relatively recent among the Yoruba. He adds that, in the past, twins were considered monstrous aberrations and were put to death in spite of the high incidence of twin births among the Yoruba. Fagg reports that beginning in 1750 the cult of the Twins began in the southwestern regions and that with the support of the Alafin of Oyo it spread to the eastern and northern Yoruban towns by the 1850s.

The Fons of Dahomey also render worship to the sacred twins, whom they call Hoho. Due to Yoruban influence, worship is rendered to the sacred twins in both Cuba and Brazil. And, due to Dahomian influence, they are also worshipped in Haiti.

The oldest of the twins is called Taiwo, a name derived from the phrase to-aiye-wo (the first who tastes the world.) The second-born twin is called Kehinde, a name derived from the phrase ko-ehin-de (the one that comes after a twin.) These twins represent good fortune, luck, and prosperity. They are represented by anthropomorphic images so linked that they cannot be separated. They are usually tied together after birth with a chain or cord, as it is believed that if they become separated their power will disappear.

Near the city of Badagry there is a very important temple dedicated specifically to the worship of the Ibeji. Here, human twins are the representatives and protégées of these gods; they too are respected and pampered.

To Yoruban parents, the birth of twins is a harbinger of good luck, good fortune, and protection. They are accustomed to go out with their children to beg alms from passersby, whom they greet in the name of the gods. The people so greeted must give them a small present as a token of their respect for the sacred twins.

If one of the twins dies, the mother has to make an image of the deceased one to be carried everywhere by the surviving twin. When the survivor becomes an adult, he has to place before his brother's image parts of his meals to assure the blessing of the Ibeji. If he should neglect this duty, the Ibeji would be enraged and would punish the survivor with death. All through their lives, twins have to render worship to their protector divinities. Sacrifices to the Ibeji consist of small portions of vegetables and beans.

The Ibeyi in Cuba

The Ibeyi are very popular in Cuba, where they are also known by the name of Jimaguas.[3] The older of the two is known by the name Taebo, from the Yoruban Taiwo, and the second one is called Kainde, from the Yoruban Kehinde. The Ibeyi are very likable, generous, and affable gods, loved by the faithful and by the other *orichas.* Even though they are mischievous because of their youth, their pranks, unlike those of Echú, are never offensive or harmful. It is believed that they have great magical powers and that they are the messengers of prosperity and good fortune.

In Cuba several *patakíes* narrate different aspects of their lives. In some *patakíes* they are the fruit of the illicit love affair between Ochún and Changó, even though in Africa and Brazil these kinship ties are not recognized. This reinterpretation of the relation between members of the pantheon is typically Afro-Cuban, as there is a great emphasis on defining the members of the celestial court by kinship bonds. The following myth describes their pleasant nature and some of their attributes:

The Ibeyi are the fruit of the passionate love of Ochún and Changó. Since their parents had no time to care for their upbringing, they roamed the villages and wilderness, bringing affection, warmth, and happiness. Men, women, and children alike welcomed them lovingly. After they tired of their restless life, they went to stay with their grandmother Yemayá. One day, the then famous drum player Changó went to visit Yemayá and found his children there. He sat them on his lap and sang songs to them about his great wars, victories, and hazardous life.

The following day, Changó, filled with rage, climbed the palm tree near Yemayá's house, whose haughty crest seemed to strike the morning air with the same rage Changó felt. The young boys went to the *ilé* to find out what had gone wrong. The boys had a striking resemblance to their parents. One of them was arrogant, daring, and filled with the zest and love of adventure his father had. The other one was soft, whimsical, and capricious like his mother. As they entered the house they saw Yemayá, Naná Burukú, Ochún, Oyá, and Oba sad and speechless, wondering about the cause of Changó's ugly mood.

"I have tried to incite him, showing him my firm breasts and my desirable body, but his anger has only increased," said Oyá.

"My throat is dry after singing to him the mellow songs that used to give him courage during the day and turned him tender at night, but silence was his only answer," murmured sweet Oba with tearful eyes.

"I offered *amalá*, his favorite food, *eguede*, and other special morsels to him, but he hasn't even noticed them," said Naná Burukú.

Elegguá, coming through the door said, "I offered firewater to him, depriving myself of that pleasure, but he has refused it."

Then the Ibeyi said, "Let us all try to make him happy."

The women immediately began to dance, moving their hips and bodies with soft tremors, swaying their heads, and singing while Elegguá beat the drums, imitating Changó. Ochún sang to the thunder god, and the rest repeated the greeting. The songs swept over the wilderness and Changó slowly came down from the palm tree, leaving anger and anguish behind him. Embracing his children he entered Yemayá's house and played the drums all night. And thus, there was singing, dancing, and happiness again. (Cros Sandoval 1975:259–60)

In another *patakí* Changó's relationship with his sons is described:

Changó, exhausted by his unending adventures and wars and his tiring work as a drummer, decided to spend some time resting in Yemayá's house. On the way he met the Ibeyi, and together they went to Yemayá's house.

Every morning Changó would ride his beautiful white horse and trot through the wilderness, beating the branches of trees with his double axe. At midday he would come home, and, after eating *amalá*, he would rest on his mat and play with his sons. At sunset he would play the drums until his fingertips were swollen by blood. The drumbeats sometimes were soft, other times sad, and other times turbulent and rapid. He played and the Ibeyi sang sacred songs and prayers.

Yemayá was extremely happy. During the day she would do the house chores, but at night she would rejoice with their songs and dances. At midnight she would go to her hiding place and play with the gold coins she kept in a gourd. Some nights she would go to bed with Changó.

The last day of Changó's visit, Yemayá decided to have a great party in his honor. She got five lambs, fifty ducks, roosters, and partridges; coconuts, plantains, and corn.

Elegguá, using a knife, beheaded the ducks, pouring their blood in a vessel containing red beads. The Ibeyi sacrificed pigeons, chickens, and hens. They severed the heads, rapidly pouring the blood in a vessel containing blue beads. Yemayá sacrificed the lambs while the women sang:

Lubeo Lubeo yembo eh, Prince Changó is fire.
Lubeo amala eh, Prince Changó, we offer you corn meal.
Lubeo aguede eh, Prince Changó, we offer you plantains.
Lubeo akuka eh, Prince Changó, wick of fire.
Lubeo obi eh, Prince Changó, we offer you coconuts.

Yemayá officiated, swaying and singing until she was out of breath. She drank the blood from the heads of the animals that had been offered. She gave the flesh of the animals to the public, which sang, *"Kabie sile Changó"* (Everything is all right).

A few women finished bleeding the lambs into a large container. Others carried the possessed Yemayá in their arms and covered her face with a piece of white cloth while praying into her ear, hoping to restore her back to consciousness. Five times she sacrificed lambs, five times she fell into a trance, and five times the miraculous prayer was intoned in her ear: By Olofi, by Olodumare, *Kofiedemi* (By Olofi, by Olodumare, forgive me).

Changó arrived hungry and tired while the banquet was being prepared and immediately began to eat. Yemayá tried to persuade him to wait and eat after the guests arrived. Changó would not wait. Yemayá abruptly told him, "What a brave man you are, you who are so afraid of Ikú."

Changó struck Yemayá in a mad rage, took her money, and left. Then he began the life of a bon vivant; wearing expensive clothes and jewels, he would go to the *güemileres* (drum festivals) every night. Men and women rendered him homage: *"Kabie sile Changó."*

Changó ran out of money. That night, at the *güemilere*, everyone turned his back on him. Humiliated, Changó went back to Yemayá's house. Elegguá, the first to see him, told him, "Get out of here, you thief." Changó got Elegguá drunk and entered the house, where he found the Ibeyi sleeping soundly on a mat next to Yemayá. He woke them up and took them outside. He told them, "I need your help, for I am a total wreck. I need to return to Yemayá's *ilé* and regain her affection. Go back to the house and sing her this song: "Yemayá *koro ni*; Yemaya *koro ni*; *ka, ma, wa, ero*; Changó *lorisa*" (Yemayá, don't be inflexible and angry; Mother, calm down; Changó is going to make you happy).

The following day, the Ibeyi sang the song in loud voices. Yemayá told them, "You are wasting your time. Changó will never be allowed in this house." She spanked them and forbade them to speak about him any more.

Changó decided to use one last strategy to recover Yemayá's love. He persuaded one of the Ibeyi to hide in the wilderness.

The following morning Yemayá and the villagers searched for the missing boy. They searched for two days.

Changó told Yemayá, "I have walked the long roads; climbed the high mountains; searched the dark caves; and from the top of the palm tree I have looked all over the land. Yet, I have found no trace of the child. I believe Ikú (death) has taken him. Since one of the twins is missing there are no Ibeyi, and I am taking the other one."

Yemayá tried to stop him, but he took the child into the woods. Yemayá, desperate, asked the villagers to stop Changó. In the ensuing confusion, Changó whistled to the other Ibeyi hiding in the woods. When the three approached the crowd, Yemayá was so elated that she forgave Changó and welcomed him back into her house and heart.

Yemayá took care of the Ibeyi until they were young men. Then, they left her home and visited other towns. They were welcomed everywhere because they were very endearing and brought good luck and prosperity. From time to time they visited their grandmother, delighting her with their stories full of humor and grace. (Cros Sandoval 1975:260–63)

In Santería, the Ibeyi are represented by lithographs of Saint Cosme and Saint Damian,[4] the Catholic saints with whom they have been associated. Anthropomorphic figurines called *erere* are also commonly used to represent them. These wooden sculptures, coarsely manufactured and frequently painted black, are dressed in red garments, the color of their father, Changó. Normally, these images are made of a single piece of wood. When they are made of two separate pieces they are always tied together. It is believed that if they are separated their magical powers will be lost. In the hollow part of the figurine, bones, dirt, pieces of horn, and roots, which have magical powers, are kept. These sculptures are frequently placed inside a clay kettle called *apote*.

The Ibeyi are invoked using *acheres*, or rattles, with small bells attached and, also, using a gourd decorated with crosses or a couple of lines painted in red on a white background. The necklace of the Ibeyi is made with the colors of Ochún and Changó, their mother and father.

The Ibeyi do not possess the believers. Nevertheless, in order for devotees to pamper the Twins and ingratiate themselves, songs and dances are dedicated to them during ritual festivities. The dancers in the chorus imitate the faltering steps of a child and take short jumps, as small children do when playing. They are always greeted with love. Believers call them Beyi *Oro alakua oye mo jojo* (the divine twins). Even though they are children, they are revered as wise and mature. Like all children, the Ibeyi love to eat candy.

As mentioned above, the Ibeyi have been identified with Saint Cosme and Saint Damian. More precisely, Taebo corresponds to San Cosme, and Kainde to San Damián. These Catholic saints were brothers at the beginning of the Christian era in Sicily. They became martyrs because they refused to worship pagan idols and defended Christianity. They are the patrons of barbers and surgeons. There is no similarity between the hagiography of these saints and the mythology of the Ibeyi. The association was probably based on the fact that the Catholic saints were brothers and that in the chromolithographs the saints appear as inseparable companions, as is the case with the Ibeyi.

Aganju in Africa

Oral traditions tell us that when the Yoruban people were migrating[5] through the arid regions north of the territory they mainly occupy today, Aganju was one of the most important gods in their pantheon. This god ruled over the desert-like earth and was the owner of volcanoes. Aganju, or Aginjou, is the Yoruban word for desert. When the Yoruban people settled in more fertile areas, the worship of this god declined in favor of the gods of agriculture and of thunder and lightning.

The following Yoruban myth speaks of Aganju's identity. He was the only child of the creator couple, Obatalá and Oduduwa. Aganju married his sister, and they had a son called Oraniyán. Later on, Oraniyán raped his mother, Yemayá, who, horrified, ran away from him. Exhausted after running for so long Yemayá lay down on the beach and died. Then, from inside her body, all the orishas streamed out.

Even though the Yoruban people acknowledge Aganju's importance, his following and cult eventually declined. In the Yoruban pantheon Aganju is considered the owner of the desert and the patron of porters.

Agayú in Cuba

In Cuba, Agayú is also called Aganyú and Agayú Sola. In some *cabildos*, Agayú is considered a very old and strong *oricha*. According to Angarica (1955:5), he represents strength, the volcano, and the sun. He is the fruit of the union of the volcano and Oro Iña, the bowels of the earth. This appears to be reminiscent of the identification in West Africa made between Aganyu and the sunny, dry, desert lands.

In other *cabildos* he is known as a boatman or fluvial porter and is associated with Saint Christopher, the patron of the city of Havana. This saint, according to legend, carried the infant Jesus across the river. Thus, he became the patron of porters and travelers. In some Cuban *ilé ochas*, Agayú's association with volcanoes and desert lands (not relevant in Cuba) became blurred and more identified with his role as a porter, especially a porter of the river, due to the influence of Saint Christopher, the Catholic saint with whom he became associated.

In Cuba, Changó and Agayú are very closely related. Changó feels great respect and love for Agayú. During festivals, whenever Changó comes down in one of his ugly moods, believers call on Agayú to control him. All Agayú has to do is look at Changó, and Changó will lower his eyes out of deference to him. Agayú is as brave a warrior as Changó, but, unlike Changó, he is thoughtful and mature and gets along very well with the other *orichas*, who greatly respect him. In Africa Aganyu and Shango are identified with a male ram, which is also used to represent them.

In some *ilé ochas*, Aganyú, or Agayú, is the father of Changó, as described in the following *pataki*:

> Agayú Solá is the porter of the river. Agayú was Changó's father, but Changó did not know it.
>
> Agayú was so feared and respected that he always left his front door wide open, certain that no one would dare break in. Since Agayú was the owner of rivers and savannas, there were always plenty of fruits and foods of all kinds in his house.
>
> One day Changó entered Agayú's house and ate everything he could put his hands on. He ate to the point of bursting. Then he lay down on Agayú's mat and took a nap. When Agayú came back and found Changó on his mat acting as if the house were his he became very angry. He piled up a lot of driftwood and made a large fire, grabbed Changó, and threw him in. Changó, however, didn't burn. How could he if Changó himself is fire?
>
> Agayú then took Changó to the seashore, with intentions to drown him. At that moment Yemayá, Changó's mother arrived. "What are you going to do? You cannot kill your own son."
>
> Agayú, fully acknowledging Changó, said, "In this world I am the bravest man there is, but you, Changó, are as brave as I am. I declare that you are my son." (Cros Sandoval 1975:264–65)

Agayú shares with his son, Changó, the ownership of the royal palm tree. They dress alike in red and white, and they are both considered kings. These two *orichas* are so close that they cannot be separated. Therefore, whoever receives Changó as his *eledá* also receives Agayú. He cannot be *asentado*; so people who need to receive him get Changó instead and, through a special liturgy, receive Agayú.

Agayú eats the same offerings that Changó receives. They are so closely associated that in some *cabildos* it is believed that Changó and Agayú are the same.

Agayú's necklace begins with a large white bead followed by nine red beads and eight yellow ones. This order is repeated until the necklace is completed.

In Cuba as in Yorubaland, Agayú is the patron of porters. Several Afro-Cuban myths, such as the following *pataki*, depict Agayú as a boatman.

> One day, Agayú, a rustic, rugged, powerful, middle-aged man, who was as strong as a bull, was watching attentively the turbulent and muddy waters of a wild river that threatened villages, beasts, and men. In deep thought, he watched the strong currents, the treacherous whirlpools, and the dangerous flooding waters. Without a word, he walked away from the expectant crowd that had gathered to see the turbulent waters. He took an ax, the trunk of a tree, and made a canoe and two heavy strong oars.
>
> "I will tame you yet," he said, in challenge, as he launched his craft into the angry waters. He crossed the current many times, until the waters started to run smoothly, completely tamed. Agayú thus became the tamer of the river. Agayú and his boat became the connection between villages on both shores of the river. Everyone who crossed the river had to pay him tribute.
>
> One early morning, an elegant, queenly woman all dressed in white came aboard Agayú's boat. Agayú silently took the woman to the other shore. When they arrived safely, the haughty woman, without saying a single word, quickly undressed and offered her firm body in payment for Agayú's services. Agayú, also in silence, possessed the haughty female. When everything was over, the woman disdainfully told him, "You have been overpaid. You have had the great honor of possessing Obatalá." She walked away as majestically as she had entered his life.
>
> After this episode, Agayú felt humiliated. From that moment on, he became suspicious and unfriendly and required that all clients give him their names and tribute on entering his boat. (Cros Sandoval 1975:265–66)

Another *pataki* narrates a different story:

> One day, a friendly little boy climbed onto Agayú's boat and playfully told him, "Agayú, take me to the other side of the river." Agayú refused to do so unless he identified himself and paid the tribute.
>
> "I don't have any money, but I do ask you to take me to the other side, where my mother is waiting for me. I have to go to her," replied the boy in a friendly voice but with a commanding tone.

Agayú answered, "I have established some rules here that I cannot break. Everyone, without exception, has to give me his or her name and pay me my tribute."

The boy replied, "That rule only applies to you and your boat. Since you are so strong and brave why don't you carry me on your shoulders? That way you will not have violated your principles."

Concealing a smile, Agayú silently placed the boy on his strong shoulders and daringly entered the strong current. However, the deeper he went in, the heavier his fragile burden became. "What in hell is the matter with you?" Agayú shouted to the boy. "You are getting heavier and heavier. You weigh like a horse."

The boy urged him, "Go on, go on."

"I cannot go any further," said Agayú on the verge of collapse.

"Look at me," the boy commanded.

"Oduduwa!" said Agayú, recognizing the great creator god.

"I now make you the owner of the river," Oduduwa told him. (Cros Sandoval 1975:146)

This *pataki*, unknown in Nigeria, is very similar to the legend of Saint Christopher, the Catholic saint with whom Agayú has been associated. In the Catholic legend, Saint Christopher is the bearer of the child Jesus and the patron of travelers. He is also the tutelary saint of the city of Havana and the patron of teamsters.

The children of Agayú are usually respected heads of families. They tend to be serious and responsible, and they are not unfriendly. They are looked up to for counsel and guidance. They are perceived as people with a strong character because Agayú is characterized by his strength. They are successful in mining activities.

Agayú's soup tureen contains two horns, four stones, and sixteen marbles. His *otán*, sacred stone, must remain submerged in the waters of the river for nine days. At the end of this time a priestess of Ochún carries the neophyte to the river to get it.

Minor Nigerian Orishas Known in Cuba

Some African Nigerian orishas are known in Cuba as *caminos* or paths of better known generic gods as discussed in the chapters dedicated to those gods. However, some Nigerian orishas who were not known throughout Yorubaland are known in Cuba. Among them are the following:

- Erinle, or Inle, is related to medicine and to *ojo de agua* (springs, fountains, or spouts). In some areas of Africa Erinle, or Eyinle, the orisha of the stream, is considered a male; in other areas a female. Samuel Johnson (1921:112) believes Erinle was originally a hunter from Ajagbusi. He never married and lived in a little hut by the river that he used to cross during his hunting expeditions. Accidentally, one day he was swept away by the river current and drowned. A tributary of the Oshun River is named after him. His devotees carry a necklace and bracelets made of brass. In Cuba, according to a *libreta de babalao*, Inle is a physician from Ilobu who had knowledge of the properties of plants even before Osain did. He has three aspects as a man: he is a king, a hunter, and a fisherman. He is the son of Yemayá and Olokun. According to Silvia Eires (January 2005), he lived with Yemayá. She cut his tongue because he liked to gossip and she was afraid that he would divulge her secrets. This is why he can only speak thru Yemayá's dilogún after a lamb is offered to her and to Inle. A person can be initiated "indirectly" into his cult via Yemayá. The neophyte is taken to the river, and offerings are given to the river's depths. A doll made of bronze is prepared and the jar containing Inle's *fundamentos* is also taken to the river. In Cuba, in some *ilé ochas* he is considered a great physician associated with Saint Rafael, the Catholics' divine physician. In chromolithographs, Saint Rafael is portrayed carrying a fish in his hand, which might have furthered the notion that the saint was also a fisherman.

- Dadá, who lives by the *ceiba* (silk-cotton tree), is the owner of vegetables. She is Changó's sister, who raised him from infancy. She is the protector of children. She was married to Babalú Ayé, who later made her sick. Agayú tried to take revenge for her. Dadá is not *asentada*; her children are initiated in Changó's worship.
- Iroko lives in the *ceiba,* the sacred silk-cotton tree, where the souls of the departed rest. His favorite food is young bulls, but he also eats roosters, hens, and white turkeys. This *oricha* likes solitude. He is not *asentado* and is received thru Obatalá.
- Kori Kote Iroke, as Dadá, is an *oricha* that protects newly born children.
- Yewá, or Yeguá, lives in the cemetery and is in charge of delivering cadavers to Oyá. Yewá is a chaste old lady. In her presence no sexual innuendoes are permissible nor any rude or loud language. Her priestesses are women who are either virgins or well over the age of procreation. Men are not initiated into her worship. Pink is her symbolic color. She has been associated with the Virgin of the Desamparados (The Virgin of the Helpless).

Conclusion to Part 2

Variations and innovations in the Afro-Cuban mythology reflect the changes undergone by the Yoruban religion in Cuba as a consequence of adaptation to the new milieu and the merging with non-Yoruban religious elements. Processes of merging and transculturation as mechanisms of cultural change have been central to Cuban history. In the case of the Yoruba-speaking people, they probably were brought to Cuba from the beginning of the colonization period and in larger numbers at the end of the eighteenth century through most of the nineteenth century. The establishment in 1839 of the *cabildo* Lukumí Changó under the patronage of Saint Barbara demonstrates that associations between Yoruban orishas and Catholic saints were occurring long before concerted efforts were undertaken to create a common doctrine for Yoruban beliefs. In Cuba, the slaves and their descendants associated African orishas with Christian saints because in some cases they perceived that similarities existed, however superficial, and because they were willing to appeal to new sources of spiritual assistance.

In general, the Afro-Cuban divinities lost some of the awe-inspiring qualities that their counterparts enjoyed in Nigeria. This development was probably caused by the loss of status of the uprooted and enslaved early practitioners and their descendants. The loss of awe-inspiring qualities may also have been due to the lack of institutional support that the worship of the *orichas* had in Cuba vis à vis Nigeria under the local divine kings, or obas. In Nigeria the obas cared for the cults and temples of the local orisha and sponsored the annual festivities to honor the orishas that were most important in the regions under their control.

Moreover, in many instances Afro-Cuban *orichas* are portrayed as amoral, deviant, deceitful, capricious, and even antisocial. They engage in behavior particularly congruent with slave society, where the individual loses all sense of control, a condition that is compatible with a chaotic perception of the social order and the universe.

Associations Between African Orishas and Catholic Saints and Virgins

In Cuba, the slaves and their descendants associated certain *orichas* with specific Christian saints and with different manifestations of the Virgin. There is little doubt that the white masters pressured their slaves to worship Catholic divinities. There is also little doubt that the slaves used Catholic images as "masks" to hide their own divinities. However, it is also very likely that in their search for meaning and access to power, they perceived that some type of common ground existed between them, however superficial. For example, the saint and the *oricha* may have shared a symbolic color or object. Obatalá is associated with the Virgin of Mercy possibly because the robe of the Virgin of Mercy is white in statues and chromolithographs. In Nigeria white is the symbolic color for Obatala, the orisha of purity.

In other instances, the basis for the association between *oricha* and saint supersedes apparent contradictions. In Cuba, a female martyr saint, Saint Barbara, is associated with Changó, the most outstanding personification of virility, rage, passion, womanizing, and behavioral excess. The basis for the association between *oricha* and saint in this case is largely symbolic and does not take into consideration the character or personality of the divinities. These are meaningful linkages nevertheless.

In chromolithographs Saint Barbara is featured in a red robe, and red is Changó's symbolic color. Moreover, in the background of chromolithographs depicting Saint Barbara, there is a burning castle. According to myths, Changó, the legendary king of Oyo, while doing magical tricks, set his own palace on fire. Furthermore, Saint Barbara was very popular among white residents in colonial Cuba; thus, her statues and chromolithographs abounded throughout the island. She is the patron saint of Spanish artillery and is associated with the thunder of canons. This very likely strengthened her association with Changó, the warrior-god of thunderstorms.

In other cases, the association is not based on any discernible similarity. One can only speculate that the presence of the statue of a particular saint in the local Catholic church prompted slaves in Cuba to adopt it as a cover for the secret representation of one of their *orichas*. In these cases, there may have been little or no common ideological or symbolic ground between the *oricha* and the saint.

One might conjecture that in such instances there was also an interest in securing the services of the supernatural patrons of the colonizers to the benefit of the "colonized." The openness of the Yoruban religion in Africa would not preclude such incorporation in the new setting.

Currently, young *santeros* who follow an Afro-centric trend in Cuba and in the United States insist that the association between *oricha* and saint is a mere disguise. They consider it to be prompted by a colonial-era fear of persecution from white masters. It is my opinion, however, that the search for equivalence in meaning takes precedence over the need for disguise. The need for logico-structural integration, as discussed by Kearney (1984) is, to paraphrase him, the frame upon which the substance of any worldview must hang. Such struggles for consistency in images and assumptions about the world are especially intense among people who are experiencing the disorientation created by the trauma of culture shock or the challenge of adapting in situations requiring bicultural or multicultural accommodations.

Problems of survival might be expected to lead to a search for all possible sources of power and mastery. Thus, the Yoruban tradition of openness and inclusion might lead to the adoption of new avenues to spiritual assistance. Equivalencies in the spiritual realm could provide meaning, structure, and pathways that might not be comprehended otherwise.

The quest for logico-structural integration helps to explain the fact that in Haitian Voodoo (Vodun), for example, which continued to evolve after the white colonial government was overthrown, the *loas*, or gods, are freely associated with Catholic saints. In Brazil's Candomblé, religious-cultural elements merged in a strikingly similar fashion based upon voluntarily assumed associations. In many instances the Yoruban *oricha* was identified, in both Brazil and Cuba, with the same Catholic saint. The name applied to these supernatural entities was also *santo*. Furthermore, the *orichas* not only were associated in Cuba and in Brazil with Catholic saints but also with non-Yoruban African supernatural entities.

At the same time, the *santo* remained essentially an African god. However, the association fostered the loss of those attributes of the *oricha* that were not relevant in the New World. Conversely, those attributes shared by both the *oricha* and the Catholic saint became more important. In a few cases some of the characteristics of the Catholic saint were assumed by the creolized supernatural entity. The most salient changes resulting from adaptation to the Cuban setting and to the association of the Yoruban divinities with Catholic and with non-Yoruban African divinities is that, in general, Yoruban divinities became more human. In certain instances, they lost some of their most powerful characteristics.

Changes in the Afro-Cuban Pantheon as Compared to the Yoruban Pantheon

The Yoruban pantheon was reduced from over two thousand orishas to a few dozen *orichas* in Cuba because of markedly changed circumstances, including severed kinship ties, shattered communities, an unfamiliar environment, a foreign economic system, loss of religious specialists, and other traumas. Specifically the following changes occurred:

Slavery destroyed African kinship ties and weakened both the cult of the ancestors and the belief in reincarnation in Cuba. Central to these beliefs in Yorubaland was the role the Supreme Being played in sealing a pact with the ancestral soul of each individual and, consequently, determining a plan, or design, regarding the purpose of a terrestrial incarnation for each individual. The loss of this belief was most costly to the importance of the belief in reincarnation in Cuba.

According to many Cuban *patakíes* (legends) the Supreme Being is an old man plagued by feebleness and frailty and is often susceptible to frivolous fears and carnal appetites. It is possible that this change from his original African nature, perceived as sublime, pure, wise, just and merciful, is linked to his being associated in some *ilé ochas* with creator gods of other African ethnic groups that had not developed the sublime abstract concept of the Supreme Being that the Yoruban people had achieved in Nigeria.

Summary of Changes

Obatalá became identified in Cuba with less-known regional creator gods of Yorubaland and with other non-Yoruban creator gods. This resulted in Obatalá's having a great number of manifestations, paths, or *caminos*, and being identified with several Catholic saints and divinities.

The cult of Orúnmila did not change very much between Africa and Cuba. His association with Saint Francis of Assisi did not particularly affect either his character or his attributes, largely because of the arrival in Cuba of very well-trained Ifa priests from Ile Ife, the sacred Yoruban city.

Eleggúa's cult in Cuba remains as important as Elegbara's is in Africa. In Santería there is a tendency to identify the more asocial and negative aspects of this god's personality with Echú, or Eshu (one of the names by which this deity is known in Africa). In Santería, Echú is one of Eleggúa's *caminos.*

The Afro-Cuban Changó, as the sole owner of the thunderbolt, completely erased other thunder-gods of Yorubaland, such as Oramfe and Jakuta. Jakuta, in Cuba, is a title or name given to Changó. Changó's preeminence in Cuba is due to the large numbers of people and well-trained priests originally from Oyo, who were able to preserve the complicated rituals and paraphernalia associated with his cult. Changó is a central figure in Cuban Santería. In Cuba, Changó underwent some sort of a humanization process. He is a boisterous, tricky womanizer and an irresponsible, habitual liar in contrast with the Yoruban Shango, who punishes liars by killing them with a thunderbolt. He is more of a trickster and a braggart in Cuba than a warrior deity who inspires terror.

In Cuba Yemayá (Yemonja in Nigeria) gained in stature, changing from being the goddess of the lagoon in Nigeria to becoming the owner of the sea. In Cuba she usurped Olokun's domain, which survives only as a manifestation of Yemayá. She is a central character in the celestial court, meddling in all the activities of the other *orichas.*

Ochún also gained in stature in Cuba. She became the sole owner of the river, displacing Oya and Oba, both of whom lost their fluvial attributes and are worshipped, instead, as the owner of the whirlpool and the domestic goddess respectively. Additionally, in Cuba, Ochún assumed the ownership of money, totally displacing Aje Saluga, who in Nigeria is the patron of merchants and money.

In Santería, Ogún, the patron of soldiers and blacksmiths, lost to Elegguá his role as the divinity that opens the road of communication between the gods and their followers. He lost prestige because soldiers and blacksmiths constituted the bulk of the following in Africa; and in Cuba slaves could not be soldiers and few were blacksmiths. In addition, the blacksmith trade on the island was less important than it was in Yorubaland, and many of the blacksmiths in the trade were not of Yoruban descent. Moreover, for some slaves the memories of the civil wars in Africa were devastating, and many blamed these wars and Ogún for their enslavement.

The Nigerian god of epidemics, Shopono, gained a following in Cuba, where he is known by a title also given to him in Africa: Babalú Ayé. In Cuba, however, this god lost most of his negative characteristics. Instead of being a cruel, vengeful, supersensitive god, he turned into a divinity so very much afflicted by physical ailments that he inspires pity and sympathy instead of fear. He becomes a god more committed to miraculous healing than to punishing transgressors and afflicting them with horrible diseases. This dramatic change in personality most likely is due to his being associated with the character of a Catholic legend that, until recently, was popularly venerated by Catholics as Saint Lazarus.

Ochosi lost preeminence in Cuba because hunting obviously did not constitute a possible activity for enslaved Africans. Oricha Oko, the god of horticulture and vegetal fertility also lost importance. This may be due to the fact that the bulk of the work done by slaves was on the sugar and coffee plantations and was not linked to subsistence farming. Moreover, some of the rituals associated with Oricha Oko's worship were considered unacceptable and immoral in the new society, especially those related to the fertility of yams, which, in Africa, entailed ritual sexual intercourse.

Naná Burukú is well known as an *oricha* in some areas such as Carlos Rojas. In other areas she was practically unknown, and her cult survived as a *camino*, or path, of Obatalá. A similar case is that of Olokun, whose cult flourished at the end of the nineteenth century and then lost ground, probably because no priest was trained in his worship. Thus, Olokun in some *ilé ochas* is considered a *camino* of Yemayá, who usurped his role as the Yoruban divinity of the sea. Additionally, individual priests sometimes changed Yoruban traditions as necessitated by circumstance and adapted them to the new setting to better serve their following and/or attract new followers.

In chapter 22 a brief but concerted effort is made to apply aspects of worldview analysis to some of the above materials. The focus is upon issues of morality, basic assumptions, and logico-structural integration.

Part 3

Santería's Moral Dimensions, Worldview Assumptions, and Logico-Structural Integration

New Ways and Current Trends

22

Moral Dimensions, Worldview Assumptions, and Logico-Structural Integration

It is important to outline some of the ideals of moral behavior that inhere in Santería. Without such interpretation much of the behavior of the *orichas* described above will appear distorted and skewed toward the more negative features of character and behavior. The reason is that the *orichas*, along with all other creations of Olodumare, reflect the coexisting characteristics of good and evil as components of their basic nature.

In many of the myths and *patakíes*, amoral activities of the gods reveal how disruptive evil can be in the lives of individuals and groups. The ranges of amoral behavior are extensive and sometimes complex. However, they are useful in helping a client or follower of Santería identify the source or sources of disorder in his or her life and, thereafter, be advised by means of the instruments of divination, *patakíes*, and proverbs to engage in specific corrective actions that will restore a better balance of "good" and order in his or her life.

Moral Dimensions

Santería has been and continues to be portrayed as a religion of resistance (Brandon 1997:91–92; De la Torre 2004:189–203). Most assuredly, that is part of its history and function. If Santería is a religion of resistance it may be so primarily because of the meaning and security provided by its positive aspects. The essential nature of worldview in the lives of a people and the power of its appeal should not be overlooked by focusng on the need to resist pressures to destroy it. Such dynamics may, indeed, be operating as a component of Santería's endurance. My view, however, is that other functions of the religion were far more important, primarily the great need of the Yoruban "Self" to be in relation with the "Other" and the "not-Self" to use Kearney's terms (1984:68–78; see also, Lowery-Palmer 1980:62–78).

Traditionally, the Yoruban ethos structured social relationships in such a way that ethical behavior was well defined and reinforced. What was good for the well-being of others was good for the self. Once again, Mbiti's comment is appropriate here: "I am because we are; and since we are, therefore, I am" (1970:141).

In general, social institutions provided some avenues for conflict resolution among members of the community. Domestic and economic problems; issues related to land or agricultural disputes, witchcraft, and other types of conflict could be resolved in socially patterned ways. Inevitably, given the lineal value orientation of the culture, those involved in conflict resolution were senior persons (primarily males; secondarily females, such as senior wives). Community conflict resolution involved community leaders, chiefs, and the council of elders. For spiritual matters, the babalawos and, ultimately, the oba king of the region could also be involved. However, in many instances these institutions failed, and the history of the area documents the frequent intrigues and conflicts leading to wars and strife.

In most instances, character, intelligence, patience, wisdom, and authority provided solutions. Within such a social system predominant modes of behavior included acceptance of and submission to legitimate authority along with cooperation among siblings and cohorts of a variety of social groups. Everyone had responsible roles in the community and each carried out his duties according to his ability. In a sense, obedience, cooperation, and harmony to the greatest extent possible were the prevailing guides to behavior. But when these guides failed, solutions were found by means of following the advice and directions of higher authorities, who, in return for respect and honor, offered wisdom and thoughtful guidance.

All of this was lost under conditions of slavery until the means were acquired within the *cabildos* and social organizations to reconstitute something of the problem-solving and life-enhancing mechanisms formerly existing in the structure of Yoruban society and its institutions. The loss of such important social means for resolving interpersonal problems and for ameliorating life conditions among slaves and their Creole descendants in Cuba functioned to greatly augment the need for such problem-solving in the form of supernatural assistance within the religious sphere.

Santería may have emerged, in part, as a religion of resistance, but the view advanced here is that the positive efforts to re-establish elements of the Yoruban ethos, social structure, and religion far outweighed the need to "resist" the pressures of slave holders and the bearers of political and economic power. The need was for survival first, in a form that was meaningful to them. Presumably, a politically motivated orientation of resistance could come only after a degree of structure and order was in place.

Santería offered the means of both creating and ordering a new "reality" for Afro-Cubans and their descendants during the colonial and republican periods in Cuba. The moral dimensions of behavior within that new reality are far less evident.

Although glimpses of morality and the ethical basis for maintaining equilibrium in life are reflected in many sections of this book, there is no immediately apparent set of commandments to enlighten outside observers about such matters in Santería. The reason is that this knowledge is embedded in every aspect of the religion and functions as a major motivating force for believers to become increasingly involved in the religion.

Previously mentioned comments by a *babalao* about Olodumare during a conference in Miami in 2001 suggest the extent to which this is true. Once again, in his words: "One needs to learn the rules of Olodumare concerning man's relationships with the *orichas* and with the *egun* [deceased] to have a satisfactory life." It may be added that one learns such rules through the instruments of divination, the most sacred of which is the board of Ifá. Ifá is the patron of the *babalaos*, in whose care the board of Ifá rests. The *babalaos*, who render cult to the god of wisdom, are the highest-ranked practitioners of Santería; they have the greatest knowledge based upon the most extensive training and reflect the most disciplined attitude toward life.

The question remains. How can a religion utilize in its practice the mythology described in previous chapters? How can such mythology elevate and reinforce ethical principles that help followers of Santería become persons better integrated into their families and communities in a way that reflects balance and goodness? The answer is that the myths of Santería do not function as outside observers might expect. There is another way to understand such content within the framework of this religion.

My interpretation is that the dark (negative/evil) side of supernatural power is reflected in these myths, along with some aspects of the good. For those who are unable to clearly identify or pinpoint the nature of the disorder that has come into their lives, such behaviors are helpful, in a sense, as projective devices. The actions of the gods revealed in such myths help to define specific types of disharmonious behavior that destroy balance and goodwill in social interaction, in families, in the workplace, and in communities. Once these are identified, the process of divination and counseling continues until prescriptions for resolution are outlined. In this process the excesses of the gods are used to caution followers and clients about such behavior in their own lives.

The *babalao* Virgilio Armenteros, M.D. (Ifá Omí) makes this point as follows: "Occasionally, the religious stories and passages in relation to the deities seem as if morality is mixed with immorality, and that is not casual. Everything carries a philosophical and interpretive message where good and evil are pointed out to us comparatively. . . . I ask myself, 'What is good if we don't know what evil is?'" (Statement written in Spanish, dated May 17, 2005)

It will be recalled that in the worldview of Santería's devotees, Olodumare is the Supreme Being who embodies the universal moral order of goodness, mercy, and justice. His power is diffused throughout the earth, in all of its inhabitants, and in all of the forces of nature. It is shared but is unevenly manifested in the *orichas*, in human beings, in properties of nature, in diverse geographical areas, in inanimate objects, and in all the plants of the earth.

In varying degrees, both supernatural entities and the practitioners of Santería have access to the means of communicating with the highest source of wisdom and purity. For example, the higher the rank of the *oricha*, the greater is the reflection of Olodumare's character and goodness. Therefore, the greater is the association with and access to the power of the Supreme Being. Such is the case with Orúnmila, the god of wisdom and the oracles, whose power resides in the divining instruments—the *opon* Ifá and the *ekuele*. Ifá, the deity "residing" in the board of Ifá and in the *odus*, legends, and proverbs related to it, is so powerful that only *babalaos*, after years of training, can gain access to the guidance of Orúnmila and Olodumare through the use of this highest and most sacred instrument of divination.

There is no way to overestimate the importance of divination in the practice of Santería. Wande Abimbola (1997) emphasizes the importance of Ifa specifically, in what may be presented here as a set of basic assumptions:

- There is a pantheon of gods; some have greater power than others; their power is specialized; Ifa is one of the most important; Ifa and Eshu are friends.
- One cannot know the cause of his misfortune without consulting Ifa; a community cannot know the source of its hard times without consulting Ifa.
- Ifa can determine such causes.
- Ifa can give advice.
- Ifa has wisdom, knowledge, and understanding.
- Ifa coordinates the work of all the gods in the Yoruban pantheon.

In short, morality per se is not to the front and center in relation to Santería's mythology. As mentioned above, the content of such myths reflects not only the range of human-like behaviors that are disruptive but, also, suggestions about acceptable ways to restore order, peace, and well-being in life. And it is the *odus* of the divining instruments, guided by the god of wisdom, that point the way toward such repair of breaches in the social fabric. In addition, in the words of the *babalao* Dr. Virgilio Armenteros: "In every *odu* there is a philosophy between the lines that the *babalao* needs to apply" (personal conversation, May 14, 2005).

Morality, however, is pervasive in the form of purity, goodness, and beauty—suffused throughout every aspect of this religious system. It appears first through cleansing rituals that incorporate all the power available from the wilderness and the plant world; then through the various forms of communication with the *orichas*—offerings, sacrifices, drumming, singing, dancing, incantation—all designed to bring goodness and power *(aché)* into the life of everyone involved. Morality may be implicit in this equation, but it is not immediately evident.

It is important to remember, also, that no matter how close to the Supreme Being in relative goodness, all supernatural powers have the ability to offset the positive (good) with negative (evil) actions. Consequently, ritual goals of emphasizing and increasing the level or amount of positive forces entering the lives of believers function at the same time to ward off or diminish the forces of evil.

At the same time, the cunning strategies employed by the *orichas* to achieve desired ends demonstrate to believers the extent to which *orichas* might work on their behalf. The cleverness of Elegguá, especially, characterizes their strengths in this regard.

Insofar as specific acts are concerned, Santería is nonjudgmental. All persons can come for help with any problems that are disrupting their lives. Ultimately, the wisdom and goodness from the "rules of Olodumare" will provide advice and guidance to restore greater order and tranquility in life—anyone's life, regardless of behaviors that might be unethical, illegal, disruptive, or dangerous in the secular realm. As indicated previously, it is only Olodumare who can judge a person's morality.

Within Santería's house-temples, however, the same type of ethical behavior is expected of members within religious lineages as might be expected in any decent biological family. Once again, the words of the *babalao* Armenteros are relevant here:

It is necessary to underline the ethical-moral elements that act as communal factors in all the Afro-Cuban temples and that are constantly verbalized by the practitioner:

- To believe in God and the *orichas* above everything else.
- To do good to everybody.
- To be a good father and godfather.
- To be a good brother and friend.
- To love and respect the family.
- To consider and respect others as one considers and respects oneself.
- To believe in spiritual evolution, which influences us.
- To zealously guard all the religious secrets that have been handed down by our ancestors, in order to avoid any deterioration that might undermine the prestige of our religion.
- To never engage in discrimination and prejudice of any kind, even though one rejects vices and aberrations, and it is necessary and obligatory to pronounce oneself against them.
- To never mix religious activities with personal interests.

According to the *babalao* Armenteros,

Morality is an ambiguous concept that adjusts itself to each society. What is moral for some might be immoral for others.

Morality in Afro-Cuban religion is directed by strong values and behavior that are framed in social conviviality, customs, and the acquired formal education.

One cannot forget that it is a religion where oral tradition predominates even though there is some written liturgical literature. Thus, to learn about it and to be initiated in Santería, it is not necessary to attend any school. One learns by getting close to religious practitioners and to accept becoming a participant in it. (Statement written in Spanish, dated May 17, 2005)

In summary, morality is intrinsic in the ethos and worldview of Santería in so many faceted ways that this, too, constitutes the material for another book; something that remains for future inquiry and discussion.

We turn now to the matter of basic assumptions and the value of a worldview approach in making them explicit.

Basic Assumptions and Propositions

As discussed earlier, Kearney describes the worldview of a people as their way of looking at reality. "It consists of basic assumptions and images that provide a more or less coherent . . . way of thinking about the world" (Kearney 1984:41). He uses the terms assumption and image interchangeably, but he differentiates first-order images and assumptions from second-order images and assumptions.

First-order assumptions are those at the core of every worldview and reflect the dimensions of the five universal categories he has outlined as Self-Other, Causality, Classification, Space, and Time. He states that, normally, these fundamental attitudes are tacitly held and not made explicit (1984:48).

An example of a first-order assumption might be that Time is cyclical rather than linear. Another example of a first-order assumption related to Causality might be that all action in the universe derives from supernatural power.

Second-order assumptions, however, are those that can be fairly easily described by individuals whose social roles require such expertise. Second-order images and assumptions are usually considered as folk knowledge, but as Kearney (1984:48) says, "In many ways they can be seen as permutations of the underlying culturally specific form of the universals. . . . Such explicit second-order images and assumptions are usually more easily cast as propositions . . . while the underlying first-order images and assumptions tend to be more abstract, less explicit, therefore, more elusive."

Kearney (1984:48) differentiates assumptions from propositions in the following way: ". . . [T]he location of an image or assumption is in the mind of the people whose world view is being analyzed, while the proposition is in the model that the anthropologist constructs to replicate that world view. Propositions are based upon images of reality that the anthropologist hypothesizes as existing in the world view of a particular individual or group. He states these hypothetical statements as propositions, which he infers from any and all social behavior and expressive productions of the people whose world view he is studying."

The insightful and revealing interpretations of Thompson (1976) and Fagg (1982) about the expression of values in Yoruban art and architecture are directly relevant here, but we are dealing now with some of the mythological material introduced in earlier chapters. The myths about the *orichas* fall into the second-order category of assumptions. They are useful, nevertheless.

It is difficult from a distance (far removed from intensive field research) to infer both first-order and second-order assumptions. They are, as Kearney indicates, more easily cast as propositions. In order to make the point about this distinction, understandings drawn from specific mythological materials are set forth below, first as second-order assumptions and then refined further as propositions. The exercise is designed to illustrate the application of Kearney's model to the analysis of mythology.

We begin with some of the assumptions in the Yoruban myth of Olodumare in chapter 9, pages 165–66. We do so while keeping in mind two important points: 1) the heterogeneity of the belief system in West Africa, and 2) the importance of the *babalaos'* traditions derived from the *odus* of Ifá. Issues surrounding the role of the Supreme Being are summarized on pages 167–170 and 175 and will not be reviewed here. Instead I simply wish to make clear that the version of the Yoruban myth of Olodumare and the descriptions of the Supreme Being previously introduced allow us to attempt to clarify the distinction between Kearney's assumptions and propositions.

ASSUMPTIONS

Important assumptions that seem to underlie the Yoruban myths and descriptions of Olodumare include the following:

- There is a Supreme Being who dwells in a realm separate from the planet.
- This Being is the source of all power and life in the universe.
- The Supreme Being created the earth.
- The power of the Supreme Being reflected in the earth created all of nature.
- The aspects of power of the Supreme Being residing in the earth and nature created the orishas.

- The power of the orishas is tied to specific aspects of nature and topography.
- The power resides unevenly in things created.
- All power reflects both positive (good) and negative (evil) characteristics.
- The Supreme Being balanced the components of both good and evil as aspects of all things created.

The observer takes into consideration (makes explicit) the second-order assumptions inherent in the mythology expressed by *babalaos* and *oriatés* whose social roles require such expertise. The observer then constructs a model to reflect that worldview as accurately as possible. This model is then stated in the form of propositions (hypothetical statements). In this case, they are inferred from the mythology alone. For more general analysis the propositions would be inferred from assumptions underlying all social behavior and expressive productions of the people whose worldview is being studied (Kearney 1984: 48).

PROPOSITIONS

Propositions inferred from second-order assumptions underlying Yoruban Olodumare mythology may be presented as follows:

- Everything in the universe is alive with the power that emanates from a Supreme Being whose dwelling place is distinct from that of the earth.
- Power is unevenly distributed, both vertically (hierarchically) and horizontally (geographically/topographically).
- Both positive (good) and negative (evil) power resides in all things created.
- It is the intention of the Supreme Being that there be balance in the created world that manifests aspects of his power.

Both heterogeneity and the traditions of *babalaos* and *oriatés* influenced by the *odus* of Ifá apply in Cuba as well as in West Africa. However, there is no question that the collection of myths from Cuba about Olodumare generates slightly divergent second-order assumptions. This suggests that some fundamental changes were occurring in the first-order assumptions of core values in Cuba as opposed to those in Yorubaland.

We see this in some cult houses, in the greater emphasis upon Olodumare as a tired weakened old god removed from the affairs of the living, as summarized on pages 172–75 at the end of chapter 9. Such changes continue, and currently in Miami there is the suggestion that Olodumare's status may be strengthening.

Kearney's analytic approach has great power in making explicit second-order assumptions reflected in mythology and in setting forth propositions based upon such inferences. It is probable that a different collection of myths about Olodumare would generate slightly divergent second-order assumptions. It is unlikely, however that first-order assumptions about the nature of Causality and Self-Other relationships underlying second-order assumptions would differ. Presumably, the propositions introduced by the observer—or by observers engaged in comparative studies—would have the capacity to identify the stability or changing nature of core beliefs as well as the stability or changing nature of second-order assumptions. The implication for the analysis of cultural continuity and change is self-evident.

Another example of the use of propositions in outlining perceptions of reality based upon mythology is provided by reference to a specific myth about the origin of good and evil introduced earlier in chapter 10, pages 176–80. This is an involved accounting that contains many images and assumptions about Santería's worldview. A listing of these would cover several pages. A set of propositions, however, conveys the same basic understanding in a more condensed form.

- There is a Supreme Being who created a world of beauty and harmony held in balance by shared responsibilities of his representatives, the gods of heaven and earth and lesser divinities.
- The balance and harmony created by the Supreme Being should not be challenged.
- Honor and respect should be shown to those whom the Supreme Being has given power, assigned rank, and specific responsibilities.
- Ruptures in the social fabric have consequences that affect the entire web of life on earth.
- Great offenses against those to whom the Supreme Being has given assigned roles and authority must be punished.
- Punishment, retaliation, and revenge further disrupt the balance of beauty and harmony in life.
- The consequences of such disruptions include the appearance and expansion of evil in the world.
- There is a way to restore order in such circumstances, but it requires contact with the offended god or gods.
- The most unlikely messenger to the gods is the one who succeeds in making contact.
- Communication with the god (or gods) requires humility, cleansing, supplication, and appropriate offerings to show honor and respect to the legitimate bearers of the power given them by the Supreme Being.

- The restoration of order is possible, but the evil that entered the world at the beginning of creation is still present and must be dealt with by all earth dwellers.

The important point to be made is that the analysis of both first-order and second-order assumptions, combined with sets of propositions, helps us understand processes of culture change in a way that cannot be achieved by means of more superficial and descriptive efforts.

Logico-Structural Integration

Kearney's concept of logico-structural integration has been utilized in previous chapters as a way to explain some of the changes described in the emergence and evolution of Santería in colonial and republican Cuba. There are two connections that need to be made in this context. The first is the connection between assumptions and behavior; the second is between assumptions, logico-structural integration, and behavior.

Kearney (1984:53) makes the connection between worldview assumptions and behavior as follows: "Our link from these abstractions to behavior is . . . that specific world views result in certain patterns of action and not others. Therefore, knowledge of a people's world view should explain aspects of their cultural behavior. . . . [M]any different kinds of behavior are predicated on relatively few world-view assumptions, such that once the assumptions are understood we are in a position to predict many other different behaviors and meanings, and to understand relationships among them."

A simple but telling example of this point is the Yoruban reluctance (or refusal) to respond to being called by name unless the person calling is seen, known, and trusted. The reason for this behavior is not immediately understood. But when a Yoruban basic assumption is made explicit about the power inherent in spoken words and the possible use of such power in malign magic, this behavior is understandable as being congruent with that assumption. Many other behaviors in Yoruban culture and in Santería, such as the positive use of incantation, singing, and drumming, reflect the underlying assumption related to causality and power in the spoken word, the singing of words, and communication by means of consecrated drums.

Kearney cites Kenneth Boulding on this matter: "[A] world view is not merely a philosophical by-product of each culture . . . but the very skeleton of concrete cognitive assumptions on which the flesh of customary behavior is hung. World view, accordingly, may be expressed, more or less systematically, in cosmology, philosophy, ethics, religious ritual . . . and so on, but it is implicit in almost every act" (Boulding 1956:143; Kearney 1984:53).

The connection between assumptions, the concept of logico-structural integration, and behavior is central to the discussion of continuities and changes identified from the comparison of orishas in Africa and the *orichas* in Cuba. The concept helps to define the ways in which worldview assumptions are interrelated and affect cultural behavior. Kearney's explanation, quoted in the preface, bears repeating here:

> The organization of world-view assumptions is shaped in two ways. The first of these is due to internal equilibrium dynamics among them. This means that some assumptions and the resultant ideas, beliefs, and actions predicated on them are *logically* and *structurally* more compatible than others, and that the entire world view will "strive" toward maximum logical and structural consistency. The second and main force giving coherence and shape to a world view is the necessity of having to relate to the external environment. In other words, human social behavior, social structure, institutions, and customs are consistent with assumptions about the nature of the world. Therefore, in given environments, some such assumptions are more functional than others, and are therefore more subject to positive selective pressures. (Kearney 1984:52)

Furthermore, "the examination of such moving equilibria among assumptions is thus tantamount to an analysis of culture change" (Kearney 1984:52). Inasmuch as Kearney (1984:59) sees worldviews as "having a tendency to strive toward consistency," internal contradictions become bothersome, "and the 'system' strives to resolve or minimize them."

In his view "logical consistency . . . represents the logical aspect of logico-structural integration." This has to do with consistency and inconsistency among propositions and not with thoughts (1984:60). In his words (1984:61), "world-view propositions are consistent or inconsistent in the same way that a well-constructed novel is 'logically' consistent."

"The 'structural' aspect of logico-structural integration refers to various types of replications in the forms of world-view images and assumptions that can be seen as permutations of more primary ones" (1984:62). These are readily apparent in the myths of Santería introduced in previous chapters. According to Kearney (1984:62), "It is these other systematic relationships existing among world-view assumptions which I refer to by the catchall term 'structural,' and hence the term 'logico-structural integration.'" Despite certain qualifications, Kearney (1984:53) asserts the following: "This model assumes . . . that there is an inherent economy of basic cognitive orientations—world view—that tend to result in logico-structural uniformities in all spheres of sociocultural behavior."

He stresses the systematic nature and internal consistency of worldviews but considers one of the most intriguing problems in worldview analysis to be the identification of inconsistencies. Kearney (1984:54) differentiates two basic types of inconsistencies—external ones and internal ones: "'External inconsistencies' in a world view result when its images or assumptions are maladaptive or otherwise inappropriate for the reality that world view presumably mirrors. Thus, at a given point in its history a world view may be a satisfactory cognition of the environment. That is, the culturally patterned perceptions of that environment and the organization of those percepts into concepts are not only internally consistent . . . but also serve to organize behavior such that it is meaningful and adaptive. The study of culture change in general . . . is fundamentally the analysis of this fit or lack of fit between world view and environment."

Internal inconsistencies, in contrast, result from contradictions among the images or assumptions of a worldview. "Such inconsistencies often result from assumptions of one historic period being retained into another in which a new social order has generated a different set of assumptions" (Kearney 1984:58).

The listing of congruencies in cultural images and behaviors in chapter 2 made clear the ease with which elements of both Yoruban religion and the popular piety of Spanish Catholicism were similar enough that merging and transculturation could occur.

Noncongruencies were acknowledged in specific instances, but in part 2 a more extensive examination of inconsistencies helped to explain the changes that occurred in the retention or loss of certain *orichas* in Santería's pantheon as well as the changes that occurred in their characteristics, personalities, and functions.

Both internal and external factors were involved in these processes. Logico-structural inconsistencies surely introduced strain that, in some cases, was not easily resolved. Examples of "structural" inconsistencies in the search for logico-structural integration are suggested in the case of Obatalá and other *orichas*, which displayed many paths, or manifestations, in Cuba.

Obatalá is a creator god, and such gods with different names were of primary importance in Africa over large areas through long periods of time. Generally, myths about Obatalá reflect underlying images of hierarchy and high status. In Cuba, however, Obatalá became identified with less-known regional creator gods as well as non-Yoruban creator gods. These myths reveal great inconsistencies in his or her character and attributes. Two interpretations are possible here.

On the one hand, with so many disparate "structural" elements to consider, logical consistency could not be achieved. It is possible that the conscious or unconscious strain toward logical-structural integration could be resolved only by accepting all of the inconsistencies in the form of a great number of *caminos*, or manifestations, of this powerful and relatively pure creator god in Santería's pantheon.

Among the array of myths about Obatalá, first-order assumptions about power, hierarchy, and status seem to have been retained, but the logical inconsistencies of second-order assumptions about gender, personality, role, function, and other attributes could not simultaneously be accepted as reflecting the character of Obatalá in Cuba. It is conceivable that logico-structural integration could be achieved only to the extent that multiple paths of Obatalá could be incorporated into his/her cult. It would seem that this type of interpretation would apply, also, to other *orichas* in Santería with a great number of logically incompatible manifestations.

On the other hand, a very different interpretation may be offered with regard to the contradictory manifestations of any particular *oricha*. This is because two of the first-order assumptions in Yoruban and Santerían worldviews are 1) that power is manifested in many different ways and 2) that both good and evil are inherent attributes of all life-forms, including gods and humans, male and female, and so forth. The power within all life-forms may be activated in both positive and negative ways: the cool and the hot; the harmless and the dangerous; through peace and rage; through nurturance and revenge; and in all the behavioral consequences implied in such duality. In the long run, these may be as unlimited as the human imagination can differentiate.

It may be that what appear to be "structural *inconsistencies*" from the worldview perceptions of an observer are "structural *consistencies*" in the worldview of devotees of Santería. These seemingly noncongruent elements may all "make sense" within the framework of Yoruban and Santerían worldviews. It is possible that a full analysis of first-order assumptions would lead to the conclusion that, from such a perspective, they are logically consistent.

In short, so far as our understanding goes at this point in time, the many paths of the oldest and most popular *orichas* in Santeria may be understood either as structural *inconsistencies* in the quest for logico-structural integration or as structural *consistencies* in the same process.

The case for the latter interpretation is strengthened somewhat, for example, by some of the different paths of Yemayá, who in Cuba is the personification of the ocean or the sea (sometimes calm; sometimes rough); as the personification of vigor and passion (either male or female); as a god who also lives in brackish waters and even in sewers and latrines. It would seem that many of Yemayá's attributes in various manifestations are meaningful as extensions from the vastness and power of the ocean and the sea into brackish water, and even sewers and latrines.

Much more work needs to be done on the matter of structural consistencies and inconsistencies in the quest for logico-structural integration. There is still the matter of *logical* consistencies and inconsistencies to be considered next.

Examples of "logical" inconsistencies in the quest for logico-structural integration are also provided by the myths discussed in part 2. These relate to analyses regarding loss of, altered, enhanced, or diminished roles of Yoruban gods in Santería's pantheon. They point to difficulties individuals must have had in relating their worldviews to the external environment in Cuba. In Kearney's terms, such difficulties represent "logical" inconsistencies.

Assumptions about the nature of the world in Africa did not match the conditions of existence in the new setting. Conditions of life in the new land were not always congruent with the need for and relationship with divinities with specific attributes and roles. In other words, the requirements of life in Cuba were no longer consistent with prior worldview assumptions about the nature of the world. The changes that occurred in assumptions about the nature of reality in Cuba contributed to changes in the pantheon of gods that made them more logically consistent with that newly perceived reality.

The consequence of such striving for logico-structural integration in the worldview of Santería's devotees would account for the changes described in the conclusion to part 2. The summary listing of those changes already provided will not be reviewed here, but they illustrate the potential value of Kearney's worldview model for understanding cultural continuity and change within the religious sphere.

It is important to note that the transplantation of Santería into the United States offered the same type of previously described ethos and consciousness of reality within its house-temples. This worldview now resides in a very different socioenvironmental setting—a setting in which there are far greater inconsistencies in ethos and worldview assumptions than were present in Cuba. Some recent and current new trends observed in the practice of Santería in very different historical and socioenvironmental contexts are discussed in the two final chapters. They are an attempt to discuss some of the changes that have occurred in Santería in Cuba and in the Diaspora after the establishment of Castro's revolutionary government; also in the Yoruban religion in Nigeria. In addition current trends observable in Santería, which has now gained a following among people who are neither African descendants nor Cuban, will be reviewed.

Santería in the Twenty-First Century

The changes experienced by the Yoruban religion in Cuba enabled it not only to survive but to serve as a vehicle for the retention of aspects of Yoruban language, music, mythology, and dance within the framework of a partially retained Yoruban worldview. Its evolution also facilitated its acceptance by Afro-Cubans of non-Yoruban descent. Many of them, attracted by its richness and complexity, abandoned the practices of their forefathers and made the Yoruban religion and its practices their own.

For similar reasons the religion attracted many Cubans of non-African ancestry. Santería provided economic, moral, and emotional nourishment by offering membership in a supportive religious lineage, a sense of control through magical manipulation of supernatural forces, and the alleviation of symptoms of ill health by reassuring the afflicted through the engagement of supernatural power for healing purposes (Cros Sandoval 1979).

Santería was also able to break through social, class, and racial boundaries. It attracted a significant following and was able to influence the cosmology, worldview, and behavior of a variety of sectors of the population.

However, in the 1950s, followers of Santería were a small minority in Cuba. From its original cradles in and around the city of Havana and the province of Matanzas, Santería had spread to other areas but not everywhere on the island. Even though some popular music borrowed rhythms and lyrics from Santería's liturgical music, most Cubans had never been directly exposed to its beliefs and practices. Moreover, Santería was perceived to reflect practices and superstitions prevalent among some segments of the mostly black underclass. Mass communication, however, contributed to the breakdown of regional isolation and facilitated the spread of Santería.

Marcos Antonio Ramos (2002:1) refers to a survey published by the Catholic University Association in 1957. It reported that 72.5 percent of the population identified itself as Catholic, while in the rural areas the percentage was only 52 percent. In that survey 68 percent of the lower class identified itself as strictly Catholic versus 88 percent of the middle class and 99 percent of the upper class. However, it seems that in the 1950s the religious interests and participation of Cubans ranged from the Catholic orthodox view to a heterodox Catholic-saint worship. A folksy Catholicism, described in chapter 2 under "Popular Piety in Colonial and Republican Cuba," was widespread among Cubans, especially among the low-income groups. This meant that the individual, although identified as a Catholic and as a member of the Catholic Church, felt free to practice concurrently Catholicism, Spiritualism, and Santería, as well as other religious practices. Moreover, among many members of the most educated classes, there was a liberal perception of religious affiliation and loyalty vocalized in the popular idiomatic expression "I am Catholic my own way." This indicated that the person could deviate from church dogma on issues such as birth control, divorce, and other matters and could also explore other religious practices. Such persons would not acquiesce to church requirements regarding weekly attendance at mass, yearly confessions, and communion without experiencing great discomfort.

By the 1950s various Protestant denominations had also developed strong roots in Cuba, and participation in Allan Kardec's spiritualist practices remained very strong. Many people explored Santería, other Afro-Cuban religions, and still other less-structured cults and religious practices, such as *muertería*. These manifestations of mixed religious beliefs and behaviors coexisted. Many individuals participated in several of the above-mentioned practices at the same time or consecutively. This ambiance did not survive the political, social, and economic turmoil of the 1960s.

Castro's Revolution dramatically and abruptly changed all aspects of Cuban life. The names of streets, buildings, and locations were changed as well as the labor and holiday calendars. History was rewritten according to socialist revolutionary goals and ideals. The revolutionary position asserted that nothing worthy had ever been achieved in Cuba before Castro took power.

As a result, the ongoing process of spontaneous cultural accommodation and evolution was drastically altered by the imposition of a totalitarian communist regime. The revolution's atheistic, materialistic, and dogmatic stance confronted and challenged the mystic/spiritual, humanist, and personalistic ambiance that had long been developing in the emerging Cuban Creole culture. This culture, characterized by the interrelatedness and melding of different ethnic traditions, was full of contradictions, ambiguities, and conflicts.

Castro's Revolution brought down the last bastions of racism (private schools, social clubs, and recreational facilities), and sought to socialize younger generations in a color-blind ethic (de la Fuente 2001:337). These policies brought about an even closer interaction between people of different races and members of formerly different social classes. These measures facilitated the exposure to Santería's followers by people who normally would not have been aware of them.

However, the revolution's de facto cult to the personality of revolutionary leaders allowed little space for the open worship of supernatural beings. The revolution did not tolerate competition in worldview or loyalty. Tolerance and exceptions, even in gray areas, became a capital offense. Open or simulated adherence to the loud revolutionary dogmatic slogans was required for survival. As Castro himself told the intellectuals in a 1961 speech: "Dentro de la Revolución todo, fuera de la Revolución nada" (Within the revolution everything: outside the revolution, nothing).[1]

In Castro's Cuba, interethnic cultural borrowing and sharing has been supplanted by a foreign, materialistic, impersonal, atheistic, and rigorously dogmatic Marxist culture. Castro's branch of Marxism clashed with the ego-integrative undercurrents of the emerging Creole culture. Thus, loyalty to family, neighbors, and friends was judged as counterrevolutionary. Love of life and its enjoyment ran counter to the proclaimed austerity of revolutionary ethics. The emerging Creole ideal personality—the family-oriented, friendly, generous, witty, and fun-loving *campechano* (Cros Sandoval 1986:61–63) that so many Cubans admired and identified with—now had to confront and reflect the new man: the revolution's authoritarian, dogmatic, yet submissive zealot. Thus, the characteristics of an incipient national identity that the Creoles had nourished was shattered by the Castro Revolution.

Santería in Cuba: The Post-revolutionary Period

The revolutionary government initially frowned upon all religious beliefs and practices. The first targets of the Castro regime were institutionalized religions such as the Catholic and Protestant churches. These churches were either structured around a central hierarchy, had international connections or headquarters, or both. They were more threatening to the revolution than Santería and other Afro-Cuban religions and were subjected to amply documented persecution (Alfonso 1985; Clark 1985; Marcos Ramos 1986, 2002).

The government seized all private schools, including those owned and operated by churches. This policy destroyed the community roots of those churches. Foreign-born priests were expelled from the island, and some churches were left unattended since there were not enough priests to care for the flock.

The regime successfully undertook policies to discourage church attendance and participation. Individuals who attended church were not eligible for scholarships to pursue lucrative careers, or obtain promotions, opportunities, and benefits. Worse yet, they were suspected of being disloyal to the revolution. In other words, any form of Christian practice was a hindrance to social advancement because it was viewed as alien and counter-revolutionary.[2]

Individuals active in churches became the targets of derisive comments and harassment. Consequently, many of the faithful, afraid of reprisals from the government, abstained from going to church and, especially, from bringing their young into its midst. Moreover, the establishment by the revolution of a

Marxist-Leninist state fostered membership in the Communist Party, whose philosophy denied any religious belief and/or practice, further weakening religion on the island.

Without a centralized hierarchy and, at that time, without foreign support, Santería and other Afro-Cuban religions and cults were less threatening to Castro's regime. Still, the government was not amenable to allowing gatherings and meetings beyond its control or sponsorship, since such group activities could evolve into a nucleus of opposition to the regime.

Freedom of association was totally repressed when, after 1959, a governmental permit was required to hold any celebration. This policy placed restrictions on the practice of Santería by requiring practitioners to apply for permits in order to celebrate festivals. In most instances, these permits, when granted, scheduled the festivals during hours that contravened traditional religious practices. The government also forbade the initiation of minors into Santería. Nevertheless, despite these restrictions, the extent of persecution and discrimination experienced by Santería's followers was far less than that suffered by Christians.

As the revolution unfolded, the regime made numerous attempts to emphasize the African legacy to Cuban culture. Such undertakings were probably designed to gain the support of the large numbers of Cubans of African descent, while encouraging the creation and development of a Third World identity. This effort also catered to the political ambitions of Castro's regime in Africa, as exemplified by military interventions in Angola, Ethiopia, and the Congo.

Toward these ends, the government generously sponsored concerts, plays, ballet exhibitions, and all types of artistic events inspired by Afro-Cuban themes, while other important roots of Cuban culture were not emphasized. In many instances, this policy enhanced the awareness and image of Afro-Cuban religions in the public sphere, but it also weakened the religion's spirituality, mysticism, and mystery. According to Katherine Hagedorn (2001:68), "The divine utterances of religious performance (which are sacred non-commercial, nonstaged and directed inward) are translated, much like an obscure language into a more broadly understood 'lingua folklorica,' the language of folkloric performance, which is secularized, staged, commodified, and directed outward, toward the audience." Government-sponsored events fostered the view that these religious practices were part of Cuban "folklore" and not expressions of faith in the supernatural.[3]

At the same time, the internal population movements that were intentionally fostered by the regime, in many instances, caused permanent disruption to the subcultural enclaves that nourished and were in turn nourished by this religion. Thus, in revolutionary Cuba, Santería gained in public presence as folklore, much to the detriment of its secretive and mysterious aura.

Currently, the government continues to regularly sponsor international conferences, workshops, exhibits, and publications about Santería. This approach has opened the religion internationally to practitioners as well as academicians.

As a result, there has been much popular and scholarly discussion about the involvement of important officials of the Castro regime in Afro-Cuban religions. Since the start of the revolution there have been persistent rumors about Fidel Castro's involvement with practices of "black magic." Photographs have substantiated these rumors, and newsreels taken during Castro's visits to Ghana and Guinea in the 1970s show him dressed in white in the midst of a river, as if participating in some type of ceremony.

The official Cuban press circulated this information and, whether intended or not, these images of Castro have given him stature as the receptacle of formidable spiritual powers. Similar to the situation of François Duvalier, the former Haitian dictator, the mystery of "black magic" has strengthened Castro's aura of invincibility. Moreover, many Santería believers relish these rumors about Castro since they do give great credibility to the efficacy of Santería's magical practices as reflected in Castro's lengthy term as a dictator.

It is worth noting that, following an opportunistic tradition, when Castro came down from Sierra Maestra in 1959 after Batista had fled the country, many of his followers wore rosaries as necklaces, portraying themselves as pious and religious people. This type of display was strange since women were primarily the ones who prayed the rosaries and practically nobody used them as necklaces, much less men. Also, during Castro's first speech in the city of Havana, two white pigeons came and stood on his shoulders, augmenting views of his stature as somebody with supernatural powers.

Actually, there is neither proof nor any witness to confirm Castro's participation in Afro-Cuban religions. Everything about his private life has been kept entirely secret. Nevertheless, it has been known since the beginning of the revolution that close associates of Castro do practice Santería.

Rolando Vallejo, who was popularly called Barbarojas (Red Beard) and was Castro's personal physician until his death, practiced Santería. It is also rumored that Castro's closest associate, Celia Sanchez, was initiated into Santería. Abelardo Hernández confided to me that when she died, a *santero* initiated in the cult of Oyá, the *oricha* of the cemetery, was called to perform a ceremony. Santería does not demand exclusivity of its followers and, as a result, there would be no dissonance between atheistic Marxism and the religious practices of Santería.

The regime's ambivalent posture toward Santería and other Afro-Cuban religions has contributed to their increased visibility throughout the island. This situation has possibly encouraged a swelling in the numbers of followers.

Moreover, the subversion of Western European Christian values and mores, upheld by the decimated upper and middle classes, has resulted in the acceptance and adoption by the majority of the population of behaviors, figures of speech, and mannerisms that formerly were considered coarse, unpolished, and characteristic of the underclass. Within these parameters, Santería, which in the past was perceived as lower-class superstition, emerged as more acceptable in the context of the proletarian and Third-World ways of the revolution. These changes supported the elimination of many prejudices against Santería; thus, the search for refuge in this religion by large segments of the population was facilitated.

Other conditions prevalent on the island during the last forty-five years have also favored the acceptance and practice of Santería by large segments of the population, regardless of racial or social background. The traumatic changes brought about by the totalitarian system have caused great feelings of loss, confusion, and cultural exhaustion. A response to the need to demonstrate loyalty to the revolution at the expense of one's own opinions, emotions, and interests has been the emergence of an ambivalent *doble moral* (dual morality).[4] This self-censorship has resulted in a loss of self-esteem and a general sense of disillusionment, alienation, and hopelessness.

In Communist Cuba, the verb *resolver* (to solve) is used constantly. It reflects the struggle and frustration present in the way Cubans live. They are engaged in the daily routine of overcoming very prosaic but important problems that constantly require their quotidian energy and attention. Concerns with the afterlife and with transcendence have no room in the lives of individuals so overwhelmed. People spend their time, day after day, trying to obtain the bare essentials of living by standing in line after line to secure a few beans, some oil, a piece of clothing, or other meager material goods for survival. The majority of Cuban people wake up every day to face the possibility of hunger, unreliable transportation to work, and frequent power shortages. These examples illustrate the helplessness and general lack of control that characterizes the life of the average Cuban on the island.

For most Cubans, the essentials of life are controlled by the regime: housing, food supplies, schooling, and transportation. In many instances, the regime's decisions are quite unpredictable. Thus, Cubans have largely become resigned to the idea that luck, not determination, hard work, or planning, is the determiner of fate. Under such circumstances, magic has grown in appeal.

In recent years, the Castro government has tried, with some degree of success, to attract some *babalaos* and to use them for intelligence gathering and rumor control. The government sponsors a group called La Asociación Cultural Yoruba that includes around 425 *babalaos.* It has given this organization a building on Paseo del Prado Avenue. A few *babalaos* from Miami have also joined this association.

The association operates as an umbrella organization of *babalaos* who act as government representatives. Foreigners, who come to Cuba to participate in conferences and workshops and who show some interest in participating in or being initiated into Santería, are referred by the government to the *babalaos* of the association. The government keeps half of the initiation fees paid by those who choose to be initiated, and the other half is paid to the priests who perform the initiation ceremonies.

These new foreign recruits are, in many instances, demanding changes in Santería's practices. The training they receive is minimal due to the pressures of time. In some instances the ceremonies of initiation have to be shortened from seven to fewer days in order to accommodate their needs. Other ceremonies are changed to accommodate their sensibilities. In general many of them do not wish to or cannot comply with the strict requirements. The role the Cuban government plays in the recruitment of these neophytes and in promoting changes in the religion is documented by Katherine Hagedorn (2001: 221): "Such changes in the comfort and transparency of the initiation ceremony are encouraged by the Cuban government, which has gotten into the business of religious tourism through what is ironically referred to as the Ochatur program."

The government supported the reopening of a *cabildo* in 1998. The site of this *cabildo* and that of the Asociación Cultural Yoruba are included in most visitor tours of the various tourist companies. In addition, the government sponsors all types of festivals in which the *babalaos* participate.

These *babalaos* are called *diplo-babalaos*, because they have access to the *diplo-tiendas*, the stores where the client carrying dollars can buy goods not available to the broader Cuban population. Juan Clark (1992:509–10) documents the fact that these stores, in the past, catered exclusively to high-level government officials and foreign diplomats. The popular name *diplo-tiendas* means precisely "stores for diplomats." Presently they are open to anybody with dollars.

Traditionally, on New Year's Day in pre-Castro Cuba, a group of *babalaos* gathered in the town of Palmira in Las Villas and in the city of Havana to announce the Letra del Año, the *odu*, or sign, that would preside and rule over the coming year. The *babalao* Jorge Torres claims that the Letra del Año has Nigerian antecedents since, during the yam festival around June 17, babalawos used to make predictions for the following year.

According to Wilfredo Fernández Jr. (March 2001), at midnight on December 31 this ceremony with Olofin is celebrated. The *babalaos* make a circle with candles and, using twelve pieces of bread instead of nuts or chains, they search for the sign of the year. The sign tells which *orichas* will play prominent roles during the coming year and what impact they will have in human and terrestrial terms. Currently, due to the growth and expansion experienced by Santería, these gatherings of *babalaos* take place in Havana, Miami, New York, Puerto Rico, Mexico, and Canada. Generally, over a hundred *babalaos* participate in each of these ceremonies.

The *babalaos* who are members of La Asociación Cultural Yoruba of Cuba meet in their locale on New Year's Day to announce the sign or letter of the year, which, in most instances, is interpreted in ways favorable to the government. Another credible and influential group of *babalaos* not associated with the Cuban government meet at La Casona (large house) on Tenth of October Avenue to make their own predictions.

The findings of one large group of Miami-based *babalaos* indicate that Yemayá and Obatalá would rule during the year 2005, with Saint Lazarus as spiritual backup. Another group of *babalaos* from Miami identified the *orichas* Oyá and Agayú. According to La Asociación Cultural Yoruba, Obatalá and Ochún were to rule, and according to the *babalaos* who meet in La Casona, Changó and Oyá were to rule.

When I discussed the discrepancy in the readings with a group of *babalaos*, Jorge Torres (January 11, 2005) responded that even though the *letras* were different, there was consistency in their advice. The *babalao* Leonel Céspedes (January 11, 2005) said that each *babalao* takes out the sign that is pertinent to his *rama* (lineage). Javier Echeverría (2003) reports that Yemayá ruled in 2002, Elegguá, in 2003, and Obatalá in 2004.

Jesus Fernández Cano (2000) documents the growth and importance of Santería in Cuba under Castro. In Fernández's view, Santería has grown in importance due to its ability to provide many believers with an identity alien to and separate from the materialistic ambiance of revolutionary Cuba. In spite of the government's attempt to manipulate and control Santería's practices, Fernández's research reveals Santería's true appeal to young Cuban professionals and even officers of Castro's regime.

In summary, Santería inside Cuba has grown in popularity both because of state policy and the appeal of magic in an uncertain world. Focused on solving problems of the here and now, Santería has once more demonstrated its efficacy in assisting people to ameliorate the circumstances of their existence and the consequences suffered while adapting to harsh new ways, much like the Yoruban religion did for African slaves in colonial Cuba.

Santería in the Diaspora

During the past forty-five years, Santería has served as an important support system for many Cubans exiled from their homeland and suffering from the stress caused by accommodation to the customs and environment of a new country. This is especially so in the United States. At the start of the revolution, many Cubans began to flee the island. Over two million Cubans have left since 1959. In all, approximately 20 percent of the Cuban people have thus "voted with their feet" (Cros Sandoval 1986:9).

It has always been easier for people who reside in or around Havana to leave the island. Government offices and embassies are located in the capital. Consequently, obtaining the required exit permits and visas is easier there. As a result, *habaneros* were over-represented in the first waves of Cuban exiles. This demographic reality influenced the spread of Santería. Havana had been one of the largest centers of the religion, and a significant number of *santeros* were able to leave Havana when the Cuban exodus began. It should be noted, however, that the uprooting experience of exile greatly affected all the Cubans who left the island, *santeros,* Christians, and agnostics alike.

Before the post-Castro exodus began, there were small nuclei of Santería believers in parts of the United States, especially in the areas of New York City and urban New Jersey. However, it was the large numbers of Cubans seeking refuge in the United States in the 1960s and 1970s that gave Santería a true visibility there. Cubans fleeing Castro settled primarily in Miami but also established important enclaves in New York, New Jersey, California, Chicago, and other areas.

Santería underwent some changes while adapting to new conditions in the United States. For instance, traditionally, *iyawós* (the newly initiated) could not look at themselves in a mirror until one year after initiation. In exile, a ceremony was developed to enable the *iyawós* to look at a mirror sooner so they could drive a car. Moreover, in the 1960s drum festivals in Miami were uncommon because *batá* drums could not cross the sea. In reality, however, it is more likely that *santeros* were afraid that their non-Cuban neighbors would call the police. Currently, with the growth of the Cuban population, *batá* drums are played in most ceremonies. It is explained that the problem of the prohibition of *batá* drums was resolved by using the airplane to carry them over.

Since the beginning of the Cuban Diaspora, Santería has enjoyed as well as suffered from much media attention. In the United States, television programs, newspapers, and popular magazines have been fascinated by Santería. The phenomenon of white *santeros* has been especially puzzling to the press. While reporting on Santería in the United States and elsewhere the media have also reported on what were perceived as bizarre sacrifices of animals.[5] With increasing appearances of sacrificed animals in rivers, by railroad tracks, at intersections, by sacred trees, and in other places in Miami and elsewhere, some alarmed residents have contacted the Humane Society. Others have called the local police to denounce the practices of Santería. The interactions between the police and *santeros* have also brought frequent, though not positive, visibility to Santería because the press has been eager to cover these esoteric practices and inform the public about them.

The story about murders committed in Matamoros, Mexico, in April 1989, by drug dealers who allegedly were members of a cult that used human sacrifices as offerings for protection, elicited the public's horrified attention to the media's coverage in national and international news.[6] Since some of the leaders of the group nominally practiced Santería and other Afro-Cuban religions, negative light was again cast on the religion. It came to the point that some *santeros* felt that they needed to defend their religion and practices.[7] A Hollywood movie called *The Believers,* with well-known actors such as Martin Sheen and Jimmy Smits, brought even more dubious public exposure and attention to this religion.

Outside of Cuba, Santería has undergone significant change. Many such changes were caused by the unique circumstances in which some of the exiled practitioners found themselves in the United States. Others resulted from Santería's adaptation to the needs of the believers and of the new following it was attracting.

One important factor was demographic. The number of blacks who left Cuba in the 1960s and 1970s was, percentage-wise, below the incidence of the black population on the island. Therefore, the Cuban population in exile was not representative of the racial configuration of the island. Thus, the Yoruban religion, brought to Cuba by African slaves, was uprooted again, now in a transculturalized, Cubanized form.

Once more displaced, the religion was brought out of Cuba by *santeros,* many of whom were of non-African descent. Consequently, many white *santeros* achieved positions of preeminence in diasporic Santería. This significant circumstance resulted in the perception of a "whitening" trend within the religion.

In many instances, this whitening trend de-emphasized some of the religion's former important functions. For many black Cubans the religion of the *orichas* is more than a religion; it is the core of their ethnic identity. This religion is an integral part of their cultural history, something uniquely theirs, which survived assimilation to the European cultural patterns that were dominant on the island. As such, it provides its followers with an important group identity as well as a degree of cultural and historical continuity. As expressed by Ezequiel Torres (June 2005), "I know my roots, I know where I come from, I know my heritage."[8]

This function is important for people of African ancestry regardless of national origin. Marta Moreno Vega, a Puerto Rican raised in New York, director of the Center for Caribbean Studies in New York, and an author expresses this function and appeal very clearly: "I was initiated into the Lucumí religion, popularly known as Santería, in 1981 in Havana, Cuba. In search of a religion that reflected my racial and cultural heritage, I was led to Cuba by the spirits of my ancestors" (2000:3). Among whites, however, this function has never been meaningful. My own extensive fieldwork in Miami has shown that the functions of Santería as a supportive social and economic network and complementary health-care system have been augmented (Cros Sandoval 1979). Practitioners, who regularly frequent *ilé ochas*, or a *santero's* house-temple, become part of an intimate, religious family that can take the place of estranged or fragmented families. These *ilé ochas* maintain an open-door policy toward their members and offer a realm of ritual activities filled with opportunities to socialize and receive moral and emotional support. Moreover, this fictive family gives assistance in solving daily problems and interpersonal conflicts.

This enhanced function of Santería has turned it into a viable mental health delivery system, which offers support, counseling, and socialization opportunities to many people who are suffering from the tensions that characterize acculturation and deculturation processes. Santería, like many other small cult groups or religious organizations—Christian and otherwise—offers believers a wide social network. They provide people who feel disoriented and alienated and who suffer from feelings of powerlessness, lack of direction, role confusion, or lack of meaningful social roles with a sense of belonging and of importance. Miami's abundant small storefront Hispanic evangelical churches, however, demand strict moral restraints, which Santería does not.

Many new *santeros* and *santeras,* looking for sources of information, found it convenient to reach out to the academic literature about Santería and the Yoruban religion. In Cuba until the 1950s, these consultations would not have been necessary and could even have been considered by senior practitioners to be almost sacrilegious. In Cuba, know-how was acquired orally, through observation, and through participation in the rituals. Knowledge was also transmitted by hand-written notebooks, or *libretas*, especially prepared by the *santero* (godfather) or the *santera* (godmother) for the godchild or neophyte.

For many priests and priestesses, leaving Cuba meant that they had to abandon their godfathers and godmothers and their consecrated religious objects. Furthermore, many newly initiated *santeros* and *santeras,* who had not yet acquired sound knowledge of rituals, magic, and dogma felt handicapped by the interruption of their training under their godparents in the traditional structured apprenticeship. Thus, many new Santería priests and priestesses started or continued their practice with limited knowledge regarding the performance of certain important rituals.

For *santeros* and *santeras* outside Cuba as well as for those on the island, the study of academic literature opened a window to Africa, to the very roots of the religion they were practicing. Moreover, many practitioners initiated contact and correspondence with African and non-African scholars. Some *santeros* and *santeras* visited Nigeria as pilgrims in search of greater understanding and meaning. Others went there to validate their credentials by undergoing specific religious experiences and rituals in their cultural/religious homeland. Finally, there were those who went for the sake of curiosity.

These circumstances opened new avenues for priests and priestesses to learn about their religion in a nontraditional manner. In the United States, Puerto Rico, and elsewhere, they began to attend and participate in conferences about Santería and the Yoruban religion. Many began writing and publishing books, manuals, newspapers, and newsletters about Santería. Thus, they became part of the literary tradition, by means of which they communicate, learn, and expand their knowledge about Santería, the Yoruban religion, and their practices. Presently, some *santeros* have their own Web sites and use the Internet to communicate, advertise their services, and engage in other activities. Often, the language used is English. This development is truly remarkable for a religion that was first practiced secretly by African slaves and later by a primarily black constituency in the shadows of society in pre-revolutionary Cuba.

In 1979 the Castro government allowed members of the exiled community to visit the island for the first time. Many *santeros* visited Cuba and have continued to do so for a variety of reasons: to renew contact with their godparents, to recover some sacred paraphernalia left behind, or to participate in some ritual they needed to experience or learn. These visits strengthened the practice of Santería outside of Cuba.

In 1980, when the Mariel boatlift occurred, many black Cubans were able to leave the island, including many of Santería's priests and practitioners. At first, some complained about the conditions of Santería outside Cuba. They viewed the religion as having become materialistic and opportunistic in exile. Many also felt that they were more knowledgeable than priests already practicing in exile. This attitude was not very different from the views expressed by professionals and technicians who had recently arrived from Cuba concerning those who were trained in the United States.

The Mariel boatlift provided an opportunity to analyze the ways in which both the culture of Cubans in exile since 1960 and that of those who had remained on the island and came in the 1980 boatlift had changed, had diverged from the cultural patterns prevalent in Cuba in the 1950s.

Many differences in cultural patterns were due to the mere passage of time. Others were caused by the difference between the adaptive strategies developed by Cubans in exile *vis-à-vis* those developed by Cubans who remained on the island. The exiled Cubans changed as a result of adjusting to the conditions prevalent in post-industrialized societies. Cubans on the island developed differently as a result of adapting to the drastic changes brought about by a radical Communist revolution combined with isolation from the outside world.[9]

In the final analysis, the exodus of so many Cubans, including *santeros* and *santeras*, greatly encouraged the visibility of Santería outside the island. This resulted in a wide and diverse following, and, as has happened so many times before, Santería changed during the process of accommodations made in the new environment.

The Religion of the Yoruba in Nigeria in the Twentieth Century

At the end of the nineteenth century, the traditional religion of the Yoruba in its Latin-American manifestations of Cuban Santería and Brazilian Candomblé was experiencing significant adaptive changes while engaging a new racially and culturally heterogeneous following. In Nigeria, however, it was in a crisis for survival. When, at the end of the eighteenth century and well into the nineteenth century, great waves of Yoruban people were being sent as slaves to Cuba and Brazil, Yorubaland was ravaged by civil wars between city-states caused in part by the fall of the Oyo Empire.

Peter McKenzie has done extensive research on Yoruban religiosity in the mid-nineteenth century, a period when wars between city-states were at their peak. McKenzie (1997: 28) believes that at that time the Yoruban religion seemed to be more focused on the worship of the earth than of the sky. To McKenzie the manifestations of the supernatural power, or ashe, were more salient in the contours and creatures of the earth than in heavenly bodies. Repeatedly, this researcher described incidents documenting the way in which Yoruban people reported manifestations of the ashe in large stones, piles of rocks, trees, groves, herbs, all types of plants, and many animals.

These findings are revealing because shortly thereafter traditional Yoruban religion would be aggressively encroached upon by Islam and Christianity, both of which are largely devoid of animistic manifestations of supernatural power. Islam had been penetrating tropical Africa from the north for centuries and had already made substantial advances in Nigeria.

The military prowess of Fulani and Hausa Muslims in the eighteenth and nineteenth centuries enabled them to make great inroads in Yorubaland. Thus, most areas of the north and northwest, in Oyo Ile, Ilorin, Ogbomosho, Iwo, new Oyo (territories where the old Oyo Empire had flourished) became and have remained strongly Muslim. The Muslim influence had been felt as far south as Ijebu Ode.

Additionally, during the nineteenth century, Christian missions began to flourish in Yorubaland. This process of growth was given a boost in 1900 with the establishment of the British Protectorate. The eastern area, comprising the territories of Ondo and Owo and the southern enclave around Lagos, became, and remains, predominantly Christian. In the southwestern area, the territories of Ogun and Abeokuta and the area around the sacred city of Ile Ife developed into a balanced Muslim and Christian region.

The traditional Yoruban religion was thus in crisis during the period when thousands of Yoruba were being taken as slaves to the New World. In the geographic area of its origin it was being challenged by Islam and Christianity, as well as by the slaving activity that resulted in thousands of Yorubans being sent to the Americas.

The Yoruban religion became most vulnerable to encroachment by Islam and Christianity at the time of the creation of the British Protectorate. At first the British deposed the obas, or local kings, but within a short period of time the old royalty was restored to power. The British used the kings to exercise indirect rule and to check the power that the unruly military leaders enjoyed as an aftermath of the long period of civil wars (Matory 1994:30–56).

Local chiefs and priests, however, lost their prestige and power under indirect rule. Thus, the civil wars, British influence, Christian missions, and Muslim preeminence greatly weakened the prestige of the traditional religion. One consequence was that many obas readily converted either to Islam or to Christianity. Another consequence was that traditional worship of the orishas suffered among the masses, given the diminished support of the obas.

At that time, the Yoruban traditional religion might have failed to be functional to many Yoruba undergoing the process of modernization. Many members of the upper and middle strata of society identified progress and modernization with the two world religions. In the northern areas of Yorubaland some realized that being Muslim was advantageous for business. In other regions, being Christian not only opened the door for business success but also for desirable public positions in the government.

The research done by David D. Laitin and J. D. Y. Peel, respectively, is most revealing. According to Peel (1983: 167), the answers that respondents gave to the question of why they converted to Islam and Christianity were very shallow: "Everyone was joining, so I joined"; "I wanted to move with them." The most revealing answers that both Peel and Laitin (1986: 37) received were those indicating that they had joined Islam and Christianity "because of civilization;" "because our eyes were opened."

In reality, the meaning of these remarks is that the two world religions were identified with progress, development, and improvements in health care. As expressed by Gbadamosi, "It became fashionable to be a Muslim or a Christian" (Laitin 1986:37). These answers may reveal a weak allegiance to the old gods; that is, keeping the old gods but keeping them underground. In the words of Apter (1992:169): "The impact of Christian conversion on [orisa]-cult member-ships is difficult to determine in any statistical sense because the 'pagan' figures were never recorded. Not all Yoruba were initiated into cults in pre-colonial society; many simply consulted the [orisa] for ritual assistance. At this popular level of participation, Christianity and ritual assistance [orisa] worship are by no means mutually exclusive. Christians still 'beg' the deities for help and at-tend the annual ceremonies. . . . That Christianity displaced [orisa] worship, however, is simply untrue. Within Ekiti kingdoms, communities, and even in-dividuals, both religions coexist."

It seems that in Nigeria a process of adjustment between the traditional Yoruba religion and the two world religions was well underway. This process shows some similarities to the process of adjustment it underwent in Cuba and Brazil. Meaningful equivalents between the cult of the orishas and deified ancestors and the cult of the saints of Muslims and Christians may have eased the pain of adaptation to the demands of these new religions.

In what must be assumed as the search for congruencies, the character and importance of certain deities changed. Eshu, the trickster, the messenger of the gods, and the god of unpredictability, was associated with Satan. As a result, Eshu was perceived as diabolic rather than mischievous. The cult of the old orisha Shopono, the deity of plagues, suffered great damage when allegations were raised against his priests for using their knowledge to spread the diseases they were supposed to treat. In contrast, according to McKenzie (1997:496), the old sky deity, Olodumare, gained prominence through identification or association with either the one Christian or Islamic god.

Nevertheless, there were certain issues in which Islam and Christianity dif-fered radically from Yoruban tradition. The two Abrahamic religions did not allow the worship of supernatural forces other than their own. The pronounced demand for exclusivity and the zealous interest in proselytizing characteristic of these religions represented attitudes that are antagonistic to the traditional religion of the Yoruba.

Despite its deep mysticism and sophisticated theology, the Yoruban religion did not require or impose rigid limits of exclusivity upon religious experiences. It did not show signs of distress in the presence of other religious systems with worldviews compatible with its own. This characteristic may have worked to the detriment of the Yoruban religion's success in fighting off the inroads that Islam and Christianity made in Nigeria—religions that required total allegiance and abandonment of old gods and ritual forms. Paradoxically, the characteristic of openness worked differently in Cuba and Brazil, where people who were baptized as Christians were attracted to the Yoruba-inspired religions and were never forced to abandon their Christian faith.

According to Laitin (1986:34–35), there are three very important differences between traditional Yoruban religion and Islam and Christianity. First, Islam and Christianity, as confessional religions, demand an individual to make a personal confession of faith to a systematic corpus of beliefs. This position is foreign to the traditional Yoruban cultural ethos.

Second, the Yoruban religion is multi-local, not universal. Among the Yoruba, "nationality," in terms of identification with one's ancestral city, practically defined religious affiliation. Yoruban traditional religion was centered on the worship of local and tutelary orishas of a particular town or region and on the cult of the ancestors. Despite their belief in an abstract, unknowable Deity, neither this Deity nor the generic gods of storms, rivers, the sea, and so forth were expanded to comprise all of mankind.

Third, Yoruban practices of worship are restricted. Many of the important rituals are held in private, not as public ritual. There is no counterpart to the weekly required church attendance or group activities in the mosque, where all are expected to participate. In other words, it is not as outwardly visible and community-oriented as are the other two religions.

In any event, based on a multiplicity of factors, traditional Yoruban religion in Nigeria lost stature after the British Protectorate was established in 1900. Currently, many community rituals are still presided over and celebrated by the present obas (kings), who, in many cases, claim they only represent cultural or folkloric manifestations. However, for many these rituals are what they were in the past, an intrinsic part of the worship of the traditional orishas.

Even though at the present time the Yoruba-speaking people are officially either Muslims or Christians, it seems that many still worship the orishas in secret and concurrently with Christianity and Islam. The Yoruba religion is practiced openly primarily in the bush. Professor Wande Abimbola decries this state of affairs in his keynote address, "The Orisha Tradition, a World View," delivered to the First Annual Orisha Tradition Conference at the University of Ile Ife in 1981 (1981:5–7):

> The system of thought and religion which we have all assembled here to speak about has now assumed the dimensions of an international culture. Let me give you a few examples. Speaking with a colleague of mine

in Puerto Rico a few days ago, I was informed that the number of Orisha
... priests and priestesses in Puerto Rico is much more than the number
of Catholic Priests in that country. In Brazil where you have a nation
with one hundred million people, more than half of the population of
that country is directly or indirectly involved with the Orisha culture. In
Cuba, especially before the last twenty years, we probably had more Ifa
priests than in Nigeria. In Trinidad, up till today, we still have Shango
priests and priestesses, some of whom are renowned scholars and pro-
fessors. All over the African Diaspora wherever you go to Colombia or
Peru or Guyana or Honduras or the United States of America, you encounter people who have devoted their lives to the propagation of Orisha
culture. But alas! In Africa, which is the birthplace of this religion, many
of the people of our generation have turned their backs to their own
culture. (Abimbola 1981)

Santería's Wider Appeal: A Culturally and Racially Heterogeneous Following

Whereas in its country of origin the Yoruban religion had long been losing
ground, in the Americas it demonstrated the flexibility to adjust to different
ecosystems and cultural contexts while integrating participants of diverse racial and socioeconomic backgrounds.

During the last decades of the twentieth century many areas of the Caribbean, South, and Central America experienced substantial movements of population. Among the underlying causes of these vast population shifts have been
political instability and upheaval, the transition from consumer to market-
crop agriculture, inadequate ownership and distribution of resources, and the
pressures of overpopulation. Consequently, the social institutions and value
systems of peasant and small-town societies that are culturally and racially
heterogeneous have been challenged and embattled. An unprecedented flight
of untrained and uneducated peasants to cities and to other countries has resulted. Moreover, a considerable number of individuals from the middle class
have abandoned their homelands in search of a better future in the United
States and elsewhere. For many, these large-scale migrations have created
great opportunities for geographic, social, and economic mobility. For others,
painful displacement, uprooting, resentment, and struggle have characterized
the experience.

Political turmoil and population displacements, of course, are not new to
these areas. During the last five centuries, Amerindian, African, and Mediterranean (predominantly Spanish, Portuguese, and French) cultural traits have

been intermingling. These processes have woven a cultural tapestry in which such values as authoritarianism, subjugation, mysticism, opportunism, and personalism have influenced survival strategies that emerged from processes of cultural contact, syncretism, reinterpretation, and, in many cases, transculturation. This background provides a fertile soil for the social and historical evolution of Santería as it develops new religious significance in the early years of the twenty-first century.

During the past four decades, significant numbers of Cuban exiles have settled in other Latin American countries in and around the Caribbean. As in the United States, the Cuban Diaspora gave Santería increased visibility. In some of these countries, such as Venezuela and Puerto Rico, Santería has developed a substantial new following.

Many Hispanic Americans are attracted to Santería partly because, in Latin America, Kardecian Spiritualism and *curanderismo* are widely practiced as complementary, and, in some instances, as health delivery systems that compete with biomedical health care. Since Santería has borrowed from spiritualist practices and beliefs, and, in addition, makes wide use of herbal remedies and magic, as *curanderismo* does, its activities are quite appealing to people who are familiar with such beliefs and practices. The belief in the interference of the souls of the deceased in human affairs is also a common denominator.

Santería, however, has a substantial number of advantages over both *curanderismo* and Spiritualism. It has a well-developed cosmology, a body of rich mythology, intact and complex divination systems, well-defined rituals, appealing music, dramatic dances, and colorful festivals. More significantly, it has had success in supporting many people who are experiencing marginal existence and alienation in the post-industrial world. Furthermore, its increased visibility in the media, linked to the Cuban Diaspora, has facilitated its acceptance and its gaining of new followers in the Caribbean, in Central America, and in South America.

In these countries, as well as in the United States, Santería's beliefs and practices help people deal with disruptions in their lives. They assist in lessening feelings of ambivalence, confusion, frustration, and lack of direction or control generated by cultures in contact and the trauma experienced by individuals who must deal with noncongruent expectations and behaviors. The characteristics of Santería's new followers suggest that it is rapidly becoming an emergent new religious complex. As a system that is both magical and religious, Santería is assisting its heterogeneous following to cope with the stresses caused by major behavioral adjustments and issues of survival in new social, political, economic, cultural, and environmental contexts.

Santería has evolved from a religion practiced mostly by black Cuban believers to a religion appealing to a larger following among growing numbers of Hispanics in the United States. It has attracted Puerto Ricans, Venezuelans, Colombians, Mexicans, Dominicans, Nicaraguans, Ecuadorians, and other Latin Americans who are adapting to life in the United States. In addition, as will be discussed next, it has also gained a new following among African-Americans. The culturally heterogeneous nature of some of the new devotees of Santería is captured by Jacob Olupona and Terry Rey (forthcoming): "An African American woman in Detroit visits her cousin, a Michigan native trained in Cuba as a babalawo . . . (diviner), who reads *ikin* (palm nuts) imported from Nigeria to advise her on her marriage prospects. A crowd of Cuban-Americans dance ritually to the animating rhythms of a *batá* (drum) ceremony at the Church of the Lukumi of the Babalu Aye in Hialeah. A Puerto Rican car driver makes his sunrise *ebó* (sacrificial) offerings at the small Ogun shrine in his Flatbush apartment before another day driving the streets of Manhattan."

The Yoruban Religion and African-Americans

Santería has also achieved a stronghold among thousands of African-Americans, but for different reasons. Many initiated African-Americans find in Santería the divinities that they believe their African ancestors had worshipped. Santería offers them a source of ethnic and racial identity similar to one that it offered the Afro-Cuban population.[10] To African-Americans, Santería is a link to Africa, to their roots. Even when they might not understand or accept the Catholic influence in Santería, some participate in its practices and join the ranks of the initiated.

While conversing with an African-American woman during a Santerían ritual in Miami, I asked her if she experienced any dissonance in having acquired knowledge of the Yoruban religion via Cubans and in participating in an African religious festival being celebrated by Cubans of European descent. Her response was revealing: "It is the way of the *orichas* that the Cubans were to be the ones to bring the religion to the United States. This might be the greatest contribution Cubans ever made to American culture." Later, she complained that white Cubans did not wear the traditional African garments to the festivals and that they served Cuban food during celebrations.

Many African-Americans who enjoy a position of preeminence among the practitioners of the Yoruban religion in the United States had their initial contact with the Yoruban religion through Santería. Oba Osejiman Adefunmi I, born Walter King and the founder of the African Theological Ministry and the African village of Olotunji in South Carolina, was initiated in Havana in 1959. Oba John Mason, who has authored several works on Yoruban religion in the United States, was brought up in this religion by his Cuban mother. In addition, some African-Americans have encountered the Yoruba's orishas via contact with people from Trinidad, where orisha worship, especially Shango's cult, is very important.

Even when their first contact with the Yoruban religion was via Santería, many African-Americans have had a tendency to abandon explicit Santerían practices by purposely discarding the Cuban "additives" in the Yoruban religion, thus adopting a "purist" stance that is also called the Yoruba Reversionist posture. Some of them have close contact with and cooperate with officials of the government of Nigeria, who are demonstrating great interest in the different expressions of the Yoruban religion in the New World.

These are some of the factors contributing to observable trends in Santería that will be discussed in the final chapter to follow.

Santería's New Ways and Current Trends

At the turn of the twenty-first century certain trends in value orientation, approach, style, and practice are noticeable in Santería. The religion's individualistic, technical, and professional orientations are of specific importance. Career ladder opportunities, a new openness, and the Afro-centric position are also very important.

Individualism

Santería has recently been exhibiting pronounced individualism. Traditionally, Santería's magical and ritual practices have been designed to increase an individual's protection and power. This focus on personal protection was probably fostered by the highly stressful conditions resulting from disrupted views of self, family, community, means of livelihood, and the like. Such confusion under slavery and, later, in the immigrant experience surely translates into the loss of a sense of mastery related to feelings of powerlessness.

This highly self-protective, individualistic stance can lead to the extremes of conducting rituals aimed at results that most outsiders would perceive to be antisocial. Yet, insiders or practitioners would consider such actions as ego-protective and ego-integrative. In this fashion, the more extreme rituals aimed at obtaining for a client the attention of someone else's spouse or those conducted to cause illness in an oppressive boss or to bring harm to an enemy are perceived as protective rather than aggressive in nature.

In Nigeria, consultation with the Ifa oracle was aimed primarily at identifying the path the individual should take in consonance with the pact his or her eleda (guardian spirit, or soul) made with Olodumare before birth. In such fashion, the advice of the oracle was sought to open the way for positive experiences and to prevent danger immanent in the agreement, thus allowing the individual to reach his or her full potential.

Since beliefs in reincarnation in Cuba were dulled and, most specifically, the possibility of reincarnation within the father's family lineage was lost, consultations in Santería are aimed at solving everyday problems of material existence; not dealing with eschatological issues. Few concerns are expressed about the ultimate destiny of the soul, about reincarnation, or the possibilities of receiving punishment or rewards in the afterlife based on one's deeds in this material life. In other words, damnation, salvation, and life after death are not central concerns.

Santería's emphasis on the individual's protection, coupled with its de-emphasis on community welfare, has earned it a reputation for amorality. However, the amorality reflected in some of Santería's myths is used in a multitude of ways in the context of the oracle to enlighten, advise, and direct human beings toward paths that will help them achieve their larger goals honorably in an ethical fashion.

Technicalism and Professionalism

Santería is becoming more and more technical. Currently, the essential quality of Santería's diversified and elaborate rituals is only validated by the knowledge of how they should be performed and what elements have to be brought into them rather than by faith and intentions. Thus, *santeros* are respected for the esoteric knowledge they accumulate and by their demonstrated ability to perform ceremonies. This knowledge is obtained by being initiated or having participated in the most complicated, uncommon, and secret rituals. It is important to have a knowledgeable godfather or godmother in order to achieve the most beneficial outcomes.

The position of godparent is extremely critical in a religion in which priests are professionals of the supernatural and must be able, because of their esoteric knowledge, to tap efficiently into supernatural power sources outside themselves on behalf of believers. Consequently, within the framework of Santería's worldview, if the *santero* is not knowledgeable, the rituals performed by him can be rendered ineffective; even worse, they can bring great tragedy to the clients. Ezequiel Torres (February 2001) comments that a *santero,* full of inspiring faith, performed a *ko bo Orí* ceremony, a rogation for the head of a client for his or her guardian *oricha* in Miami in 1991. However, the *santero* did not follow the correct steps; the ceremony was without *aché* (power), and, as a result, it was ineffective for the client.

It is impossible to say how often such failures occur; though it is assumed that experienced *santeros* surely rely on a relative success rate to attract clients. In any case, the complexity and intricacy of Santería's magical practices, which require long training and experience, are almost equivalent to professional accreditation.

Professionalism in present-day Santería is so pronounced that in some festivals the largest majority of the participants are believers who have been initiated.

Career Ladder: Opportunities for Leadership in the Priesthood

Santería offers individuals a very complex dogma, an extensive set of myths, diverse religious paraphernalia, and highly structured sets of rituals, powerful music, and dramatic dances, as well as a viable road to priesthood. Moreover, Santería offers charismatic, insightful, and ambitious individuals great economic opportunities as well as positions of prominence as ceremonial leaders and counselors. *Santeros* are exempt from many restraints to which professional practitioners of other religions are held, including the need for academic accreditation. Additionally, their earnings are tax exempt.

Santería has thus opened a wide avenue for upward social and economic mobility via its populist priesthood. This trend is especially meaningful for women, who are well accepted and represented in Santería's priestly class, except for the priesthood of *Orúnla*, the *oricha* of divination, which is limited to male *babalaos.*

Openness

Many *santeros* are looking for acceptance and understanding, or at least tolerance, from the larger society. The trend toward recognition has prompted *santeros* to bring their religious practices out into the open, in what might be considered attempts to mainstream their beliefs and make them more accessible to public awareness. Attempts to open Santería's temples were discussed in endnote 1 of chapter 7, but important points are repeated here.

In Miami, a *cabildo* Lucumí was opened in 1988, led by Miguel Ramos. Its major goals were to disseminate knowledge of Yoruban religious culture by offering courses in Yoruban language and sponsoring ritual dance training and drumming. Other *santeros* in Miami, New York, and Puerto Rico have opened *cabildos* and learning centers aimed at teaching people about their religion and the Yoruban language and at dispelling fears about its practices. These attempts have met with mixed results.

Undoubtedly Ernesto Pichardo's legal triumph with the U.S. Supreme Court has had great repercussions in Santería. Pichardo (May 2001) commented that as a consequence there is a new openness in the practice of this religion and new efforts to bring it into the mainstream of life in its new setting.

In 2001, a group of *santeros* organized a procession "like the ones in Cuba." They used cars to drive Catholic religious images and believers along one of the busiest streets of Coconut Grove, a fashionable suburban neighborhood at the edge of Miami.

In New York the recently deceased senior *santera* Lourdes Julia Quintana (Ochún Yemí) from the lineage of Aurora Lamar, organized yearly processions to the Virgin of Charity. These processions started at her home on 40th Street and 9th Avenue and paraded through Broadway each year until her death in 2004.

In Cuba today Santería's presence is felt throughout the island and is not limited to former Yoruban enclaves. During the past fifteen years, *santeros* in Cuba have been much more open about their beliefs and practices.

On the island and in the United States Santería's rituals are becoming part of the Cuban national heritage. They have inspired many types of artistic expression in music, dance, the theater, art, and literature. Recently during a *tambor* I met a young *babalao* who publishes a magazine entitled *Olofin* and who, like Pichardo, Ramos, and others, has his own Internet Web site.

Overall, Santería is more and more visible. Scholars are convening annual conferences where practitioners and experts from Africa and the Americas share their knowledge and their experiences. *Santeros*, as part of this trend, are more than eager to participate and to share still more information about their religion. In line with general advertising practices in the host country, the marketing of Santería has begun in earnest. In this way it, also, is becoming more materialistic and proselytizing than has been the case before.

However, unlike other religious organizations described by Diana Eck in a recent book entitled *A New Religious America* (2002), Santería has not chosen paths of volunteerism and community involvement as ways of becoming better known and more integrated into life in mainstream America. Aside from occasional public processions, there is little evidence that Santería is seriously into bridge-building. While Eck provides examples of "Engaged Buddhism" (Eck 2002:365–66) and similar programs of other religions, there is no observable suggestion of intimate involvement by Santería's followers or practitioners in the life of their respective communities. To what extent Santería will become involved in interfaith movements, locally, and more generally across the United States and elsewhere, remains to be seen.

Tension between *Babalaos* and *Oriatés*

In chapter 3, mention was made of points of tension between *babalaos* and *oriatés*, in which *babalaos* see *oriatés* as encroaching upon their ritual prerogatives by extending the scope of the oracle of the shells and performing rituals they feel only they should be performing. *Oriatés*, in contrast, see *babalaos* as being overly protective of privileged functions that they themselves master very well. They comment that "in Brazil's Candomblé there are no *babalaos*." This trend seems destined to continue into the future. It is reportedly based on an old conflict between Ile Ife and Oyo that Brown (2003:19–20) refers to as the Ifá-centric and Ocha-centric orientations.

These orientations rest upon different basic assumptions about the knowledge of divination and appropriate ritual access to such knowledge. These enduring and conflicting traditions offer little hope that Santería will become organized into a single body of believers. This tension brings confusion among followers but does not necessarily affect Santería's growth. From its inception, this religion has been characterized by heterogeneity in dogma and practice and also by the autonomy that each house-temple exercises in reference to others.

Afro-centrism and the Issue of Syncretism

The developments in Nigeria that weakened and even eliminated in some areas the practice and importance of traditional Yoruba religion have co-existed with processes in the New World that have nourished Santería and related traditions. Thus, despite the weakening of the Yoruba religion in Africa, the strengthening of it in the Americas has stimulated interest in its African roots.

Presently, the Afro-centric trend of African-American Yoruba Reversionism views the association of the *oricha* with the saint as a mere disguise. Furthermore, it considers Catholic and Cuban elements in the religion to be defilers of the purity of Yoruba religious traditions. Such tensions may be related to fundamental differences in the worldview of African-Americans. Their history is linked to the evolution of a largely protestant society where Mary and the saints were not worshiped. In this society, miscegenation, from the point of view of the dominant race, was unacceptable; and, the capitalist free-market-oriented-economy did not value personal relationships. The frontier experience and culture shattered the importance and viability of the extended family. Thus, long-lasting social relationships, adherence and loyalty to native towns, and friendships that transcended the passing of generations, were not common. In this culture exclusivity is based on concepts of ownership of private property, privacy in relation to self-other relationships, individualism, and entrepreneurship. Most certainly, the Yoruban worldview that was placed in contact with popular Catholicism in the Cuba of the eighteenth, nineteenth and even the twentieth century is far more distant from the protestant worldview.

Nevertheless, the Afro-centric trend is not unique to the African-American population in the U.S. and it cannot be explained only in view of worldview contrast. During the past three decades some Cuban *santeros* (many of them whites) inside and outside of Cuba have favored an Afro-centric posture in Santería similar to that of many African-Americans who practice the Yoruba religion.[1] This trend has caused the abandonment by some of the use of Catholic images, calendar, and rites.

The Afro-centric posture of resistance is common among young *santeros* who eagerly read about the Yoruban religion and Santería, research scholastic treatises, correspond with scholars, and participate in African-oriented conferences. They are attempting to de-syncretize Santería by rejecting those features that reflect Catholic and some Cuban influences. They are also trying to incorporate into Santería Yoruban practices that never took root in Cuba.

Many of them see Santería as a religion of "resistance" as expressed by Miguel A. De la Torre (2004:189–203). Even though some *santeros* have adopted this position—and it is possible that some of them have always had it—in reality, many believers still see these associations as meaningful and essential.

As mentioned previously, such searches are common among people who are experiencing social disruption or find themselves in situations requiring marked adjustments in cultural perspectives. Insofar as religious imagery is concerned, it is helpful to remember that in Haitian Voodoo (Vodun), which developed after the white French establishment was overthrown, the deities, or loas, were and continue to be associated with Catholic saints. Also, in Brazil, *orichas* were and are currently associated with Catholic saints. It is very likely that there is some psychological benefit to such linkages.

Insofar as the relationship between Santería and Catholicism is concerned, the process of the merging of beliefs and practices has been halted. In Cuba, one factor contributing to this new trend has been the Castro Revolution's suppression of the Catholic Church.

In adapting to this new situation, some religious rituals have been changed. For example, visits to the church by the recently initiated *iyawó* and Catholic masses for the souls of the departed have been largely discontinued for fear of persecution and discrimination by the Communist government, or because the local church was closed or unattended. At the same time, the deeply religious women, generally blacks, who in Cuba were devout Catholics, attended daily masses, and were at the same time successful *santeras*, did not leave Cuba in significant numbers. Those who did, in most instances, could not preserve in exile a way of life dedicated to religious activities. Thus, a fertile breeding ground for religious merging and syncretism was eliminated.

Additionally, the Catholic Church changed dramatically during the 1960s after Vatican II. In many ways these changes de-emphasized the cult of the saints to focus on the believers' developing a stronger and more intimate relationship with Christ. The Catholic Church has also taken a strong stand regarding lay participation in the life of the church. The church is placing greater demands on the faithful, making it more difficult and uncomfortable for people to take the former position of being Catholic "their own way."

It seems that the majority of Cubans in Miami are at least nominally Catholic when one observes the enormous growth experienced by the Catholic dioceses. The arrival and settlement of numerous Hispanics from many other countries and also from other parts of the United States has contributed to the strength of the Catholic presence in South Florida. Some nominally Catholic Cubans and Hispanics continue to be involved in Santería, while others practice Santería exclusively.

Although the cult of the saints, generally, has been de-emphasized, there has also been a re-evaluation of the validity of the worship of some popular saints. Among the saints whose worship among Cubans has been re-evaluated are Saint Lazarus, Saint Christopher, and Saint Barbara. All three were important in the worship of Santería in Cuba during the 1950s. They had been associated with Babalú Ayé, Agayú, and Changó respectively.[2]

In Cuba, there was a large following and devotion to the miraculous Saint Lazarus, who as noted earlier, was represented in statues and chromolithographs as a leper who walks with crutches, assisted by two dogs. This depiction of Saint Lazarus has been associated with Babalú Ayé, the Yoruban god of epidemics in both Cuba and Brazil. The association between *oricha* and saint affected the former since Babalú Ayé, in Cuba, was and is perceived as more merciful and empathic than in Africa.

As indicated in chapter 18 the authorities of the Catholic Church claim (Sosa 1994: 5, 6, 16) that Saint Lazarus was not a leper but a former bishop of the church. The pronouncement of the Catholic Church regarding this saint left many of the faithful confused.

The Catholic Church, in both Cuba and the United States, has changed its laissez-faire attitude concerning Santería. During the past thirty years, it has openly addressed the issue of popular piety, or folk manifestations of Catholicism, or folk religiosity, attempting to guide Catholics to the orthodoxy of the Catholic Church while avoiding condemnations against these other expressions of popular religiosity. I have heard very contradictory accounts about the efforts of Catholic priests to prevent *santeros* from using church premises or services for their own rituals. Some informants describe the brusk manner in which some Catholic priests ask an *iyawó* to leave when they see the *iyawó* visiting the church as a required part of initiation into Ocha.

Many Catholic priests refuse to perform religious services during the funerals of openly practicing *santeros*, whereas in the past it was common practice to invite a priest to read prayers at such funerals. Immediately after the Catholic priest had finished and departed, *santeros* proceeded with the *itutu* ceremony of Santería.

Other Catholic priests, however, are more lenient. Recently in the city of Matanzas in Cuba, *batá* drums were played to honor the Virgen del Cobre during a celebration in the Catholic Church.

In Santería, as well, some notable changes mark a new distance from Catholicism. In conversations with the *oriaté* Miguel Ramos (February 2005), Ramos mentioned that when he attended the mass offered on the eve of December 17, 2004, at the shrine of Saint Lazarus in El Rincón, Cuba, thousands of believers, including many *santeros,* heard the bishop give a sermon. Attendance was extraordinary despite the fact that the image of the leper had been removed and that only the statue of Saint Lazarus, the bishop, was worshiped.

During the last thirty years some *santeros* have discontinued the traditional celebrations in honor of an *oricha* on corresponding Catholic saint feast days. Moreover, fewer images, statues, and chromolithographs of the Catholic saints are used by *santeros.* Some, in fact, have completely discontinued their use. However, there are many *santeros* who still engage in traditional syncretic practices.

For example, Patricia Duarte wrote an article for the *el Nuevo Herald* (1983: Galería 13–14) reporting the opening of a small Greek Orthodox Church dedicated to Saint Barbara in the midst of the Little Havana neighborhood in Miami. Father Felipe, who is in charge of the church, told the journalist that many *santeros* donated money for this church, and that they frequently attended it. It is also common to find offerings of Cuban delicacies on altars where the statue of the Virgin of Mercedes is worshiped.

Moreover, every year in Miami there is a street procession to honor the Virgin of Mercy that is sponsored by a *babalocha.* This procession is attended primarily by Santería's followers. The Marian icon is carried in the streets in a procession presided over by a Catholic priest and altar boys. This same *santero* often offers drum festivals to the *orichas* in his house, where a large image of the Virgin of Mercy and other Catholic icons are kept.

Many *santeros* who assert that they are against the syncretic aspects of Santería claim that the association of the *orichas* with the Catholic saints was forced by the intolerance of colonial authorities and that it was a mask only. They argue that "one does not offer sacrifices to the statues or chromolithographs; one offers them to the *otanes*" (consecrated stones where the power of the *oricha* resides).

Nevertheless, aspects of the syncretic Cuban experience continue to be manifested in Santería. For example, there are offerings of meringue (a white-in-color Cuban delicacy) to Obatalá, the *oricha* of purity, who is considered a cool, white *oricha.* There are offerings of *capuchinos* (one-inch-long cone-shaped sponge cakes saturated with syrup) to Ochún, who, in Cuba, owns all sweet things. Also, as mentioned previously, there are offerings of red apples to Changó, because red is the symbolic color of Shango in Africa.

Some *santeros* generally admit that in their religious practices there is clearly cultural syncretism since there are no meringues, *capuchinos,* or red apples in Nigeria. Nevertheless, they claim that even though there has been some cultural borrowing, there has been no religious syncretism and that the *orichas* are, essentially and exclusively, African.

Wilfredo Fernández Jr. (March 2001), referring to the *babalaos* from the lineage of Bernardo Rojas, shared with me the following observation: "Everybody was Catholic. They were all baptized as Catholic. Some *babalaos* handled Catholic things separately, while others merged them with the African. I don't agree with those who say that participation in the Catholic Church or the worship of Catholic images was forced or simulated. I believe that since their *orichas* did not demand exclusivity, their posture was similar to that of the ancient Romans: The more gods the more power."

This statement is very similar to those made by Florencio Baró in his autobiographical account in chapter 3 describing his experience growing up in the Cuban countryside. Insofar as matters of syncretism are concerned, my position is more in line with that of Terry Rey (1999: 231–32), who comments as follows about the adoption by Voodoo-practicing (or Vodun-practicing) Haitians of the worship of Mary in association with Ezili, the African goddess of love: "Instead, historical and anthropological research reveals that Mary has been adopted and welcomed by Haitians as an important spiritual force, operating side-by-side with Ezili—each functioning in a complex mosaic among the many *lwas* and saints who may be invoked in the daily struggle to survive and the quest for health and the fullness of life."

In a recent conversation, the *babalao* Virgilio Armenteros, M.D. (January 2005) used the same argument—that his ancestors had to adopt Catholic images to disguise their beliefs. I responded that recently in a *toque de tambor* honoring La Letra del Año, which we both had attended in the home of a *babalao,* with over a hundred *babalaos* participating, there was a large statue of Saint Francis of Assisi in a prominent place. Moreover, most of the *iyalochas* had gold medals of the Virgin of Charity or Saint Barbara, as well as crucifixes hanging from their necklaces. I remarked that it was difficult to understand the need to use them as disguises nowadays. Armenteros smiled and responded, "We like to enjoy double citizenship." Later he added, "Our religion is tolerant, and it is the only one that offers a person avenues to discover the nature of the problem and the way to solve it through divination and its prescriptions."

Thus, it seems pertinent to raise a different question. The issue is not syncretism versus Afro-centrism. Instead, the issue is that Santería is a religion that does not demand exclusivity—a religion that tolerates, welcomes, and accepts other avenues of access to the sacred. The issue is inclusiveness, and inclusiveness rests upon first-order assumptions about imminent power in the universe and second-order assumptions about the nature of, the distribution of, and the means of accessing that power.

This point is clearly illustrated by a conversation I had with the *iyalocha* Norma Torrado (September 2005) concerning Santería's practices. According to Torrado, "My seniors taught me that the essence of this religion is respect (for other religious beliefs) and heart." I told her that ideally it was so, but that in practice I had observed that followers of Ocha access supernatural power in different manners and in a very pragmatic way. Furthermore, followers of Ocha had repeatedly told me that spiritual problems could be resolved by spiritualist (perfume, flowers, candles) and Catholic (masses, rosaries, candles) practices and that worldly problems could be resolved by Ocha's practices (sacrifices, drum festivals). When the problems confronted were very serious, stronger measures were sought; and followers of Ocha might resort to *palo* practices (sacrifices) to bring remedy to desperate situations. In some instances some followers might also use *Palo* when strong antisocial and/or harmful results were desired. "That is the way it is," Torrado said, nodding.

Syncretisms of elements of Yoruban beliefs with those of popular Catholicism, along with initiation in Regla de Palo the practice of Kardecian spiritualist beliefs, and membership in the Catholic Church are valid avenues to the supernatural. This appraisal is congruent with the Yoruban worldview reported by Laitin (1986:34–35) and previously discussed in chapter 23.

If some followers choose to exclude aspects of ritual and to include elements from a past sociocultural environment or from other origins, those paths are acceptable within specific lineages and may be appropriate to specific socioenvironmental and cultural contexts. Under such circumstances, tension will arise as a consequence of the jostling of basic assumptions in the quest for logico-structural integration, and it is very likely that there will be less congruence among lineages than has been the case in the past. Santería's openness is supportive of such processes. Syncretism and merging will continue, but along a very different path from that experienced in Cuba.

It might be pointed out in this regard that there are African antecedents to processes of merging and syncretism. These are reflected in both historical accounts and mythology. According to Jacob K. Olupona (2000:xviii), "In African religious heritage, there is an emphasis on pluralism and inevitably, tolerance towards other religious and cultural traditions. Clearly many traditions are eclectic; they accept differences in religious experiences of adherents."

There are weighty consequences to such debate. A great number of the initiated decry the confusion that the Afro-centric stance has caused. Some old *santeras* have complained to me about those *santeros* who currently disrespect Catholic statues. Others ignore this trend altogether. For example, during a drum celebration in early 2001, a middle-aged white woman, who had been initiated eight years before, turned to me as they began playing for Obatalá and said, "Bow, they are playing to the Santísimo [holiest]," referring to the association of Obatalá with the Catholic Supreme Being. During a discussion about this issue with the *santera* Silvia Eires (January 20, 2005) she remarked that "God is the same all over the world but manifested in different ways to different people. There is an association between the saints and the *orichas*, but they are not the same. *Orichas* lived in this world while the virgins are different manifestations of Mary." Later on, when talking about Inle, she said, "Inle se asemeja a San Rafael El Médico Divino" (Inle resembles Saint Raphael, the Divine Physician). This suggests an awareness of meaningful equivalents. A little later when I asked her about the use of holy water in Santería she said, "To me the holiest water is not from the church. It is the rain water from the first storm in May. Do you want to know why?" she asked, adding, "Because May is the month of flowers and the month of the Virgin Mary."

In many ways, the association of Santería with Catholicism opens the doors of Santería to new converts. It is attractive to people whose worldview is ecumenical and who feel comfortable finding similarities in meaning among the religious and cultural manifestations of diverse people. The association and further identification between *santo* and *oricha* seems logical and natural to people who see the *orichas* as supernatural entities that are manifested to diverse groups in different ways.

It is possible that as the members of the last generation of *santeros* brought up before 1959 pass on, the influence of Catholic practices in Santería will diminish or disappear altogether. There are many factors influencing this development: the loss of importance of the Catholic presence in Cuba, the inroads of more populist Protestant churches (Pentecostal, Evangelical, Jehovah's Witness, and others), Afro-centrism, and the prevalent agnosticism or atheism of the post-revolutionary society have taken a toll. Gone are the days when *santeros* and all others were expected to be baptized, when *novenas* had to be offered to the dead nine consecutive nights after their demise, and holy water was needed for some potions.

While the anti-Catholic posture among some practitioners and believers is very real, still, on the Island *santeros* flock to Catholic churches, especially on those important days such as December 17 when hundreds—even thousands—of people go to the chapel of El Rincón to revere Saint Lazarus. As mentioned previously, according to Miguel Ramos (January 2005) the chapel and surrounding areas were full in 2004 in spite of the fact that the statue of Lazarus, the leper, was removed years ago.

There are no attempts to discard the great influence that Kardecian Spiritualism and other African religions have had on Santería. No one seems to question these influences, which have been reinterpreted and adopted into Santería.

Spiritualism has contributed techniques to engage the souls of the departed as well as providing an eschatological view of the afterworld and reincarnation that had taken root in Cuba even before the emergence of Santería.

In the case of Regla de Palo (an Afro-Cuban religion of Congolese origin), at present we often encounter *palo cruzados* (individuals who are initiated into both Regla de Palo and Regla de Santo).[3] Some informants have commented that many people who are going to be initiated into Santería are told that they first have to be initiated into Palo. Palo magic is perceived as stronger and swifter, while Santo magic takes longer but is more reliable and trustworthy. The importance, of course, is access to power and the supernatural to the greatest extent possible. There is no tendency toward exclusiveness here.

Many practitioners boast that their religious experiences and initiations enable them to handle effectively all sorts of situations. Some use Palo, others Santería, and still others Spiritualism. This eclectic approach is prevalent among Cubans. It has probably been the result of the intense cultural merging in Cuba's historical experience.

Nevertheless, with the ease of modern travel to Africa and the proliferation of communication channels across continents through the Internet and other information sources, the practitioners and believers of Santería cannot avoid being drawn to and puzzled by Africa. Regardless of the Yoruban religion's evolution in the Americas and the Caribbean and Wande Abimbola's 1981 testimony (1981:494–95), the African roots of Santería are real. The Cuban experience with African religions is also real and meaningful. The tracing of the path of the orishas from Africa to Cuba and beyond will be of special interest to those who wish to better understand processes supporting cultural continuities as well as those contributing to cultural change.

Concluding Remarks

There are numerous indications that practitioners of Santería are very much interested in achieving better accommodations to the values and ethos of the host cultures and socioenvironmental settings in which they now reside. New organizational forms are emerging (churches, cross-cutting organizations of practitioners, Internet connections, registries, and membership lists). New ritual forms are being created, and changes are occurring in the elements of various rituals. Changes in mythology, behavioral expressions in dance, and different types of offerings and sacrifice may be expected to follow.

Syncretic processes are still in place. Cultural transfer is still occurring. Transculturation is still in progress. Worldview analysis may be especially helpful in making sense of such transformations.

As external inconsistencies in the *logical* component of logico-structural integration occur, internal inconsistencies that such changes generate in the *structural* component of this process will also be addressed. Santería will emerge in new form or, more accurately, in new forms. It is expected that worldview analysis will contribute greatly to our understandings of such changes.

Current difficulties in seeing clearly all of the trends in progress attest to the complexity of both the religion and its dynamics of change—both external and internal. It is my view, however, that Kearney's model for worldview analysis will be most helpful to scholars who apply it toward a fuller understanding of Santería's path or paths into the future.

Naugle (2002:244) emphasizes the three basic components of Kearney's model as follows: "First is the structuralist . . . identification of worldview universals. Second [is] the formation and development of these universals through external and internal causes. The third . . . [is] the impact of worldview categories, shaped by external and internal causes, on daily life and sociocultural-cultural behavior."

Kearney's model has not been fully utilized in this work, but I share with Naugle (2002:244) his appraisal that "Kearney's . . . model of worldview is rich and fertile, spawning further thought and insight." Perhaps the general approach of this initial application of the model toward understanding continuities and changes in the religion of Santería will stimulate further inquiry and greater depth of findings in the future.

Conclusion to Part 3

As the twenty-first century unfolds, Santería seems to be developing into an emergent new religion. Changes that have taken place all over the world have affected its character, the nature of the following, as well as the practices of the Yoruba religion brought to Cuba by African slaves. In the 1950's Santería could have been understood as a manifestation of the Cuban Creole culture, the product of the merging of many of the diverse cultural traditions that converged in Cuba, especially during and after the nineteenth century. Instead, Santería's evolution has demonstrated a resilience that has made it appealing to people of cultures, races, and ethnic groups beyond those of Cuba and Nigeria.

These developments occurred as a result of changes both inside and outside of Cuba, in the ancestral lands of the Yoruba people and in the rest of the world. Current dimensions of Santería demonstrate that its changes and evolution have resulted in a new following and in its projection as an emergent religious complex at the threshold of the twenty-first century.

The most significant societal trend of the latter part of the twentieth century and of the dawn of the twenty-first, is vertiginous change. Santería's origins, evolution, and current character document its ever-changing nature.

Today, some senior and junior *santeros* still cling to the traditions and the knowledge that were transmitted to them by their godparents. They practice their religion inconspicuously, secretly, just as the Yoruba did in colonial Cuba, and they shy away from the public and the media.

As Santería continues to adapt to the new conditions of a challenging century, and as new directions are explored, this religion will continue to appeal to an even more heterogeneous following, a situation that will further change its nature.

It appears that this religious system will continue to appeal to people experiencing situations of disorder, social upheaval, marginal survival, identity confusion, alienation, and illness. The new following will be among those who migrate, people whose modus vivendi has been greatly affected by the pressures of assimilation to modern society. Also, there will be followers among people who are not too concerned with the afterlife, but rather, with finding solutions to the problems here and now; people who seek to connect with supernatural forces outside of the individual in order to negotiate with them on behalf of their own needs.

As one looks into the twenty-first century and ponders the future of Santería, one also needs to consider the growth and importance of Candomblé, the Afro-Brazilian religion. Candomblé, so strikingly akin to Santería from both historical and functional perspective, has developed an impressive following in Brazil, the largest country in South America. Is it likely that Santería will follow suit?

The religion of the Yorubas, brought to Cuba by enslaved people, previously gained followers of non-African descent in the colonial era. More recently, as Cubans have abandoned the island, it has gained a wider audience. According to Miguel Ramos (March 2004), people from more than thirty different nation-states have been initiated into it. Santería is thus no longer an Afro-Cuban religion practiced exclusively by Cubans. In brief, the processes of culture change reflected in current trends of Santería, some of which have been described, essentially mean that Santería's practitioners and practices are oriented toward synchrony with the contexts in which it finds itself in a new millennium.

Santería's history, as we have seen, holds the keys to its status in the twenty-first century. In previous centuries, aspects of the religion of the Yoruba-speaking people that were brought to Cuba experienced change, evolution, and transformation. Through a process of adaptation, syncretism, and transculturation new ways emerged.

As before, Santería is further evolving into a new religious complex that assists people of different cultural backgrounds to adjust to all that they endure in an increasingly complex, impersonal, unmerciful, materialistic, ever-changing, and seemingly amoral world.

This projection of a troubled future raises the issue of changing intra-psychic processes related to changing worldviews. For a psychodynamically oriented interpretation of ego-functioning linked to Santería's worldview and the role of this religion as a mediating institution, see Halifac and Weidman (1973). The author contributed background information to this effort which, she feels, introduces ways of understanding psychological mechanisms that are more congruent with some social forms than others. These factors, too, will need to be taken into consideration as scholars in the field trace continuities and changes in Santería's trajectory into the future.

The author suggests, however, that Santería is unlikely to form a highly organized national or international church. Outside of the Island, Santería is becoming less Afro-Cuban in character, especially among the new followers. It is giving birth to different currents that cannot yet be fully described.

One of these is the Yoruba Reversionist trend, primarily with an African-American following. It reflects a Pan-African posture focused on the African Diaspora and its religious components in the New World. In some instances it appears to be racially exclusive, but however it develops, there will be many avenues of exploration in the future.

Another—and perhaps the most important factor in the success of Santería outside the island has been the presence of significant numbers of Cubans in multiethnic cities such as New York and Los Angeles and particularly in Greater Miami. During the past twenty-five years, this area has become not only a multiethnic metropolis but also the "Capital of the Caribbean and of Central America." It is the favored destination of South Americans fleeing from social and political unrest as well as poverty in their homelands.

This trend will continue because of economic opportunities created by large numbers of Spanish-speaking residents in this burgeoning metropolitan area; also, because of increasing ascendancy in political arenas. It is likely that the Afro-Cuban religion of Santería will play an important role as a mediating institution in the adaptations of such groups to such new realities in the twenty-first century.

The parameters of other currents are yet to be delineated. It is expected, however, that the merging of Santería with the beliefs and practices of Venezuelans, Nicaraguans, Puerto Ricans, Mexicans, Hondurans and others in American ethnic enclaves and in their countries of origin will introduce further significant changes in the religion.

Already, Santería is becoming more individualistic to accommodate the needs of its new sociologically and culturally mixed following. The most serious devotees are themselves becoming priests with their own following and their own ways of interpreting and reinterpreting, of practicing the religion to meet the needs of their own godchildren and clients.

It is unlikely that such trends will lead to a coherent doctrine or formally organized religion. With access to the Internet as further impetus to individualism, Santería is more likely to become one of the multitudinous approaches to health and well being that are becoming more prominent and accessible everywhere. The more people feel increasingly "marginalized" by political, economic, military, and environmental events in a global socio-economic and cultural system; the more "powerless" individuals feel themselves becoming; the more likely they will look for power-enhancing solutions to individual problems.

May the *orichas* protect them all.

Appendix A

Paths of Obatalá

- Alagguema is the name of an Obatalá manifested as an old female who owns the sacred tree, the *iroko*. In Cuba, the African native tree *iroko* does not grow, and the *ceiba*, or silk cotton tree, has taken its place. Alagguema is the word for lizards in Nigeria. In Cuba, lizards are considered messengers of Obatalá, and a chameleon is used to represent him.[1]
- Ayágguna is an Obatalá manifested as a restless young warrior who loves wars and is prone to provoke them. It is said that when Olofin distributed power, he gave Ayágguna the power of causing quarrels. A toy horse is his symbol. An informant of Lydia Cabrera (1954: 310) claims that this *oricha* is responsible for bringing to Africa the white men who enslaved blacks. This informant reports that the Ararás (Dahomians), sold black-men to whites in exchange for powder and other goods. It is precisely in Ketou and Sabe (Yoruban territories bordering with Dahomey) that this warrior *oricha*, armed with a pestle and silver sword, is worshiped. There is little doubt that the slaves from this region, where the Dahomian influence was so strong, brought the cult of Ayágguna to Cuba, where he became associated with Obatalá. This warrior *oricha* has been associated with the Catholic Saint Joseph.
- Babá Fururú, according to Lydia Cabrera (1954: 308), is an Obatalá who gives instructions to and teaches the young. In Cuba, he has been associated with the Catholic San Joaquín.
- Elefuro is a female Obatalá sometimes associated with Saint Anne.
- Iba Ibo is a very ancient Obatalá. No one is allowed to look at him. He is too powerful, and the person who dares to look at him will be instantly blinded. He represents the Eye of Providence and Divine Thought. Iba Ibo is the mystery of the talking gourd. He is known also by the names of Oba Ibo, and Igba Ibo.[2] In many *ilé ochas*, Iba Ibo is considered God in person for his great power and his role in the creation of the world.
- Ikalembo is an Obatalá accused by other Obatalás of being a drunkard. Later on, he gave the *orichas* alcoholic beverages from a small gourd, and when they got drunk, Olorún said, "The drunkards are you." It is possible that this manifestation is related to the unfortunate experience when, according to the residents of Ile Ife, Obatalá became intoxicated.

- Naná Burukú is the oldest, most important and powerful of all female Obatalás. In Dahomey, Nana Buruku is a well-known goddess. She is also well known in some regions of Yorubaland, where she is not associated with Obatala. In Adele, Dahomey, Nana Buruku is the supreme divinity of creation. In some *ilé* or cult houses in Cuba, Naná Burukú is considered as two divinities in one: Naná and Burukú, the female and the male principles respectively.[3] Possibly slaves from Dahomey, where this *oricha* has a dual character, brought the cult of Nana Buruku to Cuba. In some *santeros'* houses in Cuba, Naná Burukú is considered the mother of Babalú Ayé, the god of skin diseases and, specifically, of smallpox. [4] It seems that the worship of Naná Burukú in Cuba comes from the former French Dahomey, where she is associated with the dual principle, and also from the area of the Yoruba, where she is considered the mother of the god of smallpox. These religious traditions of diverse origin were probably reformulated in Cuba in a Naná Burukú who appears as a powerful *oricha* who controls cancer or as a very powerful manifestation of Obatalá. In some cult houses she has been associated with the Virgin of Carmen; in others with Saint Martha.
- Obalabi is a female Obatalá sometimes represented by the lithograph of Saint Rita of Cassia.
- Obalufón, Ochalufón, and Chalofón are considered to be manifestations of Obatalá by Afro-Cubans. In Nigeria, Obalufon is a deified ancestor, while Ochalufon, or Olufon, are names used for Obatala in the town of Ifon.[5] Some priests claim that Obalufón, or Ochalufón, is an Obatalá manifested as a wrinkled little old lady who trembles with cold and covers herself with a white sheet. The *orichas* respect her very much. When any of them misbehave, she calms them down by placing her hand on the angry brow. However, other informants of Lydia Cabrera (1954: 308) say Ochalufón is an old warrior, dressed in white, who shakes with tremors when he possesses a believer. Some claim he trembles because he is cold; others think he trembles from anger. Lydia Cabrera's informants say that Obalufón is a male Obatalá and the first *oricha* who talked and gave mortals the gifts of language and copulation. He is also perceived as the most peaceful of all Obatalás. This view is rather confusing, since other informants of Lydia Cabrera believe that Ochalufón and Obalufón are the same Obatalá and no longer have him as a warrior who trembles with anger. In Cuba Obalufón is considered a peaceful Obatalá who taught men how to talk. It is possible that the Afro-Cuban identification of Obalufón as a manifestation of Obatalá was based on the similarities between the name Obalufón and one of the names for Obatalá: Ochalufón. Also, it could be based on the similarities in attributes between the *oricha* who gave men the gift of language and the one who sculpts the human body. Some informants claim that Obalufón, or Och-

alufón, was associated with San Manuel while others believe he has been associated with Jesus of Nazareth.

- Obamoro is a manifestation of Obatalá as an old and powerful male *oricha*. When he possesses a believer, his whole face suffers a complete change to disguise the fact that he is the Supreme Being.
- Ochagriñán, or Osankiriyán, is the oldest of all Obatalás. He is a feeble little old man who walks with crutches. He is a very brave warrior, but at times he is seen as a very wise and peaceful old man. In Africa, Oshagiyan is the name given to Obatala in Ejigbo and Ogbomosho. There, he is considered a young warrior always on the go and armed with a silver sword. Ejigbo and Ogbomosho are close to Ijesha. Some *santeros* claim that Ochagriñan is a male Obatalá who manifests himself in the road of Osankiriyán, the road that goes to the residence of the Deity. According to many *santeros*, this manifestation of Obatalá is God himself. In the *ilé ocha* studied by Rómulo Lachateñeré (1938:38–59, 132–34, 145–51), a female Obatalá is the one who knows the road to Osankiriyán. In Cuba, Ochagriñán has been identified with Saint Joseph, the father of Jesus.
- Ochanlá or Obanlá, in Cuba, is an Obatalá manifested as a little old lady covered with a white sheet and always trembling. Reputedly, she likes to eat cocoa lard because it clears the mind and the intellect. Obanla and Oshanla are names given by the Yoruban people to Obatalá. The image of our Lady of Mercy is sometimes used to represent this *oricha*.
- Yegguá, or Yewá, a manifestation of Obatalá, is a chaste little old lady who trembles and drools. She does not tolerate fights and does not permit her followers to engage in sexual intercourse or undress in her presence. Most of her devotees are old ladies and virgins. She is claimed to own the cemetery as the goddess of death.[6] Sometimes a doll is used to represent this goddess, although the *otán,* or consecrated stone, is where the god resides. This *oricha* likes to eat virgin, female goats. According to many investigators, the statue and images of the Virgin of the Abandoned have been used to represent her. Other authorities claim that Yegguá Yewá is the first Obatalá and the mother of all the others. However, in some cult houses this honor corresponds to Naná Burukú.
- Yeku Yeku, according to some informants, is a manifestation of Obatalá as an old man. However in other cult houses, Yeku Yeku is an old lady who is so powerful that she cannot be looked at directly in the eyes because blindness would result. Every request made to this *oricha* has to be worded in the opposite. If you want health, you must ask for illness. The soup bowl that contains the *otán* of Yeku Yeku has to be opened with great care as noise and light bother this *oricha* tremendously. Many associate Yeku Yeku with Saint Clara.

- Yémmu is a manifestation of Obatalá that is considered by many *santeros* to be the mother of all other Obatalás. In other cult houses and *patakíes*, Yémmu, who is also called Yembo, is married to Obatalá and is the mother of several important *orichas*: Ogún, Elegguá, Dadá, Osun, Orúla, and Changó. In some Yoruba territories, the wife of Obatalá is called Yemowo. It is possible that the Yoruban name Iyemmu or Yemmu is derived from that name. Yémmu has been associated with the Immaculate Conception.

Appendix B

Paths of Elegbara, Elegguá, Echú

- Echú Alosi has been associated with Satan because of his evilness.
- Echú Abalome likes to be with the dead. Echú Abalombe enjoys doing business with the dead.
- Echú Achi Kuala is at the crossroads.
- Echú Aguere watches over the hills.
- Echú Akokorobiya likes to play with marbles and toys and is constantly smoking cigarettes.
- Echú Alayiki is a child and a glutton who will go to any extreme to satisfy his craving for food.
- Echú Anakilade lives in the savannas.
- Echú Añaguio Elufe is the oldest of all the Elegguás. He orders around the younger ones, who do errands for him. He owns the keys of the cemetery and has to be treated with great respect. He provides trust and security to the *babalaos.*
- Echú Arayeyi is Orúnmila's assistant and doorman.
- Echerique is the Elegguá who accompanies Osain and owns the herbs together with Osain.
- Echú Barañies is Changó's constant companion.
- Echú Baralanube is the guardian of the roads and has been associated with the Lonely Soul of the Purgatory.
- Echú Barcheno is the youngest and smallest of all. He lives and hides in the bushes to do his mischief.
- Echú Batieyo is very powerful and always carries out what he wants to do.
- Echú Beleke is often associated with the Holy Child of Atocha. He cannot be kept inside of homes where there are children because he will be jealous and kill them. He cured Olofin when the Supreme Being became sick. He is kept in a gourd.
- Echúbi is the mischievous little boy who is always hiding in the corners playing pranks. Echúbi is the leader of the sacred twins, or *jimaguas. Santeros* claim that he is of Dahomian origin.
- Echú Kaloya spends all of his time in parks, squares, and markets.
- Echú Lagguana is an adult who likes to deal with the dead. He lives on the savannas and represents hopelessness. He has been associated with the

Lonely Soul of Purgatory. This *oricha* punishes with uncontrollable bleeding those who treat him with disrespect.

- Echú Laroyé is the Elegguá who stands at the entrance of homes and lives behind the door in his own small house. He has to be the first one people greet as they enter, for if he is not happy and content he is capable of any mischief. Many times during ritual celebrations he will call the police for the mere pleasure of interrupting the celebration. He uses a whistle to communicate with the Echú who stands at street corners and with the one who lives in the savannas. It is for this reason that no one dares to whistle in the *cabildo* houses for fear Echú Laroyé will come and create problems. Echú Laroyé is also a very close friend of Ochún, whom he protects. He is a warrior. He is fond of money and dancing, and he is a glutton who loves rats and chickens. Often he disguises himself as a rat to make strange noises in the homes he lives in. He speaks through the dilogún and the *obí* (coconut), warning believers against all dangers and counseling them in matters related to money and investments. He is of great assistance to people who run their own businesses.
- Echú Majo is a thief.
- Echú Meri Leye is one of the Four Winds.
- Echú Ogguanilebbe is always hiding in the corners. He is Ogún's companion and, many times, kills dogs to quench Ogún's thirst. One should not whistle on a lonely road at night to avoid drawing his attention, since he enjoys frightening people to death.
- Echú Okuboso is life and death.
- Echú Odemara can be your friend one day and your enemy the next. He is capable of doing good and evil at the same time.
- Echú Osika is a playful boy who smokes.

Appendix C

Paths of Changó

- Obakoso is one of the best-known manifestations of Changó. The name Obakoso is taken from the historical incident of the Alafin of Oyo. It was rumored that the cruel king of Oyo, Shango, was expelled from his vast domains for his many injustices. Later, Shango committed suicide and hung himself from a tree. His close associates, who were being persecuted, denied that he had committed suicide and went on the street shouting: "Oba ko so," "the king has not hanged himself."
- Changó Obaye also lives in the palm tree, and from the top of the tree he shoots arrows of fire to the ground.
- Changó Olufina, who is very reliable and enjoys the respect of his followers, lives in the *ceiba* (silk cotton tree), which in Cuba replaced the iroko, a most sacred tree in Yorubaland.
- Changó of Ima is a path of Changó as a warrior forever struggling against the ferocious Ogún. As Changó of Ima gallops through the heavens on his horse Esinle, he causes thunder and lighting. Meanwhile, Ogún also makes terrible noises while preparing his metals and irons for the battle against Changó.
- Obbaña is the Changó of storms and warfare. In addition, he is the owner of the *batá* drums to which all initiates in Ocha are presented and to which they have to render homage.
- Changó Eyeo fights by spitting lightning and fire through his mouth. According to one *patakí*, Osain, the owner of magical herbs and Changó's godfather, gave Changó a magical gourd containing some elements to put into his mouth that gave him the power to blow smoke and fire through his lips. Many legends make reference to how Changó possesses a very powerful talisman that enables him to have such horrifying powers.
- Obbara is Changó in the role of a human derelict. He is poor and despised by all, who consider him a liar. One *patakí* relates that one day Olofin gave a party for the *orichas.* As a present, he gave pumpkins to all of his guests. Changó Obbara was not able to attend; he was so poor he did not have the proper clothes. As the gods did not like the present that Olofin gave them, in jest they took the pumpkins to Obbara, who accepted them gratefully. Upon opening the pumpkins, he found them full of gold. Olofin rewarded

Obbara's humility by ordering that, from then on, Obbara's word had to be taken as true without any argument.

- Alafi Alafi is the king of the world. This is the title given to the priest-ruler of Oyo. Many Afro-Cubans know about the historical Shango, ruler of Oyo.
- Changó Aleyé is the *oricha* who appears crowned with a double-headed ax.
- Obbalube is Oba's husband. In this *camino* or manifestation, Changó is a demanding, abusive husband. He lives with his wife in the house of his rich father-in-law.

Appendix D

Paths of Ochún

- Ochún Akuara lives in the confluence of the river and the sea. She is a queen who has no crown. Her necklace is made of pale yellow, coral, onyx, and green beads. This Ochún likes quail, and her children are called Ochún Soino (the ones born from the womb of springs).
- Ochún Aña is the lover of drums and *güemilere.*
- Ochún Bumi is the manifestation of Ochún on her way to fetch water in the river. She is the shrimp.
- Dodowa is Ochún's name in Yesá territory.
- Ibu Ikole works with the buzzard and picks up trash and dust. She guards the home. Her necklace is made of amber and coral beads.
- Ochún Ibu Eleke Oni carries a baton and covers her body with the aphrodisiac oñí. She lives by the bush and is a fighter.
- Ochún Ibu Itumu is a lesbian. She dresses as a man.
- Ochún Ibu Tinibu lives in Orun's jar.
- Ochún Ibu Yumu is represented by a pregnant woman.
- Ochún Ibu Latie Elegba lives in the middle of the river, eats in a calabash, and wears no crown.
- Ochún Ibu Okuase Oddo lives in mortar.
- Ochún Naloya is the life of the party.
- Ochún Olodi is the owner of the river. She is a woman who wears warrior garments and one whose enemies can never conquer. When she is aggravated with one of her children, she can be very vengeful and dangerous. Her crown is made of corals, and her necklace is made of coral beads, five ivory beads, and green and aqua beads. She is represented by the owl.
- Ochún Telarago is the blushing goddess who was caught by other gods at the bottom of the well making love to Orúnmila.
- Ochún Yalorde is the oldest and most important of all the Ochúns. Yalorde is the name used for Ochún in the *güemileres.*

Appendix E

Paths of Yemayá

- Yemayá/Olokun, the ocean, is an old, fearsome *oricha* who lives in the midst of the ocean and is the mother of all the Yemayás. In some cult houses Olokun is a male *oricha*, while in others he is a female. Olokun, the ocean, is much too large and powerful to come down to *güemileres* (drum festivals) and possess the head of believers. It is only on very rare occasions that a *babalao*, wearing a mask, dances for Olokun. After the dance is over, he makes supplications so his life will be spared. Olokun's name cannot be pronounced without first having touched the earth with the tip of the fingers and having kissed the dirt on the fingers. Olokun's face is horrible; and it can only be seen in dreams. Talbot (1926 2:88) reports that, according to an old tradition, the sea was the "fetish" of the Oyo Yoruba, who had been informed by their priests that any of them who saw it would die. It is possible that the last remnant feature of the cult of Olokun in Cuba reflects the beliefs of the people of Oyo who came to Cuba in important numbers and had a great impact on Santería.
- Yemayá Achaba is an arrogant woman, haughty and scornful. She carries the anchor. She wears a silver chain around her ankles and a necklace made of light blue beads. In Africa, Yemonja enjoys wearing silver bracelets. It is possible that the chains around her ankles are related to the African myth about Olokun in which he is chained to put an end to the floods that were produced by his fury.
- Yemayá Gunle is the personification of the sea that bathes the shores.
- Yemayá Tinibo is the violent and rough sea.
- Yemayá Osesu is in sewers and latrines.
- Yemayá Maye is a passionate woman.
- Yemayá Oggulle is manly and impetuous.
- Yemayá Mallelo is shy and can't stand anyone touching her face when she comes down in *güemileres*.
- Yemayá Attaramawa, according to Afro-Cubans, is a handsome woman who is conceited and arrogant.
- Yemayá Ogunte likes to eat lamb.
- Yemayá Asaba runs errands for Olokun.

- Yemayá Ibú lives in brackish waters.
- Yemayá Agána likes to walk. When she dances she limps.
- Yemayá Malléléwo is a warrior according to Castellanos and Castellanos (1992 3:56). She likes to tie up and bind everything and loves to do witch-craft. She is Ogún's wife and likes to work with him.

Appendix F

Paths of Babalú Ayé

- Azojoano Asoyorisha is the youngest of all Babalú Ayés.
- Agróniga Omobitasa is the oldest of the Babalú Ayés.
- Shakuata Agróniga is a very ancient Babalú Ayé, who is also known by the names of Ayanison and Nike.
- Ayano is the Babalú Ayé to be propitiated to avoid epidemics.
- Yonko is a cripple with only one leg.
- Chakpana is the owner of smallpox.
- Asoyi and Afrekete are other manifestations of Babalú Ayé.

Appendix G

Paths of Ogún

- Ogún Afaramulé, Ogún Ogúmbi, and Ogún Bichiriké rule over iron.
- Ogún Aguanilli is the tiller of the land, a coarse hermit who rapes women and later beats them for having dared come to him.
- Ogún Aláguedde is the blacksmith who constantly works in his shop and is a great guardian *oricha* who tirelessly watches over his protégées.
- Ogún Areré is the owner of metals, the wilderness, and the thicket. He is the patron of soldiers and is associated with Saint Peter.
- Ogún Chibirikí is a wicked Ogún who enjoys sending people to jail. He is associated with Saint Michael the Archangel.

Notes

Preface

1. The Kluckhohn-Strodtbeck Value Orientation Schedule discussed below does not deal specifically with the man/supernature set of choices. The author has assumed that the man/nature orientation also includes supernature as a component of this orientation. In Kearney's terms the supernatural is part of Self-Other and Self-not Self dimensions.

Acknowledgments

1. Santería is a term derived literally from the Spanish word *santo* (saint). "Santería" has a pejorative connotation. The religion, most appropriately, is called Regla Lucumí or Regla de Ocha, the name commonly used to refer to the Afro-Cuban religion of Yoruban origin.

Note to the Reader

1. *Bozal* consisted of broken Spanish grammar and phonetics, mixed with the grammar and phonetics of the slaves' diverse native languages. There were no patterns or uniformity in what is called *bozal*, because practically each slave developed an individualized form. Consequently, other than implying an ungrammatical mixture of two or more languages, the word *bozal* escapes definition.

Prologue

1. This *pataki* (Lucumí sacred legend or story) expresses the way some followers of Santería conceptualized the process of cultural blending that resulted in the emergence of the religion. The priests and priestesses verbally taught the *patakies* as part of the oral tradition, to their godchildren who were in training to be initiated into Santería. Later on, the *patakies* were compiled by priests in notebooks called *libretas de santeros/babalaos* (*santeros'/babalaos'* notebooks) along with general information and instructions about their religion. In a sense, these *libretas* represent the beginning of the literary tradition in Santería. In this book many *patakies*, translated from *libretas de santeros*, have been transcribed. I published many of them initially in Spanish in *La Religión Afrocubana* in 1975, but new ones have been added. I copied this particular *pataki* from Enrique Cougat's mimeographed *libreta de santero* in 1971. Cros Sandoval added the dedication to Cuba.

Introduction

1. For more information about *jigues*, see Feijoo 1986.

2. In the Spanish Caribbean the relationship between household servants and family members was generally close and warm. Most middle-class families in Cuba during

the republic could afford live-in help. These situations created opportunities for the development of close ties between members of different social classes.

3. *Bembé* is the popular name given to Afro-Cuban religious celebrations featuring drumming, dancing, and singing. They are also called *toque de tambor, tambor, toque* or *plante de santo*, and *güemilere*.

4. Tumba Francesa is a religious complex of Haitian origin and is prevalent in the southeastern areas of the province of Oriente, around Guantánamo.

5. *Botánicas* are stores where religious items are sold. *Botánicas* originally were stores that specialized in herbs and natural medicines and which were opened in the United States by Puerto Ricans. Cuban exiles transformed *botánicas* into stores catering primarily to Santería customers. There they sell nonconsecrated ritual objects, images, beads, and even animals for sacrificial purposes.

6. Palo Mayombe, also called Regla de Palo, Kimbisa, and Mayombe, is an Afro-Cuban religion derived from the religion of the people from the Congo.

Chapter 1. The Yoruban Background of Santería/Regla Lucumí

1. Some Yoruban slaves who were converted to Christianity in Sierra Leone manned many of the early Christian missions. They used the phrase "making country fashion" to refer to traditional Yoruban religion.

2. A little white girl called Zoila was kidnapped and sacrificed by "witch doctors" (presumably *paleros*) in the first decade of the twentieth century (Ortiz 1906:199, 201, 202). In addition, in 1918, in the outskirts of the city of Matanzas another little girl called Cecilia was kidnapped and sacrificed. Oscar F. Ortiz's novel *El Santo Culto* is based on that macabre incident, which was also attributed to *paleros*. Three decades later, in 1947, a seven-year-old girl was abducted from her home in Guanabacoa on December 4. (December 4 is the day the Catholic Church celebrates Saint Barbara, who has been associated in Santería with the thunder god Changó and in Regla de Palo with Nsasi or Siete Rayos.) She was brought to a place where *paleros* conducted ceremonies and installed on a throne. Her rescuers arrived before the intentions of the kidnappers were displayed. The girl grew up and is a librarian at Miami Dade College. *Paleros* were blamed for the incidents, but there is no evidence that they or *santeros* were the perpetrators.

3. Thompson (1976:P/1) comments upon the ideals of command (power), composure, and character in Yoruban leaders as being reflected in Yoruban art, particularly sculpture. However, lest readers assume that there is little room for spontaneity and creativity in Yoruban culture, it should be noted that Fagg (1982:53) emphasizes these characteristics as being related to ashe in the medium in which arts and crafts are created. He offers his readers "an awareness of the complexity, richness, and coherence of a culture that has given birth to an art of the very highest order of aesthetic sensibility."

Chapter 2. The Cuban Colonial and Republican Background of Santería/Regla Lucumí

1. Creole (Criollo or Criolla) is a term used to designate males or females, regardless of race, who were born in Cuba.

2. *Cabildos de nación* is the term used for the social organizations founded by slaves

and freemen considered to be of the same ethnic origin. These *cabildos* were religious brotherhoods, since they were organized under the protection of a tutelary saint. In Cuba, they functioned as mutual aid societies. The term *cabildo* is used for a temple of Santería.

3. Bantu-speaking farmers of the Congo River basin and adjacent Angola were among the most important ethnic groups brought to the island. The religion of these people became the foundation of the Afro-Cuban religion called Regla de Palo.

Additional important contingents of slaves were brought from Southwest Nigeria where the Yoruba-speaking people lived. Their religion became the foundation of the Afro-Cuban religion called Santería/Regla Lucumí.

Bantu-speaking people from the Calabar area, called Carabalí, were also numerous, and their religion became the foundation of the male Afro-Cuban secret society called Ñañigos or Abakwa.

Considerable numbers of Mandingos were brought from the coastal area extending from Senegal to Liberia, as well as numbers of Ashanti and Fanti from the regions where the Ghana and the Togo Republics are located. Great contingents of Minas Popós were brought from the area that is now the Republic of Benin. From the same general area, former French Dahomey, the Yoruba-speaking Ararás were brought, and their religion became the foundation of Regla Arará, which was so akin to Santería that the two merged.

Africans of other ethnic groups were brought to Cuba, but it was those ethnic groups whose religion survived in an Afro-Cuban version that had the greatest impact on Cuban culture.

4. See Guanche Pérez 1999 for a well-documented and detailed discussion about Spanish immigration in Cuba.

5. In addition to the thousands of slaves brought from different parts of Africa, many Chinese and Yucatecos (people from the Yucatan, mostly males) were brought as indentured servants. These people and their descendants have intermarried with members of the lower socioeconomic classes, especially blacks, from the time of their arrival in Cuba. The celebrated, desirable, and attractive Chinas were the product of the crossing of Spanish, African, and Chinese genes.

6. Kardec received a privileged elementary education and completed his secondary education in the prestigious school directed by the famous educator Pestalozzi in Iverdun, Switzerland. He later obtained a graduate degree in humanities and sciences and was granted a doctorate in medicine. Kardec, like his mentor Pestalozzi, was committed to improving French education by lecturing and writing books on that subject. Then he became interested in a fashionable, living room amusement—the so-called speaking table—which many considered a spiritual hoax, others a game, still others as channels for communication with the spiritual world. Part of Kardec's widespread appeal was based on his approach and the claim that his beliefs and practices of spirit communication were based on legitimate scientific research.

7. The draconian Platt Amendment was forced as an appendix to the Cuban Constitution (1901) by the interventionist government of the United States. It severely limited Cuba's sovereignty because it gave the U.S. government the right to intervene in Cuba on any occasion it felt necessary to preserve Cuban independence. The Cuban Republic

could not sign any treaty with a foreign government that could limit its sovereignty. In addition four of the largest Cuban bays were to be loaned to the United States to be used by the U.S. navy, and the Island of Pines was not included as part of the new republic. Fortunately, the United States chose only Guantánamo Bay as a base for its navy, and the Island of Pines was declared Cuban by the Hay-Quesada Treaty in the 1920s. The Platt Amendment was finally abrogated in 1936.

8. During Holy Week, celebrations took place in every city. The most renowned and elaborate were those in the colonial city of Trinidad. In Santiago de Cuba the holy burial procession came from the Church of Dolores, with Christ in a glass sarcophagus accompanied by his mother in a black vest. In Holguin there was a procession with Christ the Nazarene on his way to the cross being whipped by some men dressed in black. In Camagüey on Holy Friday, besides the procession of the burial of Christ, there was another one at ten p.m. called the Loneliness of the Virgin, which was attended by men only.

9. A similar parade takes place in Calle Ocho (Eighth Street) in Miami nowadays.

10. In Santiago de Cuba, Sancti Spiritus, and other cities there were processions of the Virgin of Charity. Many people celebrated the Virgin on September 7 and 8 at home by their altars.

11. The term mounted in Spanish, *montado* from the verb *montar* (to mount), is used in Cuba for possession by spirits or other supernatural entities. In Spanish, as in English, it has sexual connotations as does the verb possess.

12. Gypsies arrived in Spain shortly after the discovery of America. They worked in the construction of El Escorial. Many wandered southward into Andalusia, contributing even further to the cultural heterogeneity of that region, which so greatly contributed to the early colonization of the New World.

13. Some *santeros* have told me that saints and Virgins operate in a fashion similar to the Yoruban orishas, but instead of the blood of animals and certain meals, they like to be offered incense, flowers, and candles, and instead of a *tambor* (drum festival) they like believers to commit themselves to promises and penances, for instance, to wear a promise garment for a year or more, or to stop smoking for some length of time (not essentially different from *iyawós* who dress in white for a full year and have to observe many taboos for life).

14. The trend to identify the Virgin Mary with the local populations in their own semblance with her miraculously revealed self began early in colonial times in Hispanic America.

15. Castellanos and Castellanos (1988–94) constitutes a comprehensive and well-documented study of Afro-Cuban culture.

Chapter 3. The Origins of Santería/Regla Lucumí

1. *Babaoricha, iyáoricha,* and *omoricha* are terms derived from the Yoruban baba, iya and omo, which literally mean father, mother, and child of an *orisha*.

2. Regla de Ifá is the name given in Cuba to the cult dedicated to the worship of Orúla, the god of wisdom and the oracles. The priests of Orúla, or *babalaos,* constitute a religious society dedicated to the worship of Orúla and to the practice of divination using the highest divination instruments.

3. *Comparsas* and *congas* were street parades in which the participants marched and danced to the beat of African drums. Dancers in *comparsas* wore costumes and performed choreography based upon African legends and myths.

4. It should be noted that in the Yoruban kingdoms there was a tradition of reducing to slavery those community members engaged in misdeeds.

5. These mutual aid societies were the embryonic institutions for Cuban clinics, which, during the republic, rendered medical services to great numbers of urban residents at a modest price.

6. This practice demonstrates Catholic influence. In the Catholic Church the statues of the saints and other religious paraphernalia were covered with a white or purple piece of cloth during Holy Week.

7. This practice denotes the merging of Catholic and Afro-Cuban religions. The Santería calendar was based on the Catholic calendar of festivities celebrating a saint with whom an *oricha* had been associated.

8. *Casa de santo,* or *ilé ocha,* is the home of a consecrated priest where altars are kept and ceremonies are celebrated; a house-temple.

9. *Toque de palo* is a celebration of Congolese origin featuring drumming, dancing, and singing. Such celebrations are part of the Afro-Cuban religion called Regla de Palo, Mayombe, or Kimbisa.

10. According to Baró's account, it was common among slaves to identify equivalencies between African gods of different ethnic groups based on their similarities. These associations were prompted by the intermarriage of people of different African ethnic backgrounds. However, as Baró points out, different religious practices in the same household were kept separate.

11. The *bóveda* consists of a table used as an altar that is dedicated to the worship of the spirit of the dead.

12. Siete Potencias Africanas, or Seven African Powers, is a term used to refer to the *orichas* that can be *asentados* in Cuba; in other words, *orichas* that are placed inside a person's head. These *orichas* are Obatalá, Elegguá, Changó, Yemayá, Ochún, Ogún, and Oyá.

13. *Asiento* is an Afro-Cuban term derived from the Castilian Spanish verb *sentarse* (to seat). This verb is used to refer to the consecration of a neophyte to the service or worship of an *oricha.* The *oricha* is said to be placed on the head, when at the height of initiation, some secret ingredients are put into a cut made on the skin of the head.

14. *Rumbero* is the name given to a drum player who plays secular music but who, in many cases, also has the ability to play religious music. Rumba is a popular Cuban dance genre.

15. *Medio asiento* indicates the complex religious ceremonies that are part of the initiation process to Santería's priesthood. Literally, the term means that the person to be initiated has completed half of the requirements for initiation.

378 Notes to Pages 60–72

16. *Soperas* is the Spanish word for soup tureens. In Santería they are used as receptacles where the consecrated stones, or *otanes,* of the *orichas* are kept. They have taken the place of the gourds and clay kettles that were used in the past.

17. *Bejuco de sabana* (Spanish) literally means a wild vine from the savanna.

18. *Pinaldo* and *wanaldo* are the names of the ceremony that qualifies a *santero* to sacrifice four-legged animals. According to a knowledgeable informant, the ceremony qualifies *santeros* who had not been properly initiated *(santo parado).* They were individuals who, as children of knowledgeable *santeros,* had been trained by their parents but had not been properly consecrated.

19. *Yesá* is a Cubanism used to refer to people originally from the region of Ilesha in Nigeria. This term is also used to refer to the set of drums originally from that region. They are played with sticks rather than with bare hands.

20. A *palero* is a priest initiated in Regla de Palo, which is also known as Regla Mayombe. It is a religion of Congolese origin.

21. Calazán was the name of one of Lydia Cabrera's key informants, whose accounts are recorded in her book *El Monte* (1954).

22. Ocha is the name used by believers of Santería to refer to their religion. It means the holy, the sacred. Ocha is a term also used for an anniversary party, a celebration held on the anniversaries of a person's initiation into Santería.

23. Ogún is associated in Havana with Saint Peter.

24. Caña brava *(Bambusa vulgaris)* is a wild reed commonly found in the rural areas of Cuba.

25. *Guarachear* means to have fun. *Guarachas* are a popular Cuban musical genre. The beat and rhythms are fast, and the lead singer interprets a song that narrates a story while the rest of the musicians normally repeat as a choir a certain specific theme. The *guaracha* is the direct antecedent of salsa, a musical genre that is very popular today.

26. *Camino* is a path, or manifestation, of an *oricha.*

27. *Registro* is the term used for consultations with supernatural entities (*orichas* and the souls of the dead) using the divination instruments.

28. *Batá* drums are the three sacred drums that belong to Changó. In Cuba all initiates are presented to these drums. For a detailed account of the *batá* drums see Miguel Ramos 2000. Ramos is a renowned *oriaté* initiated in the cult of *Changó.*

29. Santería's followers who live in apartments with no yards place offerings to the dead in the bathrooms. There are several possible associations related to this practice. One is the importance of water for the dead, and the other is the fact that the bathroom is the most infrequently occupied part of the dwelling. There may be other reasons as well.

30. *Puyas* is a Spanish word for "dives," a satirical remark to make fun of someone.

31. Pedraza (in press). In this work the author documents the way in which processes of transculturation and merging with the dominant culture were accelerated by miscegenation.

32. In this regard, I would like to comment that despite the imposing presence of persons from Ile Ife in Cuba and the prevalence of Ifá practices on the island, the cult

of Oramfe, the thunder god of Ile Ife, never took root there. Probably he could not compete with Changó.

33. A priestess from Nigeria called Ma Monserrate arrived in Matanzas at the turn of the nineteenth century. She founded an Arará *cabildo* and a prestigious religious lineage. This lineage became the matrix of the Afro-Cuban religion called Regla Arará. The renowned priestess Ferminita Gómez later belonged to it, according to Rafael Robaina's statement in the film *When the Spirits Dance the Mambo* (Moreno Vega 2003). Regla Arará and Regla Lucumí are Afro-Cuban versions of Yoruban religion and both merged in Santería.

34. According to Brown's informants the given name of Obadimelli was Octavio Samar.

35. Many believers affirm that the *iyawó* is brought to the Catholic Church to be presented to Olofin, the Supreme Being. This practice gives weight to the position that Santería's associations with Catholicism are quite deep.

36. In 1990 I visited a small shrine from the eighth or ninth century that is dedicated to Saint Barbara in Anatolia, Cappadocia, Turkey. On the interior walls of the shrine was painted a double-ax similar to the symbol of Changó. Inquiries about this unusual painting revealed that Saint Barbara in this part of the world, which is very remote from Cuba, had been identified with an early Mediterranean thunderstorm god who shared with Changó the double-ax symbol.

37. *Novena* is a Catholic practice. Neighbors and friends of the deceased meet for nine consecutive nights after the burial to recite a rosary for the soul of the departed.

38. *Rallado en palo* is the term used to refer to those persons who have undergone the scarring that signals initiation in the Regla de Congo, which is a religion also known as Palo, Mayombe, or Kimbisa.

39. *Prenda* is the name *paleros* give to a caldron in which they place the sacred stones and other magical elements. In the *prenda* the power of the spirit of the dead person with whom they have sealed an alliance is fixed.

Chapter 5. Priesthood

1. In the following discussion there are many references to *orichas* and supplicants that may be either male or female. For purposes of simplicity, the author has chosen to utilize masculine pronouns to the greatest extent possible. In Spanish, the word *santeros* includes both male and female practitioners.

2. *Ekuele* is one of the divination instruments used exclusively by the *babalaos* or priests of Orúla. It consists of chains with pieces of metal, seeds, and beads.

3. Among *santeros* the *oriaté* is the most knowledgeable about the dilogún oracle. He is also the master of ceremony during initiation ceremonies.

4. Olofin is a most sacred consecrated object consisting of a metal cylinder about a foot in height and six inches in diameter. This sealed cylinder contains the secrets and the powers that represent Olofin, an aspect of the Supreme God. It should not be opened or else the power will be lost. In Nigeria and Cuba, Olofins were handed down from father to son during an elaborate ceremony, as disclosed to me by a nonpracticing *babalao* who is the son of a prestigious *babalao* who belonged to the Bernardo Rojas lineage. The father of this informant came from a wealthy, old, landed-gentry, Cuban family that had owned slaves. His father was an *olúo* and, when he was elevated to that

position, he received the Olofin that had belonged to a Spanish *olúo* who had died without descendants.

5. Presumably, the possibility of blackmail regarding sexuality and the revealing of secrets is considered to be great.

6. Elegguá *de amasijo* (hodgepodge, or mixture of different ingredients) is an Elegguá shaped as a cone. It is prepared by the *babalaos* and made of concrete and other elements that are the foundation of the power of this *oricha*. It can be used to do good deeds and evil deeds.

Chapter 7. Santeria's Rituals: Locus, Form, and Paraphernalia

1. In greater Miami several efforts to open a church or temple for the practice of Santería have taken place. In the 1970s Carlos Canet, a *santero* who had a daily radio program, tried to open a church. He also attempted to change some of the liturgy, emphasizing offerings of fruits (to be consumed by participants) and eliminating animal sacrifices. He did not have much success. In 1987 Ernesto Pichardo opened the Lukumí/Babalú Ayé Church. This action resulted in a conflict with the city of Hialeah, which wanted to close the church on the grounds that animal sacrifices created a health hazard. The Supreme Court of the United States overturned the city of Hialeah's ordinances on the grounds of freedom of religion in 1993.

An on-going project of a group of *oriatés* who started organizing in 2000 is to open El Templo Olorichas de las Americas to be used for communal ceremonies. Occasionally, these *oriatés* celebrate communal ceremonies attended by crowds of more than four hundred people.

2. *Canastillero* is a Spanish word for a chest of drawers. Sometimes this word is used by Afro-Cubans for their altars. Personal communication with Lydia Cabrera in 1971.

3. *Plaza* is the name given to the offerings placed on mats on the ground in front of the altars. The term *plaza* in Spanish means park and is also used to refer to the market place where all types of fruits and food are exhibited in a fashion similar to the placement of offerings on the altars.

4. Most of the *patakíes* recorded in this work were published in Cros Sandoval 1975. Different versions of some of these myths were published earlier by Fernando Ortiz, Rómulo Lachatañeré, Teodoro Díaz Fabelo, and Lydia Cabrera; their works are included in the references.

5. See Miguel Ramos 2000, for additional information on *batá* drums.

6. *Curanderos* is a Spanish word for healers who are outside of the orthodox medical health-care system. The term applies to all types of healers, whether they do or do not use some type of ritual or pharmacopoeia of Spanish, Amerindian, or African origin.

7. It is noteworthy this knowledge seeking was also pervasive among the Yoruba of Nigeria.

Chapter 8. Oracles

1. I recorded and translated the readings of the oracle of the coconut as well as those of the dilogún from a *libreta de santero* and included them in my *La Religión Afrocubana* (Cros Sandoval 1975).

2. The Yoruba believe that all the wisdom of Olodumare is available through the *odus* of divination.

3. *Jutía* is the name of a large rodent that is native to Cuba. *Jutías* normally live on tree branches. Farmers cherish their flesh. There are four different species in the island. The most abundant is the *jutia conga (Hutia Capromys pilorides)*, which lives in all the provinces of the island. The *jutia andaras (Hutia Capromys melanurus)* lives in the eastern provinces. The *jutía carabalí (Hutia Capromys prehensiles)* and the *jutía enana (Hutia Capromys nana)* are the other ones found in various locations.

4. Gleaned from personal communications with Wande Abimbola in 1986.

5. The number sixteen has great importance in both the Yoruba religion and Santería in terms of power, truth, and wisdom. The numerous references to the number sixteen in the mythology of both relate to its sacredness. It symbolizes a direct reflection of the power flowing from the Supreme Being through the god of wisdom. This god is perceived as having been present when the world and all of its inhabitants were created. The god of wisdom is conceived of as knowing all of the secrets of creation and all of the powers related to both spiritual and human characteristics of good and evil. When the god of wisdom left the earth, he is said to have given to each of his children sixteen sacred palm nuts that embodied his power, truth, and wisdom so that they "could communicate with him in order to know how to take responsibility for their lives in a world of contending powers" (Fagg 1982:196).

The permutations of first-order assumptions about causality in both Yoruban and Santerían worldviews are pervasive in symbolism related to the number sixteen. For a thorough discussion of the importance of this number in relation to the god of wisdom and the role of divination in Yorubaland, and therefore Santería, see Abimbola (1997). See also the importance of the number sixteen in Thompson's description of divination sculpture in Yorubaland (1976:CH 5/3–5).

Conclusion to Part 1

1. The behavior described here is derived from extensive research I undertook in Miami during the past three decades. The findings showed that many new followers of Santería became interested in this religion because they were experiencing health problems that their doctors were not treating successfully (psychosomatic problems, depression, compulsive behavior, maladjustment, family problems, and others). The individuals interviewed used Santería as a complementary health-care system while continuing treatment with their physicians (Cros Sandoval 1979:446).

2. Cuba became an independent republic in 1902. The young republic greatly emphasized public health; thus, efforts to bring health services to the urban population were undertaken with success. Prior to Castro's revolution, free medical services were available in most urban areas. Moreover, the private clinic system offered the middle and upper classes in-patient, ambulatory services, and medications for a modest monthly fee. Castro's regime, following the pattern of the republican governments in urban areas, introduced medical services to the rural areas where the former republic had not previously offered them.

Chapter 9. Olodamare/Olodumare, Olorun/Olorún, Olofin/Olufin: The Creator God

1. An Afro-Cuban idiom that expresses the way supernatural power is controlled and put to work by humans.

2. "At the Crossroads: Afro-Cuban Orisha Arts in Miami," a conference held at the Historical Museum of Southern Florida in May 2001.

Chapter 10. The Origin of Good and Evil

1. The *iroko* is a sacred tree in Nigeria where, it is believed, the orishas and the souls of the departed dwell. In some areas it is considered an orisha. The *iroko* does not grow in Cuba; thus, the *ceiba (Ceiba pentranda),* or silk-cotton tree, has taken its place.

2. The *tomeguín (Tiaris canora)* is a Cuban bird known as the Cuban grass quit.

3. The *pitirre (Tyrannus cubensis)* is a Cuban bird known as the giant king bird.

Chapter 15. Shango/Changó: The God of Thunder and Fire

1. Alafin is the title given to the priest-ruler in Oyo. He performs the ceremonies needed to preserve the welfare of the people of Oyo. The historic Shango was the priest/king, or alafin, of Oyo.

2. Ayan is the name of an African tree that belongs to Shango.

3. Takua, according to Afro-Cubans, is a region in Nigeria.

4. Sabalú, or Savalou, is a region in Northeast Nigeria.

5. Dajomi is a Cubanized version of the name of a French colony called Dahomey, now the Republic of Benin.

6. Obakoso is a *camino* of Changó. The term is derived from Oba ko so (the king did not hang himself) the phrase that the followers of the Alafin Shango of Oyo said it was rumored that the king had committed suicide.

7. Personal communication with Florencio Baró in November 1990.

8. The *pilón de asiento* is an artifact that belongs to Changó and is used as a throne where the person sits on the day of *medio asiento*. It is round and solid and looks like the trunk of a tree. It takes its name from the pestles used to crush cereals.

Chapter 16. Oshun/Ochún, Oya/Oyá, and Oba/Oba: Fluvial Goddesses

1. During a conversation in March 2000, Julio García Cortez told me that the present king of Oshogbo, who is a Catholic, performs the ceremonies following the cultural tradition.

2. This *pataki* is of Cuban origin and explains how Ochún became the owner of money. It depicts Ochún as a farmer. In Nigeria men did most of the farm work.

3. Yalodde, or Yalorde, is a title given to Ochún.

4. *Perras gordas y chicas* literally means in Spanish "large and small female dogs." These words were popularly used to designate small change, coins of one and five pennies.

5. Afefe is the word used in the Niger River area to designate the soft breeze that frequently blows there. Believers think that this breeze is the manifestation of the spirit of the messenger of Oyá.

Chapter 17. Olokun/Olokun and Yemonja/Yemayá: Gods of the Sea

1. Indigo blue symbolizes royalty (Thompson 1976: 3).

2. The name orungan signifies the air. Orungan is the space between the air and the solid dome of the sky.

Chapter 18. Shopono/Babalú Ayé: The God of Diseases and Plagues

1. The influence of the Lazarus of the parable has undoubtedly been very important in many believers' perceptions of this *oricha*. In contrast, the priests of this god in Africa do not portray such a pitiful image while dancing.

2. Santería's believers explain that the libertine Babalú Ayé began to lead a pious life when he became old, feeble, and in need of crutches. According to another informant, Babalú Ayé turned pious and merciful after his death, when Olofin ordered his resurrection.

Chapter 20. Osanyin/Osain: Owner of Magical and Medicinal Herbs

1. Osanyin is one of the white, or *funfun* orishas.

Chapter 21. Oshosi/Ochosi, Orisha Oko/Oricha Oko, the Ibeji/Ibeyi, Aganju/Agayú: Minor Gods of Hunting, Horticulture, the Sacred Twins, the Porter God, and Minor Orichas Known in Cuba

1. Bascom (1980: 16) mentions identical Yoruban beliefs concerning Oshosi killing his mother with an arrow.

2. Informants of Rómulo Lachateñeré (1939 3:215) say that Ochosi is associated with the Catholic San Norberto because in lithographs representing this saint he looks as if he were paralyzed by the vision of the Holy Spirit; much like Ochosi in this myth.

3. *Jimaguas* is an Afro-Cuban term for twins. According to Fernando Ortiz (1950: 86) the word *jimagua* derives from jima and akua. These Bantu words mean pregnancy and partner respectively.

4. In Haitian Voodoo (Vodun) the Marasa twin divinities were also identified with Saint Cosme and Saint Damian.

5. In the past, Africanists thought that the Yoruban people migrated from the east to their present homeland around the fifth century C.E. Presently, linguists are of the opinion that Yoruba-speaking people have lived in their present homeland for a much longer period of time. It seems that around the fifth century, there was a great influx from the east of new cultural ways into Nigeria.

Chapter 23. Santería in the Twenty-First Century

1. These are the famous final lines of Castro's speech in a gathering of Cuban intellectuals in the Biblioteca Nacional on June 30, 1961.

2. For a detailed report on religious persecution in Castro's Cuba, see Clark 1992; also, Marcos Antonio Ramos 1986, 2002.

3. Dr. Marta Moreno Vega directed the film *Cuando los Espíritus Bailan el Mambo* (2003), Center for Caribbean Studies, New York. This documentary captures the experience of Santería in present-day Cuba and the policy of Castro's regime to sponsor Santería's practices as folkloric manifestations.

4. *Doble moral* (dual morality) is the term that Cubans on the island use to define their adaptive strategy. It consists of a strict self-censorship, which entails the capacity to pretend by acting, doing, and saying precisely what the governmental authority wants, even though the person might feel and think differently.

5. Among others, see Barry Bearak, "Exotic Religions, Sacrifices, Spirits Part of Miami Life" *Los Angeles Times*, July 11, 1983; Enrique Fernandez "Exploring the Dark Continent of Santería" *The Miami Herald Tropic Magazine*, March 13, 1988; Astrid Vega, "Para Hablar con los Orichas," *El Nuevo Herald* Galería, 1–3E July 17, 1993; Associated Press Release "Animal Sacrificed as Thanks to Court" *The San Diego Union-Tribune*, June 27, 1993; Russel Miller "A Leap of Faith" *New York Times*, Jan. 30, 1994; David Hancock "Carloads of Goats Found Days Before Sacrifice Rite," *Miami Herald Local News*, 1 B November 30, 1994; Lisette Alvarez, "A Once-Hidden Faith Leaps into the Open," *New York Times*, January 27, 1997; David Brown "Voodoo Alleged in Case," *Tribune Review*, March 14, 1998; John Lantigua "Holy War Inc." *Miami New Times*, April 9–15, 1998.

6. See "La police à al poursuite des responsables des sacrifices humains," *La Presse Montreal*, April 14, 1989; Julie Morris and Steve Marshall, "Cult 'Godfather' Hunted," *USA Today*, April 13, 1989; "Cult Suspect Digs up 13th Body," *San Francisco Chronicle*, April 14, 1989. The author was interviewed by the Japanese newspaperman Takaku Kudo, as well as by CVNN TV nationwide, by French TV, and by CNN in Spanish.

7. Liz Balmaseda, "A Sacrifice of Secrecy," *Miami Herald*, April 21, 1989.

8. On many occasions Afro-Cubans have told me with pride that this religion "es lo nuestro" (it is our thing). Dr. Blanca Nieves Tamayo, a lawyer who speaks several languages and worked in Radio Martí until retirement, specifically used that phrase when she invited me to a birthday party for Marcelina, one of her guardian spirits. A famous Cuban singer also expressed herself with similar words, as did Florencio Baró.

9. These cultural differences are documented in Cros Sandoval 1986, which undertakes a comparison of the behavior, attitudes, and values of Mariel refugees and those of Cubans who left the island in the 1960s.

10. Personal conversation with an African-American who was a participant in a Santería ritual in May 1986.

Chapter 24. Santería's New Ways Current Trends

1. Some African-Americans are turned off by Santería's practices because of the use of that name to identify this Yoruba-derived religious complex. Generally, in the past, Santería had a pejorative connotation.

2. In the 1960s, during Vatican II, the Catholic Church removed Saint Christopher from the calendar of saints because there was no historical evidence of his life. Also, changes concerning Saint Lazarus took place. The church recognizes Saint Lazarus as Christ's friend and as a bishop of the early church. The medieval leper assisted by crutches and dogs, whose image was worshiped in Cuba, was identified according to the church's research as a fictional character in a parable told by Christ.

3. For more information concerning this trend of individuals being initiated and

practicing multiple Afro-Cuban religions, see: María Teresa Vélez (2000). *Drumming for the Gods: The Life and Times of Felipe García Villamil, Santero, Palero and Abakuá.* Philadelphia: Temple University Press.

Appendix A: Paths of Obatalá

1. In Dahomey, chameleons are the symbols of Lisa, the masculine principle of the dual creator divinity Mawu-Lisa. The association of Obatalá with Mawu-Lisa is logical since both divinities are related to creation.

2. According to African oral traditions, Obatala was born in Igbo. Thus, it is possible that Igba Ibo was a name used for Obatalá by people coming to Cuba from the region of Igbo. Frequently Afro-Cubans dropped the letter "gb" from Yoruban words. The Yoruban language has two double-articulated consonants; one of them is "gb." This linguistic trait may explain the origin of the name Iba Ibo, where the letter "g" was dropped both from Igba and Igbo. Moreover, Oba Ibo would mean king of Igbo.

3. In some areas of Dahomey, Nana Buruku is the mother of Mawu-Lisa, a dual divinity. Mawu signifies the feminine principle of fecundity, maternity, and forgiveness; Lisa represents the masculine principle of strength.

4. In Nago-Yoruba territory (Ketou and Abeokuta), Nana Buruku is the mother of Shapanan, a name by which the god of smallpox is also called.

5. This discrepancy is most significant since, in Africa, Obalufon is a different Oshalufon, or Olufon, names used for Obatala in the town of Ifon. According to E. Bolaji Idowu (1962:69), in Nigeria, Obalufon is a deified ancestor who possessed a powerful empire and to whom human sacrifices were frequently offered. He is known as "the god of the word" and "the god of the peace of the kingdom."

6. In Togo there is a spiritualist cult group called Yehve, which might be related to this *oricha* of death and the cemetery. At the same time, a river by the same name flows in the territory of the Egbados. However, there are no data to support the notion that the Afro-Cuban *oricha* Yegguá, or Yewá, was originally a local fluvial divinity in Nigeria.

Glossary of Lucumí and Spanish Terms

Some of the terms included in this glossary are also briefly defined in the text, when possible.

aché: Supernatural power, spiritual force that emanates from Olodumare and is manifested as luck, fate, or charisma. The Yoruba word for this supernatural power is *ashe*.

achó: Costume.

ajiaco: Typical Cuban soup made with different tubercles, plantains, and meats.

akpuon: The soloist who starts and leads the chants in the drum festivals.

akuaro: Quail.

Alafin: Changó's title as king of Oyo.

aleyo: A person who participates in Santería's rituals but who is not initiated.

amalá: Corn meal, or porridge. It is Changó's favorite meal.

Añá: A sacred drum that has been consecrated. The spirit or *oricha* that dwells in the sacred drums.

aparecidos: Ghosts.

Ara Kolé: The name given to the buzzard who saved the Earth by taking the Earth's plea to the Sky, which she had offended. It is a path, avatar, or manifestation of Ochún.

araoko: Farm, farmer.

Arará: This term is used in Cuba for the people and culture of the area of Yorubaland, neighboring the former French Dahomey, where the Benin Republic is now.

aro, arun: Illness, disease.

arubbu: Old man.

asé: Heat.

asentarse: To be initiated in the cult of an *oricha*. It literally means to seat an *oricha* in a person's head.

asiento: Ceremonies and rituals pertaining to initiation.

ataque: The Spanish word for attack. It is used idiomatically to refer to the experience of a person who has been possessed by a spirit or an *oricha*.

até Ifá: One of three names by which the divination board used by *babalaos* to consult with Ifá is known. It is also known as *opon Ifá* and *tablero de Ifá*.

awo: Money.

aya: Dog.

ayapá: Land turtle.

ayé: From the Yorubu *aje* (cowrie shell). It means the world, shells, money, the devil.

babá: Father. It is also the title given by believers to their protector *orichas.*

babalao: From the Yoruban word babalawo, this term is used to designate the priest of Orúla or Orúnmila, the god of the oracles and master of the two most prestigious oracles: the *opon Ifá* and the *ekuele.*

babalocha: A priest dedicated to any *oricha* except Orúla.

babanlas: Ancestors.

bajar: Spanish for "to descend." The word is used to refer to an *oricha* that "comes down," that is, possesses one of the believers through trance.

batá: The three sacred drums that are used in important ceremonies and to whom the newly initiated are presented. They are divine and are owned by Changó.

batey: A parkland area and center of communal activities normally situated in the heart of a plantation or farm. The owner's home and the *barracones,* or barracks, where the slaves or laborers reside, are constructed around it.

bembé: A drum festival accompanied by singing and dancing, during which the *orichas* incarnate in the believers and dance with them.

Biagué: The name by which the oracle of the coconuts is known.

bodega: A term used in Cuba to designate a general store.

botánica: A store where religious items are sold. *Botánicas* originally were stores that specialized in herbs and natural medicines and which were opened in the United States by Puerto Ricans. Cuban exiles transformed *botánicas* into stores catering primarily to Santerían customers. There they sell nonconsecrated ritual objects, images, beads, and even animals for sacrificial purposes.

bóveda: An altar dedicated to the spirits of the dead who protect the person. Offerings are given to these souls.

bozal: A mixture of Spanish and African languages used by recently arrived slaves to communicate.

brujería: Sorcery.

brujo: Spanish word for sorcerer and witchdoctor.

caballo: This term, the Spanish word for horse, is used to describe a *santero* or *santera* who has been "mounted" or possessed by an *oricha.*

cabildo: Religious brotherhoods under the tutelary protection of a saint. In colonial Cuba these social organizations of slaves and freemen of the same ethnic origin functioned as religious centers and mutual aid societies. In Cuba, the term *cabildo* is used for a temple of Santería.

cabildos de nación: Cuban social organizations formed by slaves, freemen, and their descendants who were of the same ethnic origin, or, in current terminology, of the same nation.

camino: Spanish for "way" or "road." The term refers to an avatar or manifestation of a saint or a god.

canastillero: A set of drawers. The term is used to designate Santería's altars.

casa de santo: The home of a *santero,* where some rooms are used exclusively to carry out the rituals of Santería.

cascarilla: A powder, made of eggshells, used in Santerían rituals.

ceiba: A tree that grows in Cuba, which has substituted for the Nigerian sacred tree, the iroko, which does not grow in Cuba.

chabá: A metal bracelet used by the children of Ogún, the *oricha* who is the owner of metals.

charará: Small broom made of palm brush with which Babalú Ayé's followers sweep away evil influences.

chequeté: A drink made of corn and sour orange.

coco: Literally "coconut," the term refers to the oracle that uses four pieces of coconut to divine. The oracle is also called Biagué.

collares de fundamento: The four sacred necklaces that a person receives for health or other reasons or as part of the initiation into priesthood. They are made of colored beads placed in different numerical sequences according to the *oricha* they represent. Obatalá's necklace is made of white beads; Yemayá's of blue and white beads, Changó's of red and white beads, and Ochún's of yellow or amber beads.

Criollo: Creole, that is, born in the Americas. In Cuba the term designates all those born on the island regardless of the racial or national origin of their parents.

curandero: A Spanish word, meaning healer, used to designate people who dispense health advice and services outside of the orthodox medical model. They rely heavily on magical practices and herbal medicine.

Curro: A streetwise individual who was typical of the streets of Havana during the nineteenth century.

dilogún: The oracle instrument composed of cowry shells that is used by *santeros.*

dudú: Black.

ebó or **ebbó**: Offering, sacrifice.

efún: White substance made with eggshell that is used in ritual cleansing and in other magical rituals.

egun: spirit of the dead, ghost, skeleton. This term is also used to refer to the ancestral spirits or souls of an individual's genealogical or religious (*rama*) family.

Egungun: Funeral secret societies which, in Nigeria, take care of the cult of the ancestors. They use masks to personify the ghost of the recently deceased, and they visit and counsel the relatives. Egungun is also the name of the drums used to celebrate and communicate with the dead.

ekú: The *jutia,* a Cuban rodent that lives on the branches of trees and is the size of a rabbit.

ekuele: Divination system consisting of chains called *opele* that are used by the *babalaos.*

ekui: A tamale made of black-eyed peas.

ekuté: Rat, mouse.

eledá: Guardian spirit, protector *oricha.*

eleke: Necklace.

epó: Palm nut oil.

ewe: Herbs.

eyá aranla: The hall in the temple of Ocha where people meet and where drum festivals take place. It is open to the uninitiated.

eyé: Tragedy.

eyó: War.

goricha: Soup tureen that contains the sacred stones or *otanes* that are the foundations of the power of the *orichas.*

guaguancó: A type of Afro-Cuban secular musical genre derived from Yoruban music and Andalusian *cante jondo* or *flamenco.*

guarachear: To have and to make fun.

güemilere: Term used for the drum festival, accompanied by singing and dancing, that is held to celebrate and honor the *orichas.*

habaneros: People from the city or the province of Havana.

hechicería: Spanish for "witchcraft."

iban balo: A patio or yard where the public ceremonies take place.

ibo: Road, way.

ichú: Yam.

igbá: Gourd container.

igbodú: The sanctum or room in the house or temple where the altars are placed.

ikán: Fire.

ikínes: The palm nuts used by *babalaos* when consulting the *tablero de Ifá* oracle.

Ikú: Death, Spirit of Death.

ilé: House, territory, earth, soil.

ilé ikú: Cemetery.

ilé ocha: House-temple.

ilú: Drum.

iré: Hope, good tidings.

iroko: The Nigerian tree that the Yoruban people consider sacred and where according to their beliefs the spirit of the dead and some *orichas* rest. In Cuba the *ceiba,* or silk-cotton tree, took the place of the iroko, a tree that does not grow on the island.

iroso: Infamous lie.

iruke: A horsetail used by rulers and priests in Africa as a symbol of authority. The *iruke* is a symbol of Obatalá, the king of the *orichas.*

itá: The special divination done by an *oriaté* or *italero* on behalf of a person who is undergoing the last steps toward initiation. The *itá* should yield information concerning the person's personality and character; it should offer advice concerning taboos and other religious matters; and it should also identify which specific road or manifestation of the *oricha* is going to be *asentado* in the initiate's head.

itutu: The "quieting down" ceremony that takes place when a person who has been initiated dies. The *dilogún* oracle is used to learn the wishes of the deceased concerning his or her sacred objects and other religious matters. The wishes of the deceased are carried out, and he or she is bade farewell.

iyá: Literally "mother." It is also the name of the largest of the three *batá* drums.

iyaguona: Term used for the godmother, mentor, or sponsor of a person who is going to be initiated.

iyalocha: Mother of saint or priestess of Santería.

iyaré: Senior *santera.*

iyawó: Literally, in Yoruba, the bride of an *oricha.* The term designates a recently initiated person.

iyondó: Evilness.

jimaguas: A Cubanism that means twins.

Juntas de Gobierno: Organizations formed in Spanish America to rule the colonies in the name of the king of Spain even while the king was a prisoner of Napoleon Bonaparte, who had conquered Spain.

jutía: A large, opossumlike rodent that is native to Cuba.

Kabie sile: A greeting used to welcome Changó, to please him, and to avoid his ill temper. It means "Nothing has happened."

kariocha: Literally, *ká* means "to place"; *orí* "in the head"; and *ocha* "the saint." *kariocha* is the climax of the initiation ceremony when the *oricha* is placed or is *asentado* in the head of the initiate.

ko bo orí: A ceremony performed on behalf of the sacred entity in the head of a person.

Kofiedemi: "Forgive me," a plea that believers normally address to Babalú Ayé, the *oricha* of epidemics, appealing to his mercy.

koide: Bracelet.

lépe: Conversation.

lépe lépe: Gossip.

letra: The term used to describe a combination figure, or sign, of the oracles; that is, the different ways that the shells or seeds used in divination may fall after being cast. Each of these signs has a name and brings a message, advice, and a prescription or sacrifice. The *letras* are also called *odus*.

levantamiento del plato: Literally, "the raising of the dish." The name of a ceremony which is performed a year after a priest or priestess dies.

levantar santo (to raise the saint): Term used to refer to the occasion when a neophyte takes home his *otanes* and other religious objects from the home of his or her *madrina* or *padrino*.

libreta de santero: The *santero's* notebook containing instructions about the religion that is written for a neophyte by his or her *padrino* or *madrina*. In a sense it represents the beginning of the literary tradition in Santería.

Lúbeo: Title given to Changó.

Lucumí or Lukumí: Cuban term for the Yoruban slaves and their descendants as well as for Santería, or Regla Lucumí, and the sacred language used in the liturgy of Santería.

luz (sing.), **luces** (pl.): Spanish for "light(s)." Used idiomatically to refer to lights of supernatural origin.

madrina/padrino: Spanish for godmother/godfather. These are the terms used for the *santero/santera* or *babalao* in charge of training a neophyte. They are also used for the priests who officiate in ceremonies performed for an initiated person to gain more knowledge or power.

marigwo: Palm frond; sash made of palm fronds.

medio asiento: This ceremony is part of the initiation process. It is like a marriage vow in that, upon completion, a binding contract between the neophyte and the *oricha* is established. In the province of Matanzas, the *medio asiento* used to be the crowning point, after which the neophyte was considered an *iyawó* (person recently initiated). It is considered the middle stage in the process of initiation.

meyi: Two.

Moforibale: "I revere you." Greeting used to address the *orichas*.

montarse, montado: Spanish for "to mount" and "mounted" respectively. It refers to the event wherein the *oricha*, through trance, possesses, or mounts the faithful.

monte: The thicket, the wilderness.

moyubar: To request permission.

muertería: A term used particularly in the eastern provinces of Cuba to identify religious practices and practitioners characterized by spirit possession and a general and vague cult of the dead. A *muertero* is a person who practices *muertería*.

ñame: An edible tubercle whose scientific name is *Discorea alata.*

oba: King.

obí: Coconut.

obiní: Woman.

Ocha: This name is given to the religion of the *orichas,* or Santería.

Oché: The name of the double ax that belongs to Changó.

odu, odún: The signs or configurations of the oracles, also called *letras.* Each *odu* has a proper name and contains a story or anecdote, advice, and a prescription.

olubatá: The musicians who play the consecrated *batá* drums. They have to be initiated into the cult of Aña, the *oricha* of the sacred drums.

olúo: High-ranking *babalao* or priest of Orúnmila.

omí: Water.

omiero: Sacred water.

omó: Son.

ondokó: Sexual intercourse.

opele: Divination system; also called *ekuele.*

opon Ifá: One of three names by which the divination board used by *babalaos* to consult with Ifá is known. It is also known as *até* Ifá and *tablero de* Ifá.

orí: Head.

oriaté: A *santero* who is well versed in the use of the oracle of the shells, or *dilogún,* and who also performs as master of ceremonies.

oricha: Divinity, supernatural force. The term is derived from the Yoruban "orisha," which is the name given to the gods of the Yoruban pantheon.

oricha de cabecera: The most important *oricha* that has been *asentado* in a person's head.

oro: A liturgical festival that consists of drumming and is sometimes accompanied by singing and dancing.

osun: A rooster-shaped staff made of silver that represents Osun, a guardian *oricha.*

otán (s.), **otanes** (pl.): The consecrated stone that is the material receptacle of the power of the *oricha.*

padrino: Spanish for "godfather." The term is used to describe the *santero* in charge of training a neophyte.

palero: A person initiated in Regla de Palo Mayombe, which is of Congolese origin.

pataki: A story or legend about the life and history of the *orichas* or legendary characters. It is also called *apataki.*

pilón de asiento: One of Changó's sacramental objects.

pinaldo: One of two ceremonies performed to endow the recipient with the right to sacrifice four-legged animals. The other is called *wanaldo.*

prenda: The metal kettle where the spirit of the dead, with whom a *palero* has made an allegiance, is kept. Also called *nganga.*

protección: Spanish for "protection." It is used to refer to the spirits that protect a person.

rama: Spanish for "branch." It is used to refer to lineages.

registro: To consult one of the divination systems.

regla: Spanish for "rules." The term has been used to designate Afro-Cuban religions.

Regla Abakwa: Afro-Cuban men's religious brotherhood formed by people originally from the Calabar Peninsula. It is also called Ñañigos.

Regla Arará: Afro-Cuban religion derived from the religion of the Yoruba-speaking people from the former French Dahomey.

Regla Lucumí: The name preferred by believers to refer to their Afro-Cuban religion.

Regla de Ocha: Another name for Santería, the Afro-Cuban religion derived from the religion brought to Cuba by Yoruban slaves. It is also called Regla de Santo and Regla Lucumí.

Regla de Palo: An Afro-Cuban religion derived from the religion of the people from the Congo. It is also called Kimbisa, Palo Mayombe, and Mayombe.

Regla de Santo: One of the terms used to refer to the religion of Santería.

rumbero: A musician who composes or interprets *rumbas.*

salación: A term that means that bad luck is upon you.

santera: Term used for a priestess of Santería. From the Spanish *santo*, a person who deals with *santos* (saints).

Santería: The Afro-Cuban religion, derived from the Yoruban traditional religion, that is also called Regla de Ocha and Regla Lucumí.

santero: More properly called *omoricha, babaoricha.* Such a person is a priest of Santería.

santo: Spanish for "saint," "holy," and "sacred." It is used in Cuba to describe an *oricha.*

santo parado: A term used in the past to refer to an individual who inherited the consecrated stones and other religious paraphernalia from a relative who trained him or her. The *santos parados* performed as priests but had not undergone the initiation process.

siguaraya: Sacred tree of the Lucumís *(Trichilla glabra).*

sopera: Soup tureens that are used to hold the sacred stones in which the force of the *oricha* resides.

subirse: Spanish for "to rise" or "to get on top." It refers to the situation in which an *oricha* possesses a believer. It is also called *montarse* (to mount).

suyeres: Songs and prayers dedicated to the *orichas.*

tablero de Ifá: One of three names by which the divination board used by *babalaos* to consult with Ifá is known. It is also known as *opon* Ifá and até *de Ifá.*

trillo: A dirt path through high grass or bushes.

tutú: Fresh, cold.

wanaldo: One of two ceremonies performed to endow the recipient with the right to sacrifice four-legged animals. The other is called *pinaldo.*

yefá: A powder, made of yam, used by the *babalao* to record the *odus* or configurations in the board of divination.

References

Abimbola, Wande. 1973. "The Literature of the Ifa Cult." In *Sources of Yoruba History*, edited by S. O. Biobaku, 41–62. Oxford: Clarendon Press.

———. 1975a. *Sixteen Great Poems of Ifa*. N.p: UNESCO.

———. 1975b. "Yoruba Oral Traditions." Selections from the papers presented at the *Seminar on Yoruba Tradition: Poetry in Music, Dance, and Drama* (1974). Ibadan, Nigeria: Ibadan University Press.

———. 1977. *Yoruba Divination Poetry*. London: Nok Publishers.

———. 1981. "The Orisha Tradition, a World View." In *Caribe*, Special Report on the World Conference on Orisha Tradition and Culture in Ile Ife. New York: Caribbean Cultural Center Visual Arts Research and Resource Center, Fall–Winter.

———. 1997. *Ifa Will Mend Our Broken World*. Roxbury, Mass.: Aim Books.

Abraham, R. C. 1946. *Dictionary of Modern Yoruba*. London: Hodder and Stoughton Educational.

Ade Ajayi, J. F., and Robert Smith. 1964. *Yoruba Warfare in the 19th Century*. London: Cambridge University Press.

Adesola. 1910. *The Nigerian Chronicle*, February 25, 1910.

Alfonso, Pablo M. 1985. *Cuba, Castro y los Católicos*. Miami: Ediciones Hispanamerican.

Alvarez Díaz, J., A. Arredondo, R. M. Shelton, and J. F. Vizcaino. 1964. *Cuba: Geopolítica y Pensamiento Económico*. Miami: Duplex Paper Products of Miami.

Amos, Ruben. 1982. *Leyenda del Milagroso San Lázaro*. Miami: n.p.

Angarica, Nicolas Valentin. 1955. *Manual de Orihate*. Havana: n.p.

Apter, Andrew. 1991. "The Embodiment of Paradox: Yoruba Kingship and Female Power." *Cultural Anthropology* 6, no. 2: 212–29.

———. 1992. *Black Critics and Kings*. Chicago: University of Chicago Press.

———. 1993. "Atinga Revisited: Yoruba Witchcraft and the Cocoa Economy, 1950–51." In *Modernity and Its Malcontents*, edited by Jean and John Comaroff, 111–28. Chicago: University of Chicago Press.

Atanda, J. A. 1980. *An Introduction to Yoruba History*. Ibadan, Nigeria: Ibadan University Press.

Awolalu, J. Omosade. 1972. "The Africans Traditional View of Man." *Journal of Religious Studies* 1–2: 101–18. Ibadan, Nigeria: Orita.

Awoniyi, Timothy A. 1981. "The Woed Yoruba." *Nigeria Magazine*, 134–35.

Barnes, Sandra, ed. 1997. *Africa's Ogun: Old World and New*. Bloomington: Indiana University Press.

Barnett, Miguel. [1966] 1980. *Biografía de un Cimarrón*. Havana: Editorial Letras Cubanas.

Bascom, William R. 1950. "The Focus of Cuban Santeria." *South-western Journal of Anthropology* 6, no. 1 (spring): 64–68.

———. 1951. "The Yoruba in Cuba." *Nigeria Magazine* 37: 14–20.

————. 1960. "Yoruba Concepts of the Soul." In *Men and Cultures: Selected Papers of the Fifth International Congress of Anthropological and Ethnological Sciences*, edited by A. F. C. Wallace, 401–10. London: Oxford University Press.

————. *Ifa Divination*. Bloomington: Indiana University Press.

————. 1969b. *The Yoruba of Southwestern Nigeria*. New York: Holt, Rinehart, and Winston.

————. 1980. *Sixteen Cowries: Yoruba Divination from Africa to the New World*. Bloomington: Indiana University Press.

Bastide, Roger. 1971. *African Civilizations in the New World*. New York: Harper and Row.

Beier, Ulli. 1959. *A Year of Sacred Festivals in a Yoruba Town*. Lagos: Nigeria Magazine Special Publication.

Biobaku, S. O. 1957. *The Egba and Their Neighbors, 1842–1872*. Oxford: Clarendon Press.

————. 1973. *Sources of Yoruba History*. Oxford: Clarendon Press.

Bolivar Aróstegui, Natalia. 1984. *Polowo Owo*. Havana: Editorial Ciencias Sociales.

————. 1994. *Los Orishas en Cuba*. Havana: Ediciones Pablo Milanés.

Boulding, Kenneth. 1956. *The Image: Knowledge in Life and Society* Ann Arbor: University of Michigan Press.

Brandon, George. [1993] 1997. *Santeria from Africa to the New World: The Dead Sell Memories*. Bloomington: Indiana University Press.

Brown, David H. 2003. *Santería Enthroned*. Chicago: University of Chicago Press.

Cabrera, Lydia. [1954] 1971. *El Monte*. Miami: Colección del Chicherekú.

————. 1957. *Anagó: Vocabulario Lucumí*. Havana: Colección del Chicherekú.

————. 1974. *Yemayá y Ochún: Kariocha, Iyalorichas y Olorichas*. New York: Colección del Chicherekú en el exilio.

————. 1980. *Koeko Iyawó: Aprende Novicia. Pequeño Tratado de Regla Lucumí*. Miami: Colección del Chicherekú en el exilio.

Canet, Carlos. 1973. *Lucumí: Religión de los Yoruba en Cuba*. Miami: Air Publications Center.

Cañizares, Raul. 1999. *Cuban Santeria*. Rochester, Vermont: Destiny Books.

Castellanos, Isabel. 1996. "From Ulkumí to Lucumí: A Historical Overview of Religious Acculturation in Cuba." In *Santeria Aesthetics in Contemporary Latin American Art*, edited by Arturo Lindsay, 39–51. Washington, D.C.: Smithsonian Institution Press.

Castellanos, Isabel, and Jorge Castellanos. 1988–94. *Cultura Afrocubana*. 4 vols. Miami: Ediciones Universal.

Chaviano, Diana. "Deidad Negra Oshún Encarnada en la Virgen de la Caridad." *El Nuevo Herald Galería*, 30D, May 20, 1992.

Clark, Juan. 1985. *Religious Repression in Cuba*. Miami: University of Miami North-South Center.

————. 1992. *Cuba: Mito y Realidad*. Miami–Caracas: Saeta Ediciones.

Comaroff, Jean, and John Comaroff. 1993. *Modernity and Its Malcontents*. Chicago: University of Chicago Press.

Cros Arrúe, Mercedes. 1966. *Lo Yoruba en la Santería Afrocubana*. Ph.D. dissertation. Madrid: Universidad de Madrid.

Cros Sandoval, Mercedes. 1975. *La Religión Afrocubana*. Madrid: Editorial Playor.

———. [Sandoval, Mercedes C.] 1977. "Afrocuban Concepts of Disease and Its Treatment in Miami." *Journal of Operational Psychiatry* 8, no. 2: 52–63.

———. 1979. "Santería as a Mental Health Care System." *Social Science and Medicine* 13B, no. 2: 137–51.

———. [Mercedes S. (sic)]. 1983. "Santería." *The Journal of the Florida Medical Association* 70, no. 8: 619–28.

———. 1986. *Mariel and Cuban National Identity*. Miami: Editorial Sibi.

———. 1994. "Afro-Cuban Religion in Perspective." In *Enigmatic Powers: Syncretism with African and Indigenous Peoples' Religions among Latinos*, edited by Anthony M. Stevens-Arroyo and Andrés I. Pérez Mena, 81–98. Vol. 3 of PARAL Studies Series. New York: Bildner Center Books.

———. In Press. "Santeria in the Twenty-First Century." In *Orisha Devotion and World Religion: The Globalization of Yoruba Religious Culture*, edited by Jacob Olupona and Terry Rey. Madison: University of Wisconsin Press.

Curtin, Phillip Feierman, Leonard Thompson, and Jan Vansina. 1978. *African History*. London: Longman.

Cuthrell-Curry, Mary. 2000. "African-Derived Religions in the United States." In *African Spirituality in the Americas*, edited by Jacob Olupona, 450–65. New York: Crossroads.

Dacal Moure, Ramón, and Manuel Rivero de la Calle. 1996. *Art and Archaeology of Pre-Columbian Cuba*. Pittsburgh: University of Pittsburgh Press.

Dapper, Olfert. 1686. *Description de l'Afrique*. Amsterdam: n.p.

De Gramont, Sanche. 1977. *The Strong Brown God*. Boston: Houghton Mifflin.

De la Fuente, Alejandro. 2001. *A Nation for All*. Chapel Hill: University of North Carolina Press.

De la Soledad, R., and M. J. Sanjuan. 1988. *IBO (Yorubas en Tierras Cubanas)*. Miami: Ediciones Universal.

De la Torre, Miguel A. 2004. *Santería: The Beliefs and Rituals of a Growing Religion in America*. Grand Rapids: Eerdmans.

Dennet, R. E. 1910. *Nigerian Studies*. London: MacMillan.

Díaz Fabelo, Teodoro. 1956. *Lengua de Santeros: Guiné Gongorí*. Havana: n.p.

———. 1960. *Olorún*. Havana: Departamento del Folklore del Teatro Nacional de Cuba.

Duarte, Patricia. 1983. "Santa Bárbara." *El Nuevo Herald. Galeria*. December 4, 13–14.

Echeverría, Javier. 2003. *La Letra del Año*. Documentary. Univision TV. Miami.

Eck, Diana L. 2002. *A New Religious America*. San Francisco: HarperCollins.

Ellis, A. B. 1894. *The Yoruba-Speaking Peoples of the Slave Coast*. London: Chapman and Hall.

Epega, M. L. 1935. "Ifa, the Light of My Fathers." *Nigerian Teacher* 5: 11–14.

Espinosa, Felix, and Amadeo Piñero. 1997a. *La Leyenda de Orúla*. Havana: Ediciones Cubanas.

———. 1997b. *Ifá y la Creación*. Colección Cosmogonía Yoruba. Havana: Ediciones Cubanas.

Fage, J. D. 1959. *Introduction to the History of West Africa*. Cambridge: Cambridge University Press.

Fagg, William. 1982. *Yoruba Sculpture of West Africa*. London: William Collins.

Fardon, Richard. 1995. *Counterworks*. London: ASA Decennial Conference Series.

Farrow, S. S. 1926. *Faith, Fancies, and Fetich*. London: S.P.S.K.

Feijoo, Samuel. 1986. *Mitología Cubana*. Havana: Editorial Letras Cubanas.

Fernández Cano, Jesus. 2000. "Profesionales Cubanos: Su Adhesion a la Santería." Thesis for a Licentiature Degree, Universidad de Costa Rica, San Jose.

Fernández Soneira, Teresa. 1997. *Cuba: Historia de la Educación Católica 1582–1961*. Miami: Ediciones Universal.

Forde, C. D. 1934. *Habitat Economy and Society*. London: Methuen.

———. 1951. *Yoruba-Speaking Peoples of Southwestern Nigeria*. London: International African Institute.

———. 1954. *African Worlds*, edited by D. Forde. London: Oxford University Press for International African Institute.

Fragoso Guimaraes, Carlos Antonio. 1997. *Allan Kardec*. http://www.espirito.com.br/portal/doutrina/kardec/biografia-kardec-carlos-fragoso.html.

Frobenius, Leo. 1913. *The Voice of Africa*. London: Hutchinson.

Fuja, Abayomi. 1962. *Fourteen Hundred Cowries*. London: Oxford University Press.

Garcia Cortez, Julio. 1971. *El Santo*. Mexico City: Editorial Latino Americana.

———. 1980. *Pataki*. Miami: Ediciones Universal.

———. 2000. *The Osha*. Brooklyn, N.Y.: Athelia Henrietta Press.

Geertz, Clifford. 1957. "Ethos, Worldview, and the Analysis of Sacred Symbols." *The Antioch Review* 17: 421–37.

Gibbs, James L. Jr. 1966. *Peoples of Africa*. New York: Holt, Rinehart, and Winston.

Gonzalez-Wippler, Migene. 1988. *Rituals and Spells in Santeria*. New York: Original Publications.

Greenberg, Joseph H. 1963. *The Languages of Africa*. Bloomington: Indiana University Press.

Guanche Pérez, Jesus. 1999. *España en la Savia de Cuba*. Havana: Instituto Cubano del Libro Editorial de Ciencias Sociales.

Hagedorn, Katherine. 2001. *Divine Utterances: The Performance of AfroCuban Santeria*. Washington, D.C.: Smithsonian Institution Press.

Halifax, Joan, and Hazel H. Weidman. 1973. "Religion as a Mediating Institution in Acculturation." In *Religious Systems and Psychotherapy*, edited by Richard H. Cox, 319–31. Springfield, Ill.: Charles C. Thomas.

Hanke, Lewis. 1949. *The Spanish Struggle for Justice in the Conquest of America*. Philadelphia: University of Pennsylvania Press.

Harris, Joseph E. 1998. *Africans and Their History*. New York: Penguin.

Horton, Robin. 1971. "African Conversion." *Africa* 41 (2): 85–108.

———. 1993. "Social Psychologies African and Western." In *Oedipus and Job in West African Religion*, edited by Meyer Fortes, 41–82. Cambridge: Cambridge University Press.

Howard, Phillip A. 1998. *Changing History.* Baton Rouge: University of Louisiana Press.

Hunt, Carl M. 1979. *Oyotunji Village: The Yoruba Movement in America.* Washington, D.C.: University Press of America.

Idowu, E. B. 1962. *Olodumare: God in Yoruba Belief.* London: Longman, Green.

Iliffe, John. 1995. *Africans: The History of a Continent.* Cambridge: Cambridge University Press.

Johnson, James Bishop. 1899. *Yoruba Heathenism.* London: n.p.

Johnson, S. 1921. *The History of the Yorubas.* London: Rutledge.

July, Robert W. 1970. *A History of the African People.* New York: Charles Scribner and Sons.

Kardec, Allan. 1966. [1857] 1975. *The Spirit's Book: Spiritualist Philosophy.* New York: Arno.

———. [1861] 1953. *Les Livres des Mediums/Libro de los Mediums.* Mexico City: Editorial Diana.

———. [1864] 1973. *El Evangelio Según el Espiritismo.* Venezuela: Editorial Religiosa.

———. 1966. *Devocionario Espiritista. Colección de Oraciones Escogidas.* New York: Studium Corporation.

———. 2003. *The Gospel Explained by the Spiritist Doctrine.* Philadelphia: Allen Kardec Educational Society.

Kearney, Michael M.D. 1984. *World View.* Novato, Calif.: Chandler and Sharp.

Keribo, Oyesile. 1906. *History of the Yoruba Gods.* Abeokuta, Nigeria: n.p.

Kiev, Ari. 1964. *Magic, Faith, and Healing.* New York: Free Press of Glencoe.

Klein, Herbert S. 1967. *Slavery in the Americas.* Chicago: University of Chicago Press.

Kluckhohn, Florence R. 1953. "Dominant and Variant Value Orientation." In *Personality in Nature, Society, and Culture,* edited by C. Kluckhohn, H. A. Murray, and D. M. Schneider, 342–57. New York: Alfred A. Knopf.

Kluckhohn, Florence R., and F. L. Strodtbeck. 1961. *Variations in Value Orientations.* New York: Row, Peterson.

Lachatañeré, Rómulo. 1938. *Oh Mío Yemayá.* Manzanillo, Cuba: Editorial El Arte.

———. 1939–42. "El Sistema Religioso de los Lucumis y Otras Influencias Africanas en Cuba." *Estudios Afrocubanos.* II (1939), III (1939), IV (1940), VI (1942a). Havana: Estudios Afrocubanos.

———. 1942. *Manual de Santería.* Manzanillo, Cuba: Editorial El Arte.

Laitin, David D. 1986. *Hegemony and Culture: Politics and Religious Change Among the Yoruba.* Chicago: University of Chicago Press.

Lambo, T. A. "Psychotherapy in Africa." *Psychotherapy and Psychosomatics* 24: 311–26.

Lang, Andrew. 1898. *The Making of Religion.* London: Longman, Green.

Las Casas, Bartolomé de. 1951. *Historia de las Indias,* edited by Augusto Millares Carlo. 3 vols. Mexico City: Fondo de Cultura Económica.

Long, C. H. 1964. "The West African High God: History and Religious Experience." *History of Religions* 3: 338–42.

Lowery-Palmer, Alma L. 1980. "Yoruba Worldview and Patient Compliance." Ph.D. dissertation, Department of Anthropology, University of California, Riverside.

Lucas, J. O. 1948. *The Religion of the Yorubas.* Lagos: C.M.S. Bookshop.

Marrero, Levi. 1975. *Cuba: Economía y Sociedad*. Vol. 3. Madrid: Editorial Playor.

Mason, John. 1981. *Onde Fun Orisha: Food for the Gods*. Brooklyn, N.Y.: Yoruba Theological Archministry.

———. 1985. *Four New World Religious Rituals*. Brooklyn, N.Y.: Yoruba Theological Archministry.

Matory, J. Lorand. 1994. *Sex and the Empire That Is No More*. Minneapolis: University of Minnesota Press.

Matute y Gaviria, Justino. 1866. *Noticias Relativas a la Historia de Sevilla*. Seville: n.p.

Maupoil, B. 1943. *La Geomancia a l'Ancienne Cote des Esclaves*. Vol. 12. Paris: Travaux et Memoirs de l'Institute D'Ethnologie.

Maza Miguel, Manuel P. S. J. 1993. *El Clero Cubano y la Independencia*. Santo Domingo: Centro de Estudios Sociales Padre Juan Montalvo.

Mbiti, John S. 1970. *African Religions and Philosophy*. New York: Doubleday.

McKenzie, Peter. 1997. *Hail Orisha!: A Phenomenology of a West African Religion in the Mid-Nineteenth Century*. Studies of Religion in Africa. Leiden, Netherlands: Brill.

Meillassoux, Claude. 1991. *The Anthropology of Slavery*. Chicago: University of Chicago Press.

Mercer, Paul. 1954. "The Fon of Dahomey." In *African Worlds*, edited by D. Forde, 210–34. London: Oxford University Press for International African Institute.

Millet, Jose. 2000. "El Foco de la Santeria Santiaguera." *Del Caribe* 22: 110–19.

Moreno Fraginals, Manuel. [1964] 2001. *El Ingenio: El Complejo Económico Social Cubano*. Barcelona: Editorial Crítica.

———. 1977. "Africa in Cuba: A Quantitative Analysis of the African Population in the Island of Cuba." *Annals of the New York Academy of Sciences* 292: 212–28.

Moreno Vega, Marta. 2000. *Altar of My Soul*. New York: Ballantine.

———. Director. 2003. *Cuando Los Espíritus Bailan el Mambo* (film). New York: Center for Caribbean Studies.

Murphy, Joseph. 1988. *Santeria: An African Religion in America*. Boston: Beacon Press.

———. 1993. *Santeria: African Spirits in America*. Boston: Beacon Press.

Murphy, Joseph, and Meimei Sundford (eds.). 2001. *Ochun Across the Waters: A Yoruba Goddess in Africa and the Americas*. Bloomington: Indiana University Press.

Naugle, David K. 2002. *Worldview*. Grand Rapids/Cambridge: William B. Eerdmans.

Newbury, C. W. 1961. *The Western Slave Coast and Its Rulers*. Oxford: n.p.

Nina Rodriguez, Raimundo. 1934. *Os Africanos no Brasil*. Rio de Janeiro: n.p.

Nogueira Negrao, Lisias. 1987. "Kardecism." In *The Encyclopedia of Religion*, edited by Mircea Eliade. Vol. 8. London: Macmillan.

Norbeck, Edward. 1974. *Religion in Human Life*. New York: Holt, Rinehart, and Winston.

Ogundipe, A. 1978. "Esu-Elegbara, the Yoruba God of Chance and Destiny: A Study in Yoruba Mythology." Ph.D. dissertation, Dept. of Folklore. Bloomington: Indiana University.

Olatunle, Adetokumbo. 1976. "Oyotunji, South Carolina Field Report." In *Black People and Their Culture: Selected Writings from the African Diaspora*. Washington, D.C.: Smithsonian Institution Press.

Olmstead, David L. 1953. "Comparative Notes in Yoruba and Lucumi." *Language* 29, no. 2, 157–64.

Olupona, J. K. 1983. *A Phenomenological/Anthropological Analysis of the Religion of the Ondo-Yoruba of Nigeria.* Ph.D. dissertation. Boston: Boston University.

———. 1991. *Kingship, Religion, and Rituals in a Nigerian Community: A Phenomenological Study of Ondo Yoruba Festivals.* Stockholm: Almquist and Wiksell International.

———. 1991. *African Traditional Religions in Contemporary Society,* edited by J. K. Olupona. New York: Paragon House.

———. 2000. ed. *African Spirituality: Forms, Meaning and Expressions.* New York: Crossroads.

Olupona, J. K., and Terry Rey, eds. In press. *Orisha Devotion and World Religion: The Globalization of Yoruba Religious Culture.* Madison: University of Wisconsin Press.

Ortiz de Zúñiga. 1472. *Anales Esclesiásticos y Seculares de Sevilla.*

Ortiz, Fernando. [1906] 1973. *Los Negros Brujos.* Miami: Ediciones Universal.

———. [1916] 1987. *Los Negros Esclavos.* Havana: Editorial de Ciencias Sociales.

———. 1921a. "Los Cabildos Afrocubanos." *Revista Bimestre Cubana,* 16 (1). Havana: Sociedad Económica de.

———. [1921b] 1992. *Los Cabildos y la Fiesta Afrocubana del Día de Reyes.* Havana: Editorial de Ciencias Sociales.

———. [1923] 1985. *Nuevo Catauro de Cubanismos.* Havana: Editorial de Ciencias Sociales.

———. [1951] 1985. *Los Bailes y el Teatro de los Negros en el Folklore de Cuba.* Havana: Editorial Letras Cubanas.

———. 1950. *La Africanía de la Música Folklórica de Cuba.* Havana: Publicaciones de la Dirección de Cultura del Ministerio de Educación.

———. 1952–1955. *Los Instrumentos de la Música Afrocubana.* 5 vols. Havana: Publicaciones de la Dirección de Cultura del Ministerio de Educación.

———. [1959] 1972. *Historia de una Pelea Cubana Contra los Demonios.* Las Villas, Cuba: Universidad Central de las Villas. Madrid: Formas Gráficas.

———. [1940] 1963. *Contrapunteo Cubano del Tabaco y el Azucar.* Barcelona: Editorial Ariel.

———. 1970. *Cuban Counterpoint: Tobacco and Sugar.* Translated by Harriet de Onis. New York: Vintage Books/Random House.

———. 1975. *La Música Afrocubana.* Madrid: Altamira Rotopress.

Ortiz, Oscar F. 1990. *El Santo Culto.* Hialeah, Fla.: Osor Productions.

Osamaro Ibie, Cromwell. 1986. *Ifism: The Complete Work of Orunmila.* Hong Kong: Design Printing.

Osborne, Oliver H. 1972. "Social Structure and Health Care Systems: A Yoruba Example." *Rural Africana* 17: 80–85.

Palma, Ricardo. 1949. *Tradiciones Peruanas.* Vol. 2. Buenos Aires/Mexico City: Espasa Calpe.

Palmié, Stephan. 1993. "Ethnogenetic Processes and Cultural Transfers in Afro-American Slave Populations." In *Slavery in the Americas,* edited by Wolfgang Binder, 337–63. Wurzburg: Konigshausen und Neumann.

———. 1995. "Against Syncretism: 'Africanizing' and 'Cubanizing' Discourses in North American Orisa Worship." In *Counterworks*, edited by Richard Fardon, 73–104. London: ASA Decennial Conference Series.

———. 2002. *Wizards and Scientists*. Durham, N.C.: Duke University Press.

Parrinder, E. G. 1961. *West African Religion*. London: Epworth.

Pedraza, Teresita. 1999. "This Too Shall Pass: Religion in Cuba, Resistance and Endurance." *Cuban Studies* 28: 16–39.

———. "The Afro-Cuban Religions: The Legacy of a Segmented Society." In progress. Ph.D. dissertation. Spain: University of Seville.

Peel, J.D.Y. 1983. *Ijeshas and Nigerians*. Cambridge: Cambridge University Press.

———. 2000. *Religious Encounter and the Making of the Yoruba*. Bloomington: Indiana University Press.

Pemberton III, John, and Funso S. Afolayan. 1996. *Yoruba Sacred Kingship*. Washington, D.C.: Smithsonian Institution Press.

Perez, Louis, Jr. 1986. *Cuba Under the Platt Amendment*. Pittsburgh: University of Pittsburgh Press.

Pichardo, Ernesto. 1999. Sincretism. Miami: Babalú Ayé Church of the Lucumí.

———. 1998. *The Relation of the Church to Non-Lukumi Religions*. Miami: Babalú Ayé Church of the Lucumí.

———. 1998. *Under Construction*. Third Annual South Florida Symposium on Cuba. Miami: University of Miami.

———. 1999. *Declaration on the Life of Priests*. Miami: Babalú Ayé Church of the Lucumí.

———. 2000. "Rule or Diplomacy?" CLBA JOURNAL 2000. Miami: Babalú Ayé Church of the Lucumí.

Pichardo, L. Ernesto, and Lourdes Pichardo. 1984. *Oduduwa Obatala*. Miami: Babalú Ayé Church of the Lucumí.

Prince, Raymond. 1964a. "Indigenous Yoruba Psychiatry." In *Magic, Faith, and Healing*, edited by A. Kiev, 84–120. New York: Free Press of Glencoe.

Prine, Raymond. 1964b. *Yoruba Divination and Sacrifice*. Ibadan, Nigeria: Ibadan University Press.

Ramos, Arthur. 1943. *Las Culturas Negras en el Nuevo Mundo*. Mexico City: Fondo Cultura Económica.

Ramos, Marcos Antonio. 1986. *Panorama del Protestantismo en Cuba*. San José, Costa Rica: Editorial Caribe.

———. 2002. "Religion and Religiosity in Cuba: Past, Present, and Future." *Cuba Occasional Paper Series*. Washington, D.C.: Trinity College.

Ramos, Miguel "Willie." 1982. *Ceremonia de Obaloaye*. Carolina, Puerto Rico: CECRY, Boletin Oficial del Centro de Estudios y Culto Religioso Yoruba. Año #1.

———. 1988. *Seminario de Religion Yoruba: Santeria and Eleda*. Miami: Cabildo Yoruba Omo Orisha.

———. 2000. *The Empire Beats On: Batá Drums and Hegemony in Nineteenth-Century Cuba*. Master's thesis, Sociology Department, Florida International University.

———. February 2003. "La Division de la Habana: Territorial Conflict and Cultural Hegemony in the Followers of Oyo Lukumí Religion, 1850s–1920s." *Cuban Studies,* no. 34 (February): 38–70.

Rey, Terry. 1999. *Our Lady of Class Struggle: The Cult of the Virgin Mary in Haiti.* Trenton: Africa World Press.

Rodriguez, Reyes, Andres. 2000. *Aro: la Enfermedad y la Regla de Ocha.* Santiago de Cuba: Del Caribe Numero 32/2000, pp. 72–77.

Santovenia, Emeterio S., and Raúl Shelton. [1965] 1966. *Cuba y Su Historia.* Vol. 1. Miami: Rema Press.

Shillington, Kevin. 1995. *History of Africa.* Oxford, England: Macmillan.

Sire, James W. 1989. *Naming the Elephant: Worldview as a Concept.* Downer's Grove, Ill.: InterVarsity Press.

Smart, Ninian. 1995. *Worldviews: Crosscultural Explorations of Human Beliefs.* Englewood Cliffs, N.J.: Prentice Hall.

Sosa, Juan J. Pbro. 1994. *Santa Bárbara y San Lázaro.* Miami: Committee on Popular Piety. Ministry of Worship and Spiritual Life of the Archdiocese of Miami.

———. 1999. *Sectas, Cultos, y Sincretismos.* Miami: Ediciones Universal.

Talbot, Percy Amaury. 1926. *The People of Southern Nigeria: A Sketch of Their History, Ethnology, and Languages with an Abstract of the 1921 Census.* Vols. 1–4. London: Oxford University Press.

Thompson, Robert F. 1976. *Black Gods and Kings: Yoruba Art at U.C.L.A.* Bloomington: Indiana University Press.

———. 2001. *Face of the Gods: Art and Altars of Africa and the African Americas.* Art exhibit, Art Museum at Florida International University, Miami.

Velasco, Carlos. 1915. "El Problema Religioso." In *Aspectos Nacionales,* edited by Jesús Montero. Havana: Librería "Studium."

Vélez, María Teresa. 2000. *Drumming for the Gods: The Life and Times of Felipe García Villamil, Santero, Palero, and Abakuá.* Philadelphia: Temple University Press.

Verger, Pierre. 1954. *Dieux d'Afrique.* Paris: Paul Hartman.

Wallace, Anthony F. C. 1960. *Men and Cultures.* London: Oxford University Press.

Weidman, H. H. 1973. "Implications of the Culture Broker for the Delivery of Health Care." Paper presented at the annual meeting of the Southern Anthropological Society. Wrightsville Beach, N.C., March 8–11.

———. 1975. "Concepts as Strategies for Change." *Psychiatric Annals* 5 (8): 17–19.

———. 1978. *The Miami Health Ecology Report,* vol. 1. Miami: University of Miami School of Medicine.

Wirtz, Kristina. 2000. "Las Funciones Trópicas del Parentesco en la Santería Cubana." Santiago de Cuba: *Del Caribe* no. 32/200, pp. 65–71.

Index

Note: Page numbers in italics indicate illustrations and photographs.

CPSIA information can be obtained
at www.ICGtesting.com
Printed in the USA
BVOW09s0503310517

485572BV00001B/5/P